PERSONAL NAMES IN CUNEIFORM TEXTS FROM BABYLONIA (C. 750–100 BCE)

Personal names provide fascinating testimony to Babylonia's multi-ethnic society. This volume offers a practical introduction to the repertoire of personal names recorded in cuneiform texts from Babylonia in the first millennium BCE. In this period, individuals moved freely as well as involuntarily across the ancient Middle East, leaving traces of their presence in the archives of institutions and private persons in southern Mesopotamia. The multilingual nature of this name material poses challenges for students and researchers who want to access these data as part of their exploration of the social history of the region in the period. This volume offers guidelines and tools that will help readers navigate this difficult material. The title is also available Open Access on Cambridge Core.

CAROLINE WAERZEGGERS is Professor of Assyriology at Leiden University, specialising in the social and cultural history of Babylonia in the first millennium BCE. Together with Melanie M. Groß, she directs *Prosobab*, an online prosopography of Babylonia (620–330 BCE).

MELANIE M. GROß is an Assyriologist specialising in the socio-economic history of first millennium BCE Mesopotamia. Together with Caroline Waerzeggers, she directs *Prosobab*, an online prosopography of Babylonia (620–330 BCE).

PERSONAL NAMES IN CUNEIFORM TEXTS FROM BABYLONIA (C. 750–100 BCE)

An Introduction

EDITED BY

CAROLINE WAERZEGGERS
Leiden University

MELANIE M. GROß
Leiden University

CAMBRIDGE
UNIVERSITY PRESS

CAMBRIDGE UNIVERSITY PRESS

Shaftesbury Road, Cambridge CB2 8EA, United Kingdom

One Liberty Plaza, 20th Floor, New York, NY 10006, USA

477 Williamstown Road, Port Melbourne, VIC 3207, Australia

314–321, 3rd Floor, Plot 3, Splendor Forum, Jasola District Centre,
New Delhi – 110025, India

103 Penang Road, #05–06/07, Visioncrest Commercial, Singapore 238467

Cambridge University Press is part of Cambridge University Press & Assessment, a department of the University of Cambridge.

We share the University's mission to contribute to society through the pursuit of education, learning and research at the highest international levels of excellence.

www.cambridge.org
Information on this title: www.cambridge.org/9781009291088

DOI: 10.1017/9781009291071

First published 2024

A catalogue record for this publication is available from the British Library.

Library of Congress Cataloging-in-Publication Data

NAMES: Waerzeggers, Caroline, editor. | Groß, Melanie M., editor.

TITLE: Personal names in cuneiform texts from Babylonia (c. 750-100 BCE) : an introduction / edited by Caroline Waerzeggers, Rijksuniversiteit Leiden, The Netherlands; Melanie M. Groß, Rijksuniversiteit Leiden, The Netherlands.

DESCRIPTION: Cambridge, United Kingdom ; New York, NY : Cambridge University Press, 2024. | Includes bibliographical references and index.

IDENTIFIERS: LCCN 2023023908 (print) | LCCN 2023023909 (ebook) | ISBN 9781009291088 (hardcover) | ISBN 9781009291095 (paperback) | ISBN 9781009291071 (ebook)

SUBJECTS: LCSH: Names, Personal – Akkadian – Iraq – Babylonia. | Cuneiform inscriptions, Akkadian – Iraq – Babylonia. | Akkadian language – Iraq – Babylonia – Etymology – Names. | LCGFT: Essays.

CLASSIFICATION: LCC CS2353 .P47 2024 (print) | LCC CS2353 (ebook) | DDC 935/.5–dc23/eng/20230727

LC record available at https://lccn.loc.gov/2023023908

LC ebook record available at https://lccn.loc.gov/2023023909

ISBN 978-1-009-29108-8 Hardback

Contents

List of Figures — *page* vii
List of Tables — viii
List of Contributors — x
Preface — xv
List of Abbreviations — xvi

Introduction — 1

PART I BABYLONIAN NAMES

1 Social Aspects of Babylonian Names — 19
Francis Joannès

2 Babylonian Male Names — 37
Julia Giessler

3 Babylonian Female Names — 58
Laura Cousin and Yoko Watai

4 Babylonian Family Names — 71
John P. Nielsen

5 Names of Officials ('*Beamtennamen*') — 81
Michael Jursa

6 Reading Neo-Babylonian Names — 93
Cornell Thissen

PART II NON-BABYLONIAN NAMES

7 Assyrian Names — 109
Heather D. Baker

8 Aramaic Names 121
Rieneke Sonnevelt

9 Hebrew Names 139
Kathleen Abraham

10 Phoenician and Related Canaanite Names 166
Ran Zadok

11 Arabian Names 185
Ahmad al-Jallad

12 Egyptian Names 194
Steffie van Gompel

13 Anatolian Names 213
Zsolt Simon

14 Greek Names 224
Paola Corò

15 Old Iranian Names 238
Jan Tavernier

16 Elamite Names 258
Elynn Gorris

17 Sumerian Names 273
Uri Gabbay

18 Residual, Unaffiliated, and Unexplained Names 283
Ran Zadok

Indices
Male names and persons 293
Female names and persons 306
Family names 309
Place names 311
Names of gods 313
Temple names 315
General index 316

Figures

8.1 A family tree model of Semitic languages (drawing by Rieneke Sonnevelt). *page* 122
8.2 Distribution of names in the Murašû archive from Nippur. 124
8.3 Nippur and its hinterland (drawn by Rieneke Sonnevelt, adapted from Zadok 1978, 332). 125
12.1 Example of an Egyptian name with additional Greek and Coptic writings (*DN* 165; reproduced with the kind permission of Dr Ludwig Reichert Verlag). 205

Tables

1.1 Deities of major Babylonian cities favoured in personal names *page* 25
1.2 Personal names referring to temples 26
2.1 Divine names frequently used in Babylonian male names, along with their logographic spellings 40
2.2 Shortening of Babylonian sentence names by omission of elements 50
2.3 Shortening of Babylonian compound names by omission of the theophoric element 51
2.4 Shortening of Babylonian sentence names 52
2.5 Hypocoristic short forms of Babylonian male names 54
2.6 Double names borne by Babylonian men 55
6.1 Name elements consisting of a verbal Sumerogram with a phonetic prefix 94
6.2 Name elements consisting of a verbal Sumerogram with a phonetic suffix 95
6.3 Common formats of Babylonian names with a verbal element 97
8.1 Verbs attested in Aramaic sentence names from the Neo- and Late Babylonian periods 134
8.2 Nouns attested in Aramaic nominal sentence names from the Neo- and Late Babylonian periods 134
8.3 Nouns attested in Aramaic compound names from the Neo- and Late Babylonian periods 135
9.1 Cuneiform renderings of the Hebrew gutturals 145
9.2 Hebrew nominal elements in Yahwistic personal names 155
9.3 Hebrew verbs in personal names attested in Babylonian texts 156
12.1 Egyptian graphemes, their corresponding phonemes, and their known correspondents in Neo- and Late Babylonian 207
13.1 Anatolian *Lallname* types 218
14.1 Greek theophoric names 226

14.2 Greek names according to lexical items 227
14.3 Conversion rules for Greek names into the Babylonian writing system 230
14.4 Typical endings and second elements of Greek names in Babylonian writing 231
14.5 Abbreviations of Greek royal names 232
16.1 Elamite hypocoristica in Neo-Babylonian sources 261
16.2 Neo-Elamite gods occurring in Neo-Babylonian personal names 263
16.3 Neo-Babylonian renderings of Neo-Elamite vowels 269

Contributors

KATHLEEN ABRAHAM is Professor of Hebrew and Ancient Semitic languages at the University of Leuven, and previously at Bar-Ilan University in Israel. She studies and publishes primary sources that shed light on the cultural history of Babylonia in the first millennium BCE, having a strong interest in the linguistic and social consequences of (forced) migration from the Levant at the time.

AHMAD AL-JALLAD holds the Sofia Chair in Arabic Studies at Ohio State University and specialises in the history, language, and cultures of pre-Islamic Arabia.

HEATHER D. BAKER is Associate Professor of Ancient Near Eastern History at the University of Toronto. Her research focuses on the social, economic, and political history of Assyria and Babylonia in the first millennium BCE, on Mesopotamian urbanism, and on the integration of textual and archaeological data.

PAOLA CORÒ is Associate Professor of Assyriology at the Ca' Foscari University of Venice. She combines an expertise in Assyriology with a background in Classics. Her research focuses on first millennium BCE Mesopotamia, especially cuneiform texts from the Hellenistic period. She is the author of *Prebende templari in età seleucide* (2005) and *Seleucid Tablets from Uruk in the British Museum: Text Editions and Commentary* (2018). She currently directs a Ca' Foscari-funded research project that, through a machine-learning and computer vision approach to the study of clay tablets, investigates the role and functions of 'firing holes' in the cuneiform texts from the Library of Ashurbanipal.

LAURA COUSIN studied Assyriology at the University of Paris 1 Panthéon-Sorbonne. She received her PhD in 2016 for a dissertation titled 'Babylon, City of the King in the First Millennium BCE'. She is an associate member of the UMR 7041 ArScAN-HAROC (Nanterre, France).

URI GABBAY is Professor of Assyriology in the Department of Archaeology and Ancient Near East of the Hebrew University of Jerusalem. He teaches Sumerian, Akkadian, and the culture and religion of Ancient Mesopotamia. His research focuses on Sumerian prayers and on Akkadian commentaries of the first millennium BCE.

JULIA GIESSLER is an Assyriologist specialising in Neo- and Late Babylonian sources. She studied at the University of Marburg and wrote her PhD at Freie Universität Berlin on tattoos, brandings, and other forms of body marks on humans and animals in Mesopotamia. During her work for the prosopographical online database *Prosobab*, she developed a keen interest in Babylonian onomastics.

STEFFIE VAN GOMPEL conducts PhD research into ancient Egyptian marriage and family structures at Leiden University. Her research interests include legal documents and legal traditions in Ancient Egypt and the Ancient Near East, daily life in ancient Mediterranean societies, and historical family systems in Eurasia.

ELYNN GORRIS is currently a Marie Skłodowska-Curie global fellow at the Catholic University of Louvain and Macquarie University. She specialises in the language and history of the Neo-Elamite kingdom and the broader Upper Persian Gulf region, and focuses on Neo-Elamite trade networks in her MSCA research project. She recently published a monograph: *Power and Politics in the Neo-Elamite Kingdom* (2020).

MELANIE M. GROß is an Assyriologist specialising in the socio-economic history of first millennium BCE Mesopotamia. She recently published the monograph *At the Heart of an Empire: The Royal Household in the Neo-Assyrian Period* (2020). Together with Caroline Waerzeggers, she directs *Prosobab*, an online prosopography of Babylonia (620–330 BCE).

FRANCIS JOANNÈS is Professor Emeritus of Ancient History at the University of Paris 1 Panthéon-Sorbonne, and a member of the research team Histoire et Archéologie de l'Orient cunéiforme within the Unité Mixte de Recherche Archéologies et Sciences de l'Antiquité du CNRS (MSH-Mondes, Nanterre), with a specialisation in the socio-economic history and cultural aspects of Babylonia in the first millennium BCE. He is currently working on the material culture of Babylonia and manages the 'Babylonian Texts' section of Achemenet.com, a website dedicated to the online publication of Neo-Babylonian and Achaemenid cuneiform documentation.

MICHAEL JURSA is Professor of Assyriology at the University of Vienna. His main research interest is the socio-economic history of Babylonia, in particular in the first millennium BCE.

JOHN P. NIELSEN received his PhD from the Oriental Institute of the University of Chicago and is Associate Professor in the History Department at Bradley University. He is the author of *Sons and Descendants: A Social History of Kin Groups and Family Names in the Early Neo-Babylonian Period (747–626 BC)* (2011), *Early Neo-Babylonian Personal Names from Legal and Administrative Documents (747–626 BCE)* (2015), and *The Reign of Nebuchadnezzar I in History and Historical Memory* (2018), as well as several articles and book chapters.

ZSOLT SIMON is Research Fellow at the Hungarian Research Centre for Linguistics, co-author of the *Digital Philological-Etymological Dictionary of the Minor Ancient Anatolian Corpus Languages*, and co-editor of the *Hungarian Assyriological Review*. He was formerly Sasakawa Research Fellow at the Hungarian Academy of Sciences, Junior Research Fellow at the Research Center for Anatolian Civilizations (Koç University, Istanbul), TÜBITAK Research Fellow (Koç University), and Research Fellow at the Ludwig-Maximilians-Universität München.

RIENEKE SONNEVELT carries out doctoral research at Leiden University on the spread and use of Aramaic in Babylonia during the first millennium BCE. Her thesis focuses on alphabetic epigraphs found on cuneiform clay tablets, the main direct Aramaic source from Babylonia during this period, and the socio-economic context in which they appear.

JAN TAVERNIER is Professor in Ancient Near Eastern Studies at the Université Catholique de Louvain (Belgium). His main research axes are, inter alia, Elamite history and philology, Old Persian history and philology, and the linguistic history of the Achaemenid Empire.

CORNELL THISSEN is an independent researcher and graduate of the VU University Amsterdam. He is currently finishing his PhD thesis, under the supervision of Professor Kristin Kleber, on the orthography of Babylonian names.

CAROLINE WAERZEGGERS is Professor of Assyriology at Leiden University, specialising in the social and cultural history of Babylonia in the first millennium BCE. Together with Melanie M. Groß, she directs *Prosobab*, an online prosopography of Babylonia (620–330 BCE).

YOKO WATAI is currently a visiting researcher at the Institute of Cultural Sciences of Chuo University in Tokyo, a non-permanent member of the research team Histoire et Archéologie de l'Orient cunéiforme within the Unité Mixte de Recherche Archéologies et Sciences de l'Antiquité of CNRS, and a part-time lecturer at several universities in Japan. She received her PhD from the University of Paris 1 Panthéon-Sorbonne in 2012, and was a postdoctoral fellow financed by the Japan Society for the Promotion of Science (JSPS) from 2016 to 2019. Since 2019, her research project on economic activities of women in first-millennium Babylonia has been financed by JSPS Grants-in-Aid for Scientific Research (KAKENHI, Grant Number JP 19K13361).

RAN ZADOK is Professor Emeritus of Mesopotamian, Iranian, and Judaic studies at Tel Aviv University. He specialises in the history and philology of the Fertile Crescent, especially (but not exclusively) Mesopotamia and western Iran, between 1200 and 330 BCE.

Preface

This volume offers a practical introduction to the repertoire of personal names recorded in cuneiform texts from Babylonia in the first millennium BCE. In this period, individuals moved freely as well as involuntarily across the ancient Middle East, leaving traces of their presence in the archives of institutions and private persons in southern Mesopotamia. The multilingual nature of this name material poses challenges for students and researchers who want to access this data for social historical research. This volume offers guidelines and tools to help users navigate this difficult material. The idea for this volume emerged at a training week for graduate students organised by the team of the ERC project *Persia & Babylonia* (Leiden) with Paola Corò (Venice) at Ca' Foscari University in 2018. During this week, participating students learnt about the many-faceted name material in Neo-Babylonian and Late Babylonian sources, including names in languages other than Akkadian, such as Egyptian, Anatolian, Hebrew, Aramaic, Greek, Old Persian, and Elamite. The present volume is based on the conversations held by students and teachers in Venice. We wish to thank our host Paola Corò and Ca' Foscari University for their hospitality in Venice, Nicky van de Beek for coordinating the event, and all participants of the training week for their input. This volume is published open access thanks to the financial support of the European Research Council (Consolidator Grant 682241 *Persia & Babylonia*).

Abbreviations

List of Abbreviations (Editions)

1 N =	MacCown, D. E., R. C. Haines, and D. P. Hansen. 1967. *Nippur. Part I: Temple of Enlil, Scribal Quarter, and Soundings*, Oriental Institute Publications 78. Chicago: University of Chicago Press.
ABC =	Grayson, A. K. 1975. *Assyrian and Babylonian Chronicles*, Texts from Cuneiform Sources 5. Winona Lake: Eisenbrauns.
ACLT =	Yakubovich, I. *Annotated Corpus of Luwian Texts.* http://web-corpora.net/LuwianCorpus.
AD =	Sachs, A. and H. Hunger. 1988, 1989, and 1996. *Astronomical Diaries and Related Texts from Babylonia*, 3 Vols. Vienna: Austrian Academy of Sciences.
AfO 16 =	Weidner, E. F. 1952–3. 'Keilschrifttexte nach Kopien von T. G. Pinches. Neue Folge 1. Babylonische Privaturkunden aus dem 7. Jahrhundert v. Chr. (mit 4 Tafeln)', *Archiv für Orientforschung* 16, 35–46.
AfO 50 =	Waerzeggers, C. 2003–4. 'The Babylonian revolts against Xerxes and the "End of Archives"', *Archiv für Orientforschung* 50, 150–73.
AMI NF 23 =	Stolper, M. W. 1990. 'Tobits in reverse: More Babylonians in Ecbatana', *Archäologische Mitteilungen aus Iran* NF 23, 161–76.
AnOr 8 =	Pohl, A. 1933. *Neubabylonische Rechtsurkunden aus den Berliner Staatlichen Museen*. Rome: Pontificio Istituto Biblico.

AnOr 9 = Pohl, A. 1934. *Neubabylonische Rechtsurkunden aus den Berliner Staatlichen Museen II*, Analecta Orientalia 9. Rome: Pontificio Istituto Biblico.

ÄPN = Ranke, H. 1935, 1952, and 1976. *Die Ägyptische Personennamen. Bd. I: Verzeichnis von Namen*; Bd. II: *Einleitung. Form und Inhalt der Namen. Geschichte der Namen. Vergleiche mit andren Namen. Nachträge und Zusätze zu Bd I. Umschreibungslisten*; Bd. III: *Verzeichnis der Bestandteile*. Glückstadt/ Hamburg: J. J. Augustin.

BaAr 3 = Wunsch, C. forthcoming. *Hauskäufe aus verschiedenen neubabylonischen Archiven*, Babylonische Archive 3. Dresden: ISLET.

BaAr 6 = Wunsch, C. 2022. *Judaeans by the Waters of Babylon: New Historical Evidence in Cuneiform Sources from Rural Babylonia primarily from the Schøyen Collection*, Babylonische Archive 6. Dresden: ISLET.

BaM 15 = Kessler, K. 1984. 'Eine arsakidenzeitliche Urkunde aus Warka (W 18568)', *Baghdader Mitteilungen* 15, 273–81.

BBSt. = King, L. W. 1912. *Babylonian Boundary-Stones and Memorial-Tablets in the British Museum*. London: British Museum.

BE 8/1 = Clay, A. T. 1908. *Legal and Commercial Transactions Dated in the Assyrian, Neo-Babylonian and Persian Periods, Chiefly from Nippur*, The Babylonian Expedition of University of Pennsylvania Series A, Cuneiform Texts 8, Part 1. Philadelphia: University of Pennsylvania.

BE 9 = Hilprecht, H. V. and A. T. Clay. 1898. *Business Documents of Murashû Sons of Nippur, Dated in the Reign of Artaxerxes I (464–424 BC)*, The Babylonian Expedition of University of Pennsylvania, Series A: Cuneiform Texts 9. Philadelphia: University of Pennsylvania.

BE 10 = Clay, A. T. 1904. *Business Documents of Murashû Sons of Nippur Dated in the Reign of Darius II (424–404 BC)*, The Babylonian Expedition of University of Pennsylvania, Series A: Cuneiform Texts 10. Philadelphia: University of Pennsylvania.

BE 15 = Clay, A. T. 1906. *Documents from the Temple Archives of Nippur Dated in the Reigns of Cassite Rulers (Incomplete Dates)*, The Babylonian Expedition of the University of Pennsylvania Series A, Cuneiform Texts 15. Philadelphia: University of Pennsylvania.

BIN 1 = Keiser, C. E. 1917. *Letters and Contracts from Erech Written in the Neo-Babylonian Period*, Babylonian Inscriptions in the Collection of James B. Nies 1. New Haven: Yale University Press.

BRM 1 = Clay, A. T. 1912. *Babylonian Business Transactions of the First Millennium BC*, Babylonian Records in the Library of J. Pierpont Morgan 1. New Haven: Yale University Press.

BRM 2 = Clay, A. T. 1913. *Legal Documents from Erech Dated in the Seleucid Era (312–65 BC)*, Babylonian Records in the Library of J. Pierpont Morgan 2. New Haven: Yale University Press.

CAD = Oppenheim, A. L. and Reiner, E. et al. (eds.). 1956–2010. *The Assyrian Dictionary of the University of Chicago*, 21 Vols. Chicago: Oriental Institute.

Camb. = Strassmaier, J. N. 1890. *Inschriften von Cambyses, König von Babylon (529–521 v.Chr.)*, Babylonische Texte 8–9. Leipzig: Verlag von Eduard Pfeiffer.

CEDSQM = Safaitic inscriptions documented by V. Clark and published on OCIANA. https://krc.web.ox.ac.uk/article/ociana.

CT 4 = Pinches, T. G. 1989. *Cuneiform Texts from Babylonian Tablets in the British Museum Part IV*. London: The Trustees of the British Museum.

CT 22 = Thompson, R. C. 1906. *Cuneiform Texts from Babylonian Tablets in the British Museum Part XXII*. London: The Trustees of the British Museum.

CT 44 = Pinches, T. G. 1963. *Cuneiform Texts from Babylonian Tablets in the British Museum Part XLIV: Miscellaneous Texts*. London: The Trustees of the British Museum.

CT 49 = Kennedy, D. A. 1968. *Cuneiform Texts from Babylonian Tablets in the British Museum Part XLIX: Late-Babylonian Economic Texts*. London: The Trustees of the British Museum.

CT 57 = Pinches, T. G. 1982. *Cuneiform Texts from Babylonian Tablets in the British Museum, Part LVII: Neo-Babylonian and Achaemenid Economic Texts.* London: The Trustees of the British Museum.

CTMMA 3 = Spar, I. and E. von Dassow. 2000. *Cuneiform Texts in the Metropolitan Museum of Art, Volume III: Private Archive Texts from the First Millennium BC.* New York: Brepols.

CTMMA 4 = Jursa, M. and I. Spar. 2014. *Cuneiform Texts in the Metropolitan Museum of Art, Volume IV: The Ebabbar Temple Archive and Other Texts from the Fourth to the First Millennium BC.* New York: Brepols.

CUSAS 28 = Pearce, L. E. and C. Wunsch. 2014. *Documents of Judean Exiles and West Semites in Babylonia in the Collection of David Sofer*, Cornell University Studies in Assyriology and Sumerology 28. Bethesda: CDL Press.

Cyr. = Strassmaier, J. N. 1890. *Inschriften von Cyrus, König von Babylon (538–529 v.Chr.)*, Babylonische Texte 7. Leipzig: Verlag von Eduard Pfeiffer.

Dar. = Strassmaier, J. N. 1897. *Inschriften von Darius, König von Babylon (521–485 v.Chr.)*, Babylonische Texte 10–12. Leipzig: Verlag von Eduard Pfeiffer.

DASI = Digital Archive for the Study of pre-Islamic Arabian Inscriptions, http://dasi.cnr.it/.

DN = Lüddeckens, E. and W. Brunch. 1980–2000. *Demotisches Namenbuch.* Wiesbaden: Dr Ludwig Reichert.

eDiAna = Hackstein, O. et al. (eds.). *Digital Philological-Etymological Dictionary of the Minor Ancient Anatolian Corpus Languages*, www.ediana.gwi.uni-muenchen.de/.

EE = Stolper, M. W. 1985. *Entrepreneurs and Empire: The Murašû Archive, the Murašû Firm, and Persian Rule in Babylonia*, Publications de l'Institut historique et archéologique néerlandais de Stamboul 54. Istanbul: Nederlands Historisch-Archaeologisch Instituut.

ElW = Hinz, W. and H. Koch. 1987. *Elamisches Wörterbuch*, Archäologische Mitteilungen aus Iran, Ergänzungsband 17. Berlin: Dietrich Reimer.

FuB 14 = Jakob-Rost, L. and H. Freydank. 1972. 'Spätbabylonische Rechtsurkunden aus Babylon mit aramäischen Beischriften', *Forschungen und Berichte* 14, 7–35.

GAG = Von Soden, W. 1995. *Grundriss der akkadischen Grammatik*, 3rd ed., Analecta Orientalia 33. Rome: Pontificio Istituto Biblico.

GC 1 = Dougherty, R. P. 1923. *Archives from Erech: Time of Nebuchadnezzar and Nabonidus*, Goucher College Cuneiform Inscriptions, vol. 1. New Haven: Yale University Press.

GC 2 = Dougherty, R. P. 1933. *Archives from Erech: Neo-Babylonian and Persian Periods*, Goucher College Cuneiform Inscriptions, vol. 2. New Haven: Yale University Press.

GT = Takács, G. 1999. *Etymological Dictionary of Egypt, vol. 1: A Phonological Introduction*, Handbuch der Orientalistik 84. Leiden: Brill.

HBTIN = Pearce, L. E. 2009–. *Hellenistic Babylonia: Text, Images, and Names*, http://oracc.museum.upenn.edu/hbtin/index.html.

IMT = Donbaz, V. and M. W. Stolper. 1997. *Istanbul Murašû Texts*, Publications de l'Institut Historique-Archéologique Néerlandais de Stamboul 79. Istanbul: Nederlands Historisch-Archaeologisch Instituut.

IRS = Malbran-Labat, F. 1995. *Les inscriptions royales de Suse. Briques de l'époque paléo-élamite à l'empire néo-élamite*. Paris: Réunion des Musées Nationaux.

JCS 24 = Sack, R. H. 1972. 'Some miscellaneous Neo-Babylonian', *Journal of Cuneiform Studies* 24, 105–6.

JCS 28 = Stigers, H. G. 1976. 'Neo- and Late Babylonian business documents from the John Frederick Lewis Collection', *Journal of Cuneiform Studies* 28, 3–59.

JPA = Allen, J. P. 2013. *The Ancient Egyptian Language. An Historical Study*. Cambridge: Cambridge University Press.

KRS = Safaitic inscriptions from the northeastern Jordanian bādiyah documented by G. M. H. King and published on OCIANA.

LBAT = Pinches, T. G., J. N. Strassmaier, and A. J. Sachs. 1955. *Late Babylonian Astronomical and Related Texts*, Brown University Studies 18. Providence: Brown University Press.

LGPN = Fraser, P. M. (ed.). 1987–. *A Lexicon of the Greek Personal Names.* Oxford: Clarendon Press, partially available online: www.lgpn.ox.ac.uk/.

MDP 9 = Scheil, V. 1907. *Textes élamites-anzanites, troisième série*, Mémoires de la Délégation en Perse 9. Paris: Ernest Leroux.

Nbk. = Strassmaier, J. N. 1889. *Inschriften von Nabuchodonosor, König von Babylon (604–561 v.Chr.)*, Babylonische Texte 5–6. Leipzig: Verlag von Eduard Pfeiffer.

Nbn. = Strassmaier, J. N. 1889. *Inschriften von Nabonidus, König von Babylon (555–538 v.Chr.)*, Babylonische Texte 1–4. Leipzig: Verlag von Eduard Pfeiffer.

OCIANA = Online Corpus of the Inscriptions of Ancient North Arabia, http://krcfm.orient.ox.ac.uk/fmi/webd/OCIANA.

OECT 9 = McEwan, G. J. P. 1982. *Texts from Hellenistic Babylonia in the Ashmolean Museum*, Oxford Editions of Cuneiform Texts 9. Oxford: Clarendon Press.

OECT 10 = McEwan, G. J. P. 1984. *Late Babylonian Texts in the Ashmolean Museum*, Oxford Editions of Cuneiform Texts 10. Oxford: Clarendon Press.

OIP 114 = Cole, S. W. 1996. *Nippur IV: The Early Neo-Babylonian Governor's Archive from Nippur*, Oriental Institute Publications 114. Chicago: The Oriental Institute of the University of Chicago.

OIP 122 = Weisberg, D. B. 2003. *Neo-Babylonian Texts in the Oriental Institute Collection*, Oriental Institute Publications 122. Chicago: The Oriental Institute of the University of Chicago.

PAES III = Littmann, E., D. Magie, and D. R. Stuart. 1907–21. *Publications of the Princeton University Archaeological Expeditions to Syria in 1904–1905, Division III. Greek and Latin Inscriptions in Syria, Section A. Southern Syria.* Leiden: Brill.

PBS 2/1 = Clay, A. T. 1912. *Business Documents of Murashu Sons of Nippur Dated in the Reign of Darius II*, The Museum Publications of the Babylonian Section 2/1. Philadelphia: University Museum.

PNA = Radner, K. (ed.) 1998 and 1999, and Baker, H. D. (ed.) 2000, 2001, 2002, and 2011. *The Prosopography of the Neo-Assyrian Empire*, Vols. 1/I: A; 1/II: B–G; 2/I: Ḫ–K; 2/II: L–N; 3/I: P–Ṣ; and 3/II: Š–Z. Helsinki: The Neo-Assyrian Text Corpus Project.

RINAP 3/1 = Grayson, A. K. and J. Novotny. 2012. *The Royal Inscriptions of Sennacherib, King of Assyria (704–681 BC)*, Part 1, The Royal Inscriptions of the Neo-Assyrian Period 3/1. Winona Lake: Eisenbrauns.

RINAP 4 = Leichty, E. 2011. *The Royal Inscriptions of Esarhaddon, King of Assyria (680–669 BC)*, The Royal Inscriptions of the Neo-Assyrian Period 4. Winona Lake: Eisenbrauns.

ROMCT 2 = McEwan, G. J. P. 1982. *The Late Babylonian Tablets in the Royal Ontario Museum*, Royal Ontario Museum Cuneiform Texts 2. Toronto: Royal Ontario Museum.

SAA 14 = Mattila, R. 2002. *Legal Transactions of the Royal Court of Nineveh, Part II: Assurbanipal through Sin-šarru-iškun*, State Archives of Assyria 14. Helsinki: Helsinki University Press.

SAA 18 = Reynolds, F. 2003. *The Babylonian Correspondence of Esarhaddon*, State Archives of Assyria 18. Helsinki: Helsinki University Press.

STUBM = Corò, P. 2018. *Seleucid Tablets from Uruk in the British Museum. Text Editions and Commentary*, Antichistica 16, Studi orientali 6. Venice: Edizioni Ca' Foscari.

TCL 9 = Contenau, G. 1926. *Contrats et lettres d'Assyrie et de Babylonie. Contrats de Kerkouk – Contrats Kassites – Contrats et lettres d'Assyrie – Lettres Néo-Babyloniennes*, Textes Cunéiformes 9. Paris: Paul Geuthner.

TCL 12 = Contenau, G. 1927. *Contrats néo-babyloniens I: de Téglath-phalasar III à Nabonide*, Textes Cunéiformes 12. Paris: Paul Geuthner.

TCL 13 = Contenau, G. 1929. *Contrats néo-babyloniens II: Achéménides et Séleucides*, Textes Cunéiformes 13. Paris: Paul Geuthner.

TEBR 6 = Joannès, F. 1982. *Textes économiques de la Babylonie récente, Étude des textes de TBER 6*, Études assyriologiques 5. Paris: Éditions Recherche sur les Civilisations.

TMH 2/3 = Krückmann, O. 1933. *Neubabylonische Rechts- und Verwaltungstexte, Texte und Materialien der Frau Professor Hilprecht Collection of Babylonian Antiquities im Eigentum der Universität Jena*. Leipzig: Hinrichs Verlag.

UCP 9/1 and UCP 9/2 = Lutz, H. F. 1927. *Neo-Babylonian Administrative Documents from Erech, Parts I and II*, University of California Publications in Semitic Philology. Berkeley: University of California Press.

UET 4 = Figulla, H. H. M. 1949. *Business Documents of the New-Babylonian Period*, Ur Excavations, Texts 4. London/Philadelphia: British Museum/University Museum.

UET 7 = Gurney, O. R. 1974. *Middle Babylonian Legal Documents and Other Texts*, Ur Excavations, Texts 7. London/Philadelphia: British Museum/University Museum.

VR = Rawlinson H. C. and T. G. Pinches, 1882. *The Cuneiform Inscriptions of Western Asia V: A Selection of the Miscellaneous Inscriptions of Assyria and Babylonia*. London: Jankowsky.

VS 3 = Ungnad, A. 1907. *Vorderasiatische Schriftdenkmäler 3*. Leipzig: J. C. Hinrichs.

VS 4 = Ungnad, A. 1907. *Vorderasiatische Schriftdenkmäler 4*. Leipzig: J. C. Hinrichs.

VS 5 = Ungnad, A. 1908. *Vorderasiatische Schriftdenkmäler 5*. Leipzig: J. C. Hinrichs.

VS 6 = Ungnad, A. 1908. *Vorderasiatische Schriftdenkmäler 6*. Leipzig: J. C. Hinrichs.

WVDOG 51 = Jordan, J. 1928. *Uruk-Warka nach den Ausgrabungen durch die Deutsche Orient-Gesellschaft*, Wissenschaftliche Veröffentlichung der Deutschen Orient-Gesellschaft 51. Leipzig: J. C. Hinrichs.

YNER 1 =	Weisberg, D. B. 1967. *Guild Structure and Political Allegiance in Early Achaemenid Mesopotamia*, Yale Near Eastern Researches 1. New Haven: Yale University Press.
YOS 1 =	Clay, A. T. 1915. *Miscellaneous Inscriptions in the Yale Babylonian Collection*, Yale Oriental Series, Babylonian Texts 1. New Haven: Yale University Press.
YOS 3 =	Clay, A. T. 1919. *Neo-Babylonian Letters from Erech*, Yale Oriental Series, Babylonian Texts 3. New Haven: Yale University Press.
YOS 6 =	Dougherty, R. P. 1920. *Records from Erech, Time of Nabonidus (555–538 BC)*, Yale Oriental Series, Babylonian Texts 6. New Haven: Yale University Press.
YOS 7 =	Tremayne, A. 1925. *Records from Erech, Time of Cyrus and Cambyses (538–521 BC)*, Yale Oriental Series, Babylonian Texts 7. New Haven: Yale University Press.
YOS 19 =	Beaulieu, P.-A. 2000. *Legal and Administrative Texts from the Reign of Nabonidus*, Yale Oriental Series, Babylonian Texts 19. New Haven: Yale University Press.
YOS 20 =	Doty, L. T. 2012. *Cuneiform Documents from Hellenistic Uruk*, Yale Oriental Series, Babylonian Texts 20. New Haven: Yale University Press.
YOS 21 =	Frahm, E. and M. Jursa. 2011. *Neo-Babylonian Letters and Contracts from the Eanna Archive*, Yale Oriental Series, Babylonian Texts 21. New Haven: Yale University Press.

List of Abbreviations (Museum and Excavation Numbers)

Babylon	Babylon Collection (Vorderasiatisches Museum, Berlin)
BM	British Museum (London)
FLP	Free Library of Philadelphia
K	Kuyunjik Collection (British Museum, London)
MMA	Metropolitan Museum of Art (New York)
NBC	Nies Babylonian Collection (Yale University, New Haven)
NCBT	Newell Collection of Babylonian Tablets (Yale University, New Haven)
PTS	Princeton Theological Seminary
VAT	Vorderasiatisches Museum Tontafeln (Berlin)
YBC	Yale Babylonian Collection (Yale University, New Haven)

List of Other Abbreviations and Conventions

*	reconstructed form (or reconstructed year according to post-canonical eponym)
∅	non-realised sound
< . . . >	omitted sign(s)
≪ . . . ≫	superfluous sign(s)
1.sg.	1st person singular, 'I'
2.sg.	2nd person singular, 'you'
3.sg.	3rd person singular, '(s)he'
Akk.	Akkadian
Aram.	Aramaic
Bab.	Babylonian
Bibl. Heb.	Biblical Hebrew
C	consonant
Camb	Cambyses
conj.	conjugation
Cyr	Cyrus
D	D stem
Dar	Darius I
DN	deity name
Egypt.	Egyptian
Elam.	Elamite
esp.	especially
^{f}	marker introducing a normalised female name
FN	family name
^{f}PN	female personal name
G	G stem
GN	geographical name
Heb.	Hebrew
Hiph.	Hiphil
hypocor.	hypocorism
imp.	imperative
impf.	imperfect
inf.	infinitive
Ir.	Iranian
l.e.	left edge
lo.e.	lower edge
m.	masculine
MB	Middle Babylonian

mng.	meaning
mod.	modern
MT	Masoretic Text
NA	Neo-Assyrian
Nbk	Nebuchadnezzar II
Nbn	Nabonidus
N/LB	Neo- and Late Babylonian
obj.	object
OP	Old Persian
perf.	perfect
Phoen.	Phoenician
pl.	plural
PN	personal name
prec.	precative
pres.	present tense
pret.	preterite
Pun.	Punic
r.	reverse
resp.	respectively
sg.	singular
subj.	subject
subst.	(verbal) substantive
syll.	syllabic
TN	temple name
u.e.	upper edge
Ugar.	Ugaritic
V	vowel
v.	verb
W.Sem.	West Semitic
wr.	written
Y	Y renders the Yahwistic element in English translations of Hebrew names (Chapter 9)

Introduction

Caroline Waerzeggers

Aim of This Book

One of the largest corpora of epigraphic texts from the ancient world was produced between c. 750 and 100 BCE in Babylonia, present-day southern Iraq, on clay tablets in cuneiform script. In this period, Babylonia was intensively connected to other areas of the Near East and the Mediterranean, from Greece to Iran and from Anatolia to Egypt and Arabia.[1] Increasingly, historians are finding their way to these rich materials, but not without encountering problems of accessibility. One of these problems relates to the high degree of language variety reflected in the personal name record of this text corpus.

Personal names are a fascinating testimony to Babylonia's multi-ethnic society in a globalising world, for a person's name often (albeit not necessarily) tells us something about the language community in which they grew up as a child. Personal names thus offer information on the ancient linguistic landscape; indeed, not seldomly, the onomastic material constitutes the only remaining trace of non-Babylonian communities.[2] For modern readers, however, the study of personal names often poses problems. While most languages represented in the Babylonian name material have been studied in their own scholarly traditions, few researchers enjoy training in each of these traditions to be able to deal with these materials independently.

Challenges do not only apply to the linguistic determination of non-Babylonian names. A person's name was, and is, more than a tool of identification.[3] The name is an important element in the construction of

[1] For a general introduction to the history of Babylonia in this period, see Beaulieu (2018).

[2] Puzey (2016) makes a case for the value of onomastics in linguistic landscape research generally. For the methodological challenges of reconstructing (minority) language communities from the repertoire of personal names in cuneiform texts, see the reflections by Pearce 2015 on identifying Judeans in the Babylonian text corpus.

[3] The name as a means of identification in Mesopotamia is discussed by Démare-Lafont (2014).

social identity.[4] As shown in Chapter 1, Babylonian names situated the person in a larger social group (e.g., a family unit, clan, residential, or occupational community) and transmitted values that were culturally defined and historically contingent. Decoding the dynamic meanings of a name is a complex procedure that is seldomly explained in specialist literature.

Moreover, the spelling of personal names was subject to extensive, and sometimes confusing, scribal conventions that are yet to be described in a systematic way (Chapter 6). This renders even the seemingly straightforward step of reading a name a complicated matter. In the case of non-Babylonian names, we face the additional challenge of trying to understand how Babylonian scribes transcribed the alien-sounding names in a script that was ill-suited for the task at hand.[5]

This book provides users with an introduction to the personal name repertoire in the Babylonian sources, reflecting interests both of traditional 'onomastics' (e.g., name typology, etymology, semantics, and orthography) and of 'socio-onomastics' (e.g., naming practices, patterns of name use, attitudes towards names, and religious sensibilities reflected in names). The volume showcases methodologies for working with personal names and offers practical guidelines and tools. As a guide, it offers a general overview of the current state of the field and gives suggestions for further reading in specialist literature.

Knowledge of the linguistic and cultural background of personal names allows students independent access to a rich mine of new data for writing the social and cultural history of Babylonia in its Mediterranean and Near Eastern contexts.[6] Onomastic analysis of personal names touches upon such themes as slavery and servitude, mobility and migration, acculturation and social segmentation, identity and gender, and lineage and patronage. Moreover, as some of the languages represented in the name repertoire are themselves poorly documented, the Babylonian transmission has significance beyond questions of a socio-historical nature pertaining to Babylonia proper (see, for instance, the indirectly attested Iranica discussed in Chapter 15 or the Anatolian and Elamite names in Chapters 13 and 16).

4 Aldrin (2016) discusses how onomastic studies have understood the role of personal names in the construction of identities. For a study of these matters focused on Mesopotamia, see Radner (2005) and Cousin (2020).

5 Matters of cuneiform transcription are discussed in most chapters of Part II.

6 As the Babylonian text corpus is still largely unpublished, relying on the work of others is not always an option.

The volume is meant as a first port of call for students interested in tapping into this multi-fronted source of information.

Historical Background

After the end of the Isin II period in the eleventh century BCE, text production in Babylonia came to a near halt, with few exceptions (Paulus 2014). In the next centuries, southern Mesopotamia was politically divided between communities of different cultural, social, and linguistic backgrounds. The cities were inhabited by people of Sumero–Akkadian heritage, while the borderlands – along the Zagros, the Gulf Coast, and the Arabian Desert – saw the arrival of new tribal confederacies of Aramean, Chaldean, and later also Arabian people.[7] Their occasional encroachment on urban hinterlands created tensions with the city-based population, as reported in some of the few cuneiform inscriptions that were crafted in Babylonia in this period.[8] As is well known, the personal name record from both Assyria and Babylonia reflects the increasing presence of West Semitic-speaking people in Mesopotamia.[9]

By c. 750 BCE, more cuneiform texts were again written in the cities, and the 'Kings of Babylon', even those of Chaldean descent, managed to unite the region for increasing lengths of time. The growing popularity of family names among the urban nobility reveals the emergence of a lineage society (Chapter 4). This was also the time when Assyria intensified its conquest of the Near East under Tiglath-pileser III. Babylonia inevitably came under control of its northern neighbour, at times as a vassal ruled by its own king, at other times as part of a single imperial monarchy.

A Babylonian rebel, Nabopolassar, brought the time of Assyrian suzerainty to an end. He not only 'avenged' the land of Akkad by dispelling the Assyrians from Babylonia (626 BCE), he also went on to topple the Assyrian Empire in its entirety, with the help of his Median allies. In due course, Babylonia became the next dominant power of the Near East, heir, and successor of its erstwhile oppressor, Assyria.

Babylonian society changed as a result of the imperial ambitions of its ruling class. These changes can be traced in the personal name record. First,

7 Beaulieu 2018, 171–92 and Chapters 4, 8, and 11 in this volume. The Chaldeans are thought to be ethno-linguistically Aramean: see Streck (2014, 299–300).

8 Cylinder of Nabû-šumu-iškun (Frame 1995, B.6.14.2001 i 15'b–21'); a later Babylonian chronicle reports on similar events under Nabû-šumu-iškun's predecessor Erība-Marduk (Grayson 1975, ABC 24 rev. 9–15).

9 Fales 1991; Nissinen 2014, 282–95; Streck 2014; and Chapter 8 in this volume.

according to recent scholarship, a centrifugal dynamic took place in the centre of the Empire. Families from the Babylon era were encouraged to settle in smaller, provincial towns of the imperial core – such as Uruk, Ur, and Sippar – as representatives of the state. This effort of centralisation is reflected in onomastic patterns: the Babylon-based families introduced their own naming practices to the local arena (Jursa and Gordin 2018). A second social shift that can be studied through personal names is the growing complexity of Babylonia's linguistic landscape as a result of imperial expansion. After the fall of the Assyrian Empire, refugees, deportees, and other migrants from Assyria came southward to settle, or be settled, in Babylonia. There they may have joined older émigré communities who were established in the south for political reasons when Assyria still ruled the world (Beaulieu 2019). These Assyrians are among the earliest ethno-linguistic groups whose presence can be discerned in the Babylonian text corpus thanks to their distinctive repertoire of personal names (see Chapter 7). The next decades saw the arrival of more non-Babylonian communities, often victims of war who had been taken captive during military expeditions in the West – the Levant, Syria, and Egypt (Chapters 8, 9, 10, 12, 13). Once transported to Babylonia, these deportees faced a range of different fates. Some were distributed against their will as human booty to temples, others were settled as tax-paying farmers on newly reclaimed crown land, and the most eminent among them (the defeated kings and their families, artisans, and other skilled workers of the conquered kingdoms) were kept at the palace of Babylon as distinguished, yet humiliated, hostages. Recent research shows that the Babylonian Empire's policy of forced migrations had devastating effects on the peripheries while changing the social fabric of the centre.[10] The linguistic landscape of Babylonia further diversified following the voluntary migration of traders, merchants, and settlers, amongst others, attracted by the opportunities of an expanding economy. Onomastics is the primary means of detecting the presence of these men and women in their new environments. Babylonian scribes sometimes used ethnic labels to specify the origins of foreigners. For instance, a palace scribe at the court of Nebuchadnezzar, charged with administering the dispensation of oil rations to captives, listed among the many recipients a certain Kurbannu 'the Mede' and seven 'Ionian' carpenters (*madāya*, *iamanāya*; Weidner 1939, 930, 933). But scribes did not always add such ethnonyms; in these

[10] The case of Judah and its population has received much attention of late (e.g., Alstola 2020); other communities subjected by Babylon suffered similar experiences.

cases, the personal name can offer a clue about the person's roots. As an example, we can cite the case of Pusamiski, an Egyptian man recorded in the archive of the temple of Sippar, and of Milkūmu-šarru-uṣur, an Ammonite man working in the service of the Empire as a royally appointed official. Neither of these men is explicitly labelled as Egyptian or Ammonite; instead, their foreign roots can be inferred from their names. In the case of the Egyptian man this information is of a linguistic nature: Pusamiski is a name in the Egyptian language (Psamtek).[11] In the case of Milkūmu-šarru-uṣur, it is the element Milkūmu that gives away the man's Ammonite roots: the god Milkom was venerated in the Transjordanian kingdom of Ammon, which was incorporated into the Babylonian Empire early in the sixth century BCE.[12]

Cyrus the Great of Persia conquered Babylonia in 539 BCE and added its vast realm to his emergent Empire.[13] In the following decades, Cyrus and his successors went on to create the largest and most resilient state the world had seen so far. In this new constellation of power, Babylonia lost its metropolitan status, causing its society to change and adapt again. The erstwhile capital of Babylon became the seat of a province ('satrapy') in the new state, albeit an important one with a large population and a prosperous economy. This prosperity depended to a significant degree on the labour of the deportee communities whom the Babylonian state had settled in its eastern borderland. The Persians recognised the value of these communities. Steps were taken to protect them from formal slavery by fixing their legal status as dependents of the state, while certain groups within these communities were sent back to their ancestral lands (Alstola 2020), presumably as protégés of the new regime. Archival continuities allow us to study the fate of those who stayed behind in Babylonia. Well into the fifth century, the multi-ethnic fabric of the population remains visible in the linguistic variety of the personal name repertoire captured in documentary texts (Zadok 2003). The change of regime also created new conditions for Babylonia's traditional ruling class. The Persians relied on their own 'ethno-classe' to staff the highest imperial positions, giving rise to the formation of a new colonial super-elite (Briant 1988). In the cuneiform documentation, this nobility is recognisable by their Persian names (Chapter 15). The Babylonian native elite continued to enjoy privileges but they gradually saw their position erode. After a failed revolt, they

[11] See Bongenaar and Haring (1994, 70) and Chapter 12 (this volume).
[12] For the name Milkūmu-šarru-uṣur, see Chapter 10 in this volume.
[13] For the rise of Cyrus and his conquests, see Shayegan (2018) and Kuhrt (2021).

suffered considerable setbacks (Waerzeggers 2003–4). This affected in particular the 'old guard' of Babylon-based families who had enjoyed the protection of the Babylonian kings in the past. A reversal of fortune is in evidence: the local families, whose influence had been curtailed by the efforts of centralisation by the Babylonian state, now saw an opportunity to reaffirm their positions and shape their own agendas. These developments left a clear trace in the name repertoire of Uruk.[14] It is thought that similar trends affected other provincial towns as well.

The name repertoire recorded in cuneiform texts underwent further change after Alexander's conquest of Babylon (331 BCE) and the (eventual) establishment of Seleucid rule over Babylonia. The number of Greek individuals attested in cuneiform sources increases significantly (Chapter 14). Thanks to the efforts of Julien Monerie, this corpus of Greek names is now entirely and easily accessible (Monerie 2014). In many instances, the bearers of Greek names in Babylonia were dignitaries of the Empire, but members of the native Babylonian elite are also known to have adopted Greek names. Intermarriage meant that in some families Greek and Babylonian heritage came together in the private sphere – a development that is, again, traceable in onomastic practice (Langin-Hooper and Pearce 2014).

Seleucid rule over Babylonia entered an unstable phase after the death of Antiochos IV in 164 BCE. It took a long period of conflict before the area was consolidated as a territory of the Parthian Empire by Phraates II and his successor Mithradates II (124–88 BCE).[15] Seen from the perspective of the cuneiform text corpus, however, the change of regime had little impact on the ground. By now, the practice of writing and storing cuneiform texts was much reduced. The tradition survived exclusively in an insular and inward-looking group associated with some of the major sanctuaries (e.g., in Babylon and Uruk).[16] Not long after the start of Parthian rule, in the first decades of the first century BCE, the use of cuneiform for recording everyday legal or administrative transactions came to a halt. Even though learned texts (mostly of astronomical content) continued to be written for some time, the retreat of cuneiform from everyday life means that also the repertoire of personal names, once amply attested in documentary texts, now slips out of our view.

14 Kessler (2004); Beaulieu (2019, 9–11).

15 His predecessor Mithradates I had not managed to establish stable rule despite his initial victory over the Seleucid monarch Demetrios II in 141 BCE. For the transition from Seleucid to Parthian rule in Babylonia, see Beaulieu (2018, 265–7).

16 Clancier 2011.

The Text Corpus and Its Limitations

The personal names discussed in this volume derive mostly from Babylonian cuneiform texts written on clay tablets.[17] Tens of thousands of such texts survive in a nearly uninterrupted stream of varying densities from the mid-eighth century to the early Parthian period. They offer a rich and still mostly untapped fount of data on named individuals, recorded in well-documented archival or literary contexts. The social embeddedness of these attestations allows one to tease out details about the shifting composition of Babylonian society in the course of these centuries, a time when the cultural and political significance of Babylonia in the Middle East waxed and waned.

It is important to emphasise that the cuneiform evidence, albeit rich and extensive in its own right, offers only a limited view of Babylonian society in its full extent. An obvious bias is the under-representation of women – and hence, women's names – as a result of the type of transactions usually recorded by Babylonian scribes.[18] Another shortcoming is the patchy representation of the diverse linguistic landscape. Babylonia boasted a multi-ethnic society where many different languages were spoken, some of them written in their own scripts that have not, or only sparingly, survived. The most important of these other languages and scripts is Aramaic. It is generally thought that by the mid-first millennium BCE, southern Mesopotamia had become bilingual: in the cities, and especially in the temple communities, the Babylonian language and the Sumero–Akkadian cuneiform script were used, whereas large sections of the population, rural as well as urban, used Aramaic both for spoken and written communication (Beaulieu 2006). The social standing of Aramaic increased when it became an officially sanctioned *lingua franca* of the Persian Empire.[19] The perishable materials on which the alphabetic letters were

[17] The clay tablet was not the only medium used for writing cuneiform texts in Babylonia at the time. MacGinnis (2002), Jursa (2004, 170–8), and Nielsen and Kozuh (2021) discuss the use of wooden boards in Neo-Babylonian accounting. High-end ivory writing boards were excavated in Assyria, and many scenes on Assyrian palace reliefs depict scribes writing on folding boards (Fincke 2004). These depictions give us an idea of how the wooden specimens referred to in Babylonian texts may have looked. In addition to wax boards, other surfaces (such as leather) were also used for writing cuneiform texts. Royal inscriptions were executed on a variety of materials, including architectural elements, rock faces, steles, decorative tiles, clay prisms and cylinders, votive objects (stones, jewellery, etc.), and vessels (Da Riva 2008).

[18] For the socio-economic considerations that determined whether or not a transaction was recorded on clay, see Van De Mieroop (1997), for Mesopotamia in general, and Jursa (2005, 9), for the Late Babylonian text corpus in particular.

[19] The rise and use of Aramaic as a *lingua franca* in the Assyrian, Babylonian, and Achaemenid Empires is discussed by Folmer (2020).

scratched or painted with pen and ink did not survive, leaving us with only a few traces of written Aramaic (i.e., those applied on durable materials).[20] As the choice of language/script/medium reflected faultlines in society, it becomes quickly clear that we do not only have to reckon with a textual record that favours more powerful groups in society while silencing others. Especially during Babylon's imperial age (c. 620–540 BCE) the name repertoire of non-Babylonian communities often comes to us in contexts where imbalances of power brought these groups within the perimeter of elite interests. The ration lists of the N1 archive from Nebuchadnezzar's palace are a case in point. After Babylonia lost its hegemony, first to the Persian monarchs and later to their Macedonian, Seleucid, and Parthian successors, anthroponomastics no longer reflect such disbalances of power in straightforward ways. Many of the Elamite, Persian, and Greek names attested in cuneiform records pertain to individuals who were part of the imperial super-elite of these empires. Another limitation that needs emphasising is the unequal spread of documentation across the centuries covered in this volume. After the long sixth century BCE, the overall number of surviving texts is lower. This drop in quantity does not, however, mean that the later periods are less promising for (socio-)onomastic research. The Astronomical Diaries are a case in point. These texts contain records of natural and human phenomena made by scholars of the Esagil temple of Babylon. Whereas the earlier Diaries mention very few individual persons by name (mostly kings), those from the Seleucid and Parthian periods talk more often about the actions of a range of (non-royal) historical persons, citing even their very words.[21]

State of Research

Onomastics – the study of names – is a broad field of research with a long history (Hough 2016). It encompasses not only personal names ('anthroponyms'), the topic of the current volume, but also place names, literary names, names of non-human entities such as business companies, and objects, among others. As a field of research, onomastics has an interdisciplinary outlook, combining the study of names with insights from linguistics, geography, sociology, psychology, and cultural and religious

[20] Note that as a spoken language Aramaic left its mark on Akkadian, for instance, in the shape of loanwords. The influence of Aramaic on the Babylonian dialect is nowadays thought to be less thorough and far-reaching than some decades ago.

[21] See Haubold, Steele, and Stevens (2019) (general introduction to the Astronomical Diaries); Tuplin (2019, 95–9) (prosopography of the Diaries).

studies. Broadly speaking, onomastics moved in the course of the twentieth century from favouring studies on the origins of names (e.g., etymology) to studies on naming practices (also known as 'socio-onomastics').[22]

In Assyriology too the study of names constitutes a vibrant area of interest (Pruzsinszky 2021). Like in the broader field of onomastics, one notices a shift of attention from the formal characteristics of names attested in cuneiform texts (e.g., their semiotic value or semantic meaning, linguistic features, typology, and classification) to the social and cultural significance of names and naming (Pruzsinszky 2021, 483–91).

The onomastic heritage of Babylonia in the period under consideration was first studied by Knut L. Tallqvist in his still indispensable *Neubabylonisches Namenbuch* (1905). In recent decades, Ran Zadok exploited the name repertoire (personal and otherwise) with the aim of studying Babylonia's society, geography, and linguistic landscape.[23] Significant work on naming practices was done by John P. Nielsen, who described for the first time the historical development of the system of clan names (2011). There is currently no resource comparable to the *Prosopography of the Neo-Assyrian Empire* (PNA) that supplies students with an overview of all individuals attested with a personal name in the Neo-Assyrian text corpus. Julien Monerie's dictionary of Greek names in Hellenistic Babylonian sources covers a specific sub-section of the Babylonian text corpus (Monerie 2014). John P. Nielsen assembled the personal names in early Neo-Babylonian texts (Nielsen 2015). The online database *Prosobab* collects information on persons attested in cuneiform texts under the Babylonian and Persian Empires (Waerzeggers and Groß et al. 2019).

Structure and Limitations of This Book

The focus of this book is on Babylonia (i.e., the southern Mesopotamian plain): it uses name material that is found in cuneiform records from this area dating between c. 750 and 100 BCE. The first six chapters of this volume (Part One) are concerned with naming practices in the Babylonian-speaking communities residing in the southern Mesopotamian cities. The next twelve

[22] For brief introductions to 'onomastics' and 'socio-onomastics', see Nicolaisen (2015), Ainiala (2016), Hough (2016), and Ainiala and Östman (2017).

[23] Zadok's body of scholarship is too vast to do justice to here. His major works on onomastics are his 1978 and 1979 monographs on West Semites and Jews in Babylonia and his 2009 monograph on Iranian names. Recently Gabbay and Gordin (2021, xiii–xxii) compiled a list of Ran Zadok's publications, to which the reader is referred.

chapters (Part II) are devoted to non-Babylonian personal names recorded in Babylonian texts. In these chapters, we do not attempt to describe the entire onomastic traditions of the various languages, but we focus on names borne by individuals recorded in the Babylonian sources. For example, the chapter on Assyrian names (Chapter 7) discusses such names in Babylonian texts, not the entire onomastic material of the Neo-Assyrian text corpus. Similarly, the chapter on Aramaic names (Chapter 8) focuses on such names in Babylonian texts.

Most of the Babylonians, whose names feature in Part I, resided in the urban centres, embraced Sumero–Akkadian culture, shared common religious traditions and political ideologies, and spoke and wrote the same language.[24] Despite their shared cultural values, naming practices reveal significant regional variation and social differentiation. Francis Joannès discusses the social aspects of Babylonian naming practices in Chapter 1. After outlining the fundamentals of name identification (patronym, mammonymy and papponymy, family names), the author draws attention to distinctive name types for foundlings, orphans, and slaves as well as to the existence of taboos on certain names. Chapter 2, by Julia Giessler, offers a typology of Babylonian male names and discusses naming practices, such as the use of nicknames, double names, and other variants. Chapter 3, by Laura Cousin and Yoko Watai, continues this line of investigation and presents a typology of Babylonian female names. The chapter concludes with a discussion of the role of names in the construction of social and gender identities. John P. Nielsen, in Chapter 4, points out that the name as a means of legal identification underwent change in the course of the first millennium. Whereas in older periods a two-tier filiation (name + patronym) sufficed, an extra name now added information about the individual's membership to a larger kin group. Nielsen discusses the historical origins of this onomastic practice, the typology of family names, and their social meaning in the emergent lineage society of first-millennium BCE Babylonia. Chapter 5, by Michael Jursa, deals with a particular name type often borne by royal officials that contains a reference to the king. The author discusses to what extent names of

[24] The ability to read and write cuneiform was limited to an educated elite that was associated with the temples and institutions of civic administration. While this group constituted a minority in absolute numbers, in-group literacy rates were high, as most of the male adults were able to read and write on at least a rudimentary level (Jursa 2011). Advanced writing skills were the prerogative of scholars and professional scribes (Veldhuis 2011). The status of Babylonian as a vernacular declined in favour of Aramaic in the course of the first millennium BCE (Beaulieu 2006), but within the secluded world of the temple communities Babylonian probably remained in use as a spoken language long after older scholarship posited its 'death' (Hackl 2021).

this type can be used to make assumptions about the name-bearer's allegiance to the crown. The final chapter of Part I (Chapter 6), by Cornell Thissen, delves into the conventions of orthography that determined how Babylonian scribes rendered personal names. It offers a number of useful tools to navigate the numerous (unwritten) rules.

In Part II, each chapter focuses on the name repertoire of a particular, non-Babylonian language as attested in the cuneiform texts from the period under consideration: Assyrian (Chapter 7 by Heather D. Baker), Aramaic (Chapter 8 by Rieneke Sonnevelt), Hebrew (Chapter 9 by Kathleen Abraham), Phoenician and related Canaanite languages (Chapter 10 by Ran Zadok), Arabian names (Chapter 11 by Ahmad al-Jallad), Egyptian (Chapter 12 by Steffie van Gompel), Anatolian (Chapter 13 by Zsolt Simon), Greek (Chapter 14 by Paola Corò), Old Iranian (Chapter 15 by Jan Tavernier), Elamite (Chapter 16 by Elynn Gorris), Sumerian (Chapter 17 by Uri Gabbay), and onomastica of residual languages and unexplained names (Chapter 18 by Ran Zadok). With the exception of the names in Sumerian and in some residual languages, these names mostly pertain to individuals and communities who migrated, for a variety of reasons and at different moments in the course of the first millennium BCE, to the southern part of the alluvial plain.

The chapters in Part II all adhere to the same general structure. They open with a brief discussion of the language at hand, followed by the historical background that explains why individuals bearing names in that language can be found in the cuneiform text material. The chapters continue with an overview of the principal name types and name elements in the respective language. These discussions are meant to help the identification of new attestations in the future, as the editing process of the Babylonian text corpus continues. The chapters proceed with a consideration of naming practices in the pertinent communities (socio-onomastics) and close with a discussion of spelling conventions used by Babylonian scribes to render names in the language at hand. The authors supply practical tools for identifying names of the pertinent language and point the reader to useful literature for further reading.

A Note on Conventions Used in This Volume

The contributors to this volume have made different choices with regard to the difficult question of how to normalise the Babylonian renderings of non-Babylonian names. Babylonian scribes faced limitations when trying to render foreign names in the script at their disposal. Not seldomly, they heard sounds that were alien to their own native language and for which no suitable cuneiform signs were available. This problem did not only affect names from languages unrelated to Semitic Akkadian, such as Elamite or Anatolian, but also the gutturals and vowel quality of names from the Aramaic, Hebrew, and Arabian repertoire. As a result, foreign-language names appear in the texts in a Babylonianised version (i.e., in a form that reflects the interpretation of the Babylonian scribe). This leaves scholars with a number of options when discussing these names. Some stick as closely as possible to the version as recorded in the cuneiform text, sometimes going as far as abstaining from a normalisation altogether by citing the name in transcription. This procedure is preferable especially if the original language is badly known (e.g., Elamite). Other scholars prefer to cite the name in its original language. For instance, in Chapter 15 Jan Tavernier cites the restored Old Persian name *Miθravasa- which in the Babylonian text appears as Mitriamasu (^{I}*mit-ri-a-ma-a-su*; Tavernier 2007, 253). Similarly, in Chapter 14 Paola Corò cites the Greek name Poseidōnios, which was rendered Pisidunisi (^{I}*pi-si-du-ni-si*) by the Babylonian scribe (Monerie 2014, 160). This latter approach is only possible if the original language is well documented.

Throughout the chapters, female names are marked with an initial superscript ^{f} (e.g., ^{f}Amtia). This letter ^{f} does not relate to the actual rendering or pronunciation of the name in Babylonian. It is based on the orthographic convention of the cuneiform script to mark female names with a cuneiform sign designating 'woman'.[25] In all fairness, male names were also preceded by a cuneiform marker (the so-called '*Personenkeil*'); nevertheless, we left male names unmarked in Latin-script renderings.

The scope of this volume is limited to personal names, but some chapters also include discussions of relevant ethnonyms and toponyms, especially when these are composed of personal names.

References

Ainiala, T. 2016. 'Names in society' in C. Hough (ed.), *The Oxford Handbook of Names and Naming*, Oxford: Oxford University Press, pp. 371–81.

Ainiala, T. and J.-O. Östman 2017. 'Introduction: socio-onomastics and pragmatics' in T. Ainiala and J.-O. Östman (eds.), *Socio-Onomastics: The Pragmatics of Names*. Amsterdam: John Benjamins, pp. 1–18.

[25] We did not add the superscript ^{f} when no such marker was used in the cuneiform text or when historical women with well-known non-Babylonian names are discussed (e.g., Laodice).

Aldrin, E. 2016. 'Names and identity' in C. Hough (ed.), *The Oxford Handbook of Names and Naming*, Oxford: Oxford University Press, pp. 382–94.

Alstola, T. 2020. *Judeans in Babylonia: A Study of Deportees in the Sixth and Fifth Centuries BCE*, Culture and History of the Ancient Near East 109. Leiden: Brill.

Beaulieu, P.-A. 2006. 'Official and vernacular languages: the shifting sands of imperial and cultural identities in first-millennium BC Mesopotamia' in S. L. Sanders (ed.), *Margins of Writing, Origins of Cultures*, Oriental Institute Seminars 2. Chicago: The Oriental Institute of the University of Chicago, pp. 187–216.

Beaulieu, P.-A. 2018. *A History of Babylon (2200 BC – AD 75)*. Chichester: Wiley.

Beaulieu, P.-A. 2019. 'Temple towns and nation building: migrations of priestly families in the late periods', *Journal of Ancient Near Eastern Religions* 19, 3–17.

Bongenaar, A. C. V. M. and B. J. J. Haring 1994. 'Egyptians in Neo-Babylonian Sippar', *Journal of Cuneiform Studies* 46, 59–72.

Briant, P. 1988. 'Ethno-classe dominante et populations soumises dans l'empire achéménide: le cas de l'Égypte' in A. Kuhrt and H. Sancisi-Weerdenburg (eds.), *Method and Theory*, Achaemenid History 3. Leiden: Nederlands Instituut voor het Nabije Oosten, pp. 137–74.

Clancier, P. 2011. 'Cuneiform culture's last guardians: the old urban notability of Hellenistic Uruk' in K. Radner and E. Robson (eds.), *Oxford Handbook of Cuneiform Culture*, Oxford: Oxford University Press, pp. 752–73.

Cousin, L. 2020. 'Sweet girls and strong men: onomastics and personality traits in first-millennium sources', *Die Welt des Orients* 50/2, 334–55.

Da Riva, R. 2008. *The Neo-Babylonian Royal Inscriptions: An Introduction*, Guides to the Mesopotamian Textual Record 4. Münster: Ugarit-Verlag.

Démare-Lafont, S. 2014. 'Identifiers and identification methods in Mesopotamia' in M. Depauw and S. Coussement (eds.), *Identifiers and Identification Methods in the Ancient World. Legal Documents in Ancient Societies III*, Orientalia Lovaniensia Analecta 229. Leuven: Peeters, pp. 13–31.

Fales, M. F. 1991. 'West Semitic names in the Assyrian Empire: diffusion and social relevance', *Studi Epigrafici e Linguistici sul Vicino Oriente Antico* 8, 99–117.

Fincke, J. 2004. 'The Babylonian texts of Nineveh: report on the British Museum's Ashurbanipal Library Project,' *Archiv für Orientforschung* 50, 111–49.

Folmer, M. 2020. 'Aramaic as Lingua Franca' in R. Hasselbach-Andee (ed.), *A Companion to Ancient Near Eastern Languages*, Hoboken: Wiley, pp. 373–99.

Frame, G. 1995. *Rulers of Babylonia: From the Second Dynasty of Isin to the End of Assyrian Domination (1157–612 BC)*, Royal Inscriptions of Mesopotamia Babylonian Periods, vol. 2. Toronto: Toronto University Press.

Gabbay, U. and S. Gordin 2021. *Individuals and Institutions in the Ancient Near East. A Tribute to Ran Zadok*, Studies in Ancient Near Eastern Records 27. Boston/Berlin: De Gruyter.

Grayson, A. K. 1975. *Assyrian and Babylonian Chronicles*, Texts from Cuneiform Sources 5. Locust Valley: J.J. Augustin.

Hackl, J. 2021. 'The death of Akkadian as a written and spoken language' in J.-P. Vita (ed.), *History of the Akkadian Language*, Vol. 2: *The Second and First Millennia BCE*, Handbook of Oriental Studies 152. Leiden: Brill, pp. 1459–77.

Haubold, J., J. Steele and K. Stevens. 2019. 'Introduction' in J. Haubold, J. Steele, and K. Stevens (eds), *Keeping Watch in Babylon: The Astronomical Diaries in Context*. Culture and History of the Ancient Near East 100. Leiden: Brill, pp. 1–18.

Hough, C. 2016. 'Introduction' in C. Hough (ed.), *The Oxford Handbook of Names and Naming*, Oxford: Oxford University Press, pp. 1–14.

Jursa, M. 2004. 'Accounting in Neo-Babylonian institutional archives: structure, usage, implications' in M. Hudson and C. Wunsch (eds.), *Creating Economic Order: Record-keeping, Standardization, and the Development of Accounting in the Ancient Near East*. Dresden: ISLET, pp. 145–98.

Jursa, M. 2005. *Neo-Babylonian Legal and Administrative Documents: Typology, Contents and Archives*, Guides to the Mesopotamian Textual Record 1. Münster: Ugarit-Verlag.

Jursa, M. 2011. 'Cuneiform writing in Neo-Babylonian temple communities' in K. Radner and E. Robson (eds.), *Oxford Handbook of Cuneiform Culture*, Oxford: Oxford University Press, pp. 184–204.

Jursa, M. and S. Gordin 2018. 'The ousting of the Nūr-Sîns: micro-historical evidence for state-building at the Neo-Babylonian Empire's "Augustan threshold"', *Hebrew Bible and Ancient Israel* 7, 42–64.

Kessler, K. 2004. 'Urukäische Familien versus babylonische Familien: die Namengebung in Uruk, die Degradierung der Kulte von Eanna und der Aufstieg des Gottes Anu', *Altorientalische Forschungen* 31, 237–62.

Kuhrt, A. 2021. 'The great conquests' in B. Jacobs and R. Rollinger (eds.), *A Companion to the Achaemenid Persian Empire*. Chichester: Wiley, pp. 403–13.

Langin-Hooper, S. M. and L. E. Pearce, 2014. 'Mammonymy, maternal-line names, and cultural identification: clues from the onomasticon of Hellenistic Uruk', *Journal of the American Oriental Society* 134, 185–202.

MacGinnis, J. 2002. 'The use of writing boards in the Neo-Babylonian temple administration at Sippar', *Iraq* 64, 217–36.

Monerie, J. 2014. *D'Alexandre à Zoilos: Dictionnaire prosopographique des porteurs de nom grec dans les sources cunéiformes*, Oriens et Occidens 23. Stuttgart: Franz Steiner Verlag.

Nicolaisen, W. F. H. 2015. 'Onomastics' in J. D. Wright (ed.), *International Encyclopedia of the Social & Behavioral Sciences*, 2nd ed. Oxford: Elsevier, pp. 223–6.

Nielsen, J. P. 2011. *Sons and Descendants. A Social History of Kin Groups and Family Names in the Early Neo-Babylonian Period, 747–626 BC*, Culture and History of the Ancient Near East 43. Leiden: Brill.

Nielsen, J. P. 2015. *Personal Names in Early Neo-Babylonian Legal and Administrative Tablets, 747–626 BCE*, NISABA 29. Winona Lake: Eisenbrauns.

Nielsen, J. P. and M. Kozuh 2021. '"Check the writing boards from the time of Nebuchadenzzar": An inventory of administrative writing boards in the Spurlock Museum of World Cultures', *Revue d'assyriologie et d'archéologie orientale* 115, 143–58.

Nissinen, M. 2014. 'Outlook: Aramaeans outside of Syria. 1: Assyria' in H. Niehr (ed.), *The Aramaeans in Ancient Syria*, Handbuch der Orientalistik I/106. Leiden: Brill, pp. 273–96.

Paulus, S. 2014. *Die babylonischen Kudurru-Inschriften von der kassitischen bis zur frühneubabylonischer Zeit*, Alter Orient und Altes Testament 51. Münster: Ugarit-Verlag.

Pearce, L. E. 2015. 'Identifying Judeans and Judean identity in the Babylonian evidence' in J. Stökl and C. Waerzeggers (eds.), *Exile and Return: The Babylonian Context*, Beihefte zur Zeitschrift für alttestamentliche Wissenschaft 478. Berlin: De Gruyter, pp. 7–32.

Pruzsinszky, R. 2021. 'A history of Akkadian onomastics' in J.-P. Vita (ed.), *History of the Akkadian Language, Vol. 1: Linguistic Background and Early Periods*, Handbook of Oriental Studies 152. Leiden: Brill, pp. 477–510.

Puzey, G. 2016. 'Linguistic landscapes' in C. Hough (ed.), *The Oxford Handbook of Names and Naming*. Oxford: Oxford University Press, pp. 395–411.

Radner, K. 2005. *Die Macht des Namens: Altorientalische Strategien zur Selbsterhaltung*, SANTAG 8. Wiesbaden: Harrassowitz.

Shayegan, R. M. (ed.) 2018. *Cyrus the Great: Life and Lore*. Boston: Ilex Foundation.

Streck, M. P. 2014. 'Outlook: Aramaeans outside of Syria. 2: Babylonia' in H. Niehr (ed.), *The Aramaeans in Ancient Syria*, Handbuch der Orientalistik I/106. Leiden: Brill, pp. 297–318.

Tallqvist, K. 1905. *Neubabylonisches Namenbuch zu den Geschäftsurkunden aus der Zeit Šamaššumukîn bis Xerxes*, Acta Societatis Scientiarum Fennicae 32/2. Helsinki: Societas Litteraria Fennica.

Tavernier, J. 2007. *Iranica in the Achaemenid period (c. 550–330 BC): Lexicon of Old Iranian Proper Names and Loanwords Attested in Non-Iranian texts*, Orientalia Lovaniensia Analecta 158. Leuven: Peeters.

Tuplin, C. 2019. 'Logging history in Achaemenid, Hellenistic and Parthian Babylonia: Historial entries in dated Astronomical Diaries' in J. Haubold, J. Steele, and K. Stevens (eds.), *Keeping Watch in Babylon: The Astronomical Diaries in Context*. Culture and History of the Ancient Near East 100. Leiden: Brill, pp. 79–119.

Van De Mieroop, M. 1997. 'Why did they write on clay?', *Klio* 71/1, 7–18.

Veldhuis, N. 2011. 'Levels of literacy' in K. Radner and E. Robson (eds.), *The Oxford Handbook of Cuneiform Culture*. Oxford: Oxford University Press, pp. 68–89.

Waerzeggers, C. 2003–4. 'The Babylonian revolts against Xerxes and the "end of archives"', *Archiv für Orientforschung* 50, 150–73.

Waerzeggers, C., M. Groß et al. 2019. *Prosobab: Prosopography of Babylonia (c. 620–330 BCE).* https://prosobab.leidenuniv.nl.

Weidner, E. F. 1939. 'Jojachin, König von Juda in Babylonischen Keilschrifttexten' in *Mélanges syriens offerts à Monsieur René Dussaud par ses amis et ses élèves.* Paris: Geuthner, pp. 923–35, pls I–V.

Zadok, R. 1978. *On West Semites in Babylonia during the Chaldean and Achaemenian Periods: An Onomastic Study*, revised version. Jerusalem: Wanaarta/Tel Aviv University.

Zadok, R. 1979.*The Jews in Babylonia during the Chaldean and Achaemenian Periods according to Babylonian Sources*, Studies in the History of the Jewish People and the Land of Israel Monograph Series 3. Haifa: University of Haifa.

Zadok, R. 2003. 'The representation of foreigners in Neo- and Late-Babylonian legal documents (eight through second centuries BCE)' in O. Lipschits and J. Blenkinsopp (eds.), *Judah and the Judeans in the Neo-Babylonian Period.* Winona Lake: Eisenbrauns, pp. 471–589.

Zadok, R. 2009. *Iranische Personennamen in der neu- und spätbabylonischen Nebenüberlieferung*, Iranisches Personennamenbuch 7/1B. Vienna: Verlag der Österreichischen Akademie der Wissenschaften.

PART I

Babylonian Names

CHAPTER 1

Social Aspects of Babylonian Names

Francis Joannès

Introduction

How did names acquire social meaning in Babylonia? To begin, we may recall a short presentation by Sophie Démare-Lafont about the name as an element of identification in ancient Mesopotamia (Démare-Lafont 2014). She underlined the following points concerning the definition of the name. First, a standard name consists of two or three elements, linked together in a sentence. Most names are theophoric and follow two models: either the deity is called upon for protection (e.g., Nabû-šumu-uṣur 'O Nabû, protect my name/fame') or the name-bearer is identified as a servant of the god (e.g., Arad-Bēl 'Servant of Bēl'). Second, sometimes we find 'Banana names', constructed from the reduplication of the same syllable (e.g., Dada, Zuzu). This happens mostly in Sumerian (Foster 1981) but also sometimes in Akkadian. Such names lack a lexical meaning. Third, foundlings are named after the specific circumstances of their discovery (e.g., Ša-pî-kalbi 'Out of the mouth of a dog'). And fourth, double names are attested in Neo-Babylonian times for some individuals (e.g., a man named Marduk-nāṣir-apli 'Marduk is the protector of the heir' was also known as Širku 'Gift').

In the words of Karen Radner, 'Akkadian and Sumerian personal names generally have a precise meaning' (Radner 2005, 26). The referent included in a name contributes to the social identity of the bearer. For example, some names put the person under the explicit protection of a deity, a temple, or a city (e.g., Nabû-aplu-uṣur 'O Nabû, protect the heir!'). Other names set him or her in relation with family members (e.g., Aḫūšunu 'Their brother') or with an animal (e.g., Kalbāya 'My dog'). There is also what J. J. Stamm called '*Begrüßungsnamen*': positive reminders of the circumstances at birth and the family's reaction to the newborn child (Stamm 1939). Thus, it is plausible that names formed with the verb *balāṭu* in the D stem and having the meaning 'to heal, to bring to life' – an action attributed to a deity – recalled a difficult birth. By contrast, a name like Mīnu-ēpuš-ilī 'What fault did I commit, O my god?' conveyed a negative reaction of the family – a reaction that remained attached to the person for their entire life (Stamm 1939, 164–5). In all these examples, the name and its referent revealed something about the social identity of the bearer. Only a minority of Babylonian names were 'Banana names' – that is, names constructed from the reduplication of the same syllable. Such names had no connection to the linguistic context in which they developed and operated outside the lexicon.

The Name as a Means of Identification

In Babylonia, at least since the second millennium BCE, whenever it was necessary to produce a legal identity – for instance, in legal contracts or administrative texts – people mentioned their name and the name of their father, or, alternatively, their name and their function or occupation. The mother's name was rarely used for such purposes. If she was mentioned at all, this was because she was physically present at the transaction. However, there exists one exception to this rule. In the Neo-Babylonian period, oblates (*širku*) of the Ištar temple in Uruk, born to unmarried mothers, were identified as 'PN_1, the son of $^{f}PN_2$, the released woman (*zakītu*)'.[1]

An innovation of the first centuries of the first millennium BCE was to identify persons with three, instead of two, onomastic elements: the person's name, their father's name, and a family name. This phenomenon did not affect the whole population but remained limited to the urban notability or 'bourgeoisie'. However, as this group is responsible for most archives surviving from Babylonia, the phenomenon is particularly well documented. It is often put forward as a special characteristic of Neo-Babylonian onomastic practice (see Chapter 4 in this volume).

Hence, a person can be identified with up to three onomastic elements in cuneiform texts from the first millennium BCE. The first element is a personal name. This name can be quoted in full or in an abbreviated form, often a hypocorism. For instance, the name Nabû-šumu-iddin 'Nabû gave a name' can be shortened to Iddināya (based on the component *-iddin* 'he gave') or to Šumāya (based on the component *-šumu* 'name'). The rules for deriving a hypocorism from the full name are not yet fully understood

[1] At that time, the *zakītu* women were dependent persons, attached to the temple with the legal status of oblate (*širkatu*), and being widowed or unmarried. This did not prevent them from having children. The designation *zakītu* 'released' defines their particular position in relation to the marital norm and has no pejorative value.

(see Chapter 2). The second element is the father's name. This name refers to the nuclear family and lends legitimacy to a person through direct filiation or adoption. A person who was adopted in adulthood usually retained the name of his first (biological) father, especially when being adopted for financial reasons. Thus, Iddin-Nabû, son of Nabû-bān-zēri, descendant of Nappāḫu, kept the name of his father Nabû-bān-zēri even after he was adopted by his paternal uncle Gimillu (Baker 2004). The third element is the family name. The system is fairly similar to the one in use in modern Western Europe. Chapter 4 is devoted to the topic of family names.

Papponymy and Mammonymy

The practice of naming children after members of previous generations of the family is well attested in Babylonia. Mammonymy was rare and mostly confined to Late Babylonian documentation (Wunsch 2006; Langin-Hooper and Pearce 2014). More common was papponymy, as underlined by Michael Jursa (2007, 133): 'Another tradition of some of these upper class families is papponymy: names are often reused by the grandchild generation onwards . . . The Murašû archive (Stolper 1985, 18–19) and the Tattannu archive (Jursa and Stolper 2007, 249) offer very clear evidence.' The best-known case at present is that of King Nebuchadnezzar II, whom Michael Jursa links through papponymy to a governor of Uruk during the reign of Assurbanipal, (Nabû)-kudurru-(uṣur), who would have been his grandfather (Jursa 2007). Papponymy thus seems to have developed especially during the fifth and fourth centuries, but was practised in certain social circles already in the seventh century. It is especially well documented among scholars (e.g., Ossendrijver 2011).

If papponymy was mainly practised among families of the elite, in families of a lower social stratum names referencing the father, the grandfather, or an uncle were popular, such as Abi-abi 'Grandfather', Aḫi-abia 'Brother of my father', and Abunu 'our father' (Stamm 1939, 302–3).

Orthography

In many writing systems personal names are accompanied by identifying marks to distinguish them from the rest of the words in a text. In the cuneiform script used during the Neo-Babylonian period, we find two such ideographic markers: a vertical wedge for men and the sign MUNUS for women.[2] In Assyriological parlance, the vertical wedge is known as the '*Personenkeil*'. Transliterations usually render the masculine marker as ^{I} or ^{m} and the feminine marker as ^{f} or ^{mí}, placed in superscript before the personal name. In this volume, we also mark normalised versions of female names with a superscript f; in this way, they can be easily distinguished from normalised male names, which we leave unmarked.

The name itself was often written in a non-phonetic way by using a specific set of logograms.[3] This system served three functions. First, it allowed readers to quickly differentiate a personal name from other parts of the text, which were usually written by means of phonetic signs. Second, the system allowed scribes to avoid wasting space and to optimise the layout of the text by using long or short spellings depending on available space. For instance, the name of the chief deity Marduk could be written using the short spelling ^{d}ŠÚ or the long spelling ^{d}AMAR.UTU. Such long and short options were available for many of the common elements of personal names. For instance, the element *Mušēzib-* could be rendered KAR and *mu-še-zib* and *-erība* could be written SU and *eri*$_{4}$*-ba*. Hence, acquiring knowledge of logograms specific to the repertoire of names and their variants was part of scribal training. The student practised this skill by copying out lists of names on school tablets. In certain contract types, the notion of 'page layout' was important. For instance, in property deeds the scribe was supposed to fit the chain consisting of the personal name, the father's name, and the family name on a single line. The availability of long and short spelling options was helpful to attain a neat line division. Third, the practice of writing personal names logographically offered the possibility to give the name a particular value in view of the polysemic nature of logograms. A good illustration of this practice is found in the myth of creation, *Enūma eliš*, which ends with a commentary on the fifty names of the god Marduk. The name 'is' the person: it must present itself in a particular way.

Another orthographic practice relating to Neo-Babylonian onomastics is the use of rare values of common signs in order to lend a name antiquity. This is found in royal names (see section on 'Royal Names'), but also in ancestor names. For example, the family name Sîn-taqīša-libluṭ ('O Sîn, the one you gave, may he live!') was written ^{d}A.KU-BA-TI.LA and read ^{d}E$_{4}$.GI$_{7}$-BA-TI.LA, which then was reduced by acrophony to ^{d}E.GI.BA and Egibi.

2 The masculine marker was frequently left out in front of royal names.

3 These logograms are discussed in Chapter 6.

A distinction must be made between the use of archaising spellings and the use of real ancient names. A Sumerian name – an ancient language of culture by the Neo-Babylonian period – allowed the bearer to inscribe himself in a prestigious tradition and to reinforce his social status (see Chapter 17). It is not always clear whether an archaising spelling represents a Sumerian name. For instance, the name spelled ^{I}BÀD.MAH-^{d}AMAR. UTU could be understood as a real Sumerian name, even though it has an Akkadian equivalent: Tukulti-Marduk.[4] Another example is the name spelled ^{Id}ÙRU.DÙ-MA.AN.SUM,[5] of which the Akkadian equivalent would be Nusku-iddin. Here, the scribe added a note drawing attention to the fact that the name-bearer wrote his own name (ll. 19–20): ^{Id}URU. DÙ-MA.AN.SUM A *šá* ^{I}*ta-qiš*-^{d}ME.ME *ina* ŠU^{II}-*šú* MU-*šú* IN.SAR 'Nusku-iddin son of Taqīš-Gula wrote his own name himself'. As a name, ^{Id}URU.DÙ-MA.AN.SUM is found in other archival contexts (e.g., *Cyr.* 173; VR 67 1 r. 16) but in those instances it is clearly used as an ancestor's name.[6]

Such archaising spellings were also used by scribes who wanted to show that they were scholars, even when writing practical texts. A case in point is Nabû-zēru-līšir, a scribe who travelled to Agade in order to copy ancient royal inscriptions for King Nabonidus. He had been a scholar at the court of Neriglissar and went on to work for Nabonidus. Nabû-zēru-līšir used archaic signs and spellings not only when copying ancient inscriptions of, among others, Kings Kurigalzu and Šar-kali-šarrī, but also when writing administrative documents. Curiously, in a sale contract of agricultural land (*Nbn.* 116), he gives both his paternal (Nabûnnāya) and maternal (Šamaš-abāri) ancestry.

Family and Social Status

Claiming a (prestigious) ancestor generally put an individual in the social group of the so-called *mār banê*. The most accurate French equivalent of this term would be '*notable*'; CAD M_{1} 256 s.v. *mār banî* 1.a translates it as 'free person, noble man'. As CAD also notes, during the first millennium BCE the adjective *banû* (and its superlative *babbanû* or its intensive form *bunnu*) replaced the older adjective *damqum*, which was used in the Old Babylonian period in the term *mār damqi*. In fact, during the second

4 CAD T 461 s.v. *tukultu* 1.a.2′.b′ with references.

5 TEBR 6 no. 23:2 (Nippur, reign of Artaxerxes II).

6 See the discussion by Cornelia Wunsch about the archive of ^{f}Šikkūtu, a woman from this very family (Wunsch 2003b, 89–105).

millennium BCE, the term *awīlum damqum* or *mār awīlim damqim* had the meaning 'of good family, well-to-do' in texts from Mari, Bogazköy, Alalah, and El Amarna, but not in Babylonia. On the other hand, in the Neo-Assyrian documentation *mār damqi* refers to a category of soldiers and no longer has anything to do with social hierarchy. The Neo-Babylonian expression *mār banê* has also recently been studied by Kristin Kleber (2018, 448–50), who insists that this term primarily refers to a person who does not have servile status, regardless of his or her actual social ranking.

Neo-Babylonian society was very diverse, however. As some private archives of Neo-Babylonian urban notables show, the use of family names was restricted to wealthy (but not necessarily the wealthiest) individuals. Men such as Iddin-Nabû from the Nappāḫu family in Babylon, the descendants of the Gallābu family in Ur, and those of the Ea-ilūtu-bāni family in Borsippa did own real estate, but on a modest scale. Their financial assets cannot be considered extensive either. In other words, the use of a family name was not in itself a sufficient mark of belonging to the highest political and economic elites of the country. We have to look towards the socio-economic group of the entrepreneurs in order to find the wealthiest individuals. The two best-known examples from the Neo-Babylonian period are the Egibi family of Babylon in the sixth and early fifth centuries (Wunsch 2000) and the Murašû family of fifth-century Nippur, who made their fortune in the management of military tenures in the service of the Persian crown (Stolper 1985). In the latter case, it is difficult to determine whether the name Murašû had the status of 'family name' as the name had been borne as a personal name by the first-attested head of the family, under Darius I (Cardascia 1951; Stolper 1985).

Some families took over chief political and religious functions and thus created veritable dynasties of ruling elites. For instance, the Ša-nāšišu family held positions as governors and temple administrators (*šangû*, *šatammu*, and *šākin ṭēmi*) in the cities of Babylon, Sippar, and Borsippa (Jursa 2007, 76–7; Waerzeggers 2014). During the Hellenistic period, the scholars of Uruk functioned as a true socio-professional group who claimed membership of a prestigious clan, like the family of the descendants of Sîn-leqe-unninnī.

As shown by the case of the Ša-nāšišus, some family groups in first millennium BCE Babylonia gained a situation of control over the great institutions (especially the temples) and formed a kind of oligarchy or local ruling class, a phenomenon that has many parallels in history. However, these networks did not form a permanent or undisputed elite over a long period of time: after the Babylonian revolts against Xerxes in 484 BCE, many families of central Babylonia were excluded from high office (Kessler 2004;

Waerzeggers 2003–4). Moreover, as producers of wealth, entrepreneurs did not require a firmly established family group: in Uruk, the rent farmer Šumu-ukīn of the Basia family was an outsider to the local urban elite when he rose to prominence in the beginning of the reign of Nabonidus.

Gods in Personal Names

Inhabitants of the great religious cities (*māḫāzu*) often bore names referring to their city's deity (almost always masculine, except in Uruk and Isin), his female consort, and, to varying degrees, his divine vizier. A theophoric name can thus serve as an indication of a person's geographical origin (see Table 1.1).

Another system of reference derived from the 'national', rather than the local, pantheon. This system was centred around two gods whose power extended over the whole of Babylonia: Marduk (also named Bēl) and his son Nabû. In the Neo-Babylonian period, Nabû had the same status of 'intercessor god' near the supreme deity (i.e., Marduk) that Sîn had enjoyed during the Old Babylonian period vis-à-vis Enlil. There was also a '*Beiform*' of Marduk, the god Madānu (^{d}DI.KU$_{5}$), who was Marduk's official 'throne bearer' (GU.ZA-LÁ). Madānu accounted for Marduk's power as a god of justice, a sphere that he shared with the sun god, Šamaš. A similar 'national' appeal was enjoyed by Ištar – venerated in, among other places, Uruk, Babylon, Sippar, and Agade – and by Nanāya, who was worshipped in Uruk and Borsippa.

Table 1.1 *Deities of major Babylonian cities favoured in personal names*

City	Deity favoured in personal names
Babylon	Marduk (or Bēl), Bēltia, Ištar-of-Babylon
Borsippa	Nabû, Tašmētu, Nanāya, Mār-bīti
Isin	Gula (or Bābu)
Kish	Zababa
Kutha	Nergal
Larsa	Šamaš, Aya, Bunene
Nippur	Enlil, Ninlil, Ninurta, Kusu
Sippar	Šamaš, Aya, Bunene
Ur	Sîn, Ningal, Nusku, and the 'chtonic group' (Ninazu, Ningišzidda, Niraḫ, Umunazu)
Udannu	Nergal (IGI.DU)
Uruk	Anu, Ištar (or Innin), Nanāya, Urdimmu

In view of the national pantheon, a personal name composed of, for instance, the element Nabû is less informative about a person's origins than a name referring to the god Zababa, who was strongly connected to the local pantheon of the city of Kish. We see that names consisting of a city's deity could be used as a means to reaffirm local identities against the royal centralism exercised by Babylon and its Marduk-based theology. As Karlheinz Kessler has shown, the resurgence of the god Anu in personal names at Uruk during the second part of the Achaemenid period was a way to reject the influence of Babylon (Kessler 2004). The people of Uruk foregrounded their city's male divinity Anu instead of Marduk, perhaps because Ištar had become a 'national' goddess, no longer exclusively connected with Uruk.

In the same theophoric perspective, we have to pay attention to personal names referring to the great temples, especially those of Borsippa (Ezida) and Babylon (Esagil), but also of Sippar (Ebabbar) and Uruk (Eanna).[7] The ideological reference is the same as for the god names, as the affiliation to a temple was indicative of a person's local identity (see Table 1.2).

The same is true for some personal names using city names, such as Zēr-Bābili and Ṭāb-Uruk, and maybe also, when the relation is not to a temple or a city but to sacred paraphernalia, for the rare family name Ina-ṣilli-sammi 'In the shade of the lyre' (^{I}*ina*-GISSU-^{giš}ZÀ.MÍ).

Table 1.2 *Personal names referring to temples*

Temple name	Examples of personal names
Esagil (Babylon)	Ina-Esagil-šumu-ibni, Ina-Esagil-zēri, ^{f}Banât-ina-Esagil, Esagil-amassu, Esagil-šadûnu
Eturkalamma (Babylon)	^{f}Ina-Eturkalamma-alsišu
Ezida (Borsippa)	Ezida-šumu-ibni, Ṭāb-šār-Ezida
Eimbianu (Dilbat)	^{f}Ina-Eimbianu-alsišu
Eigikalamma (Marad)	^{f}Ina-Eigikalamma-lūmuršu
Egalmaḫ (Nippur)	Arad-Egalmaḫ
Eanna (Uruk)	Eanna-iddin, Eanna-līpī-uṣur, Eanna-nādin-šumi, Ina-ṣilli-Eanna, Itti-Eanna-būdia
Ebabbar (Sippar)	Ebabbar-šadûnu

7 The name of the great temple in Uruk might have to be read Ayakku instead of Eanna; see Beaulieu (2002).

Royal Names

During the Neo-Assyrian period, some kind of taboo rested on the royal name (Livingstone 2009, 154). Giving a child a name already borne by the sovereign or a member of his family was considered an offence against the king because it could signal a conspiracy. In 521 BCE, when unrest broke out in the Persian Empire after Cambyses' sudden death, two individuals tried to ascend the throne in Babylon and lead a rebellion against Darius I. Both rebels took a royal name charged with symbolism: Nebuchadnezzar (the Babylonian form of the name is Nabû-kudurru-uṣur).[8] The first of these rebels also claimed to be the son of Nabonidus, the last king of the Neo-Babylonian dynasty. This shows that at this time it was still considered a mark of legitimacy to bear the name Nebuchadnezzar. However, a generation later, in 484 BCE, two new Babylonian usurpers rebelled against the Persian Empire, but neither of these men chose a name relating to the Neo-Babylonian dynasty; rather, they operated under their own personal names, Bēl-šimânni and Šamaš-erība.

Of the kings of the Neo-Babylonian dynasty, Nebuchadnezzar II (605–562 BCE) bore a particularly 'royal' name, as it clearly referred to Nebuchadnezzar I who had ruled between 1125 and 1104 BCE. However, in view of the fact that Nebuchadnezzar II already bore this name when he still was chief administrator (*šatammu*) of the temple of Ištar in Uruk (Jursa 2007), it is uncertain how we should interpret the ideological significance of this name. When we consider the other Neo-Babylonian kings[9] – his father Nabû-aplu-uṣur (626–605), his son Amīl-Marduk (562–560), his son-in-law Nergal-šarru-uṣur (560–556), Lâbâši-Marduk (556), Nabû-na'id (556–539), and, finally, Bēl-šarru-uṣur (co-regent with Nabonidus) – they all seem to have borne common names.[10]

Also in Babylonia, the names of kings were avoided by the general population. Available lists of Neo-Babylonian personal names show that kings had few homonyms in society despite the common nature of their names. In the words of Heather Baker:

> In Babylonia also this restriction on the use of royal names can be observed. . . . [A] number of individuals named Nabû-na'id are attested in

[8] In scholarship they are referred to as Nebuchadnezzar III and IV.

[9] Such an analysis applies well to the kings of the Neo-Babylonia dynasty founded by Nabopolassar in 626 BCE, as their names can be compared with the numerous personal names found in the texts from daily life. In the absence of such ample documentation, the situation during the preceding centuries in Babylonia (ninth to seventh centuries BCE) is less easy to determine.

[10] Note that Amīl-Marduk was probably the name adopted by Nabû-šumu-ukīn, son of Nebuchadnezzar II, upon his release from imprisonment (Baker 2002). Nabû-šumu-ukīn is known as the author of a hymn to Marduk, where he claims to have been held captive because of false accusations (Finkel 1999).

> Babylonian documents of the late seventh and earlier sixth centuries BC, but there is a notable lack of such individuals born after the accession of the king of that name. Even the latest attested person, the father of a man known in a tablet dated 522 BC was most likely born and named before Nabonidus' accession in 555 BC. (Baker 2002, 7)

Scribes often chose rare logogrammatic values to spell the names of Babylonian kings. For instance, in the case of Nabonidus the usual spelling $^{\text{(I)d}}$AG-*na-a*$^{?}$*-id* is often replaced with the more scholarly version $^{\text{(I)d}}$AG-NÍ. TUK or $^{\text{(I)d}}$AG-I. This system may have begun already in the seventh century BCE, as the name of Šamaš-šumu-ukīn (668–648 BCE) was written using a rare spelling for Šamaš ($^{\text{(I)d}}$GIS-NU$_{11}$-MU-GI.NA).

'Historical' Names

The kings of the Ur III period and even of the Empire of Akkad (later third millennium BCE) were part of Babylonian collective memory, as can be seen, for example, in the divinatory practice of linking certain configurations of the liver to 'historical' events taking place in those distant times (Glassner 2019). We also find evidence of persons being named after these ancient kings, presumably as a mark of prestige. One notes, for instance, the popularity of names such as Šarru-kīn 'Sargon' (*Nbk.* 106:2; *Nbk.* 365:1; *Cyr.* 297:1); Kurigalzu, a Kassite king (YOS 21 169:19') and Narām-Sîn (TMH 2/3 9:41–2). It is unclear why these kings were remembered and not others. In order to answer this question, we need a better understanding of the transmission of cultural memory in Babylonia. Finally, we can note a name more mythological than historical: Aṣûšu-namir (^{I}*a-ṣu-šú-na-mir*), known from the myth of Ištar's descent, is mentioned as the name of a person in the legal text YOS 7 118, from the Eanna archive of Uruk.

Slave Names

Introduction

The names of slaves follow the same general rules of formation as the proper names of free persons (Watai 2012; Hackl 2013; and Chapter 3), but some names were typical for slaves. For instance, names such as 'I grasped the feet of (a deity)' are only attested for slaves (e.g., Šēpē(t)-Bēl-aṣbat, ^{f}Šēpē(t)-Ninlil -aṣbat, ^{f}Šēpētāya; see Tallqvist 1905, 202). The main categories of slave names are discussed in the next section.

Slaves were probably given a new name when they entered a new household (Radner 2005, 31). This phenomenon is visible especially when slaves are of foreign origin: by receiving an Akkadian name, they were given a new identity. This identity put them, before all, at the service of their owner. The relationship to the master could be made explicit in the name itself, as seen in the following examples (Stamm 1939):

^{f}Bānītu-bēlu-uṣrī	'Bānītu, protect my master!'
Gabbi-(ilāni)-bēlu-uṣur	'All gods, protect my master!'
Ina-qātē-bēli-lumḫur	'May I receive (life) from the hands of my master'
Madānu-bēlu-uṣur	'Madānu protect my master!'
^{f}Nanāya-bēlu-uṣrī	'Nanāya protect my master!'
^{f}Nanāya-kilīlu-uṣrī	'Nanāya protect the tiara (the mistress)'

As observed by Heather Baker, the element Marduk is so rare in slave names that a 'deliberate avoidance' seems to be at play (Baker 2002, 8). However, while slave names with Marduk are very rare (Atkal-ana-Marduk in *Cyr.* 64 and 315 being an exception), the elements Bēl and Bēltia are regularly included in slave names. Perhaps such names did not refer to the gods Marduk and Zarpanītu, but rather to the slave's legal owners (*bēlu* 'master'; *bēltu* 'mistress'). Even when the scribe put the cuneiform sign DINGIR before the logogram EN, we cannot be sure whether this orthography reflects the actual meaning of the name. Ša-Bēl-bāni 'All what pertains to Bēl is beautiful' is an example of such an ambiguous slave name (*Dar.* 275).

Slave names rarely include references to family members (e.g., 'son', 'heir', 'brother', and 'sister'). A name such as Nabû-dūr-ēdi 'Nabû is the defence of the individual', typical for slaves, seems to highlight the plight of single people. In the absence of family solidarity, to which a slave could not aspire given his status, prayer-names seem to deliver the slave's fate into the hands of the gods and, as we have seen, perhaps also his master or mistress.

Main Categories of Slave Names

Slave names often express a prayer or a request for assistance, directed to a deity. The implicit effect of such names is that of a perpetual prayer uttered by the slave for himself or herself and maybe also for the benefit of his or her master or mistress. Some examples are:

^{f}Bānītu-supê-muḫur	'Bānītu, accept my prayers!'
Bēl-ēdu-uṣur	'Bēl, protect the single!'
Enlil-māku-pitin	'Enlil, strengthen the weak!'

Enlil-supê-muḫur	'Enlil, accept my prayers!'
^{f}Ina-Esagil-šimînni	'Listen to me in Esagil!'
^{f}Ina-Eturkalamma-alsišu	'In Eturkalamma, I cried out to him (the god)'
Nabû-alsika-abluṭ	'I cried out to you, Nabû, and I came back to life'
Nabû-alsi-ul-āmur	'I cried out to Nabû but I could not see him'
Nabû-ayyālu	'Nabû, (come to) my help!'
Nabû-killanni	'Nabû, direct me!'
Rēmu-šukun	'Have mercy on me!'

Another category of slave names consists of expressions of trust in the deity and in his or her benevolence, for example:

^{f}Ana-muḫḫi-Nanāya-taklāku	'I trust in Nanāya'
^{f}Ana-muḫḫīšu-taklāku	'I trust in him (the god)'
Bēl-išdīa-ukīn	'Bēl granted the continuation (of the family)'
Gūzu-ina-Bēl-aṣbat	'I took my joy with Bēl'
Ina-qātē-Nabû-bulṭu	'Health is in the hands of Nabû'
Ina-ṣilli-Bīt-Akītu	'Under the protection of Bīt-Akītu'
^{f}Itti-Eturkalamma-būnūʾa	'My face is turned towards Eturkalamma'
^{f}Mannu-akî-ištaria	'Who is like my goddess?'
Nabû-gabbi-ileʾʾi	'Nabû knows everything'
Nabû-lū-salim	'May Nabû be well disposed (toward me)'
Nabû-rēmuʾa	'Nabû (has) mercy on me'
Nergal-rēṣûa	'Nergal is my helper'
Ultu-pāni-Bēl-lū-šulum	'Greetings from Bēl'

Slaves also often bore names referring to flora and fauna, as can be seen in these examples:

^{f}Baltammu	'Balsam'
^{f}Bazītu	'Monkey'
Gadû, ^{f}Gadāya	'Kid'
^{f}Ḫilbunītu	'Galbanum'
^{f}Inbāya	'Fruit'
^{f}Isḫunnatu	'Bunch of grapes'
^{f}Kallabuttu	'Locust'
^{f}Murašītu	'Wild cat'
^{f}Sinūnu	'Swallow'
^{f}Suluppāya	'Date'
Šaḫû	'Pig' ([11])
^{f}Šeleppūtu	'Turtle'

11 An anonymous reviewer of this manuscript notes that Thesiger (1964, 34) observed that Iraq's Marsh Arabs use similar names for boys whose brothers had died in infancy, to avert the evil eye.

^{f}Šikkû	'Mongoose'
^{f}Šilangītu	'Fish'

Finally, there are some programmatic names, directly related to the slave's activities:

^{f}Ana-pî-maḫrat	'She is ready for the command'
Ina-nemēli-kitti-ibašši	'True profit is there'

In some cases, the foreign origin of slaves, even of those bearing Babylonian names, was indicated. For instance, in the large inheritance document of the Egibi family, one of the slaves was listed as ^{f}Nanāya-silim ^{uru}*ga-an-da-ru-i-tu*$_4$ 'from Gandar' (*Dar.* 379:44). Another example is ^{f}Nanāya-ittia *miṣrītu* 'from Egypt' (*Camb.* 334 and duplicates). In the case of Tabalāya the slave's name refers to Cilicia (Streck 2001, 114). Some slaves, finally, were simply called Ubāru 'foreigner'. For instance, in *Dar.* 492 we encounter a slave described as follows: 'Ubāru, the tattooed(?) slave whose right hand is inscribed with the name of Mušēzib-Marduk'.

Names of Foundlings and Orphans

Not everyone in Babylonia had a peaceful destiny and birth was not always considered a happy event. Perhaps a name like ^{f}Lā-magirtu ('Not welcome') illustrates this experience.[12] The names of orphans and foundlings also reflect the dramatic conditions of their birth. The name Abī-ul-īde 'I do not know my father' is interpreted as typical for fatherless children (Stamm 1939, 321). Abī-lūmur 'I want to see my father' expresses a similar situation (Streck 2001, 114). And we may consider as abandoned children those persons who had been found in the streets (*sūqu*, *sulû*) or who had been rescued from stray animals (Wunsch 2003a),[13] as reflected in such names as:

Ḫāriṣānu	'The one from the ditch (of the city)' (Streck 2001, 114)
Sūqāya / ^{f}Sūqaʾītu	'The one from the street'
Sulāya	'The one from the street'
Ša-pî-kalbi	'Out of the mouth of a dog'[14]

12 Note that Johannes Hackl (2013, 138) translates this name as 'Stubborn' and Laura Cousin and Yoko Watai translate it as 'Disobedient' (see Chapter 3, this volume).

13 This hypothesis is based on the meaning of the name borne by these individuals. In some contracts, however, those persons appear with a full father's name, from which it could be concluded that they had been fully integrated into their adoptive family.

14 Note that Streck (2001, 114) translates this name as 'Mit einer Hundeschnauze'.

Non-Babylonian Names

What did it mean to bear a foreign name in a society which attributed such value and significance to the personal name? Babylon's status as the capital city of a multi-ethnic empire attracted many individuals of allo-ethnic origin. Some of these persons migrated voluntarily to Babylonia, for instance, in order to perform a function in the service of power. Ḫanūnu 'Hannon', the chief royal merchant at the court of Nebuchadnezzar II, is a case in point. Others were brought to Babylonia as prisoners of war, deportees, or booty. This is the case with the Egyptian prisoners taken during the great battles between Nebuchadnezzar II and the Egyptians in Carchemish and Hamath. The king presented many of these prisoners as gifts to the temples of Babylonia. Several lists of personnel have been preserved where we can find phonetic renderings of their Egyptian names in cuneiform (Bongenaar and Haring 1994). These persons were not meant to increase the temple's workforce, probably did not speak Akkadian, and disappeared a few years later, presumably due to natural death.

Another community of forced immigrants is that of the deportees from the kingdom of Judah who were taken captive by the Babylonian army in 597 and especially in 587 BCE. Some recently published archives relate to this community (Pearce and Wunsch 2014). Without anticipating the chapter on Yahwistic names (see Chapter 9), we note that many instances are known of children born to the deportees who, even though sometimes bearing an Akkadian name, still retained their Judean identity within the familial group. In fact, in the majority of cases, name-giving practices preserved a strong ethnic, cultural, and social identity within the Judean community.

Most foreigners were registered with their original name, transcribed more or less approximately into cuneiform script, without any depreciative mark. This practice continued when Babylonia was no longer the centre of political power. For instance, after the conquest by Alexander the Great, one notices a significant increase of Greek names recorded in cuneiform tablets (Monerie 2014 and Chapter 14). Nevertheless, Babylonian scribes did sometimes emphasise the social status of foreigners in two different ways. Occasionally, they added an ethnic label to the personal name – for instance, Partammu 'the Persian' (*Dar.* 379:3) or Aḫšeti 'the Imbukean' (Abraham 2004 no. 46:16). Such labels allowed the scribe to characterise an individual whose name had no clear meaning for him. Another way of marking a foreign person's status was by adding a title situating the individual, like Gubāru 'Governor of Babylon and Across-the-River'. It should be noted that West Semitic names were not marked as such. Babylonian society was virtually bilingual (Aramaic–Akkadian) and West Semitic names were very common in the onomastic repertoire (see Chapter 8). The difficulties encountered by scribes when dealing with foreign names are illustrated by the multiple spellings for the name of the king Xerxes which had no understandable referent for Babylonian scribes (Tavernier 2007, 66–7).

Conclusions

In Babylonia, a person's name could express different aspects of his or her social identity. A common name type conveyed a relationship between the person and a deity, who was thanked or implored. Nabû-iddin 'Nabû gave', Bēl-rēmanni 'Bēl have mercy on me', Šamaš-iqīša 'Šamaš awarded', and Nabû-alsi-ul-abāš 'I cried out to Nabû and will not come to shame' are examples of such names. Other names expressed a special relationship between the person and a family member; for instance, Aḫūšunu 'Their brother' and [f]Ummī-ṭābat 'Mother is good'. A physical characteristic of the name-bearer, often of women, could be referred to, or a particular circumstance at birth. Kubburu 'Fat' is an example of the former name type, and Nabû-mītu-uballiṭ 'Nabû resurrected the stillborn (child)' and Ēdu-ēṭir 'Save the only (son)' are examples of the latter type.

This personal identity was coupled with a second identity, conveyed by the father's name. That name inserted the person into a nuclear family that provided him or her with a means of existence, assistance, and, possibly, renown. He or she was thus legitimised as a civilian with the status of a free person. Slaves and oblates were given a personal name but not a father's name. Instead, they were referred to by their master's name.

Finally, urban notables added a third name: an ancestor's name (or family name) which lent the individual a social position and allowed them to look for functions, activities, and matrimonial as well as professional alliances.

Further Reading

The study of Neo-Babylonian socio-onomastics is in its infancy and various future research avenues are still open. One aspect that requires more research is the practice of naming and renaming enslaved people. Female slave names have received more attention (Watai 2012; Hackl 2013) than male slave names.

Sibling naming patterns are studied by Heather D. Baker (2002), and intergenerational developments within families and larger communities by Tero Alstola (2020) and Stephanie M. Langin-Hooper and Laurie E. Pearce (2014). Ancestor names and family names have been the topic of several studies, notably by Wilfred G. Lambert (1957) and John P. Nielsen (2011). The rare phenomenon of female ancestor names is studied by Cornelia Wunsch (2006). For Neo-Babylonian onomastics, the name book by Knut L. Tallqvist (1905) remains indispensable.

References

Abraham, K. 2004. *Business and Politics under the Persian Empire: The Financial Dealings of Marduk-nāṣir-apli of the House of Egibi (521–487 BCE)*. Bethesda: CDL Press.

Alstola, T. 2020. *Judeans in Babylonia: A Study of Deportees in the Sixth and Fifth Centuries BCE*, Culture and History of the Ancient Near East 109. Leiden: Brill.

Baker, H. D. 2002. 'Approaches to Akkadian name-giving in first-millennium BC Mesopotamia' in C. Wunsch (ed.), *Mining the Archives: Festschrift for Christopher Walker on the Occasion of His 60th Birthday*, Babylonische Archive 1. Dresden: ISLET, pp. 1–24.

Baker, H. D. 2004. *The Archive of the Nappāḫu Family*, Archiv für Orientforschung Beiheft 30. Vienna: Institut für Orientalistik der Universität Wien.

Beaulieu, J.-A. 2002. 'Eanna = Ayakkum in the Basetki inscription of Narām-Sîn', *Nouvelles Assyriologiques Brèves et Utilitaires* 2002/36.

Bongenaar, A. C. V. M. and B. J. J. Haring. 1994. 'Egyptians in Neo-Babylonian Sippar', *Journal of Cuneiform Studies* 46, 59–72.

Cardascia, G. 1951. *Les archives des Murašû: Une famille d'hommes d'affaires babyloniens à l'époque perse (455–403 av. J.-C.)*. Paris: Imprimerie Nationale.

Démare-Lafont, S. 2014. 'Identifiers and identification methods in Mesopotamia' in M. Depauw and S. Coussement (eds.), *Identifiers and Identification Methods in the Ancient World. Legal Documents in Ancient Societies III*, Orientalia Lovaniensia Analecta 229. Leuven: Peeters, pp. 13–31.

Finkel, I. 1999. 'The lament of Nabû-šuma-ukîn' in J. Renger (ed.), *Babylon: Focus mesopotamischer Geschichte, Wiege früher Gelehrsamkeit, Mythos in der Moderne*, Colloquien der Deutschen Orient-Gesellschaft 2. Saarbrücken: Saarbrücker Druckerei und Verlag, pp. 323–42.

Foster, B. J. 1981. 'Ethnicity and onomastics in Sargonic Mesopotamia', *Orientalia Nova Series* 51, 297–354.

Frahm, E. 2012. 'Headhunter, Bücherdiebe und wandernde Gelehrte: Anmerkungen zum altorientalischen Wissenstransfer im ersten Jahrtausend v. Chr.' in H. Neumann (ed.), *Wissenskultur im Alten Orient: Weltanschauung, Wissenschaften, Techniken, Technologien*, Colloquien der Deutschen Orient-Gesellschaft 2. Wiesbaden: Harrassowitz, pp. 15–30.

Glassner, J.-J. 2019. *Le devin historien en Mésopotamie*, Ancient Magic and Divination 16. Leiden: Brill.

Hackl, J. 2013. 'Frau Weintraube, Frau Heuschrecke und Frau Gut: Untersuchungen zu den babylonischen Namen von Sklavinnen in neubabylonischer und persischer Zeit', *Wiener Zeitschrift für die Kunde des Morgenlandes* 103, 121–87.

Jursa, M. 2007. 'Die Söhne Kudurrus und die Herkunft der neubabylonischen Dynastie', *Revue d'assyriologie et d'archéologie orientale* 101, 125–36.

Jursa, M. and M. W. Stolper. 2007. 'From the Tattannu archive fragment', *Wiener Zeitschrift für die Kunde des Morgenlandes* 97, 243–81.

Kessler, K. 2004. 'Urukäische Familien versus babylonische Familien: die Namengebung in Uruk, die Degradierung der Kulte von Eanna und der Aufstieg des Gottes Anu', *Altorientalische Forschungen* 31, 237–62.

Kleber, K. 2018. 'Dependent labor and status in the Neo-Babylonian and Achaemenid periods' in A. Garcia-Ventura (ed.), *What's in a Name? Terminology Related to Work Force and Job Categories in the Ancient Near East*, Alter Orient und Altes Testament 440, Münster: Ugarit-Verlag, pp. 441–65.

Lambert, W. G. 1957. 'Ancestors, authors and canonicity', *Journal of Cuneiform Studies* 11, 1–14, 112.

Langin-Hooper, S. M. and L. E. Pearce. 2014. 'Mammonymy, maternal-line names, and cultural identification: Clues from the onomasticon of Hellenistic Uruk', *Journal of the American Oriental Society* 134, 185–202.

Livingstone, A. 2009. 'Remembrance at Assur: The case of the dated Aramaic memorials', *Studia Orientalia* 106, 151–7.

Monerie, J. 2014. *D'Alexandre à Zoilos: Dictionnaire prosopographique des porteurs de nom grec dans les sources cunéiformes*, Oriens et Occidens 23. Stuttgart: Franz Steiner Verlag.

Nielsen, J. P. 2011. *Sons and Descendants. A Social History of Kin Groups and Family Names in the Early Neo-Babylonian Period, 747–626 BC*, Culture and History of the Ancient Near East 43. Leiden: Brill.

Ossendrijver, M. 2011. 'Science in action: Networks in Babylonian astronomy' in E. Cancik-Kirschbaum, M. van Ess, and J. Marzahn (eds.), *Babylon: Wissenskultur in Orient und Okzident*. Berlin: De Gruyter, pp. 213–21.

Pearce, L. E. and C. Wunsch. 2014. *Documents of Judean Exiles and West Semites in Babylonia in the Collection of David Sofer*, Cornell University Studies in Assyriology and Sumerology 28. Bethesda: CDL Press.

Radner, K. 2005. *Die Macht des Namens: Altorientalische Strategien zur Selbsterhaltung*, SANTAG 8. Wiesbaden: Harrassowitz.

Stamm, J. J. 1939. *Die akkadische Namengebung, Mitteilungen der Vorderasiatisch-Ägyptischen Gesellschaft 44*. Leipzig: J. C. Hinrichs Verlag.

Stolper, M. W. 1985. *Entrepreneurs and Empire: The Murašû Archive, the Murašû Firm, and Persian Rule in Babylonia*, Uitgaven van het Nederlands Historisch-Archaeologisch Instituut te Istanbul 54. Istanbul: Nederlands Historisch-Archaeologisch Instituut.

Streck, M. P. 2001. 'Das Onomastikon der Beamten am neubabylonischen Ebabbar-Tempel in Sippar', *Zeitschrift für Assyriologie und Vorderasiatische Archäologie* 91, 110–19.

Tallqvist, K. L. 1905. *Neubabylonisches Namenbuch zu den Geschäftsurkunden aus der Zeit des Šamaššumukîn bis Xerxes*, Acta Societatis Scientiarum Fennicae 32/2. Helsinki: Societas Litteraria Fennica.

Tavernier, J. 2007. *Iranica in the Achaemenid Period (ca. 550–330 BC). Lexicon of Old Iranian Proper Names and Loanwords, Attested in Non-Iranian Texts*, Orientalia Lovaniensia Analecta 158. Leuven: Peeters.

Thesiger, W. 1964. *The Marsh Arabs*. London: Longman.

Waerzeggers, C. 2003–4. 'The Babylonian revolts against Xerxes and the "end of archives"', *Archiv für Orientforschung* 50, 150–73.

Waerzeggers, C. 2014. *Marduk-rēmanni: Local Networks and Imperial Politics in Achaemenid Babylonia*, Orientalia Lovaniensia Analecta 233. Leuven: Peeters.

Watai, Y. 2012. 'Project of prosopographical study of Neo-Babylonian women (french version)'. *Hypotheses.org*: https://refema.hypotheses.org/244.

Wunsch, C. 2000. Das Egibi-Archiv, 2 Vols., *Cuneiform Monographs 20a and 20b*. Groningen: Styx.

Wunsch, C. 2003a. 'Findelkinder und Adoption nach neubabylonischen Quellen', *Archiv für Orientforschung* 50, 174–244.

Wunsch, C. 2003b. *Urkunden zum Ehe-, Vermögens- und Erbrecht aus verschiedenen neubabylonischen Archiven*, Babylonische Archive 2, Dresden: ISLET.

Wunsch, C. 2006. 'Metronymika in Babylonien: Frauen als Ahnherrin der Familie' in G. del Olmo Lete, L. Feliu, and A. Millet-Albà (eds.), *Šapal tibnim mû illakū: Studies Presented to Joaquín Sanmartín on the Occasion of His 65th Birthday*, Aula Orientalis Supplementa 22. Sabadell/Barcelona: Editorial AUSA, pp. 459–69.

CHAPTER 2

Babylonian Male Names

Julia Giessler

Babylonian male names make up the majority of the name material in the Babylonian cuneiform sources dating to the first millennium BCE. This chapter discusses typical elements of male names and also how these elements are formed and combined. The second part of the chapter is dedicated to abbreviated forms of these names as well as to the phenomenon of some individuals having more than one legitimate name.

Typology of Male Names

Introduction

Babylonian male names are usually marked with a single vertical wedge, the so-called '*Personenkeil*' (see Chapter 1). Exceptions to this rule are the names of the Neo-Babylonian kings, which are frequently spelled without a personal marker. Female names are clearly distinguished from male ones by the female marker MUNUS. Other than that, male and female names differ only slightly with regard to grammatical features, semantics, and structure (Chapter 3).

Besides male names, family names can also be introduced by the '*Personenkeil*' or, in rare cases, even by MUNUS. Several male and a few female names are known to serve as family names concurrently.[1] While these family names hark back to ancestral names, there are also family names which derive from occupational titles or places of origin. In these cases, the '*Personenkeil*' can be replaced by or combined with the determinative LÚ, which is otherwise not used as a personal but as a professional marker in this period (see Chapter 4).

[1] Examples of family names that go back to male ancestors will be given in the course of this chapter. Family names that refer to female ancestors are Maqartu 'Precious', Qaqqadānītu '(The one) with large head', and perhaps Arrabtu '(Female) dormouse' (Wunsch 2006).

The longest personal names express complete sentences, consisting of two to four or, in rare cases, even more words.[2] On the other hand, names can also consist of single and compound terms. In modern translations of Babylonian texts, personal names are capitalised and hyphens are used to connect the constitutive elements of the name. Personal markers and determinatives are usually not displayed, but in this volume we mark female names by placing ^{f} in superscript before the name. In the course of this chapter it will also be indicated whether a name is attested only as a male name or also as a family name.

The literal meaning of personal names varies greatly. Apart from names heavy with religious meaning, profane statements, questions, and vocabulary from daily life are also used to denote individuals. Nonsense names, on the other hand, are hardly attested. Possible pet names with reduplicated syllables (so-called 'Banana names') are not common in this period. Exceptions might, for instance, be the male names Bazuzu (common) and Igigi (rare), whose literal meaning still escapes us. Compared to older periods, there are also very few names in the Babylonian onomasticon of the first millennium which cannot yet be associated with a specific language; such names are discussed by Ran Zadok in this volume (see Chapter 18).

The overwhelming majority of personal names relates directly to the name-bearers and their environment. Tangible topics such as the newborn child, its family, and the circumstances of its birth are connected with the grand scheme of things: the value of life, its creation, and, of course, the divine influence on it. Thus, the onomasticon contains a great number of recurring terms related to religion, progeny, family, and social life. Some of the most common terms will be introduced in this chapter.

Although names remain untranslated in modern text editions, knowledge about their meaning is fundamental for creating correct transliterations and transcriptions, especially when ambiguous logographic spellings are involved (see Chapter 6). Moreover, the interpretation of names also enables us to understand their social significance, as names can convey information that goes far beyond a gender dichotomy. Many names

[2] The Babylonian onomasticon comprises a few names consisting of five words, for example, Lūmur-pāni-Marduk-itti-balāṭu 'May I see the face of Marduk with life' (Baker 2004 no. 265 r. 7'), Ultu-pāni-Bēl-lū-šulum 'May well-being (come) from the face of Bēl', and Papsukkal-ša-iqbû-ul-īni 'That, which has been commanded by Papsukkal, is irrevocable' (Tallqvist 1905, 240, 271). An example from Assyria is the name of the prince Aššur-etel-šamê-erṣeti-muballissu 'Aššur, the prince of heaven and earth is the one who keeps him alive' (Pempe in PNA 1/I, 184–5).

contain relevant hints about the social status and origin of their bearers (see Chapter 1).

Interpretations of names given in the course of this chapter are based on Knut L. Tallqvist (1905), Johann J. Stamm (1939), John P. Nielsen (2015), and Cornell Thissen (2017), who collected and analysed a large amount of material from the Babylonian onomasticon. For supplementary information and further attestations, the online database *Prosobab* has been used (Waerzeggers and Groß et al. 2019).

Typical Elements of Male Names

Deities are particularly common elements of Babylonian, and generally of all Akkadian, names. In addition to the generic terms *ilu* 'god', *ilī* 'gods' (or 'my god'), and *ilānu* 'the gods', spelled mostly with the logogram DINGIR plus possible endings,[3] names of specific divinities occur in large numbers. Starting with Nabû, the most popular god in the onomasticon of this period, Knut L. Tallqvist counted a total of 84 divine names attested in personal names (1905). This included not only deities, but also divine titles, epithets, and unclear logographic spellings. The number of deities frequently used as theophoric name elements is in fact much smaller (Table 2.1).[4]

Several groups of male names show a flexible use of theophoric elements. The common name type DN-iddin '(God x) has given' is, for instance, attested with all kinds of different deities – for example, Anu-iddin, Bēl-iddin, Ea-iddin, Nabû-iddin, among others. The choice of a specific deity as theophoric name element depends on several factors (see also Chapter 1). Personal preferences, local customs, and historical trends, but also the social status of the name-bearer can play a role. Generally, men tend to include the principal god or goddess of their hometown in their names. There are also some who show a preference for deities associated with their professions, and still others who follow a theological pattern when naming their children, one by one in accordance with their birth order, after the hierarchical position of the gods in the pantheon (see Baker 2002).

[3] Plural forms can be marked by the signs MEŠ and ME or by annexing the syllable *-ni*. Spellings for 'my god' include DINGIR, DINGIR-*ía*, *-ia*, and *-ú-a*.

[4] The frequency by which the thirty most common deities occur in names is illustrated in a table provided by Tallqvist (1905, xix–xx). Regarding all periods of Akkadian, Johann J. Stamm counted 53 different theophoric elements in the onomasticon (Stamm 1939, 68–9).

Table 2.1 *Divine names frequently used in Babylonian male names, along with their logographic spellings*

Adad	^{d}IŠKUR ^{d}10	Bānītu	(syll.)	Ea	^{d}IDIM	Marduk	^{d}AMAR.UTU ^{d}ŠÚ	Ninlil	^{d}NIN.LÍL
Amurru	^{d}KUR.GAL ^{d}MAR.TU	Bēl	^{d}EN	Enlil	^{d}50	Mār-bīti	^{d}A.É ^{d}DUMU.É	Ninurta	^{d}MAŠ
Anu	^{d}60	Bēltu	^{d}GAŠAN ^{d}NIN	Gula	^{d}ME.ME	Nabû	^{d}AG ^{d}PA	Nusku	^{d}PA.KU
Aya	(syll.)	Bunene	^{d}ḪAR	Ištar	^{d}IN.NIN ^{d}INANNA ^{d}15	Nanāya	(syll.)	Sîn	^{d}30
Bābu[5]	^{d}BA.Ú ^{d}KÁ	Būru	^{d}AMAR	Madānu	^{d}DI.KUD	Nergal	^{d}IGI.DU ^{d}U.GUR	Šamaš	^{d}UTU

[5] The reading of this god's name is debated; see recently Sandowicz (2021) on this matter.

Foreign gods can be mentioned in names that also include Babylonian elements and vice versa. More information on these hybrid names, reflecting the multi-cultural setting of this period, can be found elsewhere in this book (see Chapters 7, 8, and 12).

Apart from the deities themselves, their sanctuaries are also mentioned in personal names. Eanna, Ezida, Esagil, and other temples occur, as well as smaller places of worship, such as Bīt-Akītu and Bīt-Papsukkal. Secular toponyms and localities that link name-bearers to their home towns cover a similar range. Cities across the region of Akkad, from the capital of Babylon to provincial centres such as Sippar, Nippur, and Kish, are used as elements in personal names, alongside generic terms such as *bītu* 'house' (É) and *ālu* 'city' (URU).

Within the group of kinship terms that occur as elements in names, children play a larger role than adults. The mentioning of *abu* '(biological) father' (AD)[6] and *ummu* 'mother' (AMA) is less common than that of *aḫu* 'brother' (ŠEŠ) and *aḫātu* 'sister' (mostly written syllabically), which can refer either to the newborn child itself or to its siblings. In any event, the mentioning of siblings indicates that the name-bearer was not the first-born. It is possible that the term *māru* 'son' (DUMU) likewise expresses birth order, when a child bearing such a name was born after the one designated as *aplu* 'son, heir' (A, IBILA), *kīnu* 'legitimate one' (GIN), or *kudurru* 'heir' (NÍG.DU).[7]

The terms *šumu* 'name' (MU) and *zēru* 'seed' (NUMUN) are typical for male names. As expressions for human continuity, they relate exclusively to sons who will hand down their father's heritage, including his household and family name.[8] By contrast, references to the brief biological existence of human beings are contained in all kinds of names. Related concepts of life, health, and survival concern both male and female offspring. They are integrated in names through elements such as *balāṭu* 'life', 'to live' and *bulluṭu* 'to keep alive' or 'to bring into being' (TIN), *šulmu* 'well-being' (mostly written syllabically), and *ṣillu* 'protection' (GIŠ.MI).

[6] The term *abu* can also refer to divine father figures and to owners of slaves; see Stamm (1939, § 8).

[7] For a detailed discussion regarding the meaning of these name elements, see Stamm (1939, § 7). In case of the terms *aḫu* and *aḫātu* it is often unclear whether the imagined speaker uttering the name is the name-bearer (in which case these elements refer to siblings) or the sibling(s) (in which case these elements refer to the newborn child).

[8] For a comprehensive analysis of Mesopotamian personal names as metaphors and manifestations of the individual's fame and memory, see Radner (2005).

Frequently recurring verbs in names are *amāru* 'to see' (IGI), *aqāru* 'to be precious' (KAL), *banû* 'to create' (DÙ), *bašû* 'to exist' (GÁL), *erēšu* 'to wish for' (APIN, KAM, KÁM), *ešēru* 'to be/go well' (GIŠ), *eṭēru* 'to save' (KAR, SUR), *lēʾû* 'be able, powerful' (Á.GÁL, DA), *nadānu* 'to give' (MU, SUM.NA), *nâdu* 'to praise' (I), *kânu* 'to be(come) permanent, firm, true' (GI.NA, GIN), *naṣāru* 'to protect' (ÙRU, PAB), *paḫāru* 'to gather' (BÁḪAR), *qabû* 'to name, call' (E), *râmu* 'to love' (ÁG), *šalāmu* 'to be(come) healthy, intact', and *šullumu* 'to keep healthy, intact, safe' (GI). Adjectives used as elements in names often derive from these verbs. Additionally, *damqu* 'good' (SIG_5), *dannu* 'strong' (mostly written syllabically, sometimes KAL), and *ṭābu* 'good, sweet' (DÙG.GA) are frequently used adjectives.

Sentence Names

Personal names expressing complete sentences do not necessarily follow the common word order of the Late Babylonian language (subject–object–predicate). Often, the predicate stands at the beginning of the name. The phrase 'Marduk has given (an heir)' occurs, for instance, in two different names: Marduk-(aplu-)iddin and Iddin-Marduk (also a family name). Along with the example of Aplu-iddin 'He has given an heir', it becomes clear that elements were not only exchanged but also omitted in order to create short or alternative forms of names. The practice of shortening or modifying names will be discussed in greater detail in the section on 'Shortened Names'.

Despite their variation in length and word order, Babylonian sentence names can be divided into a number of subcategories based on their contents and narrative structure.

a) Names like 'Marduk has given (an heir)' express **favourable actions** by revered entities towards the name-bearer and his social environment from the viewpoint of an anonymous narrator. The actors included in these names are usually deities, while the newborn child and its environment appear as the beneficiaries of the actions.[9] Less often masters (of slaves), the king (as superior of his officials), and cities as well as regions are mentioned as entities bestowing favour.[10]

[9] Exceptionally, relatives of the name-bearer are mentioned as agents – for example, Aḫu-ālu-uṣur 'O brother, protect the city' (Nielsen 2015, 17).

[10] For an extensive discussion of names of slaves and officials, see Chapters 1 and 5 in this volume.

This group of names shows a huge diversity in structure. Names that obey the common word order usually consist of the subject in initial position followed either by an object and a conjugated verbal form or by a genitive construction consisting of a participle plus object. Compare, for instance, the parallel names Nabû-šumu-iddin 'Nabû has given the name' (also used as a family name) and Nabû-nādin-šumi 'Nabû is the giver of the name'. Occasionally the subject is followed by two verbal forms indicating consecutive actions towards the newborn child: for example, Sîn-tabni-uṣur 'O Sîn, you have created (the child), now protect (it)' (also a family name).[11] Names in this category usually consist of three words, but more elements occur when compound nouns are involved or prepositions are added: for example, Nabû-zēr-kitti-līšir 'O Nabû, may the seed of truth thrive' and Nergal-ina-tēšî-eṭir 'O Nergal, save from confusion'. In names using a reversed sentence order, the object is usually not retained; see, for instance, the male names Ibni-Ištar 'Ištar has created', Iddin-Bēl 'Bēl has given', and Erība-Enlil 'Enlil has replaced for me'.

b) **Conditions and qualities** constitute the topic of another common group of sentence names, expressed by (verbal) adjectives. The subjects are usually deities, the king, the name-bearer, or relatives. Most of these names consist of two words, as in the male names Bēl-dannu 'Bēl is strong', Ištar-lēʾi 'Ištar is capable', and Aḫḫū-ṭābū 'The brothers are good'. Three elements occur when compounds are employed or when positive injunctions are expressed, as in the rare male names Abi-ummi-aqar 'The (maternal) grandfather is precious' and Šarru-lū-dari 'May the king be eternal', or in the family name Arkât-ilāni-damqā 'The future of the gods is good'. Four elements are exceptional: for example, the rare male name Abu-Enlil-dāri-libūr 'O father, may Enlil stay firm forever'.

c) Apart from sentences pronounced by anonymous speakers, names can also express **personal statements** of the newborn child or a parent. Examples of such male names are Ana-Bēl-atkal 'I trusted in Bēl', Nanāya-uṣalli 'I prayed to Nanāya', and Abu-ul-īde 'I do not know the (or my) father' (also used as a family name).[12] Invocations of deities frequently precede such statements, as in the male names Bēl-ina-nakutti-alsika 'O Bēl, I called out to you in distress' and Bābu-alsiki-abluṭ 'O Bābu, I called on you and I lived'. The name

[11] Another (rare) example of this sentence structure is the male name Nabû-tabni-šuklil 'O Nabû, you have engendered, now cause (the child) to be carried to full term' (Nielsen 2015, 254).

[12] Female names possibly reflecting a mother's lament in childbirth are discussed in Chapter 3 (Classification, 6).

Lūṣi-ana-nūr-Marduk 'May I go out into the light of Marduk' (also used as a family name) is a popular example of a name with atypical word order.

A particularly common element of this type of names is the wish to see (*lūmur* 'may I see'), mostly referring to a certain deity. Desired occasions and places can be named, as in the male names Nabû-ina-Esagil-lūmur 'May I see Nabû in (the temple) Esagil', Bēl-ina-kāri-lūmur 'May I see Bēl at the mooring place', Nabû-nūrka-lūmur 'O Nabû, may I see your light', and Pāni-Sîn-lūmur 'May I see the face of Sîn'. Also, the wish for siblings or for one's hometown can be expressed: for example, the male names Aḫḫē-lūmur 'May I see (the) brothers' and Ālu-lūmur 'May I see the city'.

d) **Equations** between entities occur in names expressing declarative sentences as well as questions. In order to stress the estimation of a personal god, deities are matched with relatives of the name-bearer, authorities, and protective forces, or sometimes also with each other: for example, the male names Aḫu-kî-Sîn 'The brother is like Sîn', Adad-dayyānu 'Adad is the judge', Bēl-usātu 'Bēl is (my) help', Enlil-kidin 'Enlil is protection', and Sîn-kî-Nabû 'Sîn is like Nabû'.[13] Comparisons between relatives and other phenomena are exceptional; see, for instance, the uncommon male name Aḫu-dūru 'The brother is (like) a wall'. Compound nouns occur only scarcely: for example, the rare male name Aḫī-šadi-ili 'My brother is (like) the mountain of the god'. As predicates are not employed, these names cannot always be distinguished from names based on nouns in genitive construction. When phrased as a question, they are usually recognisable by the initial interrogative particle *mannu* (or *mamma*) 'who': for example, the male names Mannu-kî-Nanāya 'Who is like Nanāya?', Mamma-kî-Ezida 'Who is like Ezida?', and Mamma-kî-šarri 'Who is like the king?'.

e) **Other questions** expressed by male names are, for instance, Ammēni-ilī 'Why, my god?', Aya-aḫu 'Where is the brother?', Mannu-izkur 'Who has proclaimed?', and Mīnu-ēpuš-ilī 'O my god, what have I done?'. Some are preceded by invocations of deities: for example, the male name Bēl-ammēni 'O Bēl, why?'.

Not all sentence names can be assigned to one of the aforementioned groups. Some are completely exceptional, while others do not entirely

[13] Such names might have been more common in older periods, as seen from the examples listed by Stamm (1939, 299–301).

match the structures and meanings of comparable names, such as the common male names Itti-DN-balāṭu 'With DN there is life', attested with various theophoric elements, and Ša-Nabû-šū 'He is the one of Nabû', also attested with the variant Ša-Bēl-šū 'He is the one of Bēl'. The latter name constitutes a borderline case: by linking the name-bearer to the god Nabû or Bēl, respectively, this name's meaning shows affinity with sentence names expressing equations between entities but its structure resembles that of names based on a genitive construction.

Compound Names (Genitive Constructions)

As the example of Ša-Nabû-šū 'He is the one of Nabû' illustrates, names based on genitive constructions do not have to be completely different from sentence names. Besides the fact that some can be interpreted as nominal sentences uttered by an anonymous speaker, parallels in meaning also occur. The relationship between deities and name-bearers or their environment is the most popular topic in both categories of names. Yet, the majority of compound names are characterised by a distinct vocabulary that indicates that we are not dealing with short forms of sentences, but with original names.

a) Some frequently attested compound names refer to the name-bearers as **servants and subordinates of deities**. This relationship can be expressed by the status terms *amīlu* 'man' and *ardu* 'servant' in male names and family names alike;[14] see Amīl-Nanāya 'Man of Nanāya', Arad-ili-rabî 'Servant of the great god', and Arad-Nergal 'Servant of Nergal' (also a family name). Alternatively, subordination is indicated metaphorically by terms like *kalbu* 'dog' and *būru* 'calf', such as in the male names Būr-Adad 'Calf of Adad' and Kalbi-Bābu 'Dog of Bābu'. Occupational titles, temple designations, and geographic references are frequently employed in family names that express subordination, but hardly ever in male names of this type.[15]
b) Compound names that refer to the birth of the name-bearer as a **present of the gods** can employ several synonymous terms for 'gift'; see the male names Nidinti-Anu 'Gift of Anu', Qīšti-Marduk

[14] Female names can likewise include the status term *amtu* 'maidservant'. Yet, an Akkadian term for 'woman' is, to my knowledge, not attested in personal names at all.

[15] An exception might be Šangû-Ninurta 'Priest of Ninurta'. This is mostly known as a family name, but at least once attested as a male name (UET 4 89:11).

'Gift of Marduk', Rēmūt-Bābu 'Gift of Bābu', and Širikti-Šamaš 'Gift of Šamaš'.

c) Another group of common compound names express **divine help and patronage**; see, for instance, the male names Gimil-Gula 'Favour of Gula', Ina-ṣilli-Esagil 'Under the protection of Esagil', also attested with the variant Ina-ṣilli-šarri 'Under the protection of the king', and Kidin-Sîn 'Protection of Sîn' (also a family name). The contents and terminology of these names sometimes equal that of the aforementioned sentence names that express equations between deities and protective forces; compare, for instance, Bēl-eṭēri 'Lord of saving' (also a family name) and Bēl-eṭēri-Nabû 'Lord of saving is Nabû' (male name), or the male names Bēl-usātu 'Bēl is (my) help' and Nabû-bēl-usāti 'Nabû is the lord of help'.

d) Widely known as a name for orphans and foundlings is Ša-pî-kalbi 'From the mouth of a dog' (see Chapter 1). Structurally similar names mention deities instead of the term *kalbu* 'dog', for example, Ša-pî-Bēl. In these cases, a metaphorical interpretation is also possible: 'The one promised by Bēl'.[16]

Single Words (Non-Compound Names)

The briefest names, consisting of only one word, show the biggest variety regarding contents. On the one hand, they can refer to concepts and ideas that also occur as elements of sentence names and compound names. These names might well be short versions of originally longer forms; see, for example, the male names Ēṭiru 'Saviour' (cf. Amurru-ēṭir 'Amurru has saved'), Dābibī 'My plea' (cf. Iššar-dābibī-nēr 'O Iššar, kill those who plot against me'), Gimillu 'Favour' (cf. Gimil-Nergal 'Favour of Nergal' or Nabû-mutīr-gimilli 'Nabû is the one who returns kindness'), Balāssu 'His life' (cf. Enlil-balāssu-iqbi 'Enlil pronounced his life'), Rībātu 'Compensation' (cf. Šamaš-erība 'Šamaš has replaced for me'), and Talīmu 'Favourite brother' (cf. Nabû-talīmu-uṣur 'O Nabû, protect the favourite brother').[17] On the other hand, brief names can be based on a totally different vocabulary than those consisting of sentences or compounds. In addition to nouns denoting phenomena from the social and natural environment, isolated adjectives and verbs are also used as names.

[16] See Stamm (1939, 259). Nielsen (2015) gives a literal translation: 'Of the mouth of Bēl'.

[17] Some of these names are also used as family names: Balāssu 'His life', Dābibī 'My plea', Gimillu 'Favour', and Šamaš-erība 'Šamaš has replaced for me'. Also, the male name Ēṭiru 'Saviour' corresponds with the family name Eṭēru 'To save'.

a) **Natural phenomena** are represented when individuals are named after plants, stones, or other materials; see, for instance, the male names Burāšu 'Juniper' and Ḫuṣābu 'Chip of wood'.
b) Also, a large group of **animal names** serve to denote individuals, both male and female (see Chapter 3 for female names). Curiously, wild beasts are more often referred to than domesticated ones, and highly symbolic animals, including lions, eagles, and the mythological Anzû bird, are completely lacking in the onomasticon. Instead we find, for instance, men called Barbaru 'Wolf', Arrab(t)u '(Female) dormouse' (both forms are also used as family names), Ḫaḫḫuru 'Raven', Uqūpu 'Monkey', Šellebu 'Fox', Murašû 'Wildcat', and Kulbību 'Ant'. Regarding domesticated animals, especially terms for offspring are used as male names; e.g., Kalūmu 'Lamb' and Mūrānu 'Puppy'. Thus, it seems that animal terms serve mainly as pet names and nicknames, mimicking physical qualities and character traits of humans. Yet, despite their informal and at times humoristic connotation, hardly any of them are actually attested as the second name of an individual (Stamm 1939, § 4). The phenomenon of second names will be further discussed under 'Nicknames and Double Names'.
c) The same holds for male names that refer directly to **physical features and other personal characteristics**, such as Dullupu 'Sleepy', Dummuqu 'To be gracious', Arrakūtu 'Very tall', Nummuru 'Brilliant', Tardennu 'Second(ary)', and Ašarēdu 'The foremost one' (also a family name). Despite their informal appearance, these names are not known as secondary names.
d) The **geographical origin** of men is reflected in names such as Bābilāya 'Babylonian', Balīḫû 'Man from Balikh' (cf. Bālīḫāya 'The Balikhian'), or Miṣirāya 'Man from Egypt'. These names are mainly used as family names, but occasionally they also denote male individuals.
e) The **time of birth** can play a role in name-giving. Some individuals are named after the month in which they were born, such as Ulūlāya 'Man born in Ulūlu', or after a festival taking place at the time, for example, Kinūnāya 'Man born during the Kinūnu festival'.
(f) An individual's **social rank** can be mirrored by names such as Batūlu 'Young man', Zikaru 'Man', Līdānu 'Bastard', and perhaps also Banūnu (West Semitic) 'Little son' (if not to be read in Akkadian: Bānûnu 'Our creator').
(g) **Occupational titles** constitute a particularly large group amongst the original one-word names. Most of them serve only as family names in

the first millennium BCE, such as Asû 'Physician', Gallābu 'Barber', and Ṭābiḫu 'Butcher' (see Chapter 4). Only a few are used as male names; see, for instance, Dayyānu 'Judge' and Ḫazannu 'Mayor'.

Variants of Male Names

Individuation by Filiation

Although personal names denote individuals, they are not unique themselves. This does not only apply to popular names. Even uncommon names lose their exceptional status when reused in memory of their original bearers. Within small communities, such as nuclear families and local work teams, the fundamental non-uniqueness of personal names can be ignored. The mentioning of simple names and even generic titles, such as 'mom' or 'boss', is usually sufficient to identify a specific member of an in-group. Otherwise, short forms and nicknames can be employed to differentiate between namesakes within a community. However, the larger a group, the more it needs unambiguous ways to identify a specific person in time and place. Especially in official contexts, for instance, when drawing up long-term contracts such as property deeds, societies need a way to ensure that witnesses, acting parties, and their descendants can be identified in the future.

Official documents from first millennium BCE Babylonia frequently use additional data when referring to individuals. Besides indications of origins like 'the Borsippean' (^{lú}BAR.SIP^{ki}), status terms such as *qallu* 'slave' (of another individual) and occupational titles like *ṭupšar bīti* 'college scribe' were used. Freeborn people are usually designated as sons or daughters of their fathers. Occasionally, maternal names are given instead of paternal ones (see Chapter 1). In addition, the urban gentry also used family names taken from occupational titles of their members or from personal names of their (alleged) ancestors (see Chapter 4). In Seleucid times genealogies expand even more, as individuals are frequently mentioned by name, patronym, grandfather's name, and family name.

Shortened Names

Shortening of names can take place for practical as well as affectionate reasons. In contrast to modern short names, Babylonian ones are not necessarily less official than their original full forms, as they are attested in all kinds of formal documents. Depending on the structure of the original name, there are different ways and degrees of shortening. The longer the original name, the more possibilities it offers for shortening. In addition to simple and multiple reductions, modifications also occur.

Names expressing complete sentences can be shortened by omitting one or more elements. Short forms created by such reductions still constitute complete and grammatically correct sentences that express the same basic meaning as the original full forms. Sometimes, however, the omission of elements led to ambiguous short forms in which the original sentence structures of the full names are not recognisable anymore. This is the case when, for instance, the male name Ana-Bēl-ēreš 'He desired Bēl' is shortened to the form Bēl-ēreš. This can be interpreted as either 'He desired Bēl' or 'Bēl-desired'. Yet, most sentence names keep a grammatically clear structure, even when shortened by more than one element. The four-part male name Nergal-ina-tēšî-eṭir 'Nergal, save from confusion!' can be shortened in two steps: firstly, to Ina-tēšî-eṭir 'Save from confusion!' and, secondly, to Tēšî-eṭir 'Save (from) confusion!' All three forms – Nergal-ina-tēšî-eṭir, Ina-tēšî-eṭir, and Tēšî-eṭir – are known to be variants used to denote the same individuals.[18] These persons are to my knowledge never called Nergal-tēšî-eṭir 'O Nergal, save (from) confusion!', although this name exists in general and appears to be another shortened variant of the full form Nergal-ina-tēšî-eṭir. Similarly, it is most likely that structurally similar names such as Šamaš-ina-tēšî-eṭir 'O Šamaš, save from confusion' or Nabû-ina-tēšî-eṭir 'O Nabû, save from confusion!' generate the same short forms as Nergal-ina-tēšî-eṭir, but such cases are, to my knowledge, not attested. Since the principles of shortening names have not been studied in detail yet, only attested variants are discussed in this chapter. All examples of short forms and nicknames given in the further course of this chapter are based on identified individuals recorded in the online database *Prosobab*; text references can be found there.

As the example of the name Nergal-ina-tēšî-eṭir, with its variants Ina-tēšî-eṭir and Tēšî-eṭir, illustrates, theophoric elements and prepositions are often omitted to create short forms. Several male names are shortened in the same way (Table 2.2).

Male names based on genitive constructions usually generate short forms by omitting the theophoric element (Table 2.3).

[18] Two persons are attested with all three variants of this name: Nergal-ina-tēšî-eṭir, son of Ina-Esagil-mukīn-apli, from the Balīḫû family (BM 77352, BM 77372, and BM 77386), and Nergal-ina-tēšî-eṭir, son of Zēria, from the Šangû-Šamaš family (e.g., BM 74583, BM 74595, and BM 74597).

Table 2.2 *Shortening of Babylonian sentence names by omission of elements*

Full form	Theophoric element omitted	Preposition omitted	Double reduction
Nergal-ina-tēšî-eṭir 'O Nergal, save from confusion'	Ina-tēšî-eṭir 'Save from confusion'		Tēšî-eṭir 'Save (from) confusion'
Nabû-bēlšunu 'Nabû is their lord'	Bēlšunu 'Their lord'		
Lâbâši-Marduk 'May I not come to shame, O Marduk'	Lâbâši 'May I not come to shame'		
Lâbâši-Sîn 'May I not come to shame, O Sîn'	Lâbâši 'May I not come to shame'		
Šulum-ana-Bābili 'Well-being to Babylon'		Šulum-Bābili 'Well-being (to) Babylon'	
Ana-Bēl-ēreš 'He desired Bēl'		Bēl-ēreš 'He desired Bēl' or 'Bēl-desired'	
Itti-Nusku-īnīa 'With Nusku is my eye'		Nusku-īnīa 'Nusku is my eye'	
Itti-Šamaš-balāṭu 'With Šamaš is life'		Šamaš-balāṭu 'Šamaš is life'	
Itti-Nabû-balāṭu 'With Nabû is life'			Balāṭu 'Life'

Table 2.3 *Shortening of Babylonian compound names by omission of the theophoric element*

Full form	Short form
Širikti-Marduk	Širiktu
'Gift of Marduk'	'Gift'
Kiribti-Marduk	Kiribtu
'Blessed by Marduk'	'Blessedness'
Nidinti-Marduk	Nidintu
'Gift of Marduk'	'Gift'
Nidinti-Bēl	Nidintu
'Gift of Bēl'	'Gift'

The particularly common type of sentence names that consist of three basic elements and that express favourable actions of revered deities can be shortened in two steps. First, the subject or the direct object of these names can be omitted. Then, further reduction is achieved by omitting either the direct object or the object of a genitive construction as seen in the examples of male names presented in Table 2.4.

The direct object of a sentence name can also be replaced by a structurally different element such as a personal suffix. The full male name Nabû-šumu-uṣur 'O Nabû, protect the name' is shortened into Nabû-uṣuršu 'O Nabû, protect him'. Names with comparable structures can probably be modified in the same way.

Other cases of modified names illustrate that elements, isolated by double reduction, can be replaced by grammatically different forms of these elements: verbs can be replaced by substantives and vice versa. Balāṭu 'Life', for instance, is not only a double reduced short form of the male name Itti-Nabû-balāṭu 'With Nabû there is life' but also a modified short form of the male name Šamaš-uballiṭ 'Šamaš has kept alive'. Curiously, the structurally equal male name Itti-Marduk-balāṭu 'With Marduk there is life' generates the modified short form Libluṭ 'May he live'. This illustrates that not all principles of modification are easily predictable.

A widespread phenomenon is the modification of short forms by annexing a meaningless syllable, also known as a hypocoristic ending. Although hypocoristic forms give the impression of pet names, they are used in official contexts just like other short forms. Several hypocoristic endings occur. It is not always possible to distinguish them from Akkadian plural markers, possessive pronouns, and other meaningful suffixes, as, for

Table 2.4 *Shortening of Babylonian sentence names*

Full form	Subject omitted	Direct object omitted	Double reduction
Nabû-nādin-aḫi	Nādin-aḫi		
‘Nabû is the giver of the brother’	‘Giver of the brother’		
Nabû-šumu-ukīn	Šumu-ukīn		
‘Nabû has established the name’	‘He has established the name’		
Marduk-šumu-iddin	Šumu-iddin		
‘Marduk has given the name’	‘He has given the name’		
Nabû-šumu-iddin		Nabû-iddin	
‘Nabû has given the name’		‘Nabû has given’	
Bēl-aḫu-ittannu		Bēl-ittannu	
‘Bēl has given the brother’		‘Bēl has given’	
Šamaš-pirʾu-uṣur			Pirʾu
‘O Šamaš, protect the offspring’			‘Offspring’
Nabû-nādin-šumi			Nādinu[19]
‘Nabû is the giver of the name’			‘Giver’

19 Note also a well-known case from Assyria: a certain Nabû-šumu-iddin, *ḫazannu* of the Nabû temple in Kalḫu, also used the name Nādinu in letters to the king (Esarhaddon); see Baker in PNA 2/II, 885–6 s.v. Nabû-šumu-iddina 15.

instance, in the male name Aḫ(ḫ)ūtu 'Brotherhood' or, hypocoristically, 'Brother'. Especially popular in the Babylonian onomasticon is a group of hypocoristic endings that coincide with the forms of the possessive suffix of the first person singular, namely the hypocoristic endings *-ia*, spelled C*i-ia*/*ía*, and *-āya*, spelled C*a-a*, or infrequently also C*a-ia*, followed by *-ea* or *-ēa*, spelled C*e-e-a* or (C)VC*-e-a*. Additionally, hypocoristic endings of West Semitic origin, including *-ā*, *-ān*, and *-ī*, also occur frequently (see Chapter 8). Table 2.5 provides a selection of differently structured male names and their hypocoristic short forms.

Nicknames and Double Names

In contrast to short names that always show at least some kind of similarity to their original full forms, nicknames and double names are completely different from the name that a person bears otherwise. Babylonian documents attest to this phenomenon frequently, sometimes directly by mentioning individuals with a 'second (or: other) name' (*šumu šanû*). More often, people use different personal names interchangeably without marking them as such. A son of Lūṣi-ana-nūr-Marduk ('May I go out into the light of Marduk') from the family Ilī-bāni ('My god is the creator') is, for instance, mostly referred to as Nādinu 'Giver', but in some documents he appears as Dādia 'My favourite' (Joannès 1989, 50–2). The frequency by which he is called Nādinu may indicate that this is his primary name. Still, the name Dādia, which is also attested as another name of a man called Nergal-ašarēdu ('Nergal is the foremost'),[20] is obviously valid in official contexts too. Male double names frequently show shifts between comprehensive and short names, as Table 2.6 shows. Shifts between names with serious content and seemingly humoristic names are, by contrast, not particularly common; however, note the example of Nergal-ušēzib 'Nergal has rescued' whose second name is Puršû 'Flea'.[21]

Not only personal names but also family names can vary. Some individuals use two family names interchangeably – one that refers to a (prebendary) profession, the other taken from the name of an ancestor. In the case of Ingallēa (meaning uncertain) and Gallābu 'Barber' the acquisition or disposal of prebends may have caused different branches of the clan to use the name that reflects their actual tenure or lack of the

[20] He is a son of Puḫḫuru 'Assembled' from the family Ilūtu-bāni 'Creator of divinity'; for references, see Joannès (1989, 370).

[21] The first three examples in this table are taken from Jursa (1999, 146); the others are taken from the *Prosobab* database.

Table 2.5 *Hypocoristic short forms of Babylonian male names*

Full form	Short form
Arad-Marduk	Ardia
'Servant of Marduk'	'Servant' (hypocor.) or 'My servant'
Ṭāb-ṣilli-Marduk	Ṭābia
'Good is the protection of Marduk'	'Good' (hypocor.)
Iddin-Nabû	Iddināya
'Nabû has given'	'He has given' (hypocor.)
Šamaš-iddin	Iddia
'Šamaš has given'	(meaning unknown, probably hypocor.)
Iqīša-Marduk	Iqīšāya
'Marduk has granted to me'	'He has granted to me' (hypocor.)
Bēl-iqīša	Iqīšāya
'Bēl has granted to me'	'He has granted to me' (hypocor.)
Šamaš-erība	Erībāya
'Šamaš has replaced for me'	'He has replaced for me' (hypocor.)
Nabû-tabni-uṣur	Tabnēa
'O Nabû, you have created (the child), now protect (it)'	'You have created' (hypocor.)
Nabû-bān-aḫi	Bānia
'Nabû is the creator of the brother'	'Creator' (hypocor.) or 'My creator'
Šamaš-aplu-iddin	Aplāya
'Šamaš has given an heir'	'Heir' (hypocor.)
Nūr-Bēl-lūmur	Nūrea
'May I see the light of Bēl'	'Light' (hypocor.)

barber's office.[22] There is also a family that abandoned their professional family name Ṭābiḫu 'Butcher' for unknown reasons in favour of a new ancestral family name Eṭēru 'To save'. According to a study by Cornelia Wunsch (2014a), this shift took place gradually over the course of several decades. Within one generation, members of the family switched back and forth from one name to the other or used both names interchangeably. It is possible that they tried to differentiate themselves from other, non-prebendary butchers called Ṭābiḫ-kāri 'Butcher at the quay or market' by using either the specified name Ṭābiḫ-Marduk 'Butcher of Marduk' or the new one, Eṭēru 'To save'. Also, some members of the clan Zērāya (hypocoristically based on *zēru* 'seed' or Zēr-Aya 'Seed of Aya') may have changed their family name to Ile??i-Marduk 'Marduk is powerful'.[23]

22 Pedersén 2005, 204–6; Nielsen 2011, 65–6.

23 Jursa 1995, 73–4. Wunsch (2014a, 757) also mentions a possible change of the family names Iddin-Papsukkal ('Papsukkal has given') and Ša-1-luḫ (reading and meaning unclear).

Table 2.6 *Double names borne by Babylonian men*

Itti-Marduk-balāṭu	Iddināya
'With Marduk there is life'	'He has given' (hypocor.)
Marduk-nāṣir-apli	Širku
'Marduk is the protector of the heir'	'Gift'
Nergal-ušēzib	Puršû
'Nergal has rescued'	'Flea' (hypocor.?)
Nādinu	Dādia
'Giver'	'My favourite'
Nergal-ašarēdu	Dādia
'Nergal is the foremost'	'My favourite'
Nabû-ittannu	Aplāya
'Nabû has given'	'Heir' (hypocor.)
Munaḫḫiš-Marduk	Nidintu
'Marduk is the one who makes prosperous'	'Gift'

Further Reading

The works of Knut L. Tallqvist (1905) and Johann J. Stamm (1939) constitute the most comprehensive studies on Akkadian names and name-giving, especially with regard to Babylonia in the first millennium BCE. While Tallqvist focusses on this period, Stamm provides diachronic analyses that illustrate the development of names and naming practices in the course of time. The structures, typical elements, and socio-cultural meanings of Babylonian names outlined in the present chapter are discussed by these authors in more detail. Also, additional examples for individual names, short forms, and variants can be found there. Despite their early composition, both publications are still most relevant for onomastic studies.

For revised readings and interpretations of personal names, the reader should consult the user-friendly volume by John P. Nielsen (2015). His alphabetically arranged list of Babylonian names of the Neo-Babylonian period does not only provide English translations but also references to attestations and further literature. With regard to family names, Cornelia Wunsch (2014b) provides a concise overview of orthography and historical developments. John P. Nielsen (2011) offers a more extensive discussion of the emergence and spread of family names in the early Neo-Babylonian period.

For a broader approach to Akkadian names, the encyclopaedic article by Dietz-Otto Edzard (1998) is recommended. His outline of Akkadian onomastics goes beyond the aforementioned publications by including names of deities and demons, places, waters, walls, and fields. Moreover, Edzard also touches upon linguistic aspects of names, including their relation to (literary) language, their morphology, and Sumerian influences.

References

Baker, H. D. (ed.) 2001. *The Prosopography of the Neo-Assyrian Empire*, 2/II: L–N. Helsinki: The Neo-Assyrian Text Corpus Project.

Baker, H. D. 2002. 'Approaches to Akkadian name-giving in first-millennium BC Mesopotamia' in C. Wunsch (ed.), *Mining the Archives: Festschrift for Christopher Walker on the Occasion of His 60th Birthday*. Dresden: ISLET, pp. 1–24.

Baker, H. D. 2004. *The Archive of the Nappāhu Family*, Archiv für Orientforschung Beiheft 30. Vienna: Institut für Orientalistik.

Edzard, D.-O. 1998. 'Name, Namengebung (Onomastik). B. Akkadisch', *Reallexikon der Assyriologie und der Vorderasiatischen Archäologie* 9, 103–16.

Joannès, F. 1989. *Archives de Borsippa: La famille Ea-ilûta-bani: Étude d'un lot d'archives familiales en Babylonie du VIIIe au Ve siècle av. J.-C.* Geneva: Librairie Droz.

Jursa, M. 1995. *Die Landwirtschaft in Sippar in neubabylonischer Zeit*, Archiv für Orientforschung Beiheft 25. Vienna: Institut für Orientalistik.

Jursa, M. 1999. *Das Archiv des Bēl-rēmanni*, Publications de l'Institut historique-archéologique néerlandais de Stamboul 86. Leiden: Nederlands Instituut voor het Nabije Oosten.

Nielsen, J. P. 2011. *Sons and Descendants: A Social History of Kin Groups and Family Names in the Early Neo-Babylonian Period, 747–626 BC*, Culture and History of the Ancient Near East 43. Leiden: Brill.

Nielsen, J. P. 2015. *Personal Names in Early Neo-Babylonian Legal and Administrative Tablets, 747–626 BCE*, NISABA 29. Winona Lake: Eisenbrauns.

Pedersén, O. 2005. *Archive und Bibliotheken in Babylon: Die Tontafeln der Grabung Robert Koldeweys 1899–1917*. Saarbrücken: Saarländische Druckerei und Verlag.

Radner, K. (ed.) 1998. *The Prosopography of the Neo-Assyrian Empire 1/I: A*. Helsinki: The Neo-Assyrian Text Corpus Project.

Radner, K. 2005. *Die Macht des Namens. Altorientalische Strategien zur Selbsterhaltung*, SANTAG 8. Wiesbaden: Harrassowitz.

Sandowicz, M. 2021. 'The name BaU revisited' in U. Gabbay and S. Gordin (eds.), *Individuals and Institutions in the Ancient Near East*. Studies in Ancient Near Eastern Records 27. Berlin: De Gruyter, pp. 215–26.

Stamm, J. J. 1939. *Die akkadische Namengebung*, Mitteilungen der Vorderasiatisch-Ägyptischen Gesellschaft 44. Leipzig: J.C. Hinrichs Verlag.

Tallqvist, K. L. 1905. *Neubabylonisches Namenbuch zu den Geschäftsurkunden aus der Zeit des Šamaššumukîn bis Xerxes*, Acta Societatis Scientiarum Fennicae 32/2. Helsinki: Societas Litteraria Fennica.

Thissen, C. 2017. 'Review of J. P. Nielsen 2015. Personal Names in Early Neo-Babylonian Legal and Administrative Tablets, 747–626 BCE', *Bibliotheca Orientalis* 74, 103–40.

Waerzeggers, C. and M. Groß et al. 2019. *Prosobab: Prosopography of Babylonia (c. 620–330 BCE)*. https://prosobab.leidenuniv.nl.

Wunsch, C. 2006. 'Metronymika in Babylonien: Frauen als Ahnherrin der Familie' in G. del Olmo Lete, L. Feliu, and A. Millet-Albà (eds.), *Šapal tibnim mû illakū. Studies Presented to Joaquín Sanmartín on the Occassion of His 65th Birthday*, Aula Orientalis Supplementa 22. Sabadell/Barcelona: Editorial AUSA, pp. 459–69.

Wunsch, C. 2014a. 'Double family names in Neo-Babylonian records: The case of the Ēṭiru and Ṭābiḫu families and their butchers' prebends' in Z. Csabai (ed.), *Studies in Economic and Social History of the Ancient Near East in Memory of Péter Vargyas*. Budapest: l'Harmattan, pp. 751–87.

Wunsch, C. 2014b. 'Babylonische Familiennamen' in M. Krebernik and H. Neumann (eds), *Babylonien und seine Nachbarn. Wissenschaftliches Kolloquium aus Anlass des 75. Geburtstages von Joachim Oelsner, Jena, 2. und 3. März 2007*, Alter Orient und Altes Testament 369. Münster: Ugarit-Verlag, pp. 289–314.

CHAPTER 3

Babylonian Female Names

Laura Cousin and Yoko Watai

A vast corpus of women's names appears in the documentation from the Neo-Babylonian and Persian periods (626–330 BCE). This chapter establishes a typology of Babylonian female names and discusses the question of whether and how female personal names contributed to the construction of a female identity, in contrast to a male identity.

Typology of Female Names

Introduction

In cuneiform writing, female names are marked with the determinative MUNUS, as opposed to male names, which are marked with a single vertical wedge (see Chapter 1). Modern transliterations usually represent the female sign by placing ^{f} in superscript in front of the name. In this volume, we maintain this convention also in normalised versions of the names. In this way, normalised names can be easily recognised as male (unmarked) or female (preceded by ^{f}).

The structure of Akkadian female names is similar to the structure of male names; that is, they are composed of one or more elements (maximum four) and constitute either a sentence or a substantive. There is, however, a grammatical difference between male and female names. A verb, an adjective, or a noun forming part of a woman's name is generally given a feminine form. For example, the name Iddin-Marduk 'Marduk gave' (i.e., Marduk gave the child who bears the name) is a male name, while the name ^{f}Bānītu-taddin 'Bānītu gave', with the feminine form of the verb *nadānu* 'to give', is a female name. Here the form of the verb (or the adjective) does not correspond to the gender of the deity, but to the gender of the name-bearer.[1] Another example of the grammatical difference between male and female names is Aḫūšunu 'Their brother', which is a male name, while ᶠAḫāssunu 'Their sister' is the equivalent borne by women.

An additional feature is that female theophoric names include the name of a goddess. There are only a few examples of female names containing the name of a male god.[2] By contrast, male names with a female theophoric element are well known, albeit not very numerous (see 'Gendered Theophoric Elements').

Finally, it should be noted that there are some names that were borne by both men and women. Examples of such names include: Silim-Bābu 'Be friendly, O Bābu!' (with the masculine form of the imperative of the verb *salāmu*), Šulum-Bābili 'Well-being of Babylon', Nidintu 'Gift', and Ša-pî-kalbi 'Out of the mouth of a dog', which refers to an abandoned child.

Classification of Sentence Names

Babylonian female names can be classified in two main types: names which constitute a sentence and names which constitute a substantive. In each type, further divisions are possible. Starting with sentence names, we discern roughly eight subcategories.

1) *Attribute names* express an attribute of the divinity, with a divine name accompanying a nominal form such as ᶠNanāya-šarrat 'Nanāya is the queen', an adjective such as ᶠNanāya-damqat 'Nanāya is good', or a stative verb such as ᶠBābu-ēṭirat 'Bābu saves'. ᶠDN-šarrat, ᶠDN-damqat, and ᶠDN-ēṭirat are very common names, but many different verbs, nouns, and adjectives, such as *ṭābu* 'good' (ᶠMammītu-ṭābat 'Mammītu is good'), *ilatu* 'goddess' (ᶠNinlil-ilat 'Ninlil is goddess'), *aqāru* 'to be precious' (ᶠAya-aqrat 'Aya is precious'), *ramû* 'to dwell' (ᶠAttar-ramât 'Attar lives'), *rêšu* 'to rejoice' (ᶠNanāya-rīšat 'Nanāya rejoices'), *dannu* 'strong' (ᶠBānītu-dannat 'Bānītu is strong'), and *kašāru* 'to compensate' (ᶠNanāya-kēširat 'Nanāya compensates'), are also used. The names of goddesses are

[1] This is clear because male names that include the name of a goddess as the theophoric element contain the masculine form of the verb, such as Gula-zēru-ibni 'Gula created the descendant' (Wunsch 2000b no. 149). Hence, the male variant of the female name ᶠBānītu-taddin is Bānītu-iddin (e.g., *Nbn.* 772:4 and Wunsch 1993 no. 181: rev. 8).

[2] Two rare examples are ᶠMarduk-ēṭirat 'Marduk saves' in *Cyr.* 331 and ᶠMārat-Sîn-banât 'The daughter of Sîn is good' in UET 4 163. Gendered theophoric elements are discussed in greater detail later in the chapter (see section 'Gendered Theophoric Elements').

omitted in some cases, such as in the names ^{f}Ina-Esagil-bēlet 'She is the lady in Esagil' and ^{f}Ina-Esagil-ramât 'She lives in Esagil'. Certain substantive names were regarded as an abbreviated form of attribute names; for example, the name ^{f}Lēʔītu was likely an abbreviated form of ^{f}Lēʔi-DN 'DN is capable' (see Hackl 2013, 164–5).

2) *Petition names* generally contain a verb in the imperative and express a plea to a divinity from the speaker, such as ^{f}Nanāya-šimînni 'Listen to me, O Nanāya!' and ^{f}Aya-bulliṭanni 'Keep me healthy, O Aya!'. The speaker in these names was probably the name-bearer or possibly her mother. In addition to *šemû* 'to listen' and *bulluṭu* 'to make healthy', petition names include diverse verbs such as *salāmu* 'to be friendly' (^{f}Bānītu-silim 'Be friendly, O Bānītu!'), *râmu* 'to love' (^{f}Rīminni-Ištar 'Love me, O Ištar!'), *dânu* 'to judge' (^{f}Nanāya-dīninni 'Judge me, O Nanāya!'), *naṣāru* 'to protect' (^{f}Nanāya-kilīlu-uṣrī 'Protect my wreath, O Nanāya!'), *maḫāru* 'to receive' (^{f}Bānītu-supê-muḫur 'Receive my prayer, O Bānītu!'), *eṭēru* 'to save' (^{f}Bānītu-eṭrīnni 'Save me, O Bānītu!'), and *bâšu* (^{f}Lā-tubāšinni 'Don't put me to shame!').

3) *Wish names* contain either the precative or imperative of a verb and express a plea to a divinity for a third person, generally the child who bears the name, such as ^{f}Lū-balṭat 'May she be healthy!', ^{f}Nanāya-bullissu 'Keep her healthy, O Nanāya!', and ^{f}Bēltia-uṣrīšu 'Protect her, O Bēltia!', but sometimes for someone else, such as in the slave name ^{f}Nanāya-bēlu-uṣrī 'Protect my master, O Nanāya!'. The verbs *naṣāru* 'to protect' and *bulluṭu* 'to make healthy' are used frequently. The verb is omitted in some names, such as ^{f}Nanāya-ana-bītišu (or ^{f}Ana-bītišu) '(Show it) to her family, O Nanāya!' and ^{f}Ana-makānišu '(Show it) to her dwelling place!'.

4) *Trust names* represent the name-bearer's expression of trust or respect for a deity ('Prospective trust'), such as ^{f}Ana-muḫḫi-Nanāya-taklāku 'I trust in Nanāya', or the reward of trust ('Retrospective trust') such as ^{f}Tašmētu-atkal 'I trusted in Tašmētu'. Other examples of the former are ^{f}DN-ittia 'DN is with me', ^{f}DN-lūmur 'I will see DN', as well as the names meaning 'DN is my . . . ', such as ^{f}DN-šadû'a 'DN is my mountain'. ^{f}Itti-Nanāya-īnāya/-būnū'a 'My eyes/face (are/is turned to) Nanāya' and ^{f}Gabbi-ina-qātē-Bānītu 'All are in Bānītu's hands' are also included in this category. The latter category, the retrospective trust name, includes ^{f}Ina-bāb-magāri-alsišu 'At the gate of favour, I invoked her', and ^{f}Šēpet(/Šēpessu)-DN-aṣbat 'I took the feet of DN', often abbreviated to ^{f}Šēpetaya.

5) *Thanksgiving names* generally contain the preterite of a verb whose subject is a deity. They express the thanksgiving from the viewpoint of the name-giver, such as ᶠTašmētu-tabni 'Tašmētu created (the child who bears the name)' or ᶠBānītu-ṣullê-tašme 'Bānītu heard my prayer'.
6) *Lament names* include ᶠĀtanaḫ-šimînni 'I am tired, listen to me!' and ᶠAdi-māti-Ištar 'How long, O Ištar?'. It may also be better to include ᶠIna-dannāti-alsišu 'In distress, I called her' in this category, rather than in trust names. The speaker in these names is generally thought to have been the name-bearer, but it seems possible that the names expressed the feelings of the mother during or after giving birth. If so, it was presumably the mother who named the newborn girl.
7) *Praise names* are also found, such as ᶠMannu-akî-Ištaria 'Who is like my Ištar?', but this type of name is rare.
8) All of the types listed here are theophoric names that refer to divinities, but a minority of sentence names do not refer to divinities. Examples include ᶠAbu-ul-tīde 'She does not know the father' and ᶠAḫātu-aqrat 'The sister is precious'.

The same classification can be applied to male names (Chapter 2), but there are some differences in the choice and preference of words and name types between female and male names. For example, some verbs such as *nadānu* 'to give' and *kânu* 'to be(come) firm' are common in male names, whereas female names with these verbs are rare. The terms *māru* 'son' and *aplu* 'son, heir' feature in many male names, but *mārtu* 'daughter' was not generally used for female names. Thanksgiving names are thus frequently attested for men, but rarely for women.

Classification of Substantive Names

Substantive names, or designation names, are grammatically nominal and are usually composed of one or, occasionally, two elements.[3] The following subcategories can be discerned:

1) *Theophoric names*. While most of the sentence names are theophoric, the majority of designation names are not. The most popular type of theophoric designation name consists of *amat-* (or *andi-*) along with a divine name, such as ᶠAmat-Nanāya 'Servant of Nanāya'. Several names which do not include a divine name are considered to be theophoric names in which the divine element is omitted. For

[3] On compound names borne by men, see Chapter 2.

example, ^{f}Ṭābatu, which means 'Good', may be an abbreviated form of the attribute name ^{f}Ṭābatu-DN '(The goddess) DN is good'; for example, ^{f}Ṭābatu-Iššar 'Iššar (Ištar) is good'. Similarly, ^{f}Inbāya or ^{f}Inbia, which consists of *inbu* 'fruit' with a hypocoristic suffix, may be a shortened form of ^{f}Inbi-DN 'Fruit of DN'.

2) *Familial relationships.* There are two types of names expressing familial relationships. The first includes names such as ^{f}Aḫāssunu 'Their sister'. Such names simply indicate the relationship of the newborn child with her siblings. The name ^{f}Aḫāssunu means that the name-bearer had two or more elder brothers or sisters. The other type consists of names such as ^{f}Aḫāt-abīšu 'Aunt' – literally, 'Sister of his father'. According to Johann J. Stamm (1939, 301–5), babies with this type of name were possibly considered to be a replacement for, or the reincarnation of, a recently deceased family member.

3) *Affectionate names.* This type of name expresses the affection of the name-giver for the baby. Examples are ^{f}Rēʔindu 'Beloved one', ^{f}Nūptāya 'Gift (of DN)', ^{f}Buʔītu 'Desired one', and ^{f}Bēlessunu 'Their lady'. This category may include certain traits which the name-giver hoped for in the baby, such as ^{f}Kāribtu 'Prayerful one' and ^{f}Emuqtu 'Wise one'.

4) *Words for animals, plants, and objects.* We find personal names inspired by animals for both genders. In the Neo-Babylonian corpus, most animal names for women refer to small wild animals, while fewer pertain to domestic animals. In the latter category, we have names such as ^{f}Immertu 'Ewe' and ^{f}Mūrānatu '(Female) puppy'.[4] It seems that the most popular animal names for women were ^{f}Šikkû (or ^{f}Šikkūtu) 'Mongoose', ^{f}Bazītu, which may refer to a kind of monkey, and ^{f}Ḫabaṣirtu (or, exceptionally with the masculine form, ^{f}Ḫabaṣīru) 'Mouse.' It is interesting to note that ^{f}Šikkû and ^{f}Bazītu were *only* chosen for women. Grammatically, the terms *šikkû* and *bazītu* are feminine, which explains why they could only be used for naming a girl. 'Mouse' was also used for naming men. Thus, small animals, in particular those which are non-domestic, are principally chosen for women. We also find 'Monkey' (^{f}Uqūpatu), 'Dormouse' (^{f}Arrabtu), and 'Wildcat' (^{f}Murašītu) as female names. The masculine forms of these animal names were also used for men. The decision to name children after

[4] By contrast, in the Mari texts from the second millennium BCE the animal names used for women mostly pertain to domestic animals (Millet-Albà 2000).

these small animals seems readily comprehensible, while it is more difficult to imagine why some babies were named 'Turtle' (^{f}Šeleppūtu) or were named after insects such as the locust (^{f}Kallabuttu), the cricket (^{f}Ṣāṣiru), and the caterpillar (^{f}Akiltu; see Cousin and Watai 2018, 246).

Plant names, mainly those of fruits and aromatic plants, such as 'Juniper' (^{f}Burāšu), 'Bunch of grapes' (^{f}Isḫunnu, ^{f}Isḫunnatu), 'Hemp' (^{f}Qunnabatu), and 'Pomegranate' (^{f}Lurindu), were popular female names. Apart from Burāšu, these names were apparently not given to men.

Names based on accessories, such as ^{f}Qudāšu and ^{f}Inṣabtu, meaning 'Ring' and 'Earring', were frequently used for women of free status. We have found no evidence of their use for men.

5) *Physical characteristics, origins, or conditions of birth* of a baby, such as ^{f}Mīṣātu 'Small one', ^{f}Ubārtu 'Foreigner', and ^{f}Sūqaʾītu 'The one found on the street', are also referred to in women's names.
6) *Negative names*, such as ^{f}Lā-magirtu 'Disobedient', appear occasionally. Johann J. Stamm (1939, 205) described this name type as 'tender censure', but the actual circumstances of naming are usually unknown.

Hypocoristics, Abbreviated, and Double Names

Certain female names were often abbreviated. The most striking example is the name ^{f}Ina-Esagil-ramât 'She (a goddess) lives in Esagil', which is frequently shortened to ^{f}Esagil-ramât with ellipsis of *ina* 'in'. Another way of shortening personal names is found in the case of a woman called ^{f}Amat-Nanāya 'Servant of Nanāya', who appears as ^{f}Amtia in another text. The suffix *-ia* (/*-ya*), usually the possessive pronoun for the first person singular, is often difficult to distinguish from the hypocoristic suffix *-ia*. For instance, ^{f}Amtia does not mean 'My female servant'; in such names, the *-ia* is a hypocoristic ending.

Archival studies reveal that some women bore two different names, both valid in legal texts. For example, a ^{f}Kurunnam-tabni 'Kurunnam created' is also called ^{f}Kuttāya (obscure meaning), a ^{f}Bēlessunu 'Their sister' is also called ^{f}Bissāya (obscure meaning), and an ^{f}Amat-Ninlil 'Servant of Ninlil' is alternatively called ^{f}Gigītu (obscure meaning).[5] The practice of double naming is further discussed in Chapter 2.

[5] For these women, see, respectively, Wunsch (2000a, 108, n. 231), Wunsch (2005, 373), and Baker (2004, 26).

Female Onomastics and the Construction of Social and Gender Identities

Social Status

A number of personal names were given to women of free status as well as slave women, as observed by Johannes Hackl (2013). Nevertheless, we can discern preferences in the name selection of free women and slave women. Overall, sentence names tended to be given to slave women (Cousin and Watai 2018). Certain names, especially those with the element *silim* accompanying a divine name, such as ^{f}Nanāya-silim 'Be friendly, O Nanāya!' and the name ^{f}Nanāya-bēlu-uṣrī 'O Nanāya, protect (my) master!', seem to have been reserved for slave women. Animal names, too, were primarily chosen for slave women; in particular, almost all women called ^{f}Šikkû 'Mongoose' and ^{f}Ḫabaṣirtu 'Mouse' were slaves. By contrast, certain names seem to have been chosen for free women, such as the aforementioned name ^{f}Ina-Esagil-ramât and the similar name ^{f}Ina-Esagil-bēlet 'She is the lady in Esagil'. Other names for free women – if not exclusively given to free women – are, for example, ^{f}Bēlessunu 'Their lady', ^{f}Buʾītu 'Desired one', ^{f}Kaššāya 'Kassite', ^{f}Inṣabtu and ^{f}Qudāšu 'Ring' or 'Earring', ^{f}Ṭābatu 'Good', ^{f}Nūptāya 'Gift (of DN)', ^{f}Amat-DN 'Servant of DN', and ^{f}Rē'indu 'Beloved one'. The name ^{f}Kaššāya 'Kassite' was used mostly by elite women, including Nebuchadnezzar II's daughter, although it is occasionally borne by non-free women as well. Thus, all names could have been given to all women regardless of social status, although each status had its own popular names. It remains to be studied which social and cultural values are reflected in these name choices for free and unfree women.

Geographical Origins

Some female names reflect the geographical origin of their bearers.[6] In the documentation from Babylon, the naophoric element – an element deriving from a temple name – 'Esagil' is frequently attested in female names, such as in ^{f}Ina-Esagil-ramât 'She lives in Esagil' and in ^{f}Ina-Esagil-bēlet 'She is the lady in Esagil'. The Esagil temple was the main sanctuary of the god Marduk, the chief god of the city of Babylon and the king of the

[6] For a more complete study of geographical names, see Francis Joannès' contribution to this volume (Chapter 1), especially the part devoted to gods in personal names.

gods in first millennium BCE Babylonia. Other temple designations were also used in female names, especially in the names borne by oblates, such as ^{f}Ina-Eturkalamma-alsišu 'In the Eturkalamma temple, I called (the god)' and ^{f}Ina-Eigikalamma-lūmuršu 'In the Eigikalamma temple, I want to see (the god)'.[7]

Theophoric elements also indicate the geographical origin of individuals (see also Chapter 1). We can take the example of three minor female deities: the goddesses Zarpanītu, Aya, and Mammītu. Women called ^{f}Amat-Zarpanītu 'Servant of Zarpanītu' come from Babylon, in light of the fact that Zarpanītu is the divine spouse of Marduk. Likewise, women, who bear names with the theophoric element Aya, such as ^{f}Aya-aqrat 'Aya is precious' and ^{f}Aya-bēlu-uṣrī 'O Aya, protect my master', often come from Sippar or Larsa, two cities which housed an Ebabbar temple dedicated to the sun god Šamaš, the husband of Aya. The same is the case with Mammītu, divine spouse of the infernal god Nergal. Women who bore a name with this theophoric element usually originated from the city of Cutha, near Babylon, where the goddess was worshipped. Moreover, names with a reference to a major deity, such as the healing goddess Bābu, the goddess Ninlil,[8] the wife of Enlil, and the love goddess Nanāya, were often borne by women from the major cities of Nippur, Borsippa, Uruk, or Babylon.

Some names are more explicit about a person's origins. We find, for example, women called ^{f}Barsipītu ('Woman from Borsippa'), ^{f}Gandarāˀītu ('Woman from Gandar'), ^{f}Isinnāˀītu ('Woman from Isin'), and ^{f}Sipparāˀītu ('Woman from Sippar').

Gendered Theophoric Elements

Whereas some personal names are neutral names applying to both sexes, many names contain gendered elements. This is especially the case with gendered theophoric elements. Like verbs and their conjugations, they help to define the names as female or male. It seems that in Babylonia a whole range of male divinities was restricted to male names, including Adad, Anu, Bēl, Ea, Enlil, Marduk, Nabû, Nergal, Ninurta, Sîn, Šamaš,

[7] The term 'oblate' refers to an individual dedicated to a divinity; their names often marked their attachment to a sanctuary (Hackl 2013, 160). The Eturkalamma temple was the sanctuary of the goddess Bēlet-Bābili in Babylon, while the Eigikalamma temple was the sanctuary of the warrior god Ninurta, in his aspect as Lugal-Marada, in the city of Marad.

[8] It should be noted that the name of the goddess Mullēšu is written syllabically in N/LB texts (e.g., Pirngruber 2020 no. 12:12).

and Uraš. The major and most powerful male divinities of first millennium BCE Babylonia were thus used to name men (Cousin and Watai 2018, 248–51).

In accordance with the fact that male theophoric elements were usually only used to compose masculine names, some female divinities predominantly occur in names borne by women. They were minor goddesses, often consorts of great gods, or goddesses related to fertility, two qualities particularly ascribed to women. To the already mentioned Aya, Mammītu, and Zarpanītu, we can add Kurunnam, the goddess of beer, and Ninlil, Enlil's consort. Some examples are ᶠKurunnam-tabni 'Kurunnam created', ᶠItti-Ninlil-īnāya 'My eyes are set on Ninlil', and ᶠAmat-Ninlil 'Servant of Ninlil'.

However, some theophoric elements referring to goddesses are used for men and women in the Neo-Babylonian period. This observation applies to major goddesses such as Ištar,[9] Nanāya, and the goddesses of medicine, Gula and Bābu. Ištar (as well as her other aspects, Anunnītu and Bānītu) was a goddess of passionate love, but also a warrior deity, a quality which complies with the Mesopotamian idea of masculinity. Finally, among goddesses who feature in both masculine and feminine names (Anunnītu, Bānītu, Bābu, Bēltu, Gula, Ištar, Nanāya, Ningal, and Tašmētu), we find several consorts of major male deities of the Babylonian pantheon (Marduk or Bēl, Nabû, and Sîn).[10]

If the study of some personal names allows preliminary conclusions about gender identity in Babylonia, a few other names seem rather atypical. At least two women bear a name with the theophoric element Marduk and two men bear a name with the theophoric element Zarpanītu; they are Arad-Zarpanītu 'Servant of Zarpanītu' and Arad-Erua 'Servant of (the goddess) Erua' (both witnesses in *Nbk.* 76 and 106), ᶠMarduk-ēṭirat 'Marduk saves' (a land owner in *Cyr.* 331), and ᶠMarduk-uballiṭ 'Marduk has kept alive' (a woman who receives rations from a temple in Joannès 1982 no. 104).

Physical Characteristics

If certain physical qualifications can be referred to in names for both sexes, others were crucial for creating gendered identities of men and women. Masculine names referring to physical features single out strength

9 We note that Ištar has a masculine gender in some contexts. For example, Ištar is identified with the planet Venus, and in some texts, the evening star is considered female while the morning star is considered male. We thank the anonymous reviewer for this suggestion.

10 For a complete overview, see Cousin and Watai (2018, 248–51).

(e.g., the family name Dannēa), power (e.g., the family name Lēʾêa), and prosperity (e.g., Nuḫšānu). Regarding women, their names recall physical aspects of baby girls and probably also of female appearance. Examples include ᶠḪibuṣu 'Chubby', ᶠKubbutu 'Plump', and ᶠṬuppuštu 'Very plump'. Some female names refer to the beauty and the attractiveness of the woman, as is the case with the names based on fruits and jewels that were discussed earlier. On the other hand, we do not find names referring to ugliness, whereas such names are attested in the Old Babylonian documentation (second millennium BCE), as in the case of ᶠMasiktum 'Ugly'.

There is also another group of names dealing with physical characteristics and anatomies, namely those referring to disabilities. This phenomenon is well attested in the Old Babylonian period, where one finds male names such as Sukkuku ('Deaf') and Upputu or Ubbudu ('Blind'[11]). In the Neo-Babylonian period we can probably identify the name of a mute woman. A female slave bore the name ᶠŠaḫḫurratu 'Deathly hush', which derives from the verb *šuḫarruru* 'to be deathly still' (Joannès 1989, 280–1).

Desired Characteristics

Three qualities reflected in personal names are shared by men and women: goodness, joy, and the value of the person. For the latter, we may refer to names formed with the verb *(w)aqāru*, with the masculine rendering Aqru and the feminine rendering ᶠMaqartu 'Precious'. The Egibi archive provides a lot of names of this type (Wunsch 1993, 2000a/b, and Abraham 2004). We can also quote the name ᶠKabtāya 'Honoured', pointing to the importance of the person. Names referring to joy include Ḫaddāya 'Joyful' for men and ᶠRīšat or ᶠRīšāya 'Joy' for women. Goodness is expressed in names built with the verbs *damāqu* and *ṭâbu*, popular for both men and women. Names like Damqu, Damqāya, and Dummuqu were used for men. Being a grammatically neutral name, ᶠDamqāya could also be applied to women. With the verb *ṭâbu*, the male name Ṭābia and the female names ᶠṬābatu, as well as the superlative ᶠṬubbutu 'The very good one', are built.

In addition, names related to personality traits could reflect the role and place of men and women in Babylonian society. Men were more likely associated with wisdom (e.g., Apkallu), loyalty and truth (e.g., Kīnāya 'The

11 See BE 15 163 for an example where the bearer of this name is a woman.

faithful'), and mercy (e.g., Ḫan(n)an(u) 'Merciful').[12] Epithets devoted to women often contain laudations. They include affectionate names, but also names symbolising their place in society. According to these names, women were supposed to be sweet (ᶠDuššuptu) and provide an anchorage for the family (ᶠḪamatāya 'Help'; ᶠIndu 'Support').[13] Furthermore, women were ideally kind (ᶠTaslimu 'Friendly'), pure (ᶠḪiptāya), and obedient (ᶠḪanašu).[14] We also find the counterpart, ᶠLā-magirtu 'Disobedient', as the name of a slave woman (*Dar.* 379). The very existence of this name suggests that such a personality trait was not desirable for a woman, *a fortiori* a slave woman.

Further Reading

For the classification and meaning of Akkadian personal names, the most important systematic studies are those by Johann J. Stamm (1939) and Dietz-Otto Edzard (1998). Concerning women's names in the first millennium BCE, Cornelia Wunsch (2006) treated metronymic ancestral names, Johannes Hackl (2013) discussed the names and naming of female slaves, and Laura Cousin and Yoko Watai (2016 and 2018) dealt with the social and gender-related aspects of female names. There are also some works on women's names attested in the Mari documentation from the second millennium BCE: see Ichiro Nakata (1995) and Adelina Millet-Albà (2000). Finally, for the names of women in the Hellenistic period, we refer to the study of Julien Monerie (2014).

References

Abraham, K. 2004. *Business and Politics under the Persian Empire: The Financial Dealings of Marduk-nāṣir-apli of the House of Egibi (521–487 BCE)*. Bethesda: CDL Press.

Baker, H. D. 2004. *The Archive of the Nappāḫu Family*, Archiv für Orientforschung Beiheft 30. Vienna: Institut für Orientalistik.

Bongenaar, A. C. V. M. 1997. *The Neo-Babylonian Ebabbar Temple at Sippar: Its Administration and Its Prosopography*, Publications de l'Institut historique-archéologique néerlandais de Stamboul 80. Leiden: Nederlands Historisch-Archaeologisch Instituut te Istanbul.

Cousin, L. 2020. 'Sweet girls and strong men: Onomastics and personality traits in first-millennium sources', *Die Welt des Orients* 50/2, 339–57.

12 References to these names can be found in, respectively, Baker 2004 no. 130; Bongenaar 1997: 162 and 228; CUSAS 28 28.

13 Joannès 1982 no. 103; Wunsch 2003 no. 48; Roth 1989 no. 16.

14 Roth 1989 no. 12; CT 22 202; VS 4 21.

Cousin, L. and Y. Watai 2016. 'Onomastics of women in Babylonia in the first millennium BC', *Orient (Journal of the Society for Near Eastern Studies in Japan)* 51, 3–27.

Cousin, L. and Y. Watai 2018. 'Onomastics and gender identity in first-millennium BCE Babylonia' in S. L. Budin, M. Cifarelli, A. Garcia-Ventura, and A. Millet-Albà (eds.), *Gender, Methodology and the Ancient Near East. Approaches from Assyriology and Beyond*. Barcelona: Universitat de Barcelona, pp. 243–55.

Edzard, D.-O. 1998. 'Name, Namengebung (Onomastik). B. Akkadisch', *Reallexikon der Assyriologie und der Vorderasiatischen Archäologie* 9, 103–16.

Hackl, J. 2013. 'Frau Weintraube, Frau Heuschrecke und Frau Gut: Untersuchungen zu den babylonischen Namen von Sklavinnen in neubabylonischer und persischer Zeit', *Wiener Zeitschrift für die Kunde des Morgenlandes* 103, 121–87.

Joannès, F. 1982. *Textes économiques de la Babylonie récente. Étude des textes de TBER*, Recherches sur les civilisations, cahier 5. Paris: Éditions Recherches sur les Civilisations.

Joannès, F. 1989. *Archives de Borsippa: La famille Ea-Ilûta-Bâni. Étude d'un lot d'archives familiales en Babylonie, du VIIIe au Ve siècle av. J.-C.*, Hautes Études Orientales 25. Geneva: Librairie Droz.

Millet-Albà, A. 2000. 'Les noms d'animaux dans l'onomastique des archives de Mari' in D. Parayre (ed.), *Les animaux et les hommes dans le monde syro-mésopotamien aux époques historiques*, Topoi supplément 2. Lyon: Maison de l'Orient Méditerranéen, pp. 477–87.

Monerie, J. 2014. *D'Alexandre à Zoilos: Dictionnaire prosopographique des porteurs de nom grec dans les sources cunéiformes*, Oriens et Occidens 23. Stuttgart: Franz Steiner.

Nakata, I. 1995. 'A study of women's theophoric personal names in the Old Babylonian texts from Mari', *Orient (Journal of the Society for Near Eastern Studies in Japan)* 30–1, 234–53.

Pirngruber, R. 2020. 'Minor archives from first-millennium BC Babylonia: the archive of Iššar-tarībi from Sippar', *Journal of Cuneiform Studies* 72, 165–98.

Roth, M. T. 1989. *Babylonian Marriage Agreements: 7th–3rd centuries BC*, Alter Orient und Altes Testament 222. Kevelaer/Neukirchen-Vluyn: Butzon u. Bercker/Neukirchener Verlag.

Stamm, J. J. 1939. *Die akkadische Namengebung*, Mitteilungen der Vorderasiatisch-Ägyptischen Gesellschaft 44. Leipzig: J.C. Hinrichs Verlag.

Wunsch, C. 1993. *Die Urkunden des babylonischen Geschäftsmannes Iddin-Marduk*, 2 Vols, Cuneiform Monographs 3a and 3b. Groningen: Styx.

Wunsch, C. 2000a and 2000b. *Das Egibi-Archiv. I. Die Felder und Gärten*, 2 Vols, Cuneiform Monographs 20a and 20b. Groningen: Styx.

Wunsch, C. 2003. *Urkunden zum Ehe-, Vermögens und Erbrecht aus verschiedenen neubabylonischen Archiven*, Babylonische Archive 2. Dresden: ISLET.

Wunsch, C. 2005. 'The Šangû-Ninurta Archive' in H. D. Baker and M. Jursa (eds), *Approaching the Babylonian Economy*, Alter Orient und Altes Testament 330. Münster: Ugarit-Verlag, pp. 365–79.

Wunsch, C. 2006. 'Metronymika in Babylonien: Frauen als Ahnherrin der Familie' in G. del Olmo Lete, L. Feliu, and A. Millet-Albà (eds.), *Šapal tibnim mû ilakkū: Studies Presented to Joaquín Sanmartín on the Occasion of His 65th Birthday*, Aula Orientalis Supplementa 22. Sabadell: Editorial AUSA, pp. 459–69.

CHAPTER 4

Babylonian Family Names

John P. Nielsen

A distinctive feature of Babylonian onomastics in the first millennium BCE is the use of family names at most cities by a segment of the population that can be described as the urban notable class. These family names are common and the conventions for their usage are well established in the abundant legal and administrative tablets that date from the so-called 'long sixth century': the period stretching from Nabopolassar's first regnal year in 625 to Xerxes I's suppression of the Babylonian revolts in 484 (Jursa et al. 2010, 2–5). The use of family names emerged during the preceding eighth and seventh centuries, and the antecedents of some families and family names can be traced even further back in time to the early first millennium or even the latter part of the second millennium. Furthermore, some of these families persisted into the latter half of the first millennium BCE, as demonstrated by the continued presence of family names in Seleucid-era tablets.

Usage of family names at all times appears to have been restricted. Non-Babylonians never had family names, and only Babylonians of a certain social status were identified in texts with family names. Where the line of social demarcation lay is difficult to determine. Slaves and people of servile status, such as temple oblates, did not have family names, but neither did some men who had sufficient wealth to purchase land associated with the temple (Nielsen 2015b, 101), suggesting that an element of familial pedigree was involved. One could not simply adopt a family name. As a consequence, an understanding of the norms of family-name usage and an ability to identify them in Neo-Babylonian texts is essential for comprehending how individuals from the urban notable class functioned politically, economically, and socially.

After a discussion of the origins of family names in Babylonian society, we will present an overview of the types of family names that were in existence and then outline the different ways in which family names were recorded in texts, before concluding with some comments on the geographical distribution of family names throughout Babylonia.

Origins

Family names first became popular in the cities of Babylon, Borsippa, and Dilbat in the eighth and seventh centuries. They probably served as a means of projecting social cohesion and marking identity among urban notables at a time when the Babylonian state was weak and decentralised. For much of this period, Assyrians and Chaldeans occupied the Babylonian throne, and the urban notables would have had an interest in communicating their local identities to these non-Babylonians in order to ensure that their traditional prerogatives were respected. The practice may have become widespread in imitation of Aramean and Chaldean tribal groups, whose members were distinguished as sons of the eponymous ancestor for which their tribe was named.

Whatever caused the practice to gain popularity, it is evident that it had antecedents in the earliest centuries of the first millennium and even the latter second millennium. The family name Arad-Ea stands out as having belonged to a prominent family from Babylon whose members often held the office of governor (*bēl pīḫati*) in the royal administration beginning in the Kassite Dynasty (Lambert 1957, 2). One member of the family could even trace an incomplete lineage back to the Kassite-era scribe Arad-Ea, from whom the family claimed descent. A Kassite-era cylinder seal from the late fourteenth century bearing the inscription of 'Uballissu-Marduk, *šatammu* . . . of Kurigalzu, king of the world, son of Arad-Ea, the *ummiān nikkassi*' is echoed in an inscription on a stele (*kudurru*) from the second quarter of the twelfth century in which a governor named Marduk-zākir-šumi was called 'son of Nabû-nādin-aḫḫē, whose grandfather was Rēmanni-Marduk the *liplippu* of Uballissu-Marduk, descendant of Arad-Ea' (Brinkman 1993).

The term *liplippu*, which the *Chicago Assyrian Dictionary* defines as 'offspring, descendant', was not used in administrative texts but did appear in inscriptions, royal genealogies, and colophons on literary and scholarly texts, and typically expressed descent from a more distant ancestor. There are a few instances of genealogies similar to the example from the Arad-Ea family in which *liplippu* was used to indicate that possessors of family names could claim a genuine, or at least a multi-generational yet fictitious, descent from an ancestor who could be traced to the second or early first millennia. Colophons on tablets from the Epic of Gilgamesh identified members of the Sîn-leqe-unninnī family from Uruk – who often were *kalû* priests, just as descendants of Arad-Ea frequently held the title *bēl pīḫati* – as *liplippu* of Sîn-leqe-unninnī. Members of the Sîn-leqe-unninnī family either wishfully or legitimately claimed descent from a figure who was credited in later Babylonian tradition as having composed the epic and who may have been responsible for editorial undertakings in the second millennium that resulted in the version of Gilgamesh as it was known in the first millennium (Beaulieu 2000, 1–16; George 2003, 28–33).

It is possible that these lines of descent included multiple ancestors whose names became family names. A stele (*kudurru*) written in the early ninth century at Borsippa concerns an *ērib bīti* priest named Nabû-aplu-iddin, son of (DUMU) Abunāya and *liplippu* of Aqar-Nabû (BBSt. 28). Aqar-Nabû was the family name of the chief administrator (*šatammu*) of the Ezida temple and *ērib bīti* priest of Nabû at Borsippa a century later, so it is certain that Nabû-aplu-iddin was an early member of this family. However, Nabû-aplu-iddin was petitioning the king for the restoration of his paternal estate (*bīt abi*), land that had belonged to his father, Abunāya. Abunāya is also attested as a family name in seventh-century texts, and this attachment to the 'house of the father' may have led to familial segmentation in which one branch of the Aqar-Nabû family became known as the Abunāya family (Nielsen 2011, 74–8).

Finally, there are the antecedents of the Šangû-Sippar family found in the Sun God Tablet from Sippar (BBSt. 36). In the waning years of the eleventh century, Ekur-šumu-ušarši, the *šangû* priest of Šamaš, petitioned the kings Simbar-Šīḫu (1025–1008 BCE) and Eulmaš-šākin-šumi for help maintaining the cult of Šamaš at Sippar following the destruction of the cult statue of Šamaš by Sutean raiders. More than a century later, during the second quarter of the ninth century, Nabû-nādin-šumi, who was the *šangû* priest of Šamaš at the time, discovered an image of Šamaš and petitioned the king for aid to remake the statue of Šamaš and fully reinstitute his cult at Sippar. Nabû-nādin-šumi had been able to recount Ekur-šumu-ušarši's earlier efforts to the king and claimed to be a descendant of that earlier *šangû* priest. He did not call himself a *liplippu* of Ekur-šumu-ušarši, but instead described himself as 'from the seed' (*ina zēri*). In spite of the difference in terminology, the sentiment embodied in both terms is the same. Furthermore, even though *šangû* priest of Sippar was only used as a title in the text, it is very likely that a familial attitude towards the title was held by Nabû-nādin-šumi and that he was an early member of what would become the Šangû-Sippar family (Bongenaar 2000, 77–8).

Types

Family names can be grouped into two basic categories: ancestral names and occupational names. Ancestral names had fallen out of favour as given names in the first millennium and were practically never used as personal names by living persons. These family names referenced an eponymous ancestor from whom the family claimed descent. In most cases the historicity of this ancestor is unverifiable, but, as the discussion of *liplippu* demonstrated, there are a few cases where it is possible to identify the historical ancestor from whom the family took its name. As a result, we cannot discount the possibility that any ancestral family name actually referenced a formerly living person, though it is likely that many such family names were based on fictive descent. The overwhelming majority of ancestral family names were masculine names preceded by a so-called *Personenkeil*, the single vertical wedge that served as a determinative before a masculine personal name in the cuneiform writing system (see Chapter 1). Interestingly, there are a few examples of feminine personal names that were in use as family names (e.g., Arrabtu '(female) Dormouse' or Maqartu 'Precious'). These names were initially preceded by the sign MUNUS, the feminine determinative in texts. With the passage of time, however, scribes began to 'masculinise' these names by replacing MUNUS with the masculine personal name determinative (Wunsch 2006, 459–69).

Unlike ancestral family names, occupational family names are not marked by a personal name determinative in texts, but rather by the occupational determinative LÚ. Many of these names were derived from titles associated with the temples and represented the full extent of the priestly hierarchy. Names taken from both high-ranking temple-enterer priesthoods (e.g., Šangû-DN 'Priest of DN' or Kutimmu 'Goldsmith') and the lower-ranking purveying priesthoods (e.g., Ṭābiḫu 'Butcher', Rēʾi-alpi 'Oxherd', or Atkuppu 'Reed-worker') were used by families. While these families often had close associations with the temples, there are other occupational family names that may reflect association with the state or military apparatus (e.g., Lāsimu 'Scout' or Rēʾi-sisê 'Horse herder'; Still 2019, 82–3). And while it is not always the case that an individual with an occupational family name held that office or title, there are examples of families that had a strong association with or even monopolised the role: the Rēʾi-alpi family, for example, dominated the ox-herder prebends at Borsippa (Jursa 2005, 93–4).

Usage

Family names were typically communicated in texts using the language of filiation and descent. They originally replaced the name of the referent's father in a simple two-tier genealogy in which the individual (PN_1) was called the 'son of' (DUMU or A) the family name (PN_2). This practice has the benefit of allowing the reader of the tablet to differentiate between an individual who had an occupational family name and one who belonged to the occupation: the former would be called 'son of' the occupation (e.g., Bēl-ibni the son of the Potter [family]), while the occupational title simply followed the name of the latter (e.g., Bēl-ibni the potter).

The use of two-tier genealogies to express family names, however, poses some challenges for modern readers. The first challenge is the occasional appearance of individuals from Chaldean or Aramean tribes in legal and administrative tablets. Tribal affiliation could be expressed in two-tier genealogies, as a sale of a house located at Uruk in 673 BCE at the Chaldean city of Šapīya reveals. The first witness was Ea-zēru-iqīša, the chief of the Chaldean tribe of Bīt-Amukāni, who was identified as the 'son' of Amukānu (wr. ^{Id}*é-a*-NUMUN-BA-*šá* A ^{I}*a-muk-a-nu*). However, the second witness, Naʾid-bēlanu, son of Aya-rimî, was probably a Chaldean as well; Naʾid-bēlanu had a Babylonian name, but his patronym, Aya-rimî, was West Semitic (Frame 2013 no. 4). The other witnesses had two-tier genealogies written in the same way as Ea-zēru-iqīša's, but their patronyms refer to their father's names and not to a family or tribal name, with the possible exception of the sixth witness, Nabû-zēru-ibni. His patronym, Nabûnnāya, was probably a family name (Nielsen 2015a, 256).

Nabû-zēru-ibni's example brings us to the second challenge: it can be unclear whether a patronym in a two-tier genealogy is a family name or the father's name, particularly if the family name is infrequently attested. It is doubtful that this was a problem in antiquity; the corpus of names in use as family names probably would have sounded quaint or old-fashioned to a Babylonian if one had been used as a personal name. The modern reader has to either develop familiarity with the corpus of personal names and family names or consult personal name lists. Nevertheless, the use of two-tier genealogies to express both family affiliation and paternity may still have led to some confusion. One solution to this problem was the appending of -*šú šá* to DUMU or A in genealogies, resulting in a writing of PN_1 DUMU-*šú šá*/A-*šú šá* PN_2. In the latter half of the first millennium the -*šú* was dropped but the *šá* was retained. This appended writing made it clear that the patronym was the father's name and not a family name. The appearance of appended two-tier genealogies did not mean that the writings DUMU or A only preceded family names; there are examples of tablets in which these writings preceded the name of an individual's father.[1] However, if the scribe used both appended and unappended two-tier genealogies in a witness list it could be an indication that the witnesses with unappended genealogies had family names while those with appended writings did not.

The other solution was the introduction of an additional tier to genealogies. In the seventh century, three-tier genealogies in which the father's name was expressed with an appended writing in the second tier and the family name was recorded in the third tier with an unappended writing (i.e., PN$_1$ DUMU-*šú šá*/A-*šú šá* PN$_2$ DUMU/A PN$_3$) became more common in texts. This practice had the benefit of preserving the name of the referent's father as well as his family name. As a result, it becomes easier to identify brothers, uncles, and even cousins from the same family. A further elaboration of the three-tier genealogy occurred in the Seleucid period; in tablets from Uruk a fourth tier appears in many genealogies. It is unclear why this change occurred, but one possible explanation could be the strong preference for names featuring the god Anu as a theophoric element that had emerged, and the fact that most of the individuals appearing in the cuneiform texts from Seleucid Uruk came from the limited circle of endogamous families that dominated temple affairs (Beaulieu 2018, 202–3). Specifying a man textually may have necessitated the addition of a fourth tier. Furthermore, women, when they do appear in texts, would also be identified by a variant of the three-tier genealogy. The patriarchal nature of Babylonian society meant that women were never affiliated directly with their family names as a 'daughter of' the family name. Instead, women were associated with their family on the basis of their relationship to a male family member. A woman was usually ^{f}PN$_1$ 'daughter of/wife of' ^{I}PN$_2$ DUMU/A PN$_3$, meaning that marriage effectively aligned her with a new family name.

Geographic Distribution

Family names were not ubiquitous throughout Babylonia. Although family names can be found on tablets dated at every Babylonian city in the Neo-Babylonian period, their usage did not become conventional

[1] For example, see the witness list in BRM 1 34: 26) IGI *ú-pa-qu* A-*šú šá* ^{md}AG-DA 27) ^{md}AG-DA A LÚ.NAGAR 28) ^{md}URAŠ-ŠEŠ.MEŠ-MU A-*šú šá* ^{m}DUMU-^{d}EN-*at-kal* 29) LÚ.DUB ^{m}NÍG.DU A ^{m}SUM.NA-^{d}PAP-SUKKAL. The genealogies in lines 26 and 28 feature patronyms preceded by the writing A-*šú šá*; lines 27 and 29 use family names preceded by A.

everywhere. Greater population size and density in urban areas may have made family names a useful means for differentiating individuals in texts, and economic and cultural networks between cities probably contributed to the spread of the practice. They were used earliest and with greatest frequency at cities in northern Babylonia, at Babylon and the nearby cities of Borsippa, Dilbat, and Kish. Further north, it is also possible to observe that family names became used more frequently at Sippar. Some of these families, most notably the Šangû-Šamaš or Šangû-Sippar family, had a long presence at Sippar that may have extended back to the eleventh century and the events commemorated in BBSt. 36. Still others, such as the Ša-nāšišu family (Bongenaar 1997, 470–5; Jursa et al. 2010, 71–2), had relocated to Sippar from Babylon. At Nippur, however, there seems to have been an almost conscientious rejection of the use of family names (Nielsen 2011, 163–5, 177–80). This was in spite of textual evidence indicating the presence of the same cultural sentiments and practices relating to revered scholars (Rubin 2022) and prebendary functions (Joannès 1992, 90; Beaulieu 1995, 88–9) at Nippur that were the basis for ancestral and occupational family names elsewhere. Those few family names that are attested in documents dated at Nippur may have belonged to non-Nippureans. Family names were nearly as uncommon in tablets dated at Uruk and Ur in southern Babylonia as they were at Nippur, but there are indications that the practice was taking hold during the seventh century (Nielsen 2011, 217–20). Prosopographical analysis reveals that individuals who were identified in texts with family names appeared in other texts without such names. Furthermore, the names of other male kin to these individuals were also recorded without mention of their family name, with a few exceptions in which it was clear they shared the same family name. Family identity was present among some of the population even if there was no compulsion to record it in texts.

Not only was there an uneven geographic distribution of family-name usage throughout Babylonia, it is also evident that some family names originated at or were strongly associated with specific cities. For example, the Ea-ilūtu-bāni, Aqar-Nabû, and Iddin-Papsukkal families had ties to Borsippa; the Šangû-Dilbat and Salāmu families were from Dilbat; and the Ekur-zakir, Ḫunzû, and Sîn-leqe-unninnī were predominantly from Uruk (Wunsch 2014, 289–314). Furthermore, branches of these families spread to other cities after the relocation of members. The Ṣāḫit-ginê family at Sippar was descended from a man from Babylon named Dayyān-Marduk (Waerzeggers 2014, 29–30), and it may be possible to trace the Iddin-Papsukkal family at Ur and Uruk back to Borsippa, where the family appears to have had its origins (Nielsen 2009,

171–82). An awareness of the associations that some families had with certain cities and the movements of certain families over time can provide context for understanding the social networks present in a tablet. Furthermore, family names can provide useful clues when damage to an unprovenanced tablet results in the loss of the name of the city at which the tablet was dated.

Further Reading

There are several resources that can be used to identify family names. Knut L. Tallqvist's *Neubabylonisches Namenbuch* (1905) is more than a century old, yet it remains a valuable tool in spite of some outdated readings of names (e.g., Mukallim should be read Šumu-libši and Nâš-paṭri should be read Ṭābiḫu). The entry for each name first provides citations of the name as a patronym before listing occurrences of individuals who had the name, differentiated by their patronyms and family names. In those instances when a name is only attested as a patronym, it is likely that the name is in fact a family name. John P. Nielsen's *Sons and Descendants* (2011) analyses the emergence of many of these families in the early Neo-Babylonian period prior to the long sixth century. The index includes separate sections for personal names and family names. These indices are expanded upon and augmented in Nielsen's *Personal Names in Early Neo-Babylonian Legal and Administrative Tablets, 747–626 BCE* (2015a). A useful list of family names appears in Cornelia Wunsch's article 'Babylonische Familiennamen' (2014), which provides the user with information about which cities each family name was attested at and also distinguishes which family names are attested in early Neo-Babylonian sources.

There are several prosopographical studies that focus on the personnel at specific temples and elucidate the involvement of some of these families in the administrative hierarchy and their interrelationships. Hans Martin Kümmel's *Familie, Beruf und Amt im spätbabylonischen Uruk: prosopographische Untersuchungen zu Berufsgruppen des 6. Jahrhunderts v. Chr. in Uruk* (1979) covers the Eanna at Uruk; for Sippar, there is Rocío Da Riva's *Der Ebabbar-Tempel von Sippar in frühneubabylonischer Zeit (640–580 v. Chr.)* (2002) and A. C. V. M. Bongenaar's *The Neo-Babylonian Ebabbar Temple at Sippar: Its Administration and its Prosopography* (1997); and, finally, Caroline Waerzeggers' *The Ezida Temple of Borsippa: Priesthood, Cult, Archives* (2010) and Bastian Still's *The Social World of the Babylonian Priest* (2019) are excellent sources for the families at the Ezida temple.

References

Beaulieu, P.-A. 1995. 'The brewers of Nippur', *Journal of Cuneiform Studies* 47, 85–96.

Beaulieu, P.-A. 2000. 'The descendants of Sîn-lēqi-unninni' in M. Dietrich and O. Loretz (eds.), *Assyriologica et Semitica. Festschrift für Joachim Oelsner anläßlich seines 65. Geburtstages am 18. Februar 1997*, Alter Orient und Altes Testament 252. Münster: Ugarit-Verlag, pp. 1–16.

Beaulieu, P.-A. 2018. 'Uruk before and after Xerxes: The onomastic and institutional rise of the god Anu' in C. Waerzeggers and M. Seire (eds.), *Xerxes and Babylonia: The Cuneiform Evidence*, Orientalia Lovaniensia Analecta 277. Leuven: Peeters, pp. 189–206.

Bongenaar, A. C. V. M. 1997. *The Neo-Babylonian Ebabbar Temple at Sippar: Its Administration and its Prosopography*, Publications de l'Institut historique-archéologique néerlandais de Stamboul 80. Leiden: Nederlands Historisch-Archaeologisch Instituut te Istanbul.

Bongenaar, A. C. V. M. 2000. 'Private archives in Neo-Babylonian Sippar and their institutional connections' in A. C. V. M. Bongenaar (ed.), *Interdependency of Institutions and Private Entrepreneurs*, Publications de l'Institut historique-archéologique néerlandais de Stamboul 87. Leiden: Nederlands Historisch-Archaeologisch Instituut te Istanbul, pp. 73–94.

Brinkman, J. A. 1993. 'A Kassite seal mentioning a Babylonian governor of Dilmun', *Nouvelles Assyriologiques Brèves et Utilitaires* 1993/106.

Da Riva, R. 2002. *Der Ebabbar-Tempel von Sippar in frühneubabylonischer Zeit (640–580 v. Chr.)*, Alter Orient und Altes Testament 291. Münster: Ugarit-Verlag.

Frame, G. 2013. *The Archive of Mušēzib-Marduk, Son of Kiribtu and Descendant of Sîn-nāṣir*, Babylonische Archive 5. Dresden: ISLET.

George, A. R. 2003. *The Babylonian Gilgamesh Epic: Introduction, Critical Edition and Cuneiform Texts*. Oxford: Oxford University Press.

Joannès, F. 1992. 'Les archives de Ninurta-aḫḫē-bulliṭ', in M. DeJong Ellis (ed.) *Nippur at the Centennial (XXXVe RAI, Philadelphia, 1988)*, Occasional Publications of the Samuel Noah Kramer Fund 14. Philadelphia: University of Pennsylvania, pp. 87–100.

Jursa, M. 2005. *Neo-Babylonian Legal and Administrative Documents: Typology, Contents and Archives*, Guides to the Mesopotamian Textual Record 1. Münster: Ugarit-Verlag.

Jursa, M., with contributions by J. Hackl, B. Janković, K. Kleber, et al. 2010. *Aspects of the Economic History of Babylonia in the First Millennium BC: Economic Geography, Economic Mentalities, Agriculture, the Use of Money and the Problem of Economic Growth*, Alter Orient und Altes Testament 377. Münster: Ugarit-Verlag.

Kümmel, H. M. 1979. *Familie, Beruf und Amt im spätbabylonischen Uruk: Prosopographische Untersuchungen zu Berufsgruppen des 6.* Jahrhunderts v. Chr. in Uruk, Abhandlungen der Deutschen Orient-Gesellschaft 20. Berlin: Gebrüder Mann Verlag.

Lambert, W. G. 1957. 'Ancestors, authors, and canonicity', *Journal of Cuneiform Studies* 11, 1–14, 112.

Nielsen, J. P. 2009. 'Trading on knowledge: The Iddin-Papsukkal kin group in southern Babylonia in the 7th and 6th centuries BC', *Journal of Ancient Near Eastern Religions* 9, 171–82.

Nielsen, J. P. 2011. *Sons and Descendants: A Social History of Kin Groups and Family Names in the Early Neo-Babylonian Period, 747–626 BC*, Culture and History of the Ancient Near East 43. Leiden: Brill.

Nielsen, J. P. 2015a. *Personal Names in Early Neo-Babylonian Legal and Administrative Tablets, 747–626 BCE*, NISABA 29. Winona Lake: Eisenbrauns.

Nielsen, J. P. 2015b. 'Taking refuge at Borsippa: The archive of Lâbâši, son of Nādinu', *Archiv für Orientforschung* 53, 93–109.

Rubin, Z. 2022. 'The sages and the sons of Nippur: An edition of *LKA 76* (VAT 13839) from Assur', *Journal of Cuneiform Studies* 74, 63–74.

Still, B. 2019. *The Social World of the Babylonian Priest*, Culture and History of the Ancient Near East 103. Leiden: Brill.

Tallqvist, K. 1905. *Neubabylonisches Namenbuch zu den Geschäftsurkunden aus der Zeit Šamaššumukîn bis Xerxes*, Acta Societatis Scientiarum Fennicae 32/2. Helsinki: Societas Litteraria Fennica.

Waerzeggers, C. 2010. *The Ezida Temple of Borsippa: Priesthood, Cult, Archives*, Achaemenid History 15. Leiden: Nederlands Instituut voor het Nabije Oosten.

Waerzeggers, C. 2014. *Marduk-Rēmanni: Local Networks and Imperial Politics in Achaemenid Babylonia*, Orientalia Lovaniensia Analecta 233. Leuven: Peeters.

Wunsch, C. 2006. 'Metronymika in Babylonien: Frauen als Ahnherrin der Familie' in G. del Olmo Lete, L. Feliu, and A. Millet-Albà (eds), *Šapal tibnim mû illakū: Studies Presented to Joaquín Sanmartín on the Occasion of His 65th Birthday*, Aula Orientalis Supplementa 22. Sabadell/Barcelona: Editorial AUSA, pp. 459–69.

Wunsch, C. 2014. 'Babylonische Familiennamen' in M. Krebernik and H. Neumann (eds.), *Babylonien und seine Nachbarn. Wissenschaftliches Kolloquium aus Anlass des 75. Geburtstages Joachim Oelsner, Jena, 2. und 3. März 2007*, Alter Orient und Altes Testament 369. Münster: Ugarit-Verlag, pp. 289–314.

CHAPTER 5

Names of Officials ('Beamtennamen')

Michael Jursa

As a distinct category of onomastics, the *Beamtenname* is defined by its containing of a reference to the name-bearer's superior, normally the king (Edzard 1998–2001, 109–10; Streck 2001). In the context of the onomastics of first millennium BCE Babylonia, this means, for all intents and purposes, names that contain the element *šarru* 'king'. Names containing as an element a king's entire name – such as the early Old Babylonian name Išbi-Erra-dannam-nādā – were no longer in use. This chapter will first investigate the typology of *šarru*-names. Then we will address the question, based on prosopography, how such typological '*Beamtennamen*' are actually represented among the names of officials, and to which degree names of this type are indicative of a specific socio-economic and administrative collocation of the name-bearers.

Typology of Names Containing the Element *šarru* 'King'

Semantically, a larger group of names expressing a wish or blessing for the king has to be distinguished from a much smaller group in which the king is essentially a stand-in for a theophoric element in that a wish is addressed to him. In the following discussion, references for names whose bearers were demonstrably royal officials will be flagged by adding the person's title or function. The absence of such a flag, however, does not necessarily mean that the person in question did not have a background in the royal administration; it only means that relevant information is lacking.

Wishes and Blessings for the King

By far the most *šarru*-names have the pattern DN-šarru-uṣur 'DN, guard the king'. Essentially the whole range of theophoric elements attested in the onomasticon appears in these names, from rare and mostly local deities[1] to the 'great' gods of the dominant Babylon theology. Of the latter gods, Nabû is the most frequently attested in *šarru*-names, with Bēl second. Temple names can take the place of the theophoric element;[2] infrequently, a variant with *ina* 'in' is found (Ina-Esagil-šarru-uṣur; BM 29311). Occasionally, the theophoric element reveals the non-Babylonian origin of the name-bearer. For instance, Yāḫû-šarru-uṣur was a Judean (CUSAS 28 2–4) and Milkūmu-šarru-uṣur probably an Ammonite (VS 3 53). Very rarely, a 'house' or 'clan' appears in the first place: the name of governor Bīt-Irʾanni-šarru-uṣur refers to the Irʾanni clan (Wunsch 1993 no. 169).

Variants of the DN-šarru-uṣur type include:

DN-šarru-bulliṭ	'DN, preserve the king' (TCL 13 153; a *rab ekalli* official)
DN-balāṭ-šarri-uṣur	'DN, guard the king's life' (BIN 1 8)
DN-kibsī-šarri-uṣur	'DN, guard the king's steps' (AnOr 8 10; a *qīpu* official)
<DN>-amāt-šarri-uṣur	'<DN>, guard the king's word' (GC 2 322)

Instead of an imperative, the verbal form can come in the preterite:

DN-šarru-ibni	'DN has created the king' (OECT 10 362)
DN-šarru-ukīn	'DN has established the king' (GC 2 298)
DN-šarru-utēr	'DN has restored the king' (BM 114616)
DN-balāṭ-šarri-iqbi	'DN ordained the king's life' (TCL 13 227; a *mašennu* official)

Rare names expressing a wish or blessing for the king are:

DN-rāʾim-šarri	'DN loves the king' (TCL 9 103)
DN-šul(l)um-šarri	'DN, (establish) the well-being of the king' (YOS 6 11)
DN-itti-šarri	'DN is with the king' (CTMMA 3 38)
Itti-DN-šarru-lūmur	'Let me see the king with the help of DN'[3]

Finally, Šarru-lū-dari 'May the king endure', attested as the name of a *qīpu* official (CTMMA 4 136), expresses a wish without explicitly addressing a divinity.

1 Some examples are Amurru-šarru-uṣur (*Nbn.* 42); Dagān-šarru-uṣur (OECT 10 150); Gabbi-ilī-šarru-uṣur 'All the gods, guard the king' (*Cyr.* 177).

2 Some examples are Esagil-šarru-uṣur (*Camb.* 276; a *rab* . . . official); Eanna-šarru-uṣur (YOS 7 89; an oblate); Bayt-il-šarru-uṣur (CUSAS 28 17); Eašarra-šarru-uṣur or Bīt-Ašarra-šarru-uṣur (Wunsch 1993 no. 357; a governor of Šaḫrīn).

3 This could also be construed as a wish for divinely sanctioned royal patronage benefitting the name-bearer. The name is attested once in Frame (1991, 38–40) (^{I}KI-^{d}EN-LUGAL-IGI). Frame normalised the name as Itti-Bēl-šarru-limmir, which would have to be understood as 'Let the king shine with (the help of) Bēl'.

Instead of the king, 'kingdom' (*šarrūtu*) can appear in names – for instance, in DN-kīn-šarrūssu 'DN, establish his kingdom', DN-šarrūssu-ukīn 'DN established his kingdom', and Tīrik-šarrūssu 'Let his kingdom be long-lasting'.[4]

Apart from the king, the crown prince is the only other member of the royal family who appears in names: DN-mār-šarri-uṣur 'DN, guard the crown prince' (BM 103477; a vice governor of the Sealand).

This name type falls out of use at the end of the fourth or very early in the third century;[5] in fact, the later Hellenistic onomasticon does not contain any *šarru*-names at all;[6] see the following section.

Blessings from the King

The second category of names – more varied than the first, but with far fewer attestations – focuses on the king not as the recipient of divine blessings implicitly requested by the bearer of the name, but as a fount of blessings in his own right. Functionally, the king replaces a divinity in such names. This is most explicit in the name Šarru-ilū'a[7] 'The king is my god' (YOS 3 159; a *rab musaḫḫirī* official), but the fact also evinces clearly from the following name pairs.[8]

Itti-šarri-balāṭu – Itti-Marduk-balāṭu	'Life comes from the king / Marduk'
Ina-ṣilli-šarri – Ina-ṣilli-Bēl	'Under the protection of the king / Bēl'
Itti-šarri-īnīa – Itti-Nabû-īnīa	'My eyes are on the king / Nabû'
Šarru-mītu-uballiṭ – Nabû-mītu-uballiṭ	'The king / Nabû has revived the dead'
Mannu-akî-šarri – Mannu-akî-Nabû	'Who is like the king / Nabû?'
Itti-šarri-būnu – Nabû-būnu-šūtur	'The good comes from the king / Nabû, the good is overwhelming'

4 Persons bearing these name types can be found, among others, in the following texts: Waerzeggers 2014 no. 121; Wunsch 1993 no. 51 (a *ša rēši* official); YOS 6 11 (a *šakin māti* official).

5 Late references: CT 44 84, CT 49 9.

6 See also http://oracc.museum.upenn.edu/hbtin/qpn-x-people (no hits for LUGAL or *šarru*; accessed 17.8.2019).

7 Spelled -DINGIR-*ú-a*, a singular suffix (also, e.g., YOS 3 94, YOS 7 120, YOS 19 164, etc.).

8 Examples of persons bearing the *šarru*-names listed here are: Itti-šarri-balāṭu in BIN 1 69 (*rab batqi,* a high-ranking royal official); Ina-ṣilli-šarri in BE 8/1 138; Itti-šarri-īnīa in JCS 28 6 (a *qīpu* of the Eulmaš temple of Agade); Šarru-mītu-uballiṭ in PTS 3313 (slave of the *qīpu* of the Eanna temple); Mannu-akî-šarri in GC 2 353; Itti-šarri-būnu in PTS 3476; Šarru-dūru in TCL 13 193; Ṣalam-šarri-iqbi in UET 4 201 (a governor); Šarru-ukīn in YOS 3 59 (recipient of an official letter); Lalê-šarri-lušbi in BM 94592. Examples of the parallel names with a theophoric element can be found in Tallqvist (1905). For Lalê-Esagil-lušbi, see BM 103452 (a *šakin māti* official).

Ṣalam-šarri-iqbi – Bēl-iqbi	'The royal image / Bēl has spoken'
Šarru-ukīn – Nabû-ukīn	'The king / Nabû has strengthened (the name-bearer)'
Lalê-šarri-lušbi – Lalê-Esagil-lušbi	'Let me be satiated by the bounteousness of the king / Esagil'
Šarru-dūru – Nabû-dūr-ēdi	'The king is (my) fortress / Nabû is the fortress of the individual'

Also in this type of name, the crown prince makes an appearance: Mār-šarri-ilūʾa 'The crown prince is my god' (YOS 7 195). Finally, it should be noted that the only Babylonian family name that invokes the king, LUGAL-A.RA.ZU(*-ú*), may belong to this name type. Its exact reading and interpretation are uncertain (Wunsch 2014, 310), but A.RA.ZU should stand for *taṣlītu* 'prayer' or for a form of *ṣullû* 'to pray'.

None of the names in this second group, which cast the king in a (quasi-) divine role, comes from a source that post-dates 484 BCE (i.e., the major break in the continuity of Late Babylonian history). The first group, which invokes divine support for the king, on the other hand, continues (though with less frequency) beyond 484 BCE until the beginning of the Hellenistic period. To some degree, these are proxy data for the development of Babylonian attitudes towards kingship. For the long sixth century, the continuing relevance of traditional sacralised kingship cannot be doubted. Thereafter, it was no longer common to consider the king on a par with the gods. The pertinent names are no longer attested, even among the numerous Babylonians who had close ties to the royal administration and who occasionally would still bear names invoking the gods' protection for the king. In the Hellenistic period, even this latter name type disappeared, probably because of the disappearance (from our view, at least) of royal officials of Babylonian origin.[9]

The Social Range of '*Beamtennamen*'

For establishing the intended message of a '*Beamtenname*' (defined here as names invoking the king), it is easiest to start with the observation that the use of these names was restricted. Kings or members of the royal family did not bear them, unless they had been named before they or their

9 Given the narrowing down of the focus of the cuneiform documentation to the spheres of the Bēl temple of Babylon and the Anu temple of Uruk in the Hellenistic period. Note, however, the name Nidinti-šarri 'Gift of the king' attested in Hellenistic Uruk. There, it is at least sometimes a 'second name', suggesting that the name was chosen for a specific reason or occasion (e.g., YOS 20, 64, OECT 9, 47).

family members gained the throne, as was the case with Nergal-šarru-uṣur (Neriglissar) and Bēl-šarru-uṣur (Belshazzar), son of Nabonidus. '*Beamtennamen*' are also conspicuously absent among the Babylonian urban upper class – that is, the propertied landowners, be they priestly rentiers or more enterepreneurially oriented landowners.[10] Only a few individuals bearing a family name had a '*Beamtenname*' as a given name or as a patronym.[11] This suggests that the message that a '*Beamtenname*' sought to project was not part of the general outlook of this class of people.

The 'bi-polar' temple administrations are the sector of state administration in first millennium BCE Babylonia that we are best informed about (Jursa 2015; 2017). There, descendants of local priestly families worked side by side with representatives of the central government. The latter were typically designated as *qīpu* '(royal) commissioner' or as *ša rēš šarri bēl piqitti* 'courtier (and) supervisor'. While both groups were dependent on royal approval, they hailed from different backgrounds. For priests, their origin in certain families was normally a precondition for their access to office.[12] The family background of the royal officials, by contrast, is less clear: they were very rarely even given patronyms, let alone family names (Jursa 2015). The crown, not their own family, was the principal point of reference that these individuals related to and from which they drew their legitimisation, as seen in their not infrequent conflicts with local priests (Jursa and Gordin 2018; Levavi 2018). This allegiance to the crown is what '*Beamtennamen*' were intended to signal.

However, it is by no means true that the majority of officials bore such names. Of the twelve royal commissioners in Sippar, only five had a '*Beamtenname*';[13] in Uruk, only five of thirteen (Kleber 2008, 30–2). Of the thirty courtiers listed in Bongenaar's Sippar prosopography (1997, 108–12), eight have a name including the element *šarru*; in Uruk, it is 30 per cent (Jursa 2011, 165, n. 34). Finally, and perhaps most significantly, among the

10 For the distinction between rentiers and entrepreneurs, see Jursa (2010, 265–315).

11 They should be considered exceptions that prove the rule. Some very rare examples are: Nabû-mukīn-zēri/Nabû-šarru-uṣur/Bēl-napšāti (OECT 10 131 and *Camb.* 388); Nabû-itti-šarri/Nabû-aḫḫē-bulliṭ/Bēl-eṭēri (CTMMA 3 38); Bēl-ibni/Nabû-šarru-uṣur/Gaḫal (Waerzeggers 2014, 371); Itti-Bēl-šarru-lūmur/Nabû-šumu-līšir/Eppēš-ilī (Frame 1991, 38); Innin-šarru-uṣur/Nergal-ušallim/Sîn-leqe-unninnī (AnOr 8 24; YOS 6 33); Innin-šarru-uṣur/Kudurru/Ḫunzû (GC 1 353); Šamaš-šarru-uṣur/Marduk-šāpik-zēri/Sîn-leqe-unninnī (YOS 7 96); Nabû-mukīn-zēri/Nabû-šarru-uṣur/Sîn-tabni (JCS 28 5).

12 For example, Kümmel 1979; Bongenaar 1997; Kleber 2008, 5–52; Waerzeggers 2010, 33–76. These studies contain convenient lists of office holders.

13 Bongenaar 1997, 47–50, with additional attestations by Da Riva (1999) and Zawadzki (2001).

twenty-one palace officials named in what is preserved of the pertinent part of Nebuchadnezzar's '*Hofkalender*', just one person had a '*Beamtenname*' (Da Riva 2013). In light of this data, the question arises as to whether it was entirely optional for officials to bear such a name.

There is no direct evidence about the moment and circumstances when an official received a '*Beamtenname*'. If such a name was selected by a person's parents, or by the name-bearer himself, this might be seen as an aspirational act – an indication of a hoped-for career or allegiance. If such a name was awarded at his actual appointment to office, it was very likely conferred upon him by the same authority that invested him with the office.

Ethnicity is likely one important factor here. From a social and ethno-linguistic point of view, the royal administration had a different setting than the city and temple administrations. In the bilingual environment of Babylonia in the sixth and later centuries, the crown was far more open to the use of Aramaic than the temple administrations or the Babylonian urban bourgeoisie. The Aramaic scribes (*sēpiru*) that appear in the documentation from the reign of Nebuchadnezzar II onwards were usually employed by the crown. In the Persian period, royal Aramaic scribes were made obligatory members of the board of temple administrators (Jursa 2012). An investigation of the largest distinct group of royal officials – the courtiers (*ša rēši*) and their fifth-century homologues, the chamberlains (*ustarbaru*) – shows that many of these men were of non-Babylonian origin. Some were Arameans or generally West Semites;[14] a significant number was of Egyptian extraction, especially after the Persian conquest (Hackl and Jursa 2015); and yet others were of Elamite or Iranian origin, or they bore names that resist etymological explanation (Jursa 2011). Arguably, many of these courtiers were at least partly deracinated professionals of administration who owed what privileges they had to the king. Their identity rested in their name and title, as the naming customs in administrative and legal documents bear out: while an ordinary Babylonian needed to be named with his patronym and, if applicable, with his family name to be fully defined from a legal point of view, for a courtier his own name and his title were sufficient: there was no legal need for further details.

Courtiers of non-Babylonian extraction must have been under pressure to integrate also with respect to their name. Such a scenario probably lies

[14] For example, Addu-yatin, vice-governor (*ša rēši šanû*) of Ḫindanu (Bongenaar 1997, 108). Other West Semitic *ša rēšis* can be found in AfO 16 42, *Cyr.* 335, *Dar.* 301, VS 6 69, YNER 1 5, BM 79363 (Sack 1994, 101), BM 103452 (AfO 50, 265). Note the Iranian courtiers in YOS 6 169 // 231, UET 4 1 // 2 66.

behind the double name of 'Maše-Emūn, son of Sa-x-tukku, the royal courtier, whose name is Iddin-Nabû' (Bloch 2018 no. 80, ca. 28 Dar I). While this man took an unmarked Babylonian name, it is highly likely that in many other cases a name was chosen that reflected the allegiances of the courtier, a '*Beamtenname*'. I would suggest that this is the raison d'être of many of these names not only for courtiers but also for royal officials in general. Sometimes, we get confirmation of this hypothesis in the form of non-Babylonian patronyms or non-Babylonian ethnic affiliations of bearers of '*Beamtennamen*'. Of a total of eighty-two bearers of '*Beamtennamen*' for whom patronyms are known, twenty men had a demonstrably non-Babylonian background.[15] Some of these individuals are:

Nabû-šarru-uṣur, the Egyptian (UCP 9/1 29)
Sîn-šarru-uṣur, son of Pasia (probably an Egyptian patronym; *Nbk.* 382)
Zababa-šarru-uṣur, son of Il-ta-ma-mu, the Elamite (YOS 19 253)
Gabbi-ilī-šarru-uṣur, son of Iltehr-hanan (an Aramaic patronym; *Cyr.* 177)
Šarru-dūru, son of ˁEdrā (an Aramaic patronym; TCL 13 193)
Bayt-il-šarru-uṣur, son of Nabû-rapa? (an Aramaic patronym; BM 74520)
Nabû-šarrūssu-ukīn, son of Nabû-iltala (an Aramaic patronym; BM 27967+; BM 94541)
Šarru-lū-dari, son of Abu-nūr (an Aramaic patronym; JCS 24 106)
Šamaš-šarru-uṣur, son of Milki-rām (a Phoenician patronym; Jursa 1998 no. 2)
Abī-râm, son of Sîn-šarru-uṣur (son with an Aramaic name; OECT 10 113)
Aḫu-lakun, son of Nergal-šarru-uṣur (son with an Aramaic name; BE 8/1 85)

The evidence is sufficient to argue that '*Beamtennamen*' will very often have been a signal of achieved or intended integration and loyalty given by, or required from, (relative) outsiders. However, while such a signal was not required from everyone – not all officials bore '*Beamtennamen*' – is it possible to say that whoever actually did bear such a name did have a close relationship to the crown?

[15] Given the size of the sample (overwhelmingly from the long sixth century), this is probably fairly representative. It does of course not follow that the remaining 75 per cent were Babylonians, their all-Babylonian onomastics notwithstanding.

It is not possible to give an entirely conclusive answer to this question: we simply do not have sufficiently clear prosopographical data to establish the institutional affiliation of every single bearer of a '*Beamtenname*'. Several points are clear, though. First, as stated earlier, the likelihood that a bearer of a '*Beamtenname*' was a member of one of the well-established urban clans, and especially of a priestly clan, is very remote. Second, the more unusual *šarru*-names are strong signals for an affiliation with the royal administration. This is true, for instance, for the types DN-balāṭ-šarri-iqbi, DN-šarrūssu-ukīn, DN-šulum-šarri, and DN-mār-šarri-uṣur. All (or nearly all) bearers of such names can be shown to have been officials based on their titles or the context of their attestations.

In other cases, we may well lack information that would allow us to place bearers of '*Beamtennamen*' in their proper context. To quote one example, a relatively large number of such names are found among the shepherds and chief shepherds working for the Eanna temple, such as the 'chief of cattle' (*rab būli*) Arad-Bēl, son of Šarru-ukīn (AnOr 8 67; etc.), and his brother Anu-šarru-uṣur, son of Šarru-ukīn, who also was a shepherd (YOS 7 140, 161). Two *šarru*-names in two generations must be indicative. Nothing in the attested activities of these men suggests a close relationship to the crown, but we know that shepherds were to some degree outsiders who had a contractual relationship with the temple, and they may well have been drawn from a segment of the Urukean population that depended on the king.

On the other hand, however, we regularly encounter *šarru*-names among temple 'oblates' (*širku*). Two examples from the Eanna temple are Anu-šarru-uṣur (TCL 13 170) and Eanna-šarru-uṣur (YOS 7 89). These individuals owed service obligations to the temple and did not have a close – or, indeed, any – relationship to the crown; in fact, we can probably exclude the existence of such a relationship. This is sufficient evidence to state that a '*Beamtenname*' is not a fail-safe indication for identifying an official. The reason why humble oblates like those mentioned earlier might bear a '*Beamtenname*' eulogising the king – a kind of name that is, after all, quite rare and thus 'marked' – cannot be established. The reason will have lain in their personal histories. One possible pathway is suggested by the following evidence: 'Ea-šarru-bulliṭ, slave of Nabû-šarru-uṣur, the courtier' (YOS 6 138) and 'Šarru-mītu-uballiṭ, slave of the *qīpu*' (PTS 3313). These slaves of two royal officials bear '*Beamtennamen*'. The message of the names – which were almost certainly given to them by their masters – reflects the values of the name-givers, the masters. It is thus conceivable that oblates with '*Beamtennamen*' had a similar background to these two slaves: they might have been manumitted slaves of officials who had been gifted to the temple to serve it as *širkus*.

Conclusions

Names built around the element *šarru* 'king' either eulogise or bless the king, or they cast him in a quasi-divine role. The second type falls out of use after the end of the long sixth century, the first becomes obsolete in the early decades of the Hellenistic period. Overall, these names are rare and therefore 'marked'. In most cases they will have indicated a close relationship to the king. When such names are borne by officials – as they often, but not universally, are – they may emphasise their allegiance to the crown with a view towards masking or cancelling an outsider's identity. We also see such names used for slaves and temple dependents; in these cases it is likely that the names were chosen by someone with authority over these people who had a close relationship to the crown. Names of this type are very rare among the members of the prestigious urban clans, especially among priests, and their occasional occurrence in such circles must be considered an exception with probably specific reasons that remain unknown. In other words, while a '*Beamtenname*' on its own is not sufficient evidence to identify an official, it is very good grounds to assume that the name-bearer is not a priest. Therefore, we can say that Amurru-šarru-uṣur, chief administrator (*šatammu*) of the Amurru temple Ekurgal (YBC 4038; Sack 1977, 43–4), is almost certainly an exception to the rule that the *šatammu* was usually chosen from the ranks of local priestly families.

Further Reading

Beamtennamen, as defined here, has hitherto not been collected in a single place. Many can be found in prosopographic resources such as Knut Tallqvist's *Neubabylonisches Namenbuch* (1905), in the indices of text editions, and in prosopographically oriented studies of temple archives. Hans Martin Kümmel's *Familie, Beruf und Amt im spätbabylonischen Uruk* (1979) and Kristin Kleber's *Tempel und Palast* (2008) cover the Eanna temple at Uruk. For Sippar, there is Rocío Da Riva's *Der Ebabbar-Tempel von Sippar in frühneubabylonischer Zeit* (2002) and Arminius C. V. M. Bongenaar's *The Neo-Babylonian Ebabbar Temple at Sippar* (1997). Finally, Caroline Waerzeggers' *The Ezida Temple of Borsippa* (2010) and Bastian Still's *The Social World of the Babylonian Priest* (2019) present information about the Ezida temple in Borsippa. Note further Michael P. Streck's review of Bongenaar's book (2001). For Neo-Babylonian officialdom, in general, see, for example, Michael Jursa (2014, 2017).

References

Bloch, Y. 2018. *Alphabetic Scribes in the Land of Cuneiform: sēpiru Professionals in Mesopotamia in the Neo-Babylonian and Achaemenid Periods*. Piscataway: Gorgias Press.

Bongenaar, A. C. V. M. 1997. *The Neo-Babylonian Ebabbar Temple at Sippar: Its Administration and Its Prosopography*, Publications de l'Institut historique-archéologique néerlandais de Stamboul 80. Leiden: Nederlands Historisch-Archaeologisch Instituut te Istanbul.

Da Riva, R. 1999. 'Zum Verwaltungspersonal des Ebabbar zur Zeit Kandalānus', *Nouvelles Assyriologiques Brèves et Utilitaires* 1999/39.

Da Riva, R. 2002. *Der Ebabbar-Tempel von Sippar in frühneubabylonischer Zeit (640–580 v. Chr)*, Alter Orient und Altes Testament 291. Münster: Ugarit-Verlag.

Da Riva, R. 2013. 'Nebuchadnezzar II's prism (EŞ 7834): a new edition', *Zeitschrift für Assyriologie und Vorderasiatische Archäologie* 103, 196–229.

Edzard, D.-O. 1998–2001. 'Name, Namengebung (Onomastik). B. Akkadisch', *Reallexikon der Assyriologie* 9, 103–16.

Frame, G. 1991. 'Nabonidus, Nabû-šarra-uṣur, and the Eanna Temple', *Zeitschrift für Assyriologie und Vorderasiatische Archäologie* 81, 37–86.

Hackl, J. and M. Jursa 2015. 'Egyptians in Babylonia in the Neo-Babylonian and Achaemenid periods' in J. Stökl and C. Waerzeggers (eds.), *Exile and Return: The Babylonian Context*, Beihefte zur Zeitschrift für die alttestamentliche Wissenschaft 478. Berlin: De Gruyter, pp. 157–80.

Jursa, M. 1998. *Der Tempelzehnt in Babylonien vom siebenten bis zum dritten Jahrhundert v. Chr.*, Alter Orient und Altes Testament 254. Münster: Ugarit-Verlag.

Jursa, M. with contributions by J. Hackl, B. Janković, K. Kleber, et al. 2010. *Aspects of the Economic History of Babylonia in the First Millennium BC: Economic Geography, Economic Mentalities, Agriculture, the Use of Money and the Problem of Economic Growth*, Alter Orient und Altes Testament 377. Münster: Ugarit-Verlag.

Jursa, M. 2011. '"Höflinge" (ša rēši, ša rēš šarri, ustarbaru) in babylonischen Quellen des ersten Jahrtausends' in J. Wiesehöfer, R. Rollinger, and G. Lanfranchi (eds.), *Ktesias' Welt. Ctesias' World*, Classica et Orientalia 1. Wiesbaden: Harrassowitz, pp. 159–73.

Jursa, M. 2012. 'Ein Beamter flucht auf Aramäisch: Alphabetschreiber in der spätbabylonischen Epistolographie und die Rolle des Aramäischen in der babylonischen Verwaltung des sechsten Jahrhunderts v. Chr.' in G. B. Lanfranchi, D. Morandi Bonacossi, C. Pappi, and S. Ponchia (eds), *Leggo! Studies Presented to Frederick Mario Fales on the Occasion of His 65th Birthday*. Wiesbaden: Harrassowitz, pp. 379–97.

Jursa, M. 2014. 'The Neo-Babylonian Empire' in M. Gehler and R. Rollinger (eds.), *Imperien und Reiche in der Weltgeschichte. Epochenübergreifende und globalhistorische Vergleiche*. Wiesbaden: Harrassowitz, pp. 121–48.

Jursa, M. 2015. 'Families, officialdom and families of royal officials in Chaldean and Achaemenid Babylonia' in A. Archi, in collaboration with A.Bramanti (eds.), *Tradition and Innovation in the Ancient Near East. Proceedings of the 57th Rencontre Assyriologique Internationale at Rome 4–8 July 2011*. Winona Lake: Eisenbrauns, pp. 597–606.

Jursa, M. 2017. 'The state and its subjects under the Neo-Babylonian Empire' in R. de Boer and J. G. Dercksen (eds.), *Private and State in the Ancient Near East. Proceedings of the 58e Rencontre Assyriologique Internationale at Leiden 16–20 July 2012*. Winona Lake: Eisenbrauns, pp. 43–67.

Jursa, M. and S. Gordin 2018. 'The ousting of the Nūr-Sîns: micro-historical evidence for state-building at the Neo-Babylonian Empire's "Augustan threshold"', *Hebrew Bible and Ancient Israel* 7, 42–64.

Kleber, K. 2008. *Tempel und Palast: Die Beziehungen zwischen dem König und dem Eanna-Tempel im spätbabylonischen Uruk*, Alter Orient und Altes Testament 358. Münster: Ugarit-Verlag.

Kümmel, H. M. 1979. *Familie, Beruf und Amt im spätbabylonischen Uruk. Prosopographische Untersuchungen zu Berufsgruppen des 6. Jahrhunderts v. Chr. in Uruk*. Berlin: Gebrüder Mann Verlag.

Levavi, Y. 2018. *Administrative Epistolography in the Formative Phase of the Neo-Babylonian Empire*, Dubsar 3. Münster: Zaphon.

Sack, R. H. 1977. 'The scribe Nabû-bāni-aḫi, son of Ibnâ, and the hierarchy of Eanna as seen in the Erech contracts', *Zeitschrift für Assyriologie* 67, 42–52.

Sack, R. H. 1994. *Neriglissar – King of Babylon*, Alter Orient und Altes Testament 236. Kevelaer/Neukirchen-Vluyn: Butzon & Bercker/Neukirchener Verlag.

Still, B. 2019. *The Social World of the Babylonian Priest*, Culture and History of the Ancient Near East 103. Leiden: Brill.

Streck, M. P. 2001. 'Das Onomastikon der Beamten am neubabylonischen Ebabbar-Tempel in Sippar', *Zeitschrift für Assyriologie und Vorderasiatische Archäologie* 91, 110–19.

Tallqvist, K. L. 1905. *Neubabylonisches Namenbuch zu den Geschäftsurkunden aus der Zeit des Šamaššumukîn bis Xerxes*, Acta Societatis Scientiarum Fennicae 32/2. Helsinki: Societas Litteraria Fennica.

Waerzeggers, C. 2010. *The Ezida Temple of Borsippa: Priesthood, Cult, Archives*, Achaemenid History 15. Leiden: Nederlands Instituut voor het Nabije Oosten.

Waerzeggers, C. 2014. *Marduk-rēmanni. Local Networks and Imperial Politics in Achaemenid Babylonia*, Orientalia Lovaniensia Analecta 233. Leuven: Peeters.

Wunsch, C. 1993. *Die Urkunden des babylonischen Geschäftsmannes Iddin-Marduk: Zum Handel mit Naturalien im 6. Jahrhundert v. Chr.*, Vol. 2, Cuneiform Monographs 3b. Groningen: Styx.

Wunsch, C. 2014. 'Babylonische Familiennamen' in M. Krebernik and H. Neumann (eds.), *Babylonien und seine Nachbarn. Wissenschaftliches Kolloquium aus Anlass des 75. Geburtstages von Joachim Oelsner, Jena, 2. und 3. März 2007*, Alter Orient und Altes Testament 369. Münster: Ugarit-Verlag, pp. 289–314.

Zawadzki, S. 2001. 'New data concerning high officers from the Neo-Babylonian period', *Nouvelles Assyriologiques Brèves et Utilitaires* 2001/60.

CHAPTER 6

Reading Neo-Babylonian Names

Cornell Thissen

Introduction

Many Neo-Babylonian names take the form of a sentence consisting of a subject (usually a deity), an object (usually the newborn child), and a verb.[1] Whenever the elements are spelled syllabically, there is usually no problem in reading and translating the name. In the first millennium BCE, however, it became increasingly common for scribes to spell the subject, object, and/or verb of personal names with logograms (Sumerograms). Sometimes a phonetic prefix or suffix was added to indicate pronunciation, but often such reading aids were not supplied.[2] In that case, verbal logograms are especially difficult to interpret for modern readers, as these signs can render a finite form (present, preterite, perfect), a non-finite form (participle, verbal adjective, infinitive), an injunctive form (precative, imperative), or even a verbal substantive. Two examples will suffice to illustrate the challenges that modern readers face when interpreting a logographically written Babylonian name.

The first example is the name spelled ^{Id}AG-A-MU. In this name, the verb spelled MU can hypothetically be interpreted as an imperative (*Nabû-aplu-idin 'Nabû, give the son!'), a preterite (Nabû-aplu-iddin 'Nabû gave the son'), a perfect (*Nabû-aplu-ittannu 'Nabû has given the son'), or a present (*Nabû-aplu-inaddin 'Nabû gives/will give the son'). However, such ambiguity did not exist in the minds of Babylonian readers, who knew that Nabû-aplu-iddin was the only permissible form of this name.

Another example is the name spelled ^{Id}IDIM-GI. This name is to be read Ea-ušallim despite the fact that the name Ea-mušallim also existed.

I am most grateful to Pieter Alkemade for commenting on, and editing, a draft of this chapter in a difficult time; I also wish to thank the editors for their work on the manuscript; all remaining errors are mine. All names discussed in this chapter are Neo-Babylonian (c. mid-eighth century BCE onwards), unless otherwise indicated.

1 The typology of Babylonian names is discussed in Chapter 2 (male names) and Chapter 3 (female names).

2 For example, the verbal element in the name Bēl-nāṣir is often spelled PAB-*ir* to avoid confusion with -uṣur or -aḫu. However, the use of the phonetic complement was not obligatory and Bēl-nāṣir is often simply written ^{Id}EN-PAB.

The names Ea-ušallim and Ea-mušallim are obviously very similar, but they were not the same: an individual was either called Ea-mušallim or Ea-ušallim, but never both. In order to avoid confusion, scribes wrote the preterite form (*ušallim*) with the logogram GI while rendering the participle syllabically (^{Id}IDIM-*mu-šal-lim* or *mu*-GI). In other words, ^{Id}IDIM-GI was never to be read Ea-mušallim.

The latter example shows that Neo-Babylonian scribes used a coherent system for writing verbal logograms in personal names. This system can be reconstructed by comparing the different spellings that the ancient scribes used to render the names of the same individuals. In this chapter I present the results of this reconstruction and propose a simple method to determine the correct reading of verbal logograms in Neo-Babylonian personal names.[3]

Phonetic Reading Aids

Scribes could and did help the reader identify the correct rendering of logograms by adding phonetic suffixes and prefixes. The following tables collect all known Neo-Babylonian name elements that consist of a verbal Sumerogram and a phonetic prefix (Table 6.1) or suffix (Table 6.2). Entries where the transcription begins with a capital letter are one-element names.[4]

Table 6.1 *Name elements consisting of a verbal Sumerogram with a phonetic prefix*

Prefix	Transcription	Prefix	Transcription
bul-TIN-*iṭ*	bulliṭ	*mu*-(*še*)-DIB	mušētiq
e-KAR	eṭir, ēṭir	*mu*-GÁL-*ši*	Mušebši
i-BA-*šá*	iqīša	*mu*-GI	mušallim
i-DÙ	ibni	*mu*-GUR	mutīr
ik-KÁD	ikṣur	*mu*-SIG$_{(1)5}$(-*iq*/*qu*)	mudammiq
iq-E	iqbi	*mu*-SILIM	mušallim
i-SU, *ta*-SU	Erībāya, tarībi	*na*-PAB	nāṣir
it-MU-*nu*	ittannu	*nu*-ZALÁG	nūr
ka-KÁD	kāṣir	*šá*-DUB	Šāpiku, Šāpik-
li-GIŠ	līšir, Līšir	*tu*-TIN-*su*	tuballissu
li-SI.SÁ	Līšir	*ú*-SIG$_{(1)5}$-*iq*	udammiq
lu-IGI	lūmur	*ú*-TIN-*su*	uballissu
lu-È	lūṣi	*ú*-URÙ(-*šú*)	uṣur(šu)

[3] The details of this reconstruction are the subject of my forthcoming PhD dissertation (VU University Amsterdam).

[4] With the exception of Bānītu, which is the name of a deity. One-element verbal names are discussed in greater detail later in the chapter.

Table 6.2 *Name elements consisting of a verbal Sumerogram with a phonetic suffix*

Suffix	Transcription	Suffix	Transcription
ÁG-*(ú)-a*	Râmûa	MU-*(na)-a*[5]	Iddināya
APIN-*eš/iš*	ēreš	MU-*na/ni/nu*	ittannu
BA-*šá(-a-(a))*	iqīša, Iqīšāya	MU-*ú-nu/nu-nu*	Iddinunu
DIB-*iq*	mušētiq	NÍG.SUM-tu_4	nidinti, Nidintu
DÙ-*(na)-(a)-a*	Ibnāya	NIGIN$_{(2)}$-*ir*	upaḫḫir
DÙ-*at/a-tú*	banâtu	PAB-*ir*	nāṣir
DÙ-*i*	bani	SIG$_{(1)5}$-*(qí)-ia*	Damqia
DÙ-*eš/iš/uš*-ilī	ēpeš-ilī (FN)	SIG$_{(1)5}$-*iq*[6]	-udammiq, -dam(i)qu-
DÙ-*ia*	Bānia	SIG$_{(1)5}$-*qa/qá/qu*	damqā/u (FN)
DÙ-*na-a/ʾ*	banā (W.Sem.)	SILIM-*im*	Mušallim(-DN), DN-ušallim, Obj.-šullim
DÙ-*ni/nu*	bāni/bānû		
DÙ-*nu-nu/nun*	bānûnu	SILIM-*lim*	šullim
DÙ-*ti/tú/*tu_4	Bānītu (DN)	SILIM.(MU)-*a*	Šullumāya
DÙ-*uš/šú*	DN-īpuš, Mīnu-ēpuš, Obj.-epuš	SIPA-*in-du*	^{f}Rēʾindu
		SU-*a*	erība, Erībāya
DUB-*ki/ku*	Šāpiku	SI.SÁ-*ri*	Līšir
E-*bi*	iqbi	SUM-*din*	Nādinu (?)
GÁL/TIL/TUK-*ši*	-libši[7], -ušabši[8], Mušebši-	SUM-*in*	iddin
GAR-*ni/nu*	šaknu	SUM(.NA)-*a*	Iddināya
GAR-*un*	iškun	SUM(.NA)-*na/ni/nu*	ittannu
GI-*a*	Šullumāya	SUM(.NA)-*ú-nu*	Iddinunu
GIN-*a/ia/iá*	Kīnāya	SUM(.NA)-*nu-nu*	Iddinunu
GIN-*in*	Mukīn-, -ukīn	SUM-*ti/tú/*tu_4	nidinti, Nidintu
GIN-*ú-a*	kīnûa	SUM-*tú-a(-a)*	Nidintāya
GIŠ-*ir*	līšir	SUR-*ir/ri/ru/rat*	ēṭir(at)
GUB-*za/zu*	azziz ?	SÙ-*ú-a*	Rīšûa (FN)
GUR-*ir*	utīr	TIN-*a*	Balāṭāya
I-*a*	Nâdāya	TIN-*iṭ*	Obj.-bulliṭ, DN-uballiṭ
I-*id*	naʾid	TIN-*(liṭ)-su/šú(-ú)*	Balāssu, Uballissu-

[5] In rare cases, when MU-a represents a patronym, it is sometimes read Šumaya.
[6] To be read Mudammiq- or -dam(i)qu- in family names.
[7] If the object is MU (*šumu* 'name'), for example, Šumu-libši, DN-šumu-libši '(DN,) May the name exist'.
[8] If the object is not MU (*šumu* 'name'), for example, Nabû-ušabši.

Table 6.2 (*cont.*)

Suffix	Transcription	Suffix	Transcription
KÁD-*ri*	Kāṣir		DN, DN/v.-bullissu
KAM-*eš*	ēreš	TIN-*ṭu*	balāṭu, Balāṭu
KAM-*tu*$_4$	Erišti-	TIN-*uṭ*	abluṭ
KAR-*a*	Ēṭirāya	TUK-*ši*	see GÁL/TIL/TUK-*ši*
KAR-*ir*/*ri*/*ru*/*rat*	Ēṭir(at)	TUKUL-*ti*	tukulti
KAR-*šú*	šūzibšu	URÙ-*ir*	nāṣir
KAR-*tu*$_4$	^{f}Ēṭirtu	ZALÁG-(*mir*)-*ir*	unammir
KU4-(*e-reb*)-*šú*	Erēbšu	ZALÁG-*e-a*	Nūrea
LAL-*iṣ*	tāriṣ	ZALÁG-*za-na*/*nu*	Nūrzānu
		lim-ZALÁG-*ir*	limmir, lummir

Some entries can denote both a full name and an element of a larger name. For instance, BA-*šá-a* can appear in a compound name of the type DN-iqīša ('DN granted'), but it can also stand on its own as the hypocoristic Iqīšaya.

Verbal Logograms Without Reading Aids

In order to identify the correct reading of the verbal logogram when it is written without phonetic complements, the following two-step method can be used. The first step is to identify the format of the name in question. In Babylonian names, the verbal element appears in nine common constellations: as the name's only element (v.), preceded or followed by a deity's name (DN-v., v.-DN), together with another verb (v.-v.), followed or preceded by an object or subject (v.-obj., obj./subj.-v.), in combination with an object or subject and a deity's name (DN-v.-obj., DN-obj./subj.-v.), or in combination with a deity's name and another verb (DN-v.-v.).[9] These categories can be further divided based on grammatical features: the verbal form used (present tense, preterite, perfect, precative, imperative, participle, verbal adjective, substantive) or the person (first, second, or third-person singular).[10] Table 6.3 presents all common name formats, along with their subtypes and some examples, but without

[9] Pronominal prefixes and suffixes are not considered separate elements, nor are vocal endings -a, -āya, -ia, etc. (e.g., Iddināya) since these are fixed to the preceding element.

[10] No plural verbal forms were used in Neo-Babylonian names, as opposed to Old Babylonian, Middle Babylonian, and Neo-Assyrian names.

Table 6.3 *Common formats of Babylonian names with a verbal element*

Name format	Subtype	Examples
v.	pres. 1/3.sg.	Upāq
	pret./perf. 1.sg.	Ātanaḫ
	pret./perf. 2.sg.	Tattannu
	pret./perf. 3.sg.	Iddināya
	part.	Nādinu, Nāṣiru, Multēširu
	imp.	Uṣuršāya
	prec.	Līšir
	verb.adj.	Nadnāya
	subst. (incl. inf.)	Nidintu
DN-v.	DN-pres. 1/3.sg.	DN-upāq
	DN-pret./perf. 1.sg.	(Ana-)DN-ātanaḫ
	DN-pret./perf. 2.sg.	DN-tattannu
	DN-pret./perf. 3.sg.	DN-iddin, DN-ittannu
	DN-part	DN-nādin, DN-nāṣir
	DN-imp.	DN-uṣranni, DN-uṣuršu
	DN-prec.	DN-līšir
	DN-verb.adj.	DN-na?id
	DN-subst.	(Itti-)DN-balāṭu/ssu
v.-DN	pres. 1/3.sg.-DN	Upāq-(ana)-DN
	pret./perf. 1.sg.-DN	Ātanaḫ-DN
	pret./perf. 3.sg.-DN	Iddin-DN, Ittannu-DN
	part.-DN	Mukīn-DN
	imp.-DN	Uṣuršu-DN
	prec.-DN	Lūṣi-ana-nūr-DN
	verb.adj.-DN	Nadin-DN, Naṣir-DN
	subst.-DN	Nidinti-DN
v.-v.	pret./perf. 2.sg.-imp.	Tattannu-uṣur, Tattannu-bullissu
	pret./perf. 2.sg.-prec	Taqbi-līšir
v.-obj.	part.-obj.	Nādin-aḫi
obj./subj.-v.	obj.-pret./perf. 1/3.sg.	Aḫu-iddin
	obj.-imp.	Aplu-uṣur
	obj./subj.-prec.	Aḫu-lūmur, Aḫu-līšir
DN-v.-obj.	DN-part.-obj.	DN-nādin-aḫi, DN-nāṣir-aḫi
DN-obj./subj.-v.	DN-obj.-pres. 1/2/3.sg.	DN-šūzubu-ile??i
	DN-obj.-pret./perf. 1/3.sg.	DN-aḫu-iddin, DN-aḫu-ittannu
	DN-obj.-imp.	DN-šumu-uṣur
	DN-obj./subj.-prec.	DN-aḫḫē-lūmur, DN-šumu-līšir
DN-v.-v.	DN-pret./perf. 2.sg.-imp.	DN-tattannu-uṣur
	DN-pret./perf. 2.sg.-prec.	DN-tultabši-līšir

additional prepositions, adverbs, etc.[11] Note that a verbal Sumerogram can be used not only as a verb but also as an object. For instance, the sign GIN can denote an object (e.g., in the name DN-kīnu-uṣur 'DN, protect the true (heir)!') and a verb (e.g., in DN-šumu-ukīn 'DN established the name (son)').

The rules for reading verbal logograms, set out later in the chapter, pertain to these nine common name formats. Before turning to this rule scheme, however, we need to consider a number of special or rare name types that cannot be fitted into this scheme.

First-Person Singular Preterite

First-person singular preterite forms are rare in Neo-Babylonian names. These elements are mostly spelled syllabically or the reading of the logogram is self-evident[12] because of extra elements (such as the preposition *ana* (*muḫḫi*) 'to' or the interrogative pronoun *mīnu* 'what?') or because the verb refers to a human action (e.g., *šasû* 'to invoke', *ṣullû* 'to pray'). Names that use this verbal element generally express a lament or a statement of devotion by one of the parents. The following list contains all attested names of this type, of which the verbal element is written with a logogram:

- Mīnu-ēpuš-ilī 'What did I do, my god?' (*ēpuš* written DÙ)
- Ana-muḫḫi-DN-āmur 'I looked towards DN' (*āmur* written IGI)
- (Ana-DN-)(obj.)-ēreš '(From DN) I requested (obj.)' (*ēreš* written KAM/APIN-*eš*)
- Ina-qibīt-DN-azziz 'By order of DN I stood (?)' (*azziz* written GUB (*za*/*zu*))
- DN-uṣalli 'I prayed to DN' (*uṣalli* written SISKUR_x)

Present Tense

Rarely, names contain a verb in the present tense instead of the more common preterite. Such names are usually spelled syllabically, in which case their interpretation is unproblematic, or the reading of the logogram is

[11] For compactness, preterite and perfect forms are sometimes combined, as are 1/3.sg., verb.adj./subst., and imp./prec. when these forms use the verbal logogram in the same way in Neo-Babylonian names. Most examples given in Table 6.3 are based on three common verbs, written with the signs MU (*nadānu* 'to give'), ÙRU (*naṣāru* 'to protect'), and GIŠ (*ešēru* 'to be well'). Occasionally other verbs are used when the specific name form is not attested for these three verbs.

[12] Self-evident to the Neo-Babylonian reader, who had common knowledge of permissible names, but maybe not to us.

self-evident because of extra elements, rare verbs, or on semantic grounds.[13] Names in this category generally express a question, a character trait of the deity, or a statement of devotion. The following list includes all attestations of this name type, of which the verbal element is written with a logogram:

- DN-kittu-irâm 'DN loves the truth' (*irâm* written ÁG)
- Ša-Marduk-ul-inni 'What is of Marduk does not change' (*tenni*/*inni* written BAL)
- Ileʾʾi-(obj.)-DN / DN-obj.-ileʾʾi 'DN is able (to . . .)' (*ileʾʾi* written DA/Á.GÁL)
- Lâbâši(-DN) 'I will not be put to shame (, DN)' (*lâbâši* written NU.TÉŠ)
- Irâš-ana-Akītu/Esagil '(S)He rejoices over Akītu/Esagil' (*irâš* written SÙ)
- DN-qajalu-išemme 'DN hears the attending' (*išemme* written ŠE.GA)
- Nabû-maqtu-idekke 'Nabû raises the fallen' (*idekke* written ZI)
- Abī-ul-(t)īde 'I do/(S)He does not know my/the father' ((*t*)*īde* written ZU)

Long Names With or Without a Theophoric Reference

Most names consist of one, two, or three elements (see Table 6.3) and the rules set out later in the chapter pertain to these common names. Three-element names without a theophoric reference (DN) and four-element names often contain a preposition, an interrogative pronoun, or another unique element that makes these names easily recognisable. There are no set rules for interpreting the verbal element of such names; only common sense or familiarity with the Babylonian name repertoire will help determine the correct reading. Some examples include:

- Lūṣi-ana-nūr-Marduk 'May he come out to the light (of?) Marduk' (*Lūṣi* written È)
- Nergal-ina-tēšî-eṭir 'Nergal, save from confusion' (*eṭir* written SUR/KAR)
- Zēr-kitti-līšir 'May the true heir prosper' (*līšir* written GIŠ/SI.SÁ)
- Nabû-ina-kāri-lūmur 'May I see Nabû in the harbour' (*lūmur* written IGI)
- Nabû-itti-ēdi-alik 'Nabû walk(s?) with the lonely!' (*alik* written DU)

[13] For instance, in the name spelled ^{Id}DN-obj.-DA, a past tense is less likely ('DN was able') than a present tense ('DN is able').

Inverted Names

There are a few names that deviate from the standard Akkadian word order (subject-object-verb). A rare name type follows the word order object/subject-verb-DN. It is found in only four names so far: Zēru-līšir-Nusku 'Nusku, may the heir be in good condition!' (subj.-prec.-DN, hapax, *līšir* written SI.SÁ), Atta-tale''i-Bēl 'You are capable, Bēl' (subj.-pres.-DN, hapax, syll.), Lētka-idi-Zarpanītu 'Zarpanītu, give your attention!' (obj.-imp.-DN, hapax, *idi* written ŠUB), and Aḫu/Aḫḫē-iddin-Marduk 'Marduk granted (a) brother(s)' (obj.-pret.-DN, *iddin* written MU/SUM.NA). The most interesting category of inverted names follows the word order DN-verb-object. The verbal element in such names takes the form of an imperative: Sîn-rīmanni-aḫu (hapax, when not a scribal error; 'Sîn, grant me a brother!'), Nabû-zuqup-kīnu 'Nabû, support the true (heir)!' (*zuqup* written GUB), Nabû-uṣur-napištī 'Nabû protect my life!' (*uṣur* written PAB/URÙ), and Nabû-šukun-rēmu 'Nabû, place compassion!' (*šukun* written GAR). The name Nabû-uṣur-napištī might hint at the reason for the inversion. This phrase was part of a well-known mirror-like expression *DN, uṣur napištī, balāṭa qīša* 'DN, protect my life, health grant (me)!' popular on seals in first millennium BCE Babylonia.[14] Poetic use is also attested for the sequence *zuqup*-object[15] and *šukun*-object,[16] which might explain the inversion in the names DN-zuqup-kīnu and DN-šukun-rēmu. In short, deviation from the normal word order in Neo-Babylonian names was a rare phenomenon and one that may have had its origin in the wish of the name-giver for poetic euphony.

Rules for Reading Verbal Sumerograms in Neo-Babylonian Names

Having dealt with the special cases, we now turn to the rules for reading the verbal element of common names when the ancient scribe rendered it *only* logographically, without phonetic markers or unique elements. As we will see, these rules depend on the name format – that is, the number of elements in the name and their order, as presented in Table 6.3. It should

[14] Reiche and Sandowicz (2009, 205–12). On seals, the verb *uṣur* is spelled both PAB and *ú-ṣur*.

[15] In the DINGIR.ŠÀ.DIB.BA incantations one finds *zu-qup* SAG.MEŠ-[*ia*] 'support [my] head!' (Lambert 1974, 282:158).

[16] The inverted expression *šukun ḫidûtam* 'make merry' is attested in the Old Babylonian version of the Gilgamesh Epic (George 2003, 278–9: iii 8).

be noted that these rules form a *discrete* orthographic system: a sign could only be used for one name within a particular name format. For instance, the spelling DN-PAB could not be used to render both DN-nāṣir (a participle of the verb *naṣāru*) and DN-uṣur (an imperative of the same verb). In personal names, perfects and verbal adjectives are never found spelled only logographically but always with at least one syllabic part.

One-Element Names Consisting of Only a Verbal Element (v.)

Nearly all one-element names are spelled syllabically or with a phonetic complement that makes their reading self-evident. The only signs that may represent a one-element name without a phonetic complement are substantives, including infinitives. Only four names are presently known that are written with only a logogram: ^{I}GI (Šullumu 'Well-being'), ^{I}KAR (Šūzubu 'To save'), ^{I}ŠU (Gimillu 'Favour'), ^{I}TIN (Balāṭu 'Life'). These logograms cannot represent verbal adjectives because none of these verbs appear in this form in either the name format verb.adj.-DN or DN-verb. adj. In other words, *Šullum-DN, *Šūzubu-DN, *Gamil-DN, and *Baliṭ/Balṭu-DN are not found in the repertoire of Neo-Babylonian names.[17]

Two-Element Names Consisting of a Verb Preceded by a Deity's Name (DN-v.)

When the logogram represents a 'birth' verb, it should be rendered in the preterite 3.sg. as the deity is the subject of the verb. 'Birth' verbs are verbs that describe the god causing the birth of the newborn child – for example, to create, give, return, replace, etc.[18] Sometimes the ancient scribe indicated the correct reading by adding a phonetic complement to the verbal logogram (e.g., DN-iqīša 'DN gave', written DN-BA-*šá*),[19] but often no such markers were used. The following list contains all attested names of this type, of which the verbal element is written only with a logogram:

- DN-ibni 'DN created' (written DN-DÙ)
- DN-iqbi 'DN commanded' (written DN-E or DN-DUG$_4$)
- DN-utīr 'DN returned' (written DN-GUR)

17 Note that *bal-ṭu*-DN, son of Ìl-(*ḫ*)*a-qa-bi* (VS 5 55:3) is West Semitic.

18 Stamm 1939 (28, 136) uses the term '*Danknamen*' for these names.

19 BA is nearly never found alone (exceptions are BIN 1 85:3 and OIP 114 35:1, both letters), which practically makes BA-*šá* a frozen sign combination. This also applies to GÁL/TIL/TUK-*ši* in the name DN-ušabši 'DN created' and GAR-*un* in the name DN-iškun 'DN placed'.

- DN-iddin 'DN gave' (written DN-MU or DN-SUM.NA)
- DN-ukīn 'DN established' (written DN-GIN or DN-GI.NA)
- DN-erība 'DN replaced' (written DN-SU)

There are four more signs that may represent 'birth' verbs in Neo-Babylonian names, but only when they are used without an object: DN-GI (DN-ušallim 'DN brought to gestation'),[20] DN-KAR (DN-ušēzib 'DN let leave to posterity'),[21] DN-SIG$_{(1)5}$ (DN-udammiq 'DN showed favour (to the parents?)'), and DN-TIN (DN-uballiṭ 'DN kept alive and in good health').

In all other names – that is, when the logogram represents a verb that is not a 'birth' verb – it should be rendered in the precative ('May DN . . . !' or 'DN, may . . . !') or as a participle ('DN is the one who . . . '):

- DN-līšir 'DN, may (the child) prosper' (written GIŠ or SI.SÁ)
- DN-lūmur 'May I see DN' (written IGI)
- DN-lēʾû 'DN is the one who is capable' (written Á.GÁL or DA)
- DN-kāṣir 'DN is the one who strengthens' (written KÁD or KÀD)
- DN-tāriṣ 'DN is the one who stretches over (to protect)' (written LAL)
- DN-ēṭir 'DN is the one who saves' (written SUR)
- DN-gāmil 'DN is the one who spares, is merciful' (written ŠU)
- DN-nāṣir 'DN is the one who protects' (written ÙRU or PAB)

Two-Element Names Consisting of a Verb Followed by a Deity's Name (v.-DN)

When the logogram represents a 'birth' verb in the D/Š-stem, it should be rendered as a participle.[22] The following list contains all attestations of this name type, of which the verbal element is written with a logogram:

- Mudammiq-DN 'The one who treats kindly is DN' (written SIG$_{(1)5}$)
- Mukīn-DN 'The one who establishes is DN' (written GIN or GI.NA)[23]
- Mušallim-DN 'The one who keeps well is DN' (written GI)

[20] CAD Š$_1$ 226 s.v. *šalāmu* 11f and CAD M$_2$ 256 s.v. *mušallimu* 2: 'bringing (pregnancy) to term'.

[21] CAD E 420–1 s.v. *ezēbu*, causative to meaning 2d; or CAD E 419 s.v. *ezēbu*, causative to meaning 2a1′ 'to (let) leave something with or to': for example, 'in the womb Enlil left his scion'. Note that when the logogram KAR is used for the verb *eṭēru*, it is usually spelled with a phonetic component *-ir/rV*, except in names that are not easily misread, such as DN-ēṭir-napištī (DN-KAR-ZI.MEŠ).

[22] The only exception to this rule is the name Uballissu-DN 'DN made him live' (preterite D 3.sg.), always spelled with the pronominal suffix attached to the verbal logogram (TIN-*su*-(*ú*)-DN).

[23] Participle *mukīn-* in Neo-Babylonian names is always written *ki-*(*i*)*-in-* (without *mu-*) when syllabically spelled.

- Mušebši-DN 'The one who brings into being is DN' (wr. GÁL(-*ši*)/TUK(-*ši*)/TIL)
- Mušēzib-DN 'The one who saves is DN' (written KAR)

When the logogram represents a 'birth' verb in the G-stem, it should be rendered in the preterite 3.sg.: Iqīša-DN, Ibni-DN, Iqbi-DN, Iddin-DN, and Erība-DN. In these names, the verbal element is spelled and translated in the same way as names of the type DN-iqīša discussed earlier.

In the remaining names of this type the verbal logograms should be rendered as a noun: Nisḫur-DN 'Benevolent attention of DN' (NIGÍN), Gimil-DN 'Favour of DN' (ŠU), and Nūr-DN 'Light of DN' (ZALÁG). These readings are based on instances where ancient scribes used both a syllabic and a logographic spelling for the same individual's name.

Two-Element Names Without DN Written with Two Logograms

Here we can observe how Neo-Babylonian scribes helped their readers make sense of onomastic logograms in other ways than by using phonetic complements. Whenever a name consists of two verbal forms (v.-v.), the first element (always a preterite or perfect 2.sg.) was spelled syllabically: for example, ^{I}*ta-at-tan*-ÙRU (Tattannu-uṣur 'You have given (the child), now protect (it)!') and ^{I}*taq-bi*-SI.SÁ (Taqbi-līšir 'You commanded (the child's birth), may it prosper!'). This practice indirectly helps the reader make sense of names with two logograms. When the first logogram can *only* represent a verb (a participle), the second logogram must be an object; vice versa, when the second logogram can *only* be an object, it follows that the first one must be a verb (a participle), because had the name consisted of two *verbal* elements, the first had been spelled syllabically. In a similar vein, when both logograms could be verbs (e.g., MU-GIN), the second logogram has to be the verb and the first one the object, in accordance with the normal word order of Akkadian sentences (subject-object-verb).

The transcription of the name then depends on whether or not the verb is a possible 'birth' verb: if it is, the verbal form needs to be rendered in the preterite 3.sg.; if it is not, it needs to be rendered in the imperative or precative. Note that the common name spelled MU-PAB/ŠEŠ is an exception: this name should be read Nādin-aḫi 'The one who gives a brother' (participle-object) rather than *Šumu-uṣur, even though the theophoric name spelled DN-MU-PAB/ÙRU is to be read DN-šumu-uṣur 'DN protect the name!'.

Three-Element Names Written DN-Logogram-Logogram

The rules for reading such names are similar to those for two-element names of the type logogram-logogram discussed in the previous section. When the first logogram can only represent a verb, the name should be read DN-participle-object. The same applies if the second logogram can only represent an object. In all other cases the name is of the type DN-object-verb. If the verb is a possible 'birth' verb, the verbal logogram should be rendered in the preterite 3.sg. If it is another type of verb, it should be rendered as an imperative or a precative (*-līšir*, *-lūmur*, or *-libši*). The following list contains all attestations of the latter name type, of which the verbal element is written with a logogram:

- (DN-)qātēšu-ṣabat '(DN,) Seize his hands!' (written DAB)
- (DN-)aḫḫē-šullim '(DN,) Keep the brothers well/in good health!' (written GI)
- (DN-)mātu-tuqqin '(DN,) Put the country in order!' (written LAL)
- (DN-)aḫu-bulliṭ '(DN,) Keep the brother alive and in good health!' (written TIN)
- (DN-)kudurru-uṣur '(DN,) Protect the heir!' (written URÙ/PAP)

Ambiguous Spellings

Sometimes scribes did not follow the rules for writing verbal Sumerograms in names. Upon closer inspection such apparent exceptions can often be explained from the context. For instance, the name spelled DN-GI should normally be read DN-ušallim (see Introduction to this chapter), but when the syllabically written name DN-*mu-šal-lim* had already been used in a previous line, the scribe could use DN-GI as a (lazy) repeat later on (BaAr 3, BM 46544:4, r. 18).

Other ambiguous spellings are found in the limited group of family names – for example, ^{Id}30-SIG$_5$ is to be read Sîn-damqu not Sîn-udammiq – or in texts with limited readership. For instance, in letters *we* may not know how to read the name ^{I}BA-DN (OIP 114 35:1; Iqīša-DN, normally spelled BA-*šá*-DN, or Qīšti-DN, normally spelled NÍG.BA-DN), but for the senders and addressees it was obvious who was meant; neither did the scribe need to be careful or unambiguous for legal reasons. The same applies to lists of personnel produced for internal administrative purposes: these individuals were well-known in the institutions that employed them. For the same reason, the name of Borsippa's chief temple administrator Nabû-nādin-šumi could be spelled in shorthand (Nabû-MU-MU; TCL 12 9:26 and TMH 2/3 12:23) instead of the 'correct' spelling Nabû-SUM.NA-MU or Nabû-*na-din*-MU. Nabû-MU-MU is normally to be read Nabû-šumu-iddin, but this individual was so well-known in the city that confusion was unlikely.

Permissible Names

Finally, we should recall that ancient readers were intimately familiar with the repertoire of names. This knowledge helped them make sense of ambiguous spellings. As an example, we can take the sign DU. This logogram could represent at least three different verbs: it could be read DU for the verb *alāku* 'to go', GIN for the verb *kânu* 'to be true, permanent', and GUB for the verb *i/uzuzzu* 'to stand'. All three verbal forms are found in Neo-Babylonian names, sometimes even in the same name format. Nevertheless, the ancient scribe and reader will have had no problem recognising the spelling DN-GIN-A as DN-mukīn-apli 'DN is the one who firmly establishes the son', and DN-DU-IGI as DN-ālik-pāni 'DN is the one who walks in front' and not *DN-kīnu/kittu-lūmur, 'May I see the true (heir)/truth!' nor *DN-mukīn-pāni 'DN is the one who establishes the front'. Although theoretically possible, these last names did not exist. Similarly, they will have identified DN-GIN-ÙRU/PAB as DN-kīnu-uṣur 'DN, protect the true/legitimate (heir)' because the name *DN-mukīn-ahi 'DN is the one who firmly establishes the brother' was not part of the Neo-Babylonian name repertoire.

FURTHER READING

Die akkadische Namengebung by Johann J. Stamm (1939) remains a useful starting point for onomastic studies. The volume has two parts: an extensive introduction and a main part that discusses the various categories of names. The introduction looks into such diverse aspects as shortening, word order, verb (tense, person, and gender), geography, theophoric element, family, and newborn child as elements in the name, renaming, and time of naming. Its main paragraph (§ 6) discusses the various ways of classifying names, a system that Stamm blurs by also introducing an alternative and arbitrary classification, group A and B. After the introduction, he structures the main part in a rather confusing mix of the categories from § 6. Aside from these arbitrary classifications, the work is still a valuable tool for students wishing to examine an unknown name (pp. 325 ff.: I. Alphabetisches Verzeichnis der Namen) and to look for verbs and nouns in names (pp. 354 ff.: II. Verzeichnis von Namensbestandteilen).

In his Neo-Babylonian name book, Knut L. Tallqvist (1905) gathered all Neo-Babylonian names recorded in cuneiform texts published at the time. After an introduction, the book offers three indices: one with all known names (personal name, patronym, and family name) and their attestations, one sorted on deities and corresponding names and one sorted on words and verbs used in Neo-Babylonian names. Additional chapters list names of countries and places, temples, canals and rivers, streets, and gates. The introduction is still worth reading, especially paragraph III on shortening of names and paragraph IV on name formats.

References

George, A. R. 2003. *The Babylonian Gilgamesh Epic: Introduction, Critical Edition and Cuneiform Texts*, Vol. 1. Oxford: Oxford University Press.

Lambert, W. G 1974. 'Dingir.šà.dib.ba incantations', *Journal of Near Eastern Studies* 33, 267–70, 272–322.

Reiche, A. and M. Sandowicz 2009. 'Neo-Babylonian seal from the Potocki Collection at the National Museum in Warsaw' in O. Drewnowska (ed.), *Here and There Across the Ancient Near East: Studies in Honour of Krystyna Łyczkowska*. Warsaw: Agade, pp. 195–220.

Stamm, J. J. 1939. *Die akkadische Namengebung*, Mitteilungen der Vorderasiatisch-Ägyptischen Gesellschaft 44. Leipzig: J.C. Hinrichs Verlag.

Tallqvist, K. L. 1905. *Neubabylonisches Namenbuch zu den Geschäftsurkunden aus der Zeit des Šamaššumukîn bis Xerxes*, Acta Societatis Scientiarum Fennicae 32/2. Helsinki: Societas Litteraria Fennica.

PART II

Non-Babylonian Names

CHAPTER 7

Assyrian Names

Heather D. Baker

Introduction

The Assyrian dialect of Akkadian in the first millennium BCE is closely related to the Babylonian dialect. This, together with their common cultural background and the high degree of interaction and mobility between the two regions means that the personal name repertoires of Assyria and Babylonia overlap to a significant degree. For example, Neo-Assyrian sources mention many individuals who can be identified as Babylonians, whether active in Assyria (as deportees, visitors, or settlers) or in Babylonia (as mentioned, for example, in Assyrian royal inscriptions, or in the Babylonian letters of the official correspondence). Their personal names, for the most part, are indistinguishable from those of the Assyrians themselves. These circumstances make it somewhat challenging to distinguish names of genuinely Assyrian derivation and to identify them in the Babylonian sources.

The Babylonian name repertoire is well established, thanks to the wealth of published Neo-Babylonian everyday documents. For Assyria, *The Prosopography of the Neo-Assyrian Empire* (PNA) includes not only biographies of all named individuals but also concise analyses of the linguistic background of individual names, together with the attested spellings (Radner 1998, 1999; Baker 2000, 2001, 2002, 2011). The series includes more than 21,000 disambiguated individuals bearing in excess of 7,300 names. The names themselves represent numerous linguistic backgrounds, including Akkadian (Assyrian and Babylonian), Aramaic, Hebrew, Moabite, West Semitic, Phoenician, Canaanite, Arabic, Egyptian, Greek, Iranian, Hurrian, Urarṭian, Anatolian, and Elamite. PNA covers texts of all genres in so far as they mention individuals by name; it forms the basis for any attempt to distinguish between Neo-Assyrian and Neo-Babylonian personal names. The focus of this chapter is on presenting the methodology and issues involved in identifying Assyrian names in Babylonian sources, with due consideration of the historical context. The names discussed here are intended to be representative cases; they do not constitute a complete repertoire of Assyrian names documented in Babylonian texts.[1]

Before addressing current approaches to identifying Assyrian names in Babylonian sources, it is worth highlighting a key difference in Assyrian and Babylonian naming practices: while family names are commonly used in Babylonia by members of the traditional urban elite (see Chapter 4), they were never adopted in Assyria. Also, these same members of the Babylonian urban elite regularly identified themselves by their father's name in everyday documents, whereas in Assyria, with the exception of members of scribal/scholarly families, genealogical information is far less common, being limited to the occasional inclusion of the father's name. This means that the disambiguation of individuals is generally easier for Neo-Babylonian sources than for Neo-Assyrian ones, especially in the case of common names. One final point to bear in mind: feminine personal names make up around 7 per cent of the total number of names catalogued in PNA, so it is hardly surprisingly that Assyrian feminine personal names can only very rarely be identified in Babylonian texts.

Historical Background

As far as the onomastic material is concerned, the fall of Nineveh in 612 BCE forms a watershed for the presence of Assyrian name-bearers in Babylonia. Evidence prior to the fall of Assyria is slight: John P. Nielsen's 2015 study, covering early Neo-Babylonian documents dated between 747 and 626 BCE, includes only six individuals bearing names that are clearly Assyrian according to the criteria discussed later in the chapter. They are: Aššur-ālik-pāni 'Aššur is the leader' (^{I}AN.ŠÁR–*a-lik–pa-ni*), Aššur-bēlu-uṣur 'O Aššur, protect the lord!' (^{I}AN.ŠÁR–EN–URÙ), Aššur-dannu 'Aššur is strong' (^{I}AN.ŠÁR-*dan-nu*), Aššur-ēṭir 'Aššur has saved' (^{Id}AŠ-SUR), Aššur-ilāʾī 'Aššur is my god' (^{I}AN.ŠÁR-DINGIR-*a-a*), and Mannu-kî-Arbail 'Who is like Arbaʾil?' (^{I}*man-nu-ki-i*-LIMMÚ-DINGIR) (Nielsen 2015, 41–2, 196; cf. Zadok 1984, 5). Aššur-bēlu-uṣur is a particularly interesting case since he served as *qīpu* ('(royal) resident') of the Eanna temple of Uruk at some time between 665 and 648 BCE (Beaulieu 1997, 55–6). The question has been raised of whether he was

[1] For ease of reference, I cite personal names in the form in which they are listed in PNA, albeit with divine elements Aššur and Issar instead of Aššūr and Issār. Parpola (PNA 1/I, xxiv–xxv) argues for Aššūr, though see Zadok (1984, 3) for a differing view. See later in the chapter concerning Issār / Issar.

posted there or belonged to a local family, but, as Karen Radner notes, the office of *qīpu* denoted the king's representative as an 'outsider', in contrast to the other high temple officials who were drawn from the local urban élite (Radner 2017, 84; cf. Kleber 2008, 26–7). In general, though, this scarcity of Assyrian names in Babylonian sources prior to the fall is interesting because a lot of Assyrians were stationed or active in Babylonia during this period of more or less continuous Assyrian domination. The onomastic evidence suggests either that such people seldom bore diagnostically Assyrian names, or, if they did, then they did not integrate or mix with local people in a way that led to them featuring in the local transactions that dominate the extant sources from Babylonia.

The inhabitants of Assyria continued to worship the god Aššur long after the fall of Assyria in 612 BCE, as is clear from the Parthian onomasticon as late as the third century CE (Marcato 2018, 167–8). In fact, based partly on the evidence of the Cyrus Cylinder, Karen Radner has recently suggested that the post-612 BCE rebuilding of the Aššur temple at Assur may be attributed to Assyrians who had fled to Babylonia but who returned to Assur after the conquest of Babylon by Cyrus in 539 BCE (Radner 2017). Be that as it may, there is no direct contemporary evidence for actual deportations of Assyrians following the fall of their empire, though it seems clear that a great many people either fled or migrated into Babylonia from the north after 612 BCE. Evidence for this comes mainly in the form of Assyrian personal names in Babylonian texts written during the Neo-Babylonian and Achaemenid periods. In the case of Uruk, there is evidence for a flourishing cult of Aššur, with a temple or chapel dedicated to him in that city (Beaulieu 1997). Moreover, one of the texts discussed by Paul-Alain Beaulieu refers to ^{lú}ŠÀ-*bi*–URU.⸢KI*⸣.MEŠ 'people of Libbāli (= Assur)' (Beaulieu 1997, 61). This evidence for an Assyrian presence in the south is complemented by the mention of some toponyms of Assyrian origin in Babylonian sources (Zadok 1984, 3). While Karen Radner attributed the establishment of the cult of Aššur in Uruk to fugitives who fled Assur following its conquest in 614 BCE (Radner 2017, 83–4), Paul-Alain Beaulieu considers the Urukean cult of Aššur to date back to the late Sargonid period, when Uruk was an important ally of Assyria (Beaulieu 2019, 8).

Text Corpora

The Neo-Babylonian and Achaemenid-period text corpora that contain Assyrian personal names derive especially from the temple sphere, including the archives of Eanna at Uruk and Ebabbar at Sippar.

While these two cities dominate the material under discussion, Assyrian names have also been identified in archival texts written in other Babylonian cities, including Babylon and Nippur (Zadok 1984, 10–11). A detailed examination of the archival background of the relevant texts, which would assist in further contextualising the Assyrian name-bearers, is outside the scope of the present study; the individual archives and their contents are treated in summary form by Michael Jursa (2005).

Principles for Distinguishing Assyrian Names from Babylonian Names

For the sake of the present exercise, we may distinguish three major groups of Akkadian names of the first millennium BCE: (1) distinctively Neo-Assyrian personal names, (2) distinctively Neo-Babylonian personal names, and (3) names that were common to both Assyria and Babylonia. Only names belonging to the first group are of interest here, so our challenge is to define this group more precisely with reference to the other two groups. This process of distinguishing Neo-Assyrian from Neo-Babylonian personal names centres on four key features which may occur separately or in combination, namely: (i) Assyrian divine elements, (ii) Assyrian toponyms, (iii) Assyrian dialectal forms, and (iv) vocabulary particular to the Neo-Assyrian onomasticon. I shall deal with each of these features in turn in the following pages.

Names with Assyrian Divine Elements

With regard to Assyrian divine elements, Ran Zadok has remarked: 'It should not be forgotten that the Assyrians worshipped Babylonian deities (as early as the fourteenth century), but the Babylonians did not worship Assyrian deities. Therefore, if a name from Babylonia contains an Assyrian theophoric element its bearer should be regarded as an Assyrian' (Zadok 1984, 2). This is a sound methodological principle, although in practice it is of restricted application since there are few Assyrian deities that were not traditionally worshipped in Babylonia: the two pantheons overlap to a considerable extent. The following paragraphs deal with the relevant divine names, their spellings, and their reading.

Aššur and Iššar (Ištar)

The name of the god Aššur is commonly written AN.ŠÁR in Neo-Assyrian royal inscriptions from the reign of Sargon II on, although it is first attested considerably earlier, in the thirteenth century BCE (Deller 1987; Beaulieu 1997, 64, n. 22). However, in Babylonian sources personal names that contain the divine element AN.ŠÁR pose a problem of interpretation. As Simo Parpola notes in the introduction to the first fascicle of PNA, Aramaic spellings confirm that the divine name Ištar was pronounced Issar in Assyria, reflecting 'the regular Neo-Assyrian sibilant change */št/* > */ss/*'.[2] He also observes that the Babylonian version Iššar was sometimes shortened to Šar, attributing this to aphaeresis of the initial vowel and arguing that this 'implies a stressed long vowel in the second syllable'.[3] When this happens, the writing ^{d}ŠÁR (Iššar) is indistinguishable from AN.ŠÁR (Aššur).[4] The reading ^{d}ŠÁR = Iššar is confirmed in some cases by syllabic writings attested for the same individual. Ran Zadok understands Iššar to be a Babylonian rendering of Assyrian Issar; therefore, in his view these names are unquestionably of Assyrian background (Zadok 1984, 4). Thus, in Babylonian texts we face the challenge of deciding whether the signs AN.ŠÁR represent Aššur or Ištar. In some instances a clue is offered by the predicative element of the name since some predicative elements work with the divine name Aššur but not with Ištar (Zadok 1984, 4, 7–8). An example of this is the name type DN-mātu-taqqin 'O DN, keep the country in order!', which is attested with the god Aššur but not with Ištar: PNA lists Aia-mātu-taqqin, Aššur-mātu-taqqin, and Nabû-mātu-taqqin (PNA 1/I, 91, 194–6; PNA 2/II, 846). Conversely, some names formed with AN.ŠÁR have a feminine predicate and therefore the divine element must be read ^{d}ŠÁR = Iššar rather than Aššur, as in the case of ^{Id}ŠÁR-*ta-ri-bi* 'Issar has replaced', a name which also has unequivocal writings with ^{d}*iš-tar-* and ^{d}*iš-šar-* (Zadok 1984, 4). Sometimes a predicate is attested with both Aššur and Issar, and thus it provides no guide as to the reading of the divine name. In the case of the temple É AN.ŠÁR, its identification as a shrine of Aššur rather than Ištar is supported by the fact that it is listed among the minor temples of Uruk, making it unlikely that the great temple of Ištar (i.e., Eanna) is intended (Beaulieu 1997, 61).

2 Parpola in PNA 1/I, xxv; see also Zadok (1984, 4) Beaulieu (1997, 61), and Bongenaar (1997, 109).

3 Hence Parpola renders the name element Iššār (as does PNA), while most scholars prefer Iššar. In fact, it is not just the initial vowel that is dropped but also the following consonant: Parpola (1988: 76) cites several such instances in Neo-Assyrian.

4 In Neo-Assyrian sources the divine element Issar is almost invariably written $^{(d)}$15 (only 23 out of 289 writings in cuneiform of Issar names in PNA are written differently, with INNIN or *iš-tar*).

A further complication is the possibility that AN.ŠÁR might alternatively represent the deity Anšar, although Paul-Alain Beaulieu has argued convincingly against this on the grounds that Anšar was a primeval deity of only abstract character and was not associated with any known cult centre (Beaulieu 1997, 61). Note the attempt to 'Assyrianise' the Babylonian Epic of Creation by replacing Marduk with Aššur and equating Aššur (written ^{d}AN.ŠÁR) with Anšar, which resulted in genealogical confusion since Anšar was originally Marduk's great-grandfather (Lambert 2013, 4–5). Anyway, a reading Anšar can certainly be discounted: the name ^{I}*man-nu–a-ki-i*–É–AN.ŠÁR (Mannu-akî-bīt-Aššur 'Who is like the Aššur temple?'), attested alongside other Aššur names, supports the idea that we are dealing with a deity worshipped in Babylonia at the time (Zadok 1984, 3). While it cannot be entirely ruled out that the name-givers intended to reference the original Aššur temple in Assyria as preserved in the folk memory of people of Assyrian descent living in sixth century Uruk, rather than the Aššur temple/chapel in Uruk, the name nevertheless attests to the continuing reverence of Aššur in Babylonia. It is also worth noting that this particular name type, Mannu-(a)kî-DN/GN/TN and variants, is considerably more common in Assyria than in Babylonia: PNA catalogues 47 such names borne by around 370 individuals (PNA 2/II, 680–700), compared with 7 names and less than 10 name-bearers listed by Knut L. Tallqvist in his *Neubabylonisches Namenbuch* (Tallqvist 1905, 99).

Names with the theophoric element written $^{(d)}$*aš-šur* = Aššur are unambiguous. Note the potential confusion between the names ^{Id}AŠ–SUR = Aššur-ēṭir 'Aššur has saved' (Nielsen 2015, 42) and $^{I/lú}$DIL–SUR = Ēdu-ēṭir 'He has saved the only one' (Nielsen 2015, 112), which are written with identical signs apart from the determinative(s); the latter occurs as a family name.

Ištar-of-Nineveh (Bēlet-Ninua)

The goddess Ištar-of-Nineveh, in the form Bēlet-Ninua ('Lady of Nineveh'), occurs in Babylonian sources as an element of the family name Šangû-(Bēlet-)Ninua:

- PN_1 A-*šú šá* PN_2 A ^{lú}SANGA-^{d}GAŠAN-*ni-nú-a* (*Nbn.* 231:3–4, 14–15)
- PN_1 A-*šú šá* PN_2 A ^{lú}SANGA-*ni-nú-a* (VS 3 49:18–19)

In her study of Nineveh after 612, Stephanie Dalley points to these two Neo-Babylonian texts as evidence for the continuation of Nineveh after its fall in 612 BCE (Dalley 1993, 137). These instances allegedly involve a man who is called 'son of the priest of the Lady of Nineveh'. However, this reflects a misunderstanding of the Neo-Babylonian convention for representing genealogy: the man in question is actually a member of the family called 'Priest-of-Bēlet-Ninua' (Šangû-Bēlet-Ninua), a clear parallel to other Neo-Babylonian family names of the form Šangû-DN, 'Priest of DN'. It is uncertain exactly when the cult of Ištar-of-Nineveh was introduced into Babylonia; however, the goddess's temple in Babylon is already mentioned in the topographical series Tintir which was likely compiled in the twelfth century BCE (George 1992, 7). Thus, while there is no way of knowing when the eponymous ancestor entered Babylonia (assuming he, like the cult itself, came from Assyria), this family name cannot be taken as evidence for the continuation of the city of Nineveh after 612 BCE.

The question has been raised as to whether the toponym that forms part of the divine name Bēlet-Ninua is actually Nineveh or a local place, Nina (reading *ni-ná-a* instead of *ni-nú-a*) in Babylonia (Zadok 1984, 10). However, there are reasons to suppose that this family name does actually refer to the Assyrian goddess Ištar-of-Nineveh. First, the name of Bēlet-Ninua's temple in Babylon, Egišḫurankia, is the same as that of her temple in Assur, according to Andrew R. George, who understands Ninua in the divine name to represent Nineveh and not Nina (George 1993, 95, nos. 409 and 410). Second, her temple in Babylon is mentioned in an inscription of Esarhaddon (RINAP 4 48 r. 92–3), and it seems most unlikely that this would refer to the goddess of a very minor Babylonian settlement.

Eššu

In his study of Assyrians in Babylonia, Ran Zadok cites a number of names with the theophoric element Eššu (written *-eš-šu/šú* and *-*^{d}*áš-šú*), including Ardi(/Urdi?)-Aššu and Ardi(/Urdi?)-Eššu, Dalīli-Eššu, Dān-Eššu, Gubbanu(?)-Eššu, Kiṣir-Eššu, Sinqa-Eššu, Tuqnu-Eššu and Tuqūnu-Eššu, Ubār-Eššu, and Urdu-Eššu (Zadok 1984, 9). However, it should be noted that Eššu names do not feature prominently in the extant Neo-Assyrian onomasticon: only a single such name, Šumma-Eššu, is recorded (PNA 3/II, 1286 s.v. 'Šumma-Ēši or Šumma-Eššu'). On the other hand, some of the Eššu names listed above have predicates that are typically Assyrian rather than Babylonian, namely Kiṣir-, Sinqa-, Tuqnu-/Tuqūnu-, and Urdu- (see later in chapter). This suggests an Assyrian background for these particular names, even though they are not yet attested in Assyrian sources.

We then have to confront the question of how to interpret the theophoric element Eššu. According to Ran Zadok, Eššu is 'probably the same element as ˀš which is contained in names appearing in Aramaic dockets ... and an Aramaic tablet ... from the NA period' (Zadok 1984, 9). These Aramaic dockets with ˀš feature on tablets which give the personal name also in Assyrian cuneiform, and in all instances where it is preserved the divine element is written ^{d}15, to be read Issar. For example, the names of the sellers of a house, Upāqa-ana-Arbail 'I am attentive to Arbaˀil' (^{I}*pa-qa-a-na-arba-ìl*) and Šār-Issar 'Spirit of Issar' (^{I}IM-15), feature in an Aramaic caption on the edge of tablet SAA 14 47:15′–16′, dated in 617* BCE: *pqnˀrbˀl* / *srˀš*.[5] If the association between Eššu and Aramaic *ˀš(r)* is correct, we are dealing with a variant of the divine name Ištar. This is compatible with the elements Kiṣir-, Sinqa-, Tuqūnu- and Urdu- listed earlier, which are all attested in Neo-Assyrian sources in names formed with Issar.

In PNA the name Šumma-Eššu (written ^{I}*šum-ma–eš-šú*) was translated 'Truly Eši! [= Isis]' and interpreted as 'Akk. with Egypt. DN' (Luukko, PNA 3/II, 1286). Although this is the only instance of an Eššu name in PNA, a number of other names of supposed Egyptian derivation are listed that contain the element Ēši/Ēšu, understood as 'Isis', namely: Abši-Ešu (^{I}*ab-ši-e-šu*), Dān-Ešu (^{I}*da-né-e-šu*), Ēšâ (^{I}*e-ša-a*), Eša-rṭeše (^{I}*e-šar-ṭe-e-*[*še*]), and Ḫur-ši-Ēšu (^{I}*ḫur-si-e-šú*, ^{I}*ḫur-si-ie-e-šú*, ^{I}*ḫur-še-še*, ^{I}*ḫur-še-šu*). However, given that in Babylonian sources the element Eššu is written with -šš- and is particularly associated with typical Neo-Assyrian predicates, as noted earlier, it seems that regardless of whether Eššu is associated with Aramaic ˀš (= Issar), it should be kept separate from the Egyptian element Ēši/Ēšu, which is written with -š- and does not occur with those predicates.

Names Formed with Assyrian Toponyms

In addition to the names discussed here which contain Assyrian divine elements, there are a number of occurrences in Babylonian sources of personal names formed with Assyrian toponyms, notably Arbaˀil (modern Erbil): Arbailāiu 'The one from Arbaˀil' and Mannu-(a)kî-Arbail 'Who is like Arbaˀil?' (Zadok 1984, 8–9; 1985, 28). The feminine name

[5] The omission of the *-r-* here remains unexplained, although some Aramaic captions do have *ˀsr* as expected, for example, *ˀšrdrqˀl* in SAA 14 39 l.e. 1, representing the name Issar-dūr-qalli that is written in cuneiform in l. 6.

ᶠUrbil-ḫammu 'Arbaʾil is the master' (*ᶠur-bi-il-ḫa-am-mu*), borne by a slave, can be added to these (Zadok 1998). The family name Aššurāya 'Assyrian' (*ᴵaš-šur-a-a*), based on the city name Assur, is also attested. Since none of the members of this family bore Assyrian names, Ran Zadok suggests that the family's ancestor migrated to Babylonia before the Neo-Babylonian period (Zadok 1984, 2). As I noted already, the Assyrians did not use family names, so the adoption of Aššurāya as a family name must reflect the 'Babylonianisation' of the descendants. Related to this phenomenon is the presence of Assyrian toponyms in Babylonian sources, such as Aššurītu, written ᵘʳᵘ*áš-šur-ri-tú* (Zadok 1984, 3); there is no telling when such toponyms were originally introduced into Babylonia.

Names with Assyrian Dialectal Forms

Examples in this category include names formed with the Assyrian precative *-lāmur* 'may I see' (Bab. *-lūmur*), and nouns in Assyrian dialectal form, such as *urdu* 'servant' (Bab. *ardu*). The Assyrian D-stem imperative *-balliṭ* 'keep alive!' (Bab. *-bulliṭ*) comprises another potentially distinctive form, though I know of no example of the name type DN-balliṭ attested in Babylonian sources to date. Examples of names with Assyrian dialectal forms include:

- Pāni-Aššur-lāmur 'May I see the face of Aššur' (ᴵIGI–AN.ŠÁR–*la-mur*; Beaulieu 1997, 59–60). The use of Neo-Assyrian dialect was not always consistent since ᴵIGI–AN.ŠÁR–*lu-mur* is also attested (Zadok 1984, 6). In UCP 9/2 57 the name is written with both *-lāmur* (l. 8) and *-lūmur* (l. 4) (Beaulieu 1997, 59).
- Pāni-Bēl-lāmur 'May I see the face of Bēl' (*ᴵpa-ni–*ᵈEN–*la-mur*; Beaulieu 1997, 59–60).
- Urdu-Eššu 'Servant of Eššu' (*ᴵur-du-eš-šú*, Zadok 1984, 2). The common use of the logogram ÌR often makes it impossible to tell whether a name includes *urdu* or *ardu*.

In addition, the Neo-Assyrian onomasticon – unlike the Neo-Babylonian – includes names formed with the imperative of *riābu* 'to replace' (Rīb(i)-DN) as well as with the preterite (Erība-DN), though note that logographic writings with ᴵSU- as first element are ambiguous. A number of elements particular to Assyrian occur only with Assyrian divine names, according to Ran Zadok: 'It is worth pointing out that the exclusively Assyrian forms *urdu* "slave", *rīb* (Bab. *erība*), *bēssunu* (Bab.

bēlšunu) and *iššiya* (reflecting NA *issiya*) "with me"; Bab. *ittiya*) are recorded in N/LB only as the predicates of *-eššu* and ᵈŠÁR names' (Zadok 1984, 4–5).

Names Formed with Vocabulary Characteristic of the Assyrian Onomasticon

In discussing the divine name Eššu, I identified a number of Assyrian names formed with characteristic vocabulary items, namely (with translations following PNA): Kiṣir-DN ('Cohort of DN'), Mannu-(a)kî-DN ('Who is like DN?'), Sinqi-DN ('Test of DN'), Tuqūn-DN ('Order of DN'), Tuqūnu-ēreš ('He [a deity] has desired order'), and Tuqūnu-lāmur ('Let me see order!'). To these we can add Unzaraḫ-[. . .] (ᴵ*un-za-ra-aḫ*-[. . .]; Zadok 1998); compare the names Unzarḫu ('Freedman'?), Unzarḫu-Aššur, and Unzarḫu-Issar (PNA 3/II, 1387–8).

Orthography and Phonology

In the writing of Assyrian names in Neo-Assyrian sources, the divine determinative is often omitted, whereas in Neo-Babylonian this is only rarely the case. In Babylonian the divine name Ea is rather consistently written ᵈ*é-a*, whereas in Assyrian it is often written ⁽ᵈ⁾*a-a* and, more rarely, *ia*, rendered Aia (Parpola in PNA 1/I, xxv–xxvii). Note that Aia is not to be confused with the goddess Aya (⁽ᵈ⁾*a-a*), spouse of the sun god Šamaš. Otherwise, in terms of phonology, the main difference between the writing of Assyrian and Babylonian names lies in the treatment of the sibilants. We have already seen how the Assyrian divine element Issar (Ištar) was rendered Iššar in Babylonian. The sibilant *š* in Babylonian names may be rendered *s* in Neo-Assyrian: for example, the common Neo-Babylonian name Šumāya was sometimes rendered Sumāya, written ᴵ*su-ma-a-a* and ᴵ*su-ma-ia* in Neo-Assyrian sources (PNA 3/I, 1157–8). This tendency of Assyrian scribes to 'Assyrianise' Babylonian names may hinder the identification of Babylonians in the Assyrian sources. The same is true of the converse: if a Babylonian scribe were to render an Assyrian name by, for example, changing *-lāmur* to *-lūmur*, then there would be no way of identifying the individual as Assyrian in the absence of an Assyrian theophoric element or of further corroborating evidence.

Further Reading

There are very few resources that are directly concerned with the theme of this chapter. The principal resource for the study of Neo-Assyrian names in general is the six-fascicle series *The Prosopography of the Neo-Assyrian Empire*, edited by Karen Radner and Heather D. Baker and with contributions by numerous scholars. For the study of Assyrian names in Babylonian texts, Ran Zadok's articles 'Assyrians in Chaldean and Achaemenian Babylonia' (1984) and 'More Assyrians in Babylonian Sources' (1998) are indispensable, while Paul-Alain Beaulieu's study 'The cult of AN.ŠÁR/Aššur in Babylonia after the fall of the Assyrian Empire' (1997), with its focus on Uruk and the personnel of the Aššur temple in that city, adds new insights and material. Paul-Alain Beaulieu's recent article on 'Assyria in Late Babylonian Sources' (2017) presents a concise account of the 'afterlife' of Assyria in Babylonian sources, including the cult of Aššur.

References

Baker, H. D. (ed.) 2000. *The Prosopography of the Neo-Assyrian Empire*, 2/I: Ḫ–K. Helsinki: The Neo-Assyrian Text Corpus Project.

Baker, H. D. (ed.) 2001. *The Prosopography of the Neo-Assyrian Empire*, 2/II: L–N. Helsinki: The Neo-Assyrian Text Corpus Project.

Baker, H. D. (ed.) 2002. *The Prosopography of the Neo-Assyrian Empire*, 3/I: P–Ṣ. Helsinki: The Neo-Assyrian Text Corpus Project.

Baker, H. D. (ed.) 2011. *The Prosopography of the Neo-Assyrian Empire*, 3/II: Š–Z. Helsinki: The Neo-Assyrian Text Corpus Project.

Beaulieu, P.-A. 1997. 'The cult of AN.ŠÁR/Aššur in Babylonia after the fall of the Assyrian Empire', *State Archives of Assyria Bulletin* 11, 55–73.

Beaulieu, P.-A. 2017. 'Assyria in Late Babylonian sources' in E. Frahm (ed.), *A Companion to Assyria*. Oxford: Wiley-Blackwell, pp. 549–55.

Beaulieu, P.-A. 2019. 'Temple towns and nation building: migrations of Babylonian priestly families in the late periods', *Journal of Ancient Near Eastern Religions* 19, 3–17.

Bongenaar, A. C. V. M. 1997. *The Neo-Babylonian Ebabbar Temple at Sippar: Its Administration and its Prosopography*, Publications de l'Institut historique-archéologique néerlandais de Stamboul 80. Istanbul: Nederlands Historisch-Archeologisch Instituut te Istanbul.

Dalley, S. 1993. 'Nineveh after 612 BC', *Altorientalische Forschungen* 20, 134–47.

Deller, K. 1987. 'Assyrische Königsinschriften auf "Perlen"', *Nouvelles Assyriologiques Brèves et Utilitaires* 1987/101.

George, A. R. 1992. *Babylonian Topographical Texts*, Orientalia Lovaniensia Analecta 40. Leuven: Peeters.

George, A. R. 1993. *House Most High: The Temples of Ancient Mesopotamia*, Mesopotamian Civilizations 5. Winona Lake: Eisenbrauns.

Jursa, M. 2005. *Neo-Babylonian Legal and Administrative Documents: Typology, Contents and Archives*, Guides to the Mesopotamian Textual Record 1. Münster: Ugarit-Verlag.

Kleber, K. 2008. *Tempel und Palast. Die Beziehungen zwischen dem König und dem Eanna-Tempel im spätbabylonischen Uruk*, Alte Orient und Altes Testament 358. Münster: Ugarit-Verlag.

Lambert, W. G. 2013. *Babylonian Creation Myths*, Mesopotamian Civilizations 16. Winona Lake: Eisenbrauns.

Marcato, M. 2018. *Personal Names in the Aramaic Inscriptions of Hatra*, Antichistica 17, Studi orientali 7. Venice: Edizioni Ca' Foscari.

Nielsen, J. P. 2015. *Personal Names in Early Neo-Babylonian Legal and Administrative Tablets, 747–626 BCE*, NISABA 29. Winona Lake: Eisenbrauns.

Parpola, S. 1988. 'The Neo-Assyrian Word for Queen', *State Archives of Assyria Bulletin* 2/2, 73–6.

Radner, K. (ed.) 1998. *The Prosopography of the Neo-Assyrian Empire*, 1/I: A. Helsinki: The Neo-Assyrian Text Corpus Project.

Radner, K. (ed.) 1999. *The Prosopography of the Neo-Assyrian Empire*, 1/II: B–G. Helsinki: The Neo-Assyrian Text Corpus Project.

Radner, K. 2017. 'Assur's "Second Temple Period". The restoration of the cult of Aššur, c. 538 BCE' in C. Levin and R. Müller (eds), *Herrschaftslegitimation in vorderorientalischen Reichen der Eisenzeit*, Orientalische Religionen in der Antike 21. Tübingen: Mohr Siebeck, pp. 77–96.

Tallqvist, K. L. 1905. *Neubabylonisches Namenbuch zu den Geschäftsurkunden aus der Zeit Šamaššumukîn bis Xerxes*, Acta Societatis Scientiarum Fennicae 32/2. Helsinki: Societas Litteraria Fennica.

Zadok, R. 1984. 'Assyrians in Chaldean and Achaemenian Babylonia', *Assur* 4/3, 1–28.

Zadok, R. 1985. *Geographical Names According to New- and Late-Babylonian Texts*, Répertoire Géographique des Textes Cunéiformes 8. Wiesbaden: Dr. Ludwig Reichert.

Zadok, R. 1998. 'More Assyrians in Babylonian sources', *Nouvelles Assyriologiques Brèves et Utilitaires* 1998/55.

CHAPTER 8

Aramaic Names

Rieneke Sonnevelt

Introduction

The Aramaic onomasticon found in Babylonian sources linguistically belongs to the West Semitic languages while it is written in cuneiform script used to express Late Babylonian Akkadian, an East Semitic language (see Figure 8.1). Among the languages classified as West Semitic, four are recognisable in the Late Babylonian onomasticon: Arabic names, generally viewed as representing the Central Semitic branch; Phoenician; Hebrew (or Canaanite); and Aramaic names representing its Northwest Semitic subgroup.[1]

Aramaic names make up the largest part of the West Semitic onomasticon in the Neo- and Late Babylonian documentation. They will be the focus of this chapter. Chapter 9 deals with Hebrew names, Chapter 10 with Phoenician names, and Chapter 11 with Arabic names from this period. The Aramaic onomasticon of the preceding Neo-Assyrian era, which has been researched by Fales, is not included here.[2] A given name may be recognised as Aramaic on the basis of patterns and trends regarding patronym, the occurrence of an Aramaic deity, and the socio-economic context of the attestation. Despite the fact that these factors provide valuable background information (see section on 'Aramaic Names in Babylonian Sources'), the most secure way of deciding on the Aramaic nature of a name is based on linguistic criteria:

- phonological: phonemes of Semitic roots are represented in a way specific for Aramaic;
- lexical: words are created from roots that solely appear in Aramaic;

1 For a somewhat more detailed classification along these lines, see Huehnergard and Rubin 2011, 263. The matter is debated; however, linguists may prefer a model that accounts for the similarities between West Semitic – the Canaanite languages (particularly Hebrew and Phoenician) and the Aramaic language group – in contrast to languages such as Arabic and Ethiopic that form a southern group (see also Gzella 2011, 425–6; 2015, 16–22).

2 See 'Further Reading' section for references, and Chapter 7.

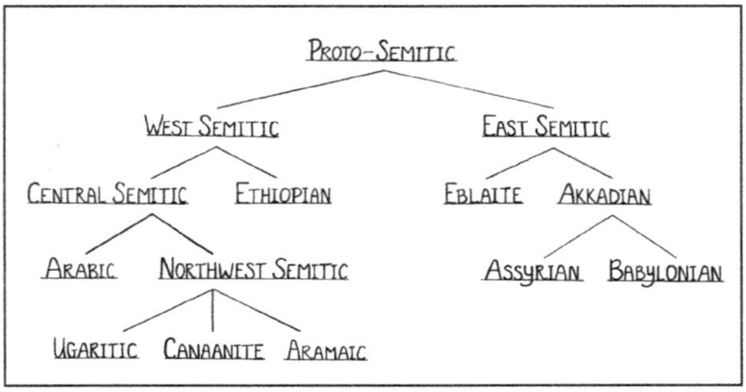

Figure 8.1 A family tree model of Semitic languages (drawing by Rieneke Sonnevelt).

- morphological: forms and patterns used are peculiar for Aramaic;
- structural: names are constructed with, for instance, Aramaic verbal components.[3]

Opinions differ as regards the nature of the Aramaic language in Babylonia during the Neo-Babylonian era. Aramaic attestations from this timeframe are – together with those from the preceding Neo-Assyrian period – variously evaluated as belonging to Old Aramaic as found in sources from Aramaean city states, as manifestations of local and independent dialects, or as (precursors of) Achaemenid Imperial (or Official) Aramaic.[4]

Defining the variety of Aramaic used in Babylonia is hindered by the fact that direct evidence from this area is generally scarce and textual witnesses from its state administration, which presumably was bilingual Akkadian–Aramaic, are non-extant. Aramaic texts mainly appear as brief epigraphs written on cuneiform clay tablets.[5] Moreover, a small number of alphabetic texts were impressed into bricks by those working on royal buildings in Babylon.[6]

[3] Zadok 1977, 21–8; Coogan 1976, 4–5. For an overview of the basic grammatical system of Aramaic, see Gzella (2015, 23–37).

[4] Depending on a diachronic or synchronic linguistic perspective and the extent to which factors of geopolitical nature and/or typology of genre are taken into account (Folmer 2011a, 129–31).

[5] For an overview of tablets with Aramaic epigraphs, c. 300 in total, see Zadok (2003, 558–78) and Oelsner (2006, 27–71). The chronological distribution shows an increase of tablets with epigraphs in the Late Babylonian period (Zadok 2003, 570).

[6] Contrary to Aramaic epigraphs on clay tablets, the impressions on bricks merely consist of names. Most of these are Akkadian, while 30 per cent qualify as Aramaic. Examples of the latter are: *bytʾldlny*, Bīt-il-dilinī 'Bīt-il, save me'; *zbdy*, Zabdī which is a hypocoristic form of 'DN has given'; *nbwntn*, Nabû-natan 'Nabû has given'; and *nbwʿzry*, Nabû-ezrī 'Nabû is my help' (Sass, Marzahn, and Ze'evi 2010, 173–7).

Chronologically, the major part of the Aramaic onomasticon appears in cuneiform texts dating to the latter half of the fifth century – a period in which the use of Aramaic as chancellery language of the Achaemenid Empire seems to have been established in all parts of its vast territory. Achaemenid Imperial Aramaic is attested in a large variety of literary genres across socio-economic domains and is written in alphabetic script on various media, such as papyri, ostraca, funerary stones, and coins.[7] Overall, the orthography of this language variety is marked by consistency (especially in administrative letters), its syntax displays influences from Persian and Akkadian, and its lexicon contains an abundance of loanwords from various languages.[8]

Aramaic Names in Babylonian Sources

Aramaic names can be found in cuneiform economic documents from all over Babylonia, but they appear most frequently in texts from the villages Yāhūdu, Našar, and Bīt-Abī-râm, dating to the sixth and early fifth centuries,[9] and in the extensive Murašû archive originating from the southern town of Nippur and its surroundings, which covers the second half of the fifth century.[10] By contrast, the proportion of West Semitic names in city-based cuneiform archives is relatively marginal: about 2 per cent of the c. 50,000 individuals appearing in this text corpus bear an Aramaic name if the Murašû documentation is disregarded; this amounts to 2.5 per cent if the latter archive is included.[11] The proportion of Aramaic names in the Murašû archive is ten times higher than the norm (see Figure 8.2).[12]

One of the reasons behind the marked difference in the proportion of non-Babylonian names between the rural archives and the Babylonian

[7] Gzella 2015, 165–8; Folmer 2011b, 588–90. [8] Folmer 2011b, 593–6.

[9] The text editions published by Laurie E. Pearce and Cornelia Wunsch (2014) in CUSAS 28 are preceded by an analysis of the names that includes data found in the forthcoming second volume. The latter texts mostly originate from the settlement of Bīt-Abī-râm.

[10] The 700+ Murašû documents are published in different text editions (BE 8/1, 9, and 10; PBS 2/1; IMT; EE) and various articles. As these texts have served as the leading corpus in Ran Zadok's investigation into West Semitic names, this chapter draws heavily on his onomastic authority.

[11] The documentation from Yāhūdu, Našar, and environs (CUSAS 28) has not been included in this count either (Zadok 2003, 489).

[12] In the Murašû corpus 2,180 individuals are attested. They are considered as bearers of a West Semitic name if their given name and/or their patronym qualifies thus. The category labelled 'ambiguous' contains names that may be Akkadian or Aramaic. The category labelled 'various' includes Iranian (2%), Arabian (1–2%), Phoenician (0.1%), Egyptian, Lydian, Cimmerian, and other names (Zadok 1977, 24).

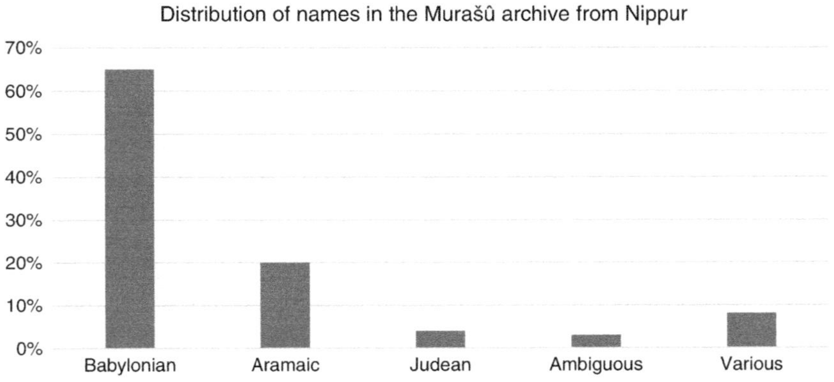

Figure 8.2 Distribution of names in the Murašû archive from Nippur.

sources in general is the fact that the former are characterised by less formative influence – and thus representation – of Babylonian elites, who formed a relatively homogenous social group. They lived in the city; were directly or indirectly connected to its institutions, most notably the temples; and virtually always bore Babylonian personal names, patronyms, and family names (see Chapter 1).[13] Unsurprisingly, they appear as protagonists in the urban documentation, while individuals with non-Babylonian names tend to have the passive role of witnesses.[14]

Onomastic diversity thus correlates with a decidedly rural setting. This is underlined by the fact that Murašû documents not written up in Nippur, but in settlements located in its vicinity, display larger proportions of both parties and witnesses with non-Babylonian names.[15] Likewise, texts from the rural settlements of Yāhūdu, Našar, and Bīt-Abī-râm contain a substantive amount of West Semitic names. Indeed, the multilingual situation in Babylonia's south-central (or possibly south-eastern) region, whence these two cuneiform corpora originate,[16] already stood out during

[13] Nielsen 2011; Still 2019; Zadok 2003, 481–4. Contrary to the widespread use of family names among elites from other Babylonian cities, Nippureans hardly adhered to this practice. According to John P. Nielsen (2011, 163–72) this is one of the manifestations of antagonism between Nippur and the cities to its north, which resulted from various historical incidents.

[14] Out of 2 per cent of individuals with non-Babylonian names, only 0.8 per cent appear as protagonists (Zadok 2003, 552).

[15] Sonnevelt 2021.

[16] There are various indications suggesting that the settlements of Yāḫūdū, Našar, and other places attested in this corpus were located in Babylonia's south (like Nippur) or south-east (Waerzeggers 2015, 181).

earlier centuries. Letters in the archive of Nippur's 'governor' written between c. 755 and 732 BCE attest to the connections between powerful leaders of Aramaean tribes and feature many Aramaic-named individuals, as well as Aramaisms.[17] Moreover, a letter dated to king Assurbanipal's reign (seventh century BCE) mentions speakers of multiple different languages living in the Nippur area (roughly indicated by the brackets in Figure 8.3).[18]

Various forms of migration contributed to the multi-ethnic character of the population in this region. First, non-Babylonian sections – among which were Aramaean groups – migrated into the territory east of the Tigris (the area indicated by the arrows in Figure 8.3).[19] Second, the diverse populace was a result of forced migration. For instance, the Babylonian

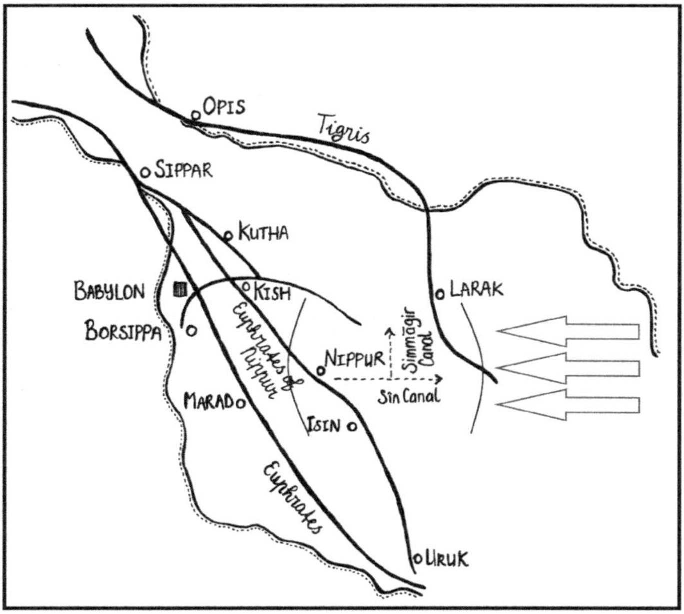

Figure 8.3 Nippur and its hinterland (drawn by Rieneke Sonnevelt, adapted from Zadok 1978, 332).

17 Cole 1996 (OIP 114), 1–14.

18 King Assurbanipal reigned from 669 to 627 BCE. SAA 18 192: r. 6' mentions the speakers of 'the many tongues' (Zadok 1977, 1).

19 Beaulieu 2013, 45–7.

king Nabopolassar (626–605 BCE) took many prisoners of war – most of them Aramaeans – from settlements in upper Mesopotamia and the middle Euphrates region and relocated them to the Nippur area in 616 BCE. Not long before, Nippur itself had been an Assyrian town where a garrison was stationed; it was only besieged and conquered between 623 and 621 BCE. Campaigns led by subsequent kings, most notably Nebuchadnezzar II (604–562 BCE), resulted in deportations of communities from Syria and the Levant and their resettlement in the same region around Nippur.[20] The state provided the deportees with fields and in return levied taxes and/or rents and conscripted the landholders as troops. The process is documented in its early stages in the cuneiform texts from Yāhūdu and its environs. Also, the Murašû archive depicts individuals active in this so-called land-for-service system.[21] Due to these migratory flows, not only the onomasticon is diverse: many toponyms in this region are non-Akkadian or Akkadian – West Semitic hybrids as well. They may refer to Aramaean tribes, eponymous forefathers, or places of origins in Syria or the Levant.[22] Finally, Aramaic epigraphs are quite well-attested in these archives.

During the Achaemenid period, the southern region functioned as a passageway between the Persian heartland and the Empire's western provinces. Through the Kabaru Canal the Babylonian waterways were directly connected with Susa, the Persian capital in Elam. Except for thus being of geopolitical importance, this area hosted travellers from Babylonia and far beyond who began the last stage of their trip to the capital here, upon changing boats in the settlement of Bāb-Nār-Kabari.[23]

Spelling and Normalisation

The normalisation of West Semitic names written in Babylonian Akkadian, for which no academic standard has been formulated, is challenging. First, it is not always straightforward whether a name is Akkadian

[20] Alstola 2020; Zadok 1977, 9–14.

[21] For the advancement and (re)organisation of the land-for-service system in the Achaemenid period, as well as the role of the Murašûs and their agents in this sector, see Stolper (1985) and van Driel (1989).

[22] Toponyms are mostly non-Akkadian in the Nippur region during the Late Babylonian period: 25% Akkadian, 36% West Semitic, 17% Akkadian – West Semitic hybrid, 5% ambiguous, 17% other (Zadok 1978; Lämmerhirt 2014, 116–17). A toponym referring to place of origin in Syria is Ḫamat; examples of Levantine twin towns are Ashkelon, Gaza, and Qadesh (Pearce 2014, 13, n. 27; Waerzeggers 2015, 190).

[23] The journey from Babylonia to Susa seems to have followed a fixed itinerary (Waerzeggers 2010, 790, 796).

or Aramaic; for instance, ^{I}*ba-ni-a* can be read as Akkadian Bānia and as West Semitic Banī, a hypocoristic form of the sentence name 'DN-established'. Second, there are many ways to approach the transcription of Aramaic names, based on the question of whether an attempt should be made to reconstruct the characteristics of an Aramaic name and, if so, to what extent. This could pertain to relatively straightforward issues, such as phonemes not represented in Akkadian (for instance, the gutturals) or those rendered differently (for instance, /w/ written /m/, as visible in the Judean theophoric element Yāma). However, it also relates to features such as vowel quality, vowel length, and stress, which are often not easy – or are downright impossible – to reconstruct due to incongruity of the writing systems and the inconsistency in which Aramaic names are converted into Akkadian.[24] Therefore, taking the Akkadian spelling as a point of departure and including only the most basic features rendered by it in a relatively consistent manner is my preferred modus operandi for transcription.

At the same time, some degree of harmonisation is necessary as, for instance, the spelling of the perfect in the Aramaic name DN-natan shows: ^{I}DN-*na-tan-nu*/-*ni*/-*na* (the final CV-sign merely indicates that the previous syllable is stressed). Abstraction on the basis of the Aramaic verbal form avoids a plethora of names that are in fact orthographic varieties. Moreover, although vowel length is not included in transcription when uncertain, a frequent and clear trend is taken into account: as the final long vowel of the perfect 3. sg. m. of verbs ending in ˀ/y/h is nearly always represented, the transcription of, for example, ^{I}DN-*ba-na-*ˀ is DN-banā. These examples demonstrate that there will always be a margin of error and that a hybrid transcription is inevitable – something that does not seem unfitting in view of the sources.[25]

Typology of Aramaic Names

The Theophoric Element

Besides the general theophoric element, this section deals with specific Aramaean deities. When these occur with Akkadian complements, the names are viewed as hybrids; in order to qualify as an Aramaic name, the linguistic criterion is decisive.

24 Due to inconsistency, it is, for example, impossible to be certain about vowel length and distinguish between *qatīl*, *qātil*, or *qatil* formations (see n. 61).

25 For a more detailed proposal, please see 'The transcription of West Semitic names' found in the guide to the Prosobab database via 'Conventions used' under the heading 'Spelling of names'. Or access directly via https://prosobab.leidenuniv.nl/guide.php%23conventions.

ˀl and ˀlh

The most frequently attested theophoric element is *ˀl* (*ˀil*) 'god'. In cuneiform script, this element is written DINGIR, the logogram and determinative for the Babylonian word *ilu* 'god', which also has the phonetic value *an*.[26] It is broadly acknowledged that the (plural) logogram DINGIR.MEŠ is employed for the same purpose in the Late Babylonian period.[27] In other words, a name like Barik-il 'God's blessed one' can be rendered ^{I}*ba-ri(k)-ki*-DINGIR as well as ^{I}*ba-ri(k)-ki*-DINGIR.MEŠ. Similarly, Raḫim-il 'God's loved one' is spelled both ^{I}*ra-ḫi-im*-DINGIR and ^{I}*ra-ḫi-im*-DINGIR.MEŠ. The same orthographic variation applies to the element *ˀl* in the name of the deity Bīt-il: for example, Bīt-il-ḫanna 'Bīt-il is gracious' (^{I}É-DINGIR-*ḫa-an-na*) and Bīt-il-adar 'Bīt-il has helped' (^{I}É-DINGIR.MEŠ-*a-dar-ri*).[28]

The element *ˀlh* (*ˀilah*) is less frequently attested. Examples are Abī-ilah and Ilah-abī 'God is my father' (^{I}AD-*ìl-a* and ^{I}*ìl-a*-AD).[29] It tends to appear as final component, followed by possessive suffix 1.sg. *-ī*, for example, in the names Mannu-kî-ilaḫī 'Who is like my god?' (^{I}*man-nu-ki-i-i-la-ḫi-ˀ*) and Abī-ilaḫī 'My father is my god' (^{I}AD-*la-ḫi-ˀ*; ^{I}AD-*i-la-ḫi-ˀ*).[30]

Aramaean Deities

A common theophoric element in Aramaic names is Addu or Adad, the storm god, written ^{d}*ad-du* and ^{d}IŠKUR respectively:[31] Addu-rapā 'Addu has healed' (^{Id}*ad-du-ra-pa-ˀ*), Adad-natan 'Adad has given' (^{Id}IŠKUR-*na-tan-nu*). Despite being a Mesopotamian god, the epicentre of Adad's veneration remained northern Syria. Here, he took the primary place among the Aramaean deities. The fact that Adad has a strong familial

26 In most instances, the sign is to be read DINGIR. This is clear when (a) the name of the same person is written in both ways (e.g., ^{I}*a-zi*-DINGIR and ^{I}*a-zi-lu*); (b) the non-theophoric element is a verb (e.g., ^{I}*ia-da-ˀ*-DINGIR); (c) the syllable before the sign ends in a vowel other than -a (e.g., ^{I}*su-mu*-DINGIR instead of non-existent ^{I}*su-mu-an*). Only a few names remain ambiguous: ^{I}*ra-ma*-DINGIR/*an*; ^{I}*sa-ra*-DINGIR/*an*; ^{I}*šá-lam*-DINGIR/*an*. The element *ˀl* can be rendered phonetically as *il-*; *-i-lu*; *-i-li*; *-il-lu*; -C*i-lu*; *-i-il* (Zadok 1977, 28–9).

27 In the Murašû corpus, more than 90% of the *ˀl*-names are written DINGIR.MEŠ (Clay 1908, 319–20; Coogan 1976, 43–4; Zadok 1977, 31–3; Streck 2017, 192).

28 In the same vein, *ˀl* appearing in Aramaic epigraphs corresponds to both DINGIR and DINGIR.MEŠ; for example, *bytˀlḥsny* = ^{Id}É-DINGIR-*ḫi-is-ni-ˀ* (CUSAS 28 53), Bīt-il-ḫisnī 'Bīt-il is my strength', and *hzhˀl* = ^{I}*ḫa-za-ˀ*-DINGIR.MEŠ (PBS 2/1 145), Ḫazā-il 'God has seen'.

29 Cole 1996 (OIP 114) 100:17 and 80:6, respectively (see comments on the latter for more examples, p. 171f).

30 The Akkadian equivalent is Abī-ilāya, written ^{I}AD-*i-la-a-a* or ^{I}AD-DINGIR-*a-a*.

31 Zadok 1977, 45–8; Coogan 1976, 43.

association with the deities Apladda and Būr is visible in father – son pairings Būr-Adad or Adad-Būr in the corpus from Yāhūdu, Našar, and surrounding settlements.[32] Adgi, a West Semitic form of Adad, is attested with an Aramaic predicate in the Murašû archive.[33]

Tammeš, whose Akkadian equivalent is Šamaš, is attested with a wide variety of Aramaic complements, especially in Nippur, one of which is Zaraḫ-Tammeš 'Tammeš has shone' (^{I}*za-ra-aḫ-*^{d}*tam-meš*). Although various phonetic cuneiform spellings are employed to render the initial West Semitic consonant /s/, ^{d}*tam-meš* is the most current orthography in Neo- and Late Babylonian sources.[34]

The name of the moon god Iltehr (based on *ʾil* and **sahr*) is akin to Akkadian Sîn. This is visible in tablets from the village of Neirab, a settlement of deportees originating from the like-named 'centre of the moon' cult in Syria.[35] In those tablets, we find the name of the same person Iltehr-idrī 'Iltehr is my help' spelled both ^{Id}*še-e-ri-id-ri-ʾ* and ^{Id}30*-er-id-ri-ʾ*. However, typically Iltehr is written ^{d}*il-te-(eḫ-)ri* in cuneiform texts.[36]

Another Aramaean deity from the heavenly realm is ʿAttar (*ʿttr*), with cognates in a range of Semitic languages. In Akkadian this is Ištar, which has the variant form Iltar:[37] Attar-ramât 'Attar is exalted' (^{Id}*at-tar-ra-mat*), Iltar-gadā 'Iltar is a fortune' (^{I}*ìl-ta-ri-ga-da-ʾ*). The Neo-Assyrian sources show that the consonantal cluster *-lt-* often shifted to *-ss-*, which was pronounced *-šš-*. Although these examples show that this shift did not carry through consistently in Babylonia, it may be visible in the name Iššar-tarībi 'Iššar replaced'.[38]

Amurru is a popular theophoric element in Aramaic names from the sixth and fifth centuries, although the deity had a low status in the Mesopotamian pantheon. From the late third until the middle of

[32] They mostly co-occur with Akkadian complements (Zadok 1977, 26, 62; Pearce and Wunsch 2014, 13).

[33] Zadok 1977, 48.

[34] Less frequently, it is spelled ^{d}*il-ta(m)-meš*. ^{d}UTU.MEŠ followed by an Aramaic component may also render Tammeš. Occasionally ^{d}UTU fulfils this function. See Zadok (1977, 39–42).

[35] See Tolini 2015 on the Neirab tablets. [36] Zadok 1977, 42; Coogan 1976, 47.

[37] See also Chapter 7 on Iššar. The gender of this deity varied according to time and location. Predicates in Assyrian sources are generally masculine; Attar-ramat has a feminine component. The latter is more in line with the overall pattern that Ištar or *ʿttr* broadly functioned as the appellative 'goddess' in the Ancient Near East. It may be due to this situation that Akkadian names with the feminine theophoric element *iltu* are rather scarce (Zadok 1977, 34–8).

[38] There is a case in which the same person is referred to as ^{Id}*iš-šar-ta-ri-bi* and ^{Id}*iš-tar-ta-ri-bi*, which poses the question of whether -ss- pronounced -šš- is based on -lt-, or whether it is a variant of -št-. According to Zadok (1977, 36), ^{d}*iš-tar* may be a purely graphic representation, which is in line with the way the above-mentioned name is alphabetically written on BM 101523 from Sippar: *ʾšrtrby*.

the second millennium it was used as a device by Sumerians and Babylonians to identify Amorites whose distinct linguistic and cultural presence was becoming more prominent. As the Amorites started to assimilate, the need of othering disappeared and groups of West Semitic origins adopted Amurru in name-giving practice as a way to self-identify.[39] Amurru being the most frequent West Semitic theophoric element in the onomasticon from Našar and neighbouring villages is a manifestation of this trend.[40] Also attested in these villages is the deity Bīt-il, who was venerated in an area close to Judah and whose name-bearers may have been deported simultaneously.[41]

Other West Semitic deities that appear with Aramaic complements are Našuh or Nusku (for instance, in the Neirab documentation),[42] Qōs,[43] Rammān,[44] and Šēʾ.[45] Šamê, 'Heaven', also appears with various Aramaic complements.[46] Attestations of the Aramaean deity ʿAttā are scarce and ambiguous. It may be linked to ʿAnat in a similar way as Nabê is connected with Nabû and Sē with Sîn.[47]

Verbal Sentence Names

Most frequent is the sentence name that has a perfect verbal form, also referred to as the suffix conjugation, as its predicate. The subject, which is a theophoric element, often appears as initial component. Generally, the verbal forms are in the G-stem. Some examples are Nabû-zabad 'Nabû has given' (^Id^AG-*za-bad-du*), Sîn-banā 'Sîn has established' (^Id^30-*ba-na-ʾ*), Aqab-il 'God has protected' (^I^*a-qab-bi*-DINGIR.MEŠ), and Yadā-il 'God has known' (^I^*ia-da-ʾ-il*).[48]

Names in which a deity is addressed by means of a perfect 2. sg. m. (indicated by the suffix *-tā*) are specific for the Late Babylonian period. They are followed by the object suffix 1.sg. (*-nī*): Dalatānī 'You

39 Beaulieu 2005, 41–5.

40 Interestingly, Amurru is not attested in Yāhūdu. Amurru mostly co-occurs with logographically written Akkadian complements, less often with Aramaic ones (Pearce and Wunsch 2014, 12–3; Zadok 1977, 76). From the fifth century onward, the deity appears with some Arabian complements (Zadok 1977, 26–7).

41 Pearce and Wunsch 2014, 13; Alstola 2020, 270.

42 Zadok 1977, 26.

43 Pearce and Wunsch 2014, 148 (no. 30); Zadok 2014, 121.

44 Zadok 1977, 49–50.

45 Zadok 1977, 43–4.

46 Zadok 1977, 39–40.

47 Zadok 1977, 32–8. Less well-attested deities are: ʿAl (e.g., in ^I^*ḫa-lu-ú-mi-il-ki*); Gad (e.g., in ^I^*ga-di-i* and ^I^AD-*gi-e-du*); GVs/š (e.g., in ^I^*gu-še-ia* and ^I^*gu-sa-a-a*); Kuna (e.g., in ^I^*ku-na-ra-pi-e*); and Mār (e.g., in ^I^*ma-ri-la-rim*). See Zadok (1977, 58–67).

48 Zadok 1977, 79–89; Coogan 1976, 107–8; Cole 1996 (OIP 114) 3, 6, 10, 59.

have saved me' (^{I}*da-la-ta-ni-*ʾ), Ḫannatānī 'You have favoured me' (^{I}*ḫa-an-na-ta-ni-*ʾ).

Other predicates have the form of an imperfect, which is also referred to as the prefix conjugation:[49] Addu-yatin 'May Adad give' (^{Id}*ad-du-ia-at-tin*), Idā-Nabû 'May Nabû know' (^{I}*id-da-ḫu-*^{d}AG), Aḫu-lakun 'May the brother be firm' (^{I}ŠEŠ-*la-kun*), Tammeš-linṭar 'May Tammeš guard' (^{Id}*tam-meš-li-in-ṭár*).[50]

Finally, verbal sentence names can contain an imperative: Adad-šikinī 'Adad, watch over me!' (^{Id}IŠKUR-*ši-ki-in-ni-*ʾ), Nabû-dilinī 'Nabû, save me!' (^{Id}AG-*di-li-in-ni-*ʾ).

Sentence names that consist of three elements sporadically occur. They are influenced by Akkadian fashion and even may incorporate an Akkadian element. An example hereof is the first element of the following name, which contains an Aramaic predicate with a G-stem imperfect 2.sg. m.:[51] Ša-Nabû-taqum '(By help?) of Nabû you will rise' (^{I}*šá-*^{d}AG-*ta-qu-um-mu*).

Nominal Sentence Names

In nominal sentence names the subject generally takes the initial position. The object is often followed by the possessive suffix 1.sg. *-ī*; sometimes 2.sg. *-ka*:[52] Abu-lētī 'The father is my strength' (^{I}AD-*li-ti-*ʾ), Abī-ilaḫī 'My father is my god' (^{I}AD-*i-la-ḫi-*ʾ),[53] Tammeš-ilka 'Tammeš is your god' (^{Id}*tam-meš-ìl-ka*), Nanāya-dūrī 'Nanāya is my bulwark' (^{Id}*na-na-a-du-ri-*ʾ),[54] Iltehr-naqī 'Iltehr is pure' (^{Id}*il-te-eḫ-ri-na-aq-qí-*ʾ), and Nusku-rapē 'Nusku is a healer' (^{Id}PA.KU-*ra-pi-e*).

Sentence names that form a question are of nominal nature as well. They either start out with the interrogative pronoun *ʿayya* 'where?' or with *man*

[49] *laqtul* functioned as a precative (wish-form) before it started to be used as imperfect (Zadok 1977, 91–6).

[50] The vowel of the prefix shifts to /i/ when the theme vowel of the verb is /a/, as formulated in the Barth – Ginsberg Law and visible in Idā-DN. Probably of similar nature is the shift from *laqtal* to *liqtal* attested in DN-linṭar (Zadok 1977, 94–5). The *laqtul*-formation, which is most often employed for the imperfect, developed into the common form of the imperfect in later stages of the Aramaic language in the region (Zadok 1977, 178).

[51] Zadok 1977, 110–11. [52] Zadok 1977, 96–104; Coogan 1976, 113–14.

[53] Other common Aramaic kinship terms are *ʾaḫ* 'brother', *ʿamm* 'paternal uncle', *ḫāl* 'maternal uncle', *dād* 'uncle' or 'favourite' (Zadok 1977, 51–8).

[54] Note that names of this type – consisting of a deity's name and a substantive – are hardly attested before the first millennium BCE; during the first millennium, it is typical for Aramaic names (Zadok 1977, 101).

'who?'[55]: Aya-abū 'Where is his father?' (^{I}*a-a-bu-ú*), Mannu-kî-ḫāl 'Who is like the maternal uncle?' (^{I}*man-nu-ki-i-ḫa-la*).

Compound Names

This type of name consists of two nominal components in a genitive construction. Nominal components can be regular nouns, kinship terms, deities, or passive participles:[56] Abdi-Iššar 'Servant of Iššar' (^{I}*ab-du-*^{d}*iš-šar*), Aḫi-abū 'His father's brother' (^{I}ŠEŠ-*a-bu-ú*), and Barik-Bēl 'Bēl's blessed one' (^{I}*ba-ri-ki-*^{d}EN).

Hypocoristica

The hypocoristic suffix *-ā*, written *-ʾ* or *-h* in Aramaic and -*Ca-a*/*ʾ* in Akkadian, is added to most nominal sentence names and compound names. It may be like the Aramaic definite article that is of similar form and is suffixed to nouns as well. Hypocoristic *-ā* became so popular during the first millennium BCE that it replaced other hypocoristic suffixes common during the previous millennium. Moreover, it started to be attached to Arabian and Akkadian names as well.[57] Aramaic examples – with a translation of their nominal bases – are: Abdā 'Servant' (^{I}*ab-da-ʾ*), ^{f}Bissā 'Cat' (^{f}*bi-is-sa-a*), Ḫarimā 'Consecrated' (^{I}*ḫa-ri-im-ma-ʾ*), Zabudā 'Given' (^{I}*za-bu-da-a*), and Iltar-gadā (Iltar + fortune; ^{I}*il-tar-ga-da-ʾ*).

Hypocoristic names with suffix *-ī* tend to be Aramaic. It may be based on the gentilic or suffix 1.sg. and is written *-y* in Aramaic, which is rendered -*Ci-i*/*ia*/*iá* or -*Ci*(-*ʾ*) in Akkadian:[58] Abnī 'Stone' (^{I}*ab-ni-i*), Namarī 'Leopard' (^{I}*na-ma-ri-ʾ*), Raḫimī 'Beloved' (^{I}*ra-ḫi-mì-i*), and Barikī 'Blessed' (^{I}*ba-ri-ki-ia*). Its phonological variant is *-ē*.

One of the hypocoristic suffixes partly replaced by *-ā* is *-ān*, written -*Ca-an*(-*nu*/*ni*), -*Ca-*(*a-*)*nu*/*ni*:[59] Nabān 'Nabû' (^{I}*na-ba-an-nu*), Binān 'Son' (^{I}*bi-na-nu*).

A great deal of variety is achieved by adding combinations of two of these suffixes to nominal formations.[60]

55 Zadok 1977, 104–5; Coogan 1976, 76. 56 Zadok 1977, 105–10.

57 Hypocoristic suffixes current before the first millennium BCE were *-ay(ya)*, *-at*, and *-ān* (Zadok 1977, 148–53).

58 For example, the same individual from Nippur is referred to as ^{I}*zab-di-e* and ^{I}*zab-di-ia* (Zadok 1977, 153–6).

59 Sometimes suffix -ān may be adjectival: ^{I}*ḫa-ra-an-na*, derived from *ḥwr* 'to be white', probably means 'the white one' (Zadok 1977, 157–62).

60 Combinations are also made with other suffixes, like -t, -at, -īt, etc. (Zadok 1977, 163–70).

One-Word Names

Nearly all names that consist of one word are affixed with a hypocoristic marker. Exceptions are attested in various formations, which often are hard to distinguish due to inconsistent Babylonian spelling.[61]

Naming Practices

As regards naming practice, it is striking that Babylonian theophoric elements appearing in the Aramaic onomasticon are not the ones prominent in contemporaneous Babylonian names. For instance, hardly any Aramaic names in the Murašû documentation contain the theophoric element Enlil, while this Babylonian deity enjoyed immense popularity in the Nippur area at the time.[62] This also is the case for Enlil's son Ninurta (attested only once) and for Marduk, Nergal, and Sîn. Babylonian gods that are found in greater numbers in Aramaic names are Nabû, who takes second position after Tammeš in Nippur's Aramaic onomasticon, as well as Bēl and Nanāya. Interestingly, Nabû primarily appears in patronyms, which indicates a decline of his prevalence.[63]

In feminine names, a tendency of different order stands out. Although suffixes *-t*, *-at*, *-īt*, and *-ī/ē* are attested, there seems to have been a strong preference for feminine names ending in *-ā*:[64] ᶠBarukā 'Blessed' (*ᶠba-ru-ka-ʾ*), ᶠGubbā 'Cistern' (*ᶠgu-ub-ba-a*), ᶠḪannā 'Gracious' (*ᶠḫa-an-na-a*), ᶠNasikat 'Chieftess' (*ᶠna-si-ka-tu$_4$*), ᶠDidīt 'Favourite' (*ᶠdi-di-ti*), and ᶠḪinnī 'Gracious' (*ᶠḫi-in-ni-ia*).

Tools for Identifying Aramaic Names in Cuneiform Sources

Various Aramaic verbs have surfaced in the examples. A more extensive – although not exhaustive – overview of verbs commonly attested in Aramaic names is presented in Table 8.1.

Nouns that regularly appear in nominal sentence names are presented in Table 8.2.[65]

61 For example, *qatīl*, *qātil*, and *qatil* are hard to distinguish; the same holds for *qatūl* and *qattūl*. For all possible formations, see Zadok (1977, 111–48).

62 The handful of examples known mostly contain very common verbal elements, such as *barik* and *yahab* (Zadok 1977, 72).

63 The same pattern is visible in the documentation from other Babylonian cities: Šamaš, who was very popular in Sippar, hardly appears in West Semitic names found in documents from this city (Zadok 1977, 69–76, 175–7).

64 Zadok 1977, 170–2.

65 *ʿidr, *simk, *ḥinn/ḥann, *šūr, and *gad are frequently attested in hypocoristica (Zadok 1977, 101).

Table 8.1 *Verbs attested in Aramaic sentence names from the Neo- and Late Babylonian periods*

Regular verbs	Irregular verbs	
brk – to bless	*ˀmr* – to say	*ngh* – to shine
gbr – to be strong	*ˀty* – to come	*nṭr* – to guard
zbd – to give, grant	*bny* – to build, create	*nsˀ* – to raise
zbn – to redeem	*brˀ* – to create	*nṣb* – to place
zrḥ – to shine	*gˀy* – to be exalted	*ntn* – to give
sgb – to be exalted	*gbh* – to be exalted	*ˁny* – to answer
smk – *to* support, sustain	*ḥwr* – to see	*pdy* – to ransom, redeem
srḥ – to be known	*ḥzy* – to see	*ṣwḥ* – to shout
ˁdr – to help, support	*ḥnn* – to be gracious, favour	*qwm* – to rise
ˁqb – to protect	*ḥsy* – to seek refuge	*qny* – to get, create, build
rḥm – to love, have mercy	*ybb* – to weep	*rwm* – to be high
rkš – to bind, harness, tie up	*ydˁ* – to know	*rˁy* – to be pleased, content
šlḥ – to send	*yhb* – to give	*rpˀ* – to heal
šlm – to be well	*ypˁ* – to be brilliant	*šly* – to be tranquil
šmˁ – to hear	*yqr* – to be esteemed	*šˀl* – to ask
tmk – to support	*mny* – to count	*šry* – to release

Table 8.2 *Nouns attested in Aramaic nominal sentence names from the Neo- and Late Babylonian periods*

*ˀayal	help	*ˀyl*
*gad	fortune	*gd*
*dūr	wall/bulwark	*dwr*
*hayl	strength, wealth	*ḥyl*
*ḥinn/ḥann	favour, grace	*ḥnn*
*layt	strength	*lˁy*
*simk	support	*smk*
*ˁidr	help	*ˁdr*
*šūr	wall/bulwark	*šwr*
*tamk	support	*tmk*

Nouns that typically appear in compound names are given in Table 8.3.

The outline of elements of which Aramaic names may consist (presented in the section 'Typology of Aramaic Names') and these tables may give a taste of what such names could look like. If one suspects a name to be Aramaic, either the indices of Ran Zadok (1977, 339–81) may be checked, or

Table 8.3 *Nouns attested in Aramaic compound names from the Neo- and Late Babylonian periods*

*ˀab	father	*ˀb*
*ˀaḥ	brother	*ˀḥ*
*ˀamat	female servant	*ˀmt*
*bVr	son	*br*
*bitt	daughter	*brt*
*gē/īr	patron, client	*gr*
*naˁr	servant, young man	*nˁr*
*ˁabd	servant	*ˁbd*

Zadok 2014, which includes attestations from later publications as well (the latter in a searchable PDF). As names have not been transcribed, use the Akkadian spelling for a search.

Further Reading

As has become clear, Zadok (1977) remains the most extensive analysis of West Semitic personal names in sources from the Neo- and Late Babylonian periods. In Zadok (2014) individuals with mainly Aramaic names from the Murašû corpus are set within their socio-economic and geographic frameworks. West Semitic names attested in documents from Yāhūdu, Našar, and Bīt-Abī-râm, published by Laurie E. Pearce and Cornelia Wunsch (2014), are found in the analysis of the onomasticon (pp. 31–93); West Semitic deities are dealt with in the introduction (pp. 12–15). The presence of Aramaean and Chaldean groups in Babylonia is dealt with by Paul-Alain Beaulieu (2013); previous literature on the subject is found in n. 40 (p. 45). On the Aramaic onomasticon and Aramaean ethnic identity in Assyria, see Fales (1991, 1993, and 2018).

References

Alstola, T. 2020. *Judeans in Babylonia: A Study of Deportees in the Sixth and Fifth Centuries BCE*, Culture and History of the Ancient Near East 109. Leiden: Brill.

Beaulieu, P.-A. 2005. 'The god Amurru as emblem of ethnic and cultural identity' in W. H. van Soldt (ed.), *Ethnicity in Ancient Mesopotamia*. Leiden: NINO, pp. 31–46.

Beaulieu, P.-A. 2013. 'Arameans, Chaldeans, and Arabs in cuneiform sources from the Late Babylonian period' in A. Berlejung and M. P. Streck (eds.), *Arameans, Chaldeans, and Arabs in Babylonia and Palestine in the First Millennium BC*, Leipziger Altorientalische Studien 3. Wiesbaden: Harrassowitz, pp. 31–55.

Clay, A. T. 1908. 'Aramaic indorsements on the documents of the Murašû sons' in R. F. Harper, F. Brown, and G. F. Moore (eds.), *Old Testament and Semitic Studies in Memory of William Rainey Harper*. Chicago: University of Chicago Press, pp. 285–332.

Cole, S. W. 1996. *Nippur IV – The Neo-Babylonian Governor's Archive from Nippur*, Oriental Institute Publications 114. Chicago: The Oriental Institute of the University of Chicago.

Coogan, M. D. 1976. *West Semitic Personal Names in the Murašû Documents*. Missoula: Scholars Press for Harvard Semitic Museum.

van Driel, G. 1989. 'The Murašûs in context', *Journal of the Economic and Social History of the Orient* 32, 203–29.

Fales, F. M. 1991. 'West Semitic names in the Assyrian Empire: Diffusion and social relevance', *Studi Epigrafici e Linguistici sul Vicino Oriente Antico* 8, 99–117.

Fales, F. M. 1993. 'West Semitic Names in the Šēḫ Ḥamad Texts', *State Archives of Assyria Bulletin* VII/2, 139–50.

Fales, F. M. 2018. 'The composition and structure of the Neo-Assyrian Empire: Ethnicity, language and identities' in R. Rollinger (ed.), *Conceptualizing Past, Present and Future*, Melammu Symposia 9. Münster: Ugarit-Verlag, pp. 443–94.

Folmer, M. L. 2011a. 'Old and imperial Aramaic' in H. Gzella (ed.), *Languages from the World of the Bible*. Berlin: De Gruyter, pp. 128–59.

Folmer, M. L. 2011b. 'Imperial Aramaic as an administrative language of the Achaemenid period' in S. Weninger, G. Khan, M. P. Streck, and J. C. E. Watson (eds.), *The Semitic Languages: An International Handbook*, Handbücher zur Sprach- und Kommunikationswissenschaft 36. Berlin: De Gruyter Mouton, pp. 587–98.

Gzella, H. 2011. 'Northwest Semitic in general' in S. Weninger, G. Khan, M. P. Streck, and J. C. E. Watson (eds.), *The Semitic Languages: An International Handbook*, Handbücher zur Sprach- und Kommunikationswissenschaft 36. Berlin: De Gruyter Mouton, pp. 425–51.

Gzella, H. 2015. *A Cultural History of Aramaic: From the Beginnings to the Advent of Islam*. Leiden: Brill.

Huehnergard, J. and A. D. Rubin 2011. 'Phyla and waves: Models of classification of the Semitic languages' in S. Weninger, G. Khan, M. P. Streck, and J. C. E. Watson (eds.), *The Semitic Languages: An International Handbook*, Handbücher zur Sprach- und Kommunikationswissenschaft 36. Berlin: De Gruyter Mouton, pp. 259–78.

Jursa, M. with contributions by J. Hackl, B. Janković, K. Kleber, et al. 2010. *Aspects of the Economic History of Babylonia in the First Millennium BC: Economic Geography, Economic Mentalities, Agriculture, the Use of Money and the Problem of Economic Growth*, Alter Orient und Altes Testament 377. Münster: Ugarit-Verlag.

Lämmerhirt, K. 2014. 'Die Bevölkerung der Region Nippur in neu- und spätbabylonischer Zeit' in M. Krebernik and H. Neumann (eds.), *Babylonien und seine Nachbarn in neu- und spätbabylonischer Zeit*, Alter Orient und Altes Testament 369. Münster: Ugarit-Verlag, pp. 113–33.

Nielsen, J. P. 2011. *Sons and Descendants: A Social History of Kin Groups and Family Names in the Early Neo-Babylonian Period, 747–626 BC*, Culture and History of the Ancient Near East 43. Leiden: Brill.

Oelsner J. 2006. 'Aramäische Beischriften auf neu- und spätbabylonischen Tontafeln', *Welt des Orients* 36, 27–71.

Pearce, L. E. 2014. 'Identifying Judeans and Judean identity in the Babylonian evidence' in. J. Stökl and C. Waerzeggers (eds.), *Exile and Return: The Babylonian Context*, Beihefte zur Zeitschrift für die alttestamentliche Wissenschaft 478. Berlin: De Gruyter, pp. 7–32.

Pearce, L. E. and C. Wunsch 2014. *Documents of Judean Exiles and West Semites in Babylonia in the Collection of David Sofer*, Cornell University Studies in Assyriology and Sumerology 28. Bethesda: CDL Press.

Sass, B., J. Marzahn, and N. Ze'evi 2010. *Aramaic and Figural Stamp Impressions on Bricks of the Sixth Century BC from Babylon*. Wiesbaden: Harrassowitz.

Sonnevelt, R. 2021. 'Ribāt's dossier from Nippur – a diplomatic study of Aramaic epigraphs on cuneiform clay tablets', *Archiv für Orientforschung* 54, 126–38.

Still, B. 2019. *The Social World of the Babylonian Priest*, Culture and History of the Ancient Near East 103. Leiden: Brill.

Stolper, M. W. 1985. *Entrepreneurs and Empire: The Murašû Archive, the Murašû Firm, and Persian Rule in Babylonia*. Istanbul: Nederlands Historisch-Archaeologisch Instituut.

Streck, M. P. 2017. 'Late Babylonian in Aramaic epigraphs on cuneiform tablets' in A. Berlejung, A. M. Maier, and A. Schüle (eds.), *Wandering Aramaeans: Aramaeans Outside Syria – Textual and Archaeological Perspectives*, Leipziger Altorientalische Studien 5. Wiesbaden: Harrassowitz, pp. 169–94.

Tolini, G. 2015. 'From Syria to Babylon and back: The Neirab archive' in J. Stökl and C. Waerzeggers (eds.), *Exile and Return: The Babylonian Context*, Beihefte zur Zeitschrift für die alttestamentliche Wissenschaft 478. Berlin: De Gruyter, pp. 58–93.

Waerzeggers, C. 2010. 'Babylonians in Susa: The travels of Babylonian businessmen to Susa reconsidered' in B. Jacobs and R. Rollinger (eds.), *Der Achämenidenhof. The Achaemenid Court*, Classica et Orientalia 2. Wiesbaden: Harrassowitz, pp. 777–813.

Waerzeggers, C. 2015. 'Review of L. E. Pearce and C. Wunsch 2014. *Documents of Judean Exiles and West Semites in Babylonia in the Collection of David Sofer*', *STRATA. Bulletin of the Anglo-Israel Archaeological Society* 33, 179–94.

Zadok, R. 1977. *On West Semites in Babylonia During Chaldean and Achaemenian Periods: An Onomastic Study*. Jerusalem: Wanaarta.

Zadok, R. 1978. 'The Nippur region during the Late Assyrian, Chaldean and Achaemenian periods, chiefly according to written sources', *Israel Oriental Studies* 8, 226–332.

Zadok, R. 2003. 'The representation of foreigners in Neo- and Late Babylonian legal documents (eighth through second centuries BCE)' in O. Lipschits and J. Blenkinsopp (eds.), *Judah and the Judeans in the Neo-Babylonian Period*. Winona Lake: Eisenbrauns, pp. 471–589.

Zadok, R. 2014. 'West Semitic groups in the Nippur region between c. 750 and 330 BCE' in J. Stökl and C. Waerzeggers (eds.), *Exile and Return: The Babylonian Context*, Beihefte zur Zeitschrift für die alttestamentliche Wissenschaft 478. Berlin: De Gruyter, pp. 94–156.

CHAPTER 9

Hebrew Names

Kathleen Abraham

Introduction to the Language and Its Background

Historical and Ethno-Linguistic Background

Following Nabopolassar's and Nebuchadnezzar II's western campaigns, major Levantine cities – Jerusalem, Tyre, and Ashkelon, among others – surrendered to Babylonia's sovereignty. The Babylonian kings forcibly took rebellious local rulers and citizens in exile to Babylonia. As a result, a significant number of Hebrew and other (North)west Semitic anthroponyms and toponyms start to appear in the Babylonian records of the long sixth century, as well as a small number of Philistine names.

There is some evidence for the presence of a Judean person (or was he Israelite?) in Babylonia already in the late seventh century BCE, before Nebuchadnezzar II's deportations. The man's name is rendered ^{I}*gir-re -e-ma* in cuneiform, which Ran Zadok (1979, 8, 34) identifies as a Yahwistic name containing the West Semitic noun *gīr* and therefore meaning 'Client of Y', but Tero Alstola raises some problems with such an identification (2020, 230, n. 1164). There are no other attestations of Yahwistic names in Babylonian records from pre-exilic times.

Not all bearers of Yahwistic or Hebrew names in Babylonia necessarily arrived from Judah with Jehoiachin in 597 BCE or with the great deportations of 587 BCE. Some may have come from Israel, either directly in the late eighth century BCE, or via Assyria after the fall of the Neo-Assyrian Empire a century later. Indeed, in principle at least, it is possible that the Assyrians deported some people from the territory of the former kingdom of Israel to Babylonia (732–701 BCE). Moreover, there is indirect evidence that descendants of Israelite deportees, who had settled in Assyria (especially in the Lower Ḫabur area), migrated from there to Babylonia after the collapse of the Neo-Assyrian Empire. The above-mentioned Gīr-Yāma as well as the members of the family of Yašeʕ-Yāma (^{I}*ia-še-ʔ-ia*

-a-ma, Isaiah), who lived in Sippar (531/0 BCE), were probably such migrating Israelites (Zadok 2014, 110–11).

The Babylonian exile marks a watershed in the linguistic history of Hebrew. By the tenth century BCE, two Hebrew-speaking states flourished in the central hill country of Palestine: Israel to the north, in the Samarian hills and portions of central Transjordan and Galilee, and Judah to the south, in the Judean hills, with its capital at Jerusalem. Hebrew spoken in the north significantly differed from that in the south. The Israelites deported by the Assyrians spoke the former, whereas the Judeans deported by the Babylonians spoke the latter. The southern form of Hebrew constitutes the classical phase of the language and is primarily represented by Standard Biblical Hebrew and numerous inscriptions from Judah. In the Hebrew of post-exilic Judah (sixth–second centuries BCE), represented by later biblical literature, we find numerous linguistic features, prototypes of Rabbinic Hebrew, that are entirely absent from the earlier literature. Thus, beneath the surface of pre-Rabbinical Hebrew, for which the Bible is our major source, a remarkable plurality of linguistic traditions extends over some 800 years. It is important to bear this in mind when interpreting cuneiform Hebrew names in the light of Biblical Hebrew and onomastics.

Basic Characteristics of Hebrew Names

It may be argued that a name that is linguistically Hebrew or includes a Yahwistic theophoric element should be classified as a 'Hebrew name'. [1] The bulk of Hebrew names in the cuneiform corpus are Yahwistic names.

Applying the aforementioned definition of 'Hebrew' to the foreign onomasticon of Babylonia is easier said than done. If Hebrew names are *stricto sensu* names with nominal or verbal elements that reflect Hebrew grammar or lexicon, Hawšiʿ 'He saved' from Nippur would have a typical Hebrew name (//MT Hôšēaʿ הוֹשֵׁעַ). In view of the Hiphil-formation it is linguistically Hebrew rather than Aramaic, which has Aphel-formations (hence, *ʾwšʿ* and *ʾwšʿyh* at Elephantine). Moreover, 'the root Y-Š-ʿ is foreign to Aramaic' (Muraoka and Porten 1998, 20–1; cf. 113–16). However, the name could also be borne by any of the other Canaanite-speaking

[1] In this chapter, Y renders the Yahwistic element in English translations of Hebrew names. Readers less familiar with the linguistic terminology common in the study of Hebrew can take advantage of C. H. J. Van der Merwe et al., *A Biblical Hebrew Reference Grammar*. Sheffield: Sheffield Academic Press, 1999, 2017 (2nd ed.). Note that Cornelia Wunsch's new volume of texts mentioning Judeans in Babylonia (BaAr 6) could not be taken into consideration here as it appeared after this chapter was submitted.

population groups and is, for instance, attested among the Transjordan Ammonites (*hwšʿl*, Al-Qananweh 2004, 71). Consequently, the major problem that confronts anyone interested in detecting linguistically Hebrew names in the cuneiform corpus of first millennium BCE Babylonia is to distinguish them from Aramaic, Phoenician, and Transjordan equivalents.

Yahwistic names in Babylonian cuneiform sources (i.e., names with the theophoric element YHWH), are Hebrew in the theological sense of the word, 'seeing that no other ethnic group in pre-Hellenistic Mesopotamia worshiped Yhw' apart from those originating from Judah (Zadok 2014, 111–12).

Besides linguistically and theologically Hebrew names, Šabbātay and Ḥaggay can be classified as 'culturally' Hebrew. They refer to religious practices characteristic of the (Biblical) Judean community, such as the observance of Sabbath and religious feasts. The problem is that they were not exclusively borne by Judean exiles or their descendants in Babylonia, and Ḥaggay is also attested among, for instance, Ammonites and Phoenicians (Al-Qananweh 2004, 73–4; Alstola 2020, 56–7). Therefore, when the individuals bearing these names had blood relatives with Yahwistic names, their Judean background is probable and the name may be classified as '(culturally) Hebrew'. Otherwise, one has to investigate their circle of acquaintances as well as the archive and overall socio-economic context in which they appear for connections with Judah or Judeans before labelling their name 'Hebrew'.

Some non-Yahwistic anthroponyms in the cuneiform corpus have parallels in the Bible, but this does not guarantee that they are Hebrew *stricto sensu*. At the most, such a name hints at the bearer's Judean descent. Famous biblical figures such as Abraham, Jacob, Benjamin, Menahem, Ezra, and Menashe bore non-Yahwistic names that are, linguistically speaking, not just Hebrew but West Semitic in general. Often parallels exist already in Ugaritic, Amorite, and/or Canaanite-Amarna onomastics from the second millennium BCE. The names listed above, all attested in Babylonian sources from the first millennium BCE, are excluded from this chapter on linguistic grounds, even when advanced prosopographic research established a Judean background for the individuals behind them.

Overall, having a Yahwistic or linguistically Hebrew name or patronym in the Babylonia of the long sixth century BCE signifies Judean (exceptionally, Israelite) descent, but the reverse is not necessarily true. Ethnic Judeans in Babylonia gave their children not only Yahwistic/Hebrew names, but also West Semitic/Aramaic and even Babylonian/Akkadian and Iranian names.

Applied Writing Systems of Hebrew in Cuneiform

Sketch of the Problem

The complicated process of detecting and decoding foreign names in the Babylonian sources, and subsequently encoding them into English, can be illustrated by the name spelled ^{I}*a-mu-še-eḫ* in a tablet from the Murašû archive (EE 113). He is the father of Mattan-Yāma (^{I}*ma-tan-ia -a-ma*) 'Gift of Y' and, since the latter has a clear Hebrew–Yahwistic compound name, it is likely that we may find his name to be Hebrew as well. This assumption is further corroborated by the fact that he occurs in the company of other men with Yahwistic names, such as Yāḫû-zabad (^{Id}*ia-a-ḫu-u-za-bad-du*) 'Y has granted' and Yāḫû-laqīm (^{Id}*ia-a-ḫu-ú-la -qí-im*) 'Y shall raise' in an archive that is known for its many Yahwistic names.

In order to crack the cuneiform spelling ^{I}*a-mu-še-eḫ*, we have to consider certain features related to the cuneiform writing system. First, there is the Neo-/Late Babylonian convention to write *w* as *m*. Second, there is the established Babylonian practice to render the West Semitic consonants *h* and ʿ, for which the cuneiform syllabary did not have a specific sign, with *ḫ*-signs or leave them unmarked. Finally, there is the problem of rendering diphthongs in cuneiform script and the avoidance of final consonant clusters. Considering all these points, ^{I}*a-mu-še-eḫ* can be analysed as a cuneiform writing for the Hebrew name Hawšiʿ 'He saved'.

Converting this information in an acceptable English (Latin-script) form is a difficult balancing act, for which see section on 'Spelling and Normalisation'.

Cuneiform Orthographies of YHWH

The man who owed barley to the Babylonian Murašû family, according to a cuneiform tablet excavated at Nippur (EE 86), is called ^{Id}*ia-a-ḫu-u-na-tan-nu* (Yāḫû-natan) 'Y has given'. On the tablet's right edge his name recurs, but this time it is written in alphabetic script as *yhwntn*. Similarly, the debtor's name in CUSAS 28 10 from Yāhūdu is spelled ^{I}*šá-lam-mi -ía-a-ma* (Šalam-Yāma) 'Y completed/is well-being' in cuneiform and *šlmyh* in alphabetic script on the same tablet. These and other alphabetic spellings reveal that ^{d}*ia-a-ḫu-u-* and *-iá-a-ma* are cuneiform renderings of the Yahwistic theophoric element.

Actually, the divine name is spelled in numerous ways by the Babylonian scribes 'who probably wrote what they heard' (Millard 2013, 841) and were not restricted by orthographic traditions. It appears in different forms depending on whether it is the first or the last component of the anthroponym.[2] Alphabetic and cuneiform spellings do not necessarily correspond, and their relation to the actual pronunciation(s) of the divine name remains an open question.

The superscripted ^{d} preceding the Yahwistic element in some cases is a modern convention for transcribing the DINGIR sign which Babylonian scribes used to indicate that what follows is the name of a deity. When writing the names of their own gods, such as Marduk or Nabû, they rigorously included it, but for foreign gods they had a more compromising attitude. Therefore, when actually used, it highlights the scribe's awareness and recognition of the divine nature of YHWH. When absent, it may imply different things – such as, for instance, his ignorance, his denial, or his carelessness. Nebuchadnezzar's scribes at Babylon c. 591 BCE did not use the DINGIR sign, but their colleagues at Nippur and Yāhūdu at around the same time did (583 and 572 BCE).[3] It shows that the latter 'were aware of the divine nature of Yhw at the very beginning of their encounter with the exiles' (Zadok 2014, 111, n. 18). Whether this awareness grew or declined over time, and how far it was influenced by geographical and demographic factors, needs further study.

Characteristics and Limitations of the Cuneiform Writing System

Cuneiform scribes were not required to be consistent in spelling, and the cuneiform script allowed many variations. Despite that, orthographic conventions and historic spellings reduced the scribes' choices, in particular in writing anthroponyms. They used traditionally fixed logograms to write divine names and recurrent name elements. Predicates such as *iddin* 'he gave', *aplu* 'firstborn son', and *zēru* 'offspring' were more often spelled with logograms (respectively MU, A or IBILA, and NUMUN) than syllabically (i.e., in the way they were pronounced).

Logograms do not show in Hebrew names (and only rarely in West Semitic ones). A few exceptions confirm this rule. Some Babylonian scribes recognised Hebrew kinship terms leading to the use of ŠEŠ and AD for Hebrew *ʾaḫ* 'brother' and *ʾab* 'father' (EE 98:13; PBS 2/1 185:2). In addition, we have one instance each of the logogram DÙ for the Hebrew verb root B-N-Y 'to create' (CUSAS 28 37:12) and perhaps also of the logogram MU for Hebrew N-T-N 'to give' (Zadok 2014, 123).

[2] Details in Pearce and Wunsch (2014, 14–29), with literature.

[3] Zadok 2002, 27 no. 2 (but without ^{d}!), and nos. 3–8; Zadok 2014, 109–10, n. 4; CUSAS 28 1.

The cuneiform scribes' relative consistency when writing Babylonian names contrasts with the high orthographic variation of foreign names. To give an idea, Laurie E. Pearce and Cornelia Wunsch (2014, 27) count twelve different writings of the name Rapaˀ-Yāma 'Y healed' in the Yāhūdu corpus alone. Some are insignificant for linguistic analysis; for instance, the variation among homophonous signs (*ú*/*u*, *ia*/*ía*, etc.). In other cases, they may hint at contrasting linguistic relations: ^{I}*ba-ra-ku-ia-a-ma* 'Y has blessed' (Barak-Yāma; Hebrew G *qatal*-perf.) vs. ^{I}*ba-ri-ki-ia-a-ma* 'Blessed by Y' (Barīk-Yāma; Aramaic passive participle); ^{I}*šá-lam-ia-a-ma* 'Y is well-being' (Šalam-Yāma; Hebrew G *qatal*-perf.) vs. ^{I}*šá-lim-ma-a-ma* 'Kept well by Y' (Šalīm-Yāma; Aramaic passive participle) vs. ^{I}*ši-li-im-iá-a-ma* 'Y made recompense' (Šillim-Yāma; Hebrew D *qittil*-perf.).

Related to the matter under consideration is the degree of the scribes' phonemic awareness. Were they able to hear and identify the specific Hebrew phonemes and sounds, such as the peculiar West Semitic *ś* (שׂ) in Maˁśēh-Yāma 'Y's work'? Does their occasional rendering with *lt* (e.g., ^{I}*ma-al-te-e-ma*) suggest they heard a fricative-lateral pronunciation of the phoneme (Zadok 2015a; cf. Zadok 2002, 31 no. 38; 2014, 116)? Did they hear the *ayin* (ˁ) in the names ˁAzar-Yāma (initial) 'Y helped' and Šamaˁ-Yāma (internal) 'Y heard', the *aleph* (ˀ) in ˀAṣīl-Yāma (initial) 'Noble is Y', the *heh* (h) in Hawšiˁ (initial) 'He saved' and in Yāhû (internal), or the diphthong in some of the names just cited? Did they hear a difference between the *k* in Kīn-Yāma 'True is Y' and its fricative allophone (ḵ) in Yəhôyākîn – assuming that the spirantisation of at least some of the *bgdkpt* had already started in the Hebrew of the sixth century BCE?

Even if they understood the names or at least heard them correctly, the scribes were not always able to document them properly with the tools at their disposal. Which cuneiform sign or combination of signs could they use to write down, for instance, the Hebrew gutturals?

Ran Zadok extensively dealt with these problems in 1977, in the appendix to his monumental book *On West Semites in Babylonia* (pp. 243–64), and again in 1988, in the course of his research on *The Pre-Hellenistic Israelite Anthroponomy* (cf. Millard 2013, 844). With the publication of the documents from Yāhūdu in 2014 the pool of (Yahwistic) Hebrew names significantly increased, but the rules laid down by him are still in force and only minor additions are in place (Zadok 2015a).

As enhancement to Ran Zadok's findings, we include here a table (Table 9.1) that visualises the conventional cuneiform renderings of the West Semitic (incl. Hebrew) gutturals in first millennium BCE names from Babylonia. It is based on his data, but differentiates between zero- and

Table 9.1 *Cuneiform renderings of the Hebrew gutturals*

		Initial	Internal	Final
ayin	ḫ	^{I}*ḫu-uz-za-a* = ˁUzzāya	^{I}*šá-ma-ḫu-ia-a-ma* = Šamaˁ-Yāma	^{I}*a-mu-še-eḫ* = Hawšiˁ
	ˀ	-	^{I}*šá-ma-ˀ-ia-ma* = Šamaˁ-Yāma ^{I}*a-muš-ˀ-a-ma* = Hawšiˁ-Yāma	^{Id}KUR.GAL-*šá-ma-ˀ* = Amurru-šamaˁ
	V	^{I}*a-za-ra-ia-a-ma* = ˁAzar-Yāma	^{I}*šá-me-e-a-ma* = Šamaˁ-Yāma ^{Id}*ia-a-ḫu-ú-i-zi-ri* = Yāḫû-ˁizr(ī)	^{Id}*ia-ḫu-ú-šu-ú* = Yāḫû-šūˁ
	Ø	^{I}*az-za-ra-ia-a-ma* = ˁAzar-Yāma	^{I}*šá-am-iá-a-ma* = Šamaˁ-Yāma ^{Id}*iá-ḫu-ú-uz-zi-ri* = Yāḫû-ˁizr(ī)	-
	g		^{I}*pa-ra-gu-šú* = Parˁōš 'Flea' (< *Parġōš*)	
aleph	V	^{I}*ú-uḫ-li-a-ma* = ˀUhl(ī)-Yāma ^{I}*a-ṣí-li-a-ma* = ˀAṣīl-Yāma	^{I}*ra-ap-pa-a-a-ma* = Rapaˀ-Yāma	-
	Ø	^{I}*ur-mil-ku* = ˀŪr-Milk(i)	^{I}*ra-pa-ia-a-ma* = Rapaˀ-Yāma ^{I}*ḫu-ú-mar-ra* = <Yā>ḫû-ˀamar	-
	ˀ	-	^{I}*ra-pa-ˀ-ia-a-ma* = Rapaˀ-Yāma	^{I}*ra-pa-ˀ*
ḥeth	Generally ḫ			
heh	ḫ	^{I}*ḫu-ú-na-tan^{an}-na* = <Yā>ḫû-natan	^{I}*ia-ḫu-ú-na-ta-nu* = Yāḫû-natan ^{I}*ú-uḫ-li-a-ma* = ˀUhl(ī)-Yāma	-
	ˀ	-	^{Id}*ia-ˀ-ú-šu-ri* = Yāḫû-šūr(ī) ^{I}*ia-ˀ-ú-kin$_{7}$* = Yāḫû-kīn (for king Jehoiachin)	-
	Ø	^{I}*a-mu-še-eḫ* = Hawšiˁ (unless Aram. ˀAwsiˁ) ^{I}*uš-šu-ḫi-a-ma* = Hōšiˁ-Yāma (unless Aram. ˀŌšiˁ-Yāma)	^{I}*ia-a-ḫi-in-nu* = Yāḫ<û>-ḥīn	-
	k	-	^{I}*ia-ku-ú-ki-nu* = Yāḫû-kīn (for king Jehoiachin)	-

vowel-spellings, in view of writings such as ^{I}*aq-bi-ia-a-ma* (zero) vs. ^{I}*a-qa-bi-a-ma* (vowel) for the initial *ayin* in ˁAq(a)b-Yāma 'Protection is Y/Y protected'. Illustrations from esp. Yahwistic names are provided, except for Amurru-šamaˁ (common West Semitic).

It may happen that the zero and multiple spellings for Hebrew gutturals, long vowels, and consonant clusters leave the modern scholar with more than one choice. In principle, ^{I}*ḫi-il(-lu)-mu-tu*, for which no exact biblical parallel exists, derives from the verb roots Ġ-L-M (> ˁ-L-M) 'to be young' (cf. biblical toponym *ˁAlemet* עָלֶמֶת, Zadok 1988, 67) or Ḥ-L-M (cf. the biblical name *Ḥēlem* חֵלֶם 'Strength', Zadok 1979, 31; 1988, 116). More examples are adduced elsewhere in the chapter (e.g., *qatl*/*qitl*-nouns vs. G perf.; and *ḥiriq compaginis* vs. 1.sg. genitive suffix).

Babylonisation of Hebrew Names
Babylonian scribes occasionally reinterpreted Yahwistic names through re-segmentation of name components, assonance, inter-language homophony, and metathesis. Laurie E. Pearce and Cornelia Wunsch (2014, 28, 42–3, 61, 66) notice four occurrences in the Yāhūdu corpus which they analyse in detail. In all these examples, a fine line distinguishes between Judeans reshaping their names to recognisable Babylonian forms (perhaps even with the specific aim of obliterating their Judean identity) and Babylonian scribes nativising foreign names to approximate Akkadian names.

Spelling and Normalisation

Encoding Hebrew names, transmitted in cuneiform script, in Latin script is a difficult balancing act. Some scholars avoid the problem by simply citing the names in their original cuneiform spelling. Otherwise, the choices range from normalisations that are faithful to the cuneiform form (Amušeḫ) to those that are based on historical-linguistic reconstructions (Hawšiˁ) or inspired by biblical parallels with its Tiberian vocalisation (Hôšēˁa הוֹשֵׁעַ); conventional English renderings thereof (Hosea) are acceptable only for popularising publications. In any case, conversion rules for Hebrew and Aramaic names should be the same because they share the same linguistic features. Consistency is desirable, but probably not always attainable.

Particularly complex is transcribing the divine name, as we do not know its original Hebrew articulation and the cuneiform transcriptions are many and confusing. As a result, in the scholarly literature, we find Yāma, Yāw, Yāḫû, among others. In this contribution, I use Y as an abbreviation of the Hebrew divine name in English translations, adopting a neutral stance on this complex issue.

The Name Material in Babylonian Sources

Text Corpora and Statistics

Babylonian sources with Hebrew names are chiefly administrative and legal documents from the sixth and fifth centuries BCE that can be connected to three main types of archives (royal, private, and temple). Most Hebrew names are recorded in the first two types. Very few occur in Babylonian temple archives. A couple appear in documents whose archival context cannot be established. The archival classification provides us with valuable information on the name-bearers' socio-economic or legal background. Remarkably, Hebrew names are absent from the Neo-Babylonian corpus of historiographic texts. There are also virtually no Hebrew names in the published corpora of administrative and private letters (except perhaps for ᶠBuqāšu in Hackl et al. 2014 no. 216).

Four corpora of cuneiform administrative and legal texts stand out, described in much detail by Tero Alstola (2020, chps 2–5), including bibliographic references to editions and secondary literature. In chronological order, these are:

(1) The royal archives from Babylon, excavated in Nebuchadnezzar's palace, primarily consisting of ration lists (archive N1). They refer to the Judean king Jehoiachin and his entourage in 591 BCE.

(2) A group of six cuneiform documents, originating from Rassam's excavations at Abu Habbah (ancient Sippar), that pertain to the descendants of Ariḫ, a family of Judean royal merchants in Sippar in the years 546–493 BCE.

(3) The corpus of c. 200 documents, acquired on the antiquities market, that were drafted at various villages in the rural area south(-east) of Nippur over a period of 95 years, from 572 to 477 BCE. The main villages are Yāhūdu, Našar, and Bīt-Abī-râm.

(4) The private archive of the Babylonian Murašû family found in situ in Nippur. It consists of c. 730 documents dated to the second half of the fifth century BCE (452–413 BCE). Drafted in Nippur-city or in villages in the nearby countryside, they record the business activities of the descendants of Murašû, in the course of which they encountered men of Judean descent, many bearing Yahwistic/Hebrew names. The Murašû archive 'constitutes the last significant corpus of cuneiform evidence on Judeans in Babylonia. Only a single text survives from the fourth century BCE' (Alstola 2020, 222).

The information that we can draw from these sources is dictated by their archival and archaeological origin (or lack thereof). They were written by and chiefly for the Babylonian members of the urban elite. The only exception seems to be the documents from the environs of Yāhūdu. Here, Judeans do not just appear against the backdrop of other people's transactions or as an object, but they are the leading characters, leasing land, paying taxes, etc. Even so, they are still presented by indigenous Babylonian scribes who, by recording their foreign names and activities, may have served the royal administration more than the Judeans. Anyway, no sources written by the Judean deportees themselves or their descendants survive. A complicating factor, furthermore, is the incomplete publication of some of the sources, and the scribes' limited knowledge of Hebrew grammar and culture.

Among the c. 2,500 names in the Murašû archive from Nippur in central Babylonia, Ran Zadok identified seventy Hebrew names (of which thirty-six are Yahwistic): less than 3 per cent. He suspects 'that this may be just an accident of documentation and it does not necessarily mean that the largest concentration of Judeans in Babylonia was in the Nippur region' (Zadok 2002, 63).

In and around Yāhūdu, approximately 159 individuals with Yahwistic/Hebrew names can be identified among the roughly 1,000 individuals recorded in c. 200 documents. This means that about 15 per cent of all names there are Yahwistic, with the largest concentration of them occurring in the town of Yāhūdu itself (c. 35 per cent). Variations in counting occur among scholars, but the overall picture remains the same (cf. Pearce 2015, 20).

Only a handful of Hebrew names are recorded in Uruk and its region, while none are mentioned in Ur, so that one may conclude that 'very few Judeans resided in southern Babylonia, despite the rich Babylonian documentation from there' (e.g., the vast Eanna temple archive from Uruk) (Zadok 2014, 113; Jursa and Zadok 2020, 21, 28–31).

Judeans with Yahwistic/Hebrew names or patronyms also dwelt in the capital and in most of the major cities of northern Babylonia (Sippar, Borsippa, Opis, and Kish). The evidence comes primarily from the royal administration in Babylon and the mercantile community in Sippar. Hebrew names are, however, virtually absent from the private archives of the urbanite North Babylonians and the temple archive of Sippar. For example, among the 1,035 individuals that can be identified in the Nappāḫu family archive from Babylon none bore West Semitic names in general, or Hebrew names in particular. Similarly, only one Hebrew name pops up among the 1,130 individuals in the Egibi family archive, and Hebrew names are rare in the vast Borsippean family archives. No more than eight Yahwistic names occur in the thousands of documents from Sippar's temple.

Typology of Names

Ran Zadok has written extensively on the West Semitic name typology, and the reader is referred to his studies for details (especially Zadok 1977, 78–170 and Zadok 1988, 21–169). The following sections present a summary of those formations that are relevant for the study of the cuneiform Yahwistic names and the linguistically Hebrew profane names. The examples are illustrative, not exhaustive.

Yahwistic Verbal Sentence Names

Most cuneiform Yahwistic names are verbal sentences, with the name components predominantly put in the order predicate–subject, and without an object (cf. biblical Yahwistic names).

The verbal predicates display the following characteristics: (1) They are always in the G-stem, except the Hiphil in Hawšiʕ 'He saved', and a few disputable cases;[4] (2) Perfect (*qtl*) is the norm, with only a few predicates in the imperfect (*yqtl*; e.g., Yigdal-Yāma 'Y will be(come) great', Išrib-Yāma 'Y will propagate'), imperative (e.g., Qī-lā-Yāma 'Hope for Y!' < Q-W-Y),[5] active participle (e.g., Yāḫû-rām 'Y is exalted', Nāṭi-Yāma 'Y bends down'), and passive participle (e.g., Ḥanūn-Yāma 'Favoured by Y'); (3) The predicate is always in the 3.sg. (except for those in the imperative), and without object suffixes or other extensions, a few exceptions notwithstanding.[6]

Yahwistic Nominal Sentence Names and Genitive Compound Names

In the Yahwistic nominal sentence names the predicate–subject sequence prevails. The predicates are all nouns, except for the adjective in ʾAṣīl-Yāma 'Noble is Y'. An adjective is also present in ^{I}*ṭu-ub-ia-ma* if understood as Ṭōb-Yāma 'Good is Y' (rather than Ṭūb-Yāma 'Goodness is Y').

[4] For instance, ^{I}*ši-li-im-iá-ma* 'Y is well-being/Y completed' (G-*qatil*-perf. with attenuation a > i; cf. biblical *Šelemyāh* שְׁלֶמְיָה), or 'Y has made recompense' (D-stem; cf. biblical *Šillēm* שִׁלֵּם); ^{I}*na-aḫ-im-ia-a-ma* 'Y comforted' (G-*qatil*-perf.; cf. biblical *Nəḥemyāh* נְחֶמְיָה, or Aramaic D-stem); and ^{I}*iq-im-ia-a-ma* from the hollow root Q-W/Y-M, which could either be a G-stem Yaqīm-Yāma 'Y will stand up (vindicate)' or a Hiphil Yāqīm-Yāma 'Y will raise' (cf. names from other hollow verbs, Zadok 1988, 24, 39–40).

[5] See CUSAS 28 77 s.v. Qīl-Yāma. My transliteration of the name shows the name elements, namely the verb Q-W-Y + preposition *lā* + divine name. Cf. Biblical Hebrew *Qēlāyāh* (Zadok 1988, 43). There is also an interesting parallel in an Aramaic ostracon from Idumea, fourth century BCE: *qwhlʾl* (Schwiderski 2008, Bd. 1, 723 and Bd. 2, 216 s.v. IdOstr-EN:113(4)).

[6] For example, ^{I}*ḫa-na-**ni**-ʾ-ia-a-ma* 'Y consoled **me**', ^{I}*ši-kin*^{in}*-**ni**-a-ma* 'Y manifest yourself **to me**!'; cf. non-Yahwistic ^{I}*ši-ki-**na*** 'Manifest yourself!' with the extension *-nā* for exhortation.

The distinction between *qatl* and *qitl* forms is not always clear, partly because *qatl* could become *qitl* because of the attenuation *a* > *i*, already in Biblical Hebrew names, especially after *ayin* or near liquids and nasals (e.g., *ˁazr* > *ˁizr*, *malk* > *milk*). Moreover, the cuneiform scribes may not always have been aware of, or careful enough about, these differences. They may also have heard variant pronunciations for the same name from different speakers.

Further noteworthy is the wavering between segholite (CVCC) and bisyllabic (CVCVC, anaptyctic?) spellings – as, for instance, in the orthographies of Ṣid(i)q-Yāma 'Justice is Y'. Thus we have a *qitl* spelling (CVCC) in ^{I}*ṣi-id-qí-iá-a-ma* along with *qitil* spellings (CVCVC) in ^{I}*ṣi-di-iq-a-ma* and ^{I}*ṣi-di-qí-ia-a-ma*. As a result, it is hard to determine whether the bisyllabic spellings in the following names reflect verbal (G *qatal*-perf.) or nominal (*qatl*) predicates: Mal(a)k-Yāma 'Y rules/The king is Y', ˁAz(a)z-Yāma 'Y is strong/Strength is Y', ˁAq(a)b-Yāma 'Y protected/Protection is Y', ˁAt(a)l-Yāma 'Y is pre-eminent/The prince is Y', Šal(a)m-Yāma 'Y completed/Peace is Y', and Yāḫ̮û-ˁaz(a)r 'Y helped/Help is Y'.

Uncertainty arises about the exact relationship between the elements in names such as Ṣid(i)q-Yāma: genitive 'Y's justice' or predicative 'Y is justice'.

Finally, the choice between a *ḥiriq compaginis* or 1.sg. possessive pronoun cannot be sufficiently determined on the basis of the cuneiform orthographies. For instance, the spellings ^{I}*ṣi-di-qí-ia-a-ma* and ^{I}*ṣi-id-qí-iá-a-ma* do not reveal whether we have Ṣidqi-Yāma 'Justice is Y' or Ṣidqī-Yāma 'My justice is Y'.

Yahwistic Interrogative Sentence Names

Under this category falls the name Mī-kā-Yāma 'Who is like Y?'.

Yahwistic Names With a Prepositional Phrase

The name Bâd-Yāma (^{I}*ba-da-ia-a-ma*) 'In the hand/care of Y' in a text from the Murašû archive belongs here, and perhaps also ^{I}*qí(-il)-la-a-ma*, ^{Id}*i-ḫu-ú-li-ia*, and ^{I}*ia-a-ḫu-lu-nu*/*ni*, if they indeed reflect Hebrew *lā* 'for', respectively, *lî* 'for me' and *lānû* 'for us' (CUSAS 28 77, 90; Zadok 1979, 18–19).

Abbreviated Yahwistic Names

Included in this category are one-element names in which the divine name is shortened by means of suffixes (hypocoristica). Laurie E. Pearce and Cornelia Wunsch (2014, 20) list the following abbreviated forms of the final Yahwistic elements: -*Ca-a-a*, -*Ce-e-ia-a-ˀ*, -*Ci-ia-a-ˀ*, *Ci-ia*/*ía*, -*Cu-ia*, -*ia-*[*a*]*-ˀ*, and -*ia-a-ˀ*. However, not all names ending in, for instance, -*Ci-ia*/*ía* or -*Ca-a-a* in cuneiform texts are abbreviated Yahwistic names. These endings are common hypocoristic endings in Babylonian and West Semitic onomastics. Accordingly, names such as ^{I}*ḫa-an-na-ni-ía*, ^{I}*pa-la-ṭa-a-a*, and ^{I}*zab-di-ia* are not abbreviated Yahwistic names, unless additional (con)textual data confirm this.

A clear example is that of Ḥanannī 'He has been merciful to me', whose father bore the Iranian name Udarnā. We would not consider him a worshipper of YHWH in tablet BE 10 84 from the Murašû archive, where his name is spelled ^{I}*ḫa-an-na-ni-*^{ʔ}, were it not for two other tablets from the same archive where his name is rendered with the theophoric element fully spelled ^{I}*ḫa-na-ni/nu-ia-a-ma* 'Y has been merciful to me' (BE 9 69; PBS 2/1 107). One of his brothers was called Zabdia (^{I}*zab-di-ia*) 'Gift': did he have an abbreviated Yahwistic name – for example, Zabad-Yāma 'Given by/Gift of Y' (cf. PBS 2/1 208: ^{I}*za-bad-ia-a-ma*) – or a plain West Semitic one derived from the root Z-B-D with a hypocoristic ending *-ia*? Similar illustrative cases of individuals bearing both a full Yahwistic name and a hypocoristic thereof derive from the Yāhūdu corpus: Banā-Yāma (^{I}*ba-na-a-ma*) 'Y created', son of Nubāya, is also known as Bānia (^{I}*ba-ni-ia*) 'He created'; Nīr(ī)-Yāma (^{I}*ni-i-ri-ia-a-ma*) 'Y's light/Y is (my) light', son of ʔAḥīqar, as Nīrāya (^{I}*ni-ir-ra-a*, ^{I}*ni-ir-ra-a-a*) 'Light'; and Samak-Yāma (^{I}*sa-ma-ka-*^{ʔ}*-a-ma*) 'Y supported', father of Rēmūtu, as Samakāya (^{I}*sa-ma-ka-a-a*) 'He supported'.[7]

Finally, the Yāhūdu and Murašû corpus attest names with an abbreviated form of the divine name in initial position: ^{I}*ia-a-ḫi-in(-nu)*, Yāḫ<û>-ḥīn 'Y is grace' and ^{I}*ḫu-ú-na-tan*^{an}*-na*, <Yā>ḫû-natan 'Y has given'.

Non-Yahwistic Hebrew Names and Hypocoristica

The non-Yahwistic names are typically one element names with(out) hypocoristic suffixes, rarely two-element names. The hypocoristic endings are feminine *-ā*, adjectival *-ān* > *-ōn*, adjectival *-ay*(*ya*), and ancient suffixes *-ā*, *-ī*/*ē*, *-ūt*, or *-ī+ā* (= *ia*).

There are two categories depending on the predicate: names with an isolated verbal predicate and those based on nouns. ^{f}Barūkā 'Blessed', Hawšiʕ 'He saved', Ḥanan(nī) 'He consoled (me)', Yamūš 'He feels/removes' (Zadok 2015b), Natūn 'Given', Naḥūm (^{I}*na-ḫu-um-mu*) 'Consoled', Satūr 'Hidden/Protected', and ʕAqūb (^{I}*a-qu-bu*) 'Protected' belong to the first group. ʔAškōlā 'Bunch of grapes', Ḥaggay '(Born) on a feast', Ḥannān(ī/ia) 'Consolation', Ḥillumūt 'Strength', Mattania 'Gift', Naḥḥūm (^{I}*na-aḫ-ḫu-um*) 'Consolation', ʕAqqūb (^{I}*aq-qu-bu*) 'Protection',

7 Perhaps also Naḥim-Yāma (^{I}*na-aḫ-im-ia-a-ma*) 'Y comforted', son of Šamaʕ-Yāma, also known as Naḥimāya (^{I}*na-aḫ-ḫi-im-ma-a*), CUSAS 28 72.

Pal(a)ṭay 'Refuge', Parʿōš 'Flea', ᶠPuʿullā 'Achievement', Šabbātay '(Born) on Sabbath', Šamaʿōn 'Sound', and Šapān '(Rock) badger' belong to the second group, but the line is sometimes hard to draw due to defective cuneiform orthographies: for example, ᴵ*ši-li-im* for Šil(l)im 'He is (kept) well' or Šillīm 'Loan'. Yašūb-ṭill(ī) '(My) Dew will return'[8] and Yašūb-ṣidq(ī) '(My) Justice will return' are extensions of the first group. For most of the above-listed names recorded Yahwistic compounds exist.

The nominal patterns are: (1) simple patterns (*qatl*, *qitl*, and *qatal*), (2) patterns extended by gemination or reduplication of the root consonants (*qall*, *qittul*, *qutull*, *qattāl*, *qittīl*, and *qattūl* caritative formations), (3) patterns extended by prefixes (*maqtal*), and (4) four-radical nouns. Admittedly, it is often difficult to determine the exact pattern from the cuneiform orthographies. Should ᴵ*ḫa(-an)-na-nu*, ᴵ*ḫa-na(-an)-nu*, ᴵ*ḫa-na-an-ni-ˀ*, and ᴵ*ḫa-an-na-ni-ia* be read Ḥanan(nī) 'He has been merciful (to me)' or Ḥannān(ī/ia) '(My) Consolation'? Content-wise, the nominal predicates refer to physical or mental features, animals, plants, and time of birth.

The isolated verbal predicates are in the G passive particple (*qatūl*), G perf. (*qatal*), and impf. (*yaqtul*), D perf. (*qittil*), or Hiphil perf. (*haqtil*).

Meticulous linguistic analysis is needed before securely classifying these names as specifically Hebrew (and not, for instance, Canaanite, Aramaic, or Phoenician). A case in point is Šapān (ᴵ*šap-an-nu vel sim.*, Zadok 2002, 12, 42). It is exclusively Hebrew, because phonetically it is strikingly different from its Phoenician equivalent where unstressed *a* shifted to *ō*, as seen in the name's occurrence in Neo-Assyrian sources ᴵ*sa-pu-nu*. From a prosopographical point of view, it is noteworthy that his father bore a Babylonian name (Bēl-ēṭir). Similar grammatical and prosopographical data may help in the ethno-linguistic classification of other non-Yahwistic names. However, phonological rules in particular are tricky as a means to separate Hebrew from other (North) west Semitic names, in particular Aramaic names.

Female Names

Most Hebrew female names attested in cuneiform originate from the Yāhūdu corpus: ᶠYapaʿ-Yāḫû 'Y appeared' was the wife of Rapaˀ-Yāma and granddaughter of Samak-Yāma; ᶠYāḫû-ḥīn 'Y is grace' was the daughter of ᴵ*ma-le-šú* (unclear) and granddaughter of Mī-kā-Yāma. ᶠPuʿullā 'Achievement' was a female slave bearing a Hebrew name. ᶠNanāya-kānat

8 More likely Hebrew 'dew' (*ṭall*) than Aramaic *ṭall* 'shadow', because of the *š* in *yašūb*. In Aramaic the verb would have sounded **yatūb* with *t*, as in the female name Neo-/Late Babylonian ᶠ*tu-ba-a* (if derived from the same root).

'Nanāya is reliable', finally, bore a hybrid name that will be discussed in further detail later in the chapter.

Outside this corpus, only three women with Hebrew names are attested. $^{f?}$Abī-Yāma 'My father is Y', mentioned in a text without archival context (Zadok 2002, 45 no. 156), was the daughter of ^{I}*i-ri-*$^{?}$ (unclear). ^{f}Barūkā 'Blessed', a slave and wife of Kuṣura (Babylonian name), is known from the Murašû archive (EE 100). ^{f}Yāḫû-dimr(ī) 'Y's strength/Y is (my) strength' bore a hybrid name (see #4 in section 'Hybrid Names').

Slave Names

Judeans in Yāhūdu owned slaves with Babylonian (^{f}Ana-muḫḫi-Nanāya-taklāku), Babylonian–Aramaic (^{f}Nanāya-biʿī), and Egyptian (^{f}Ḫuṭuatā) names, as well as the following Hebrew names: ʿAbd(i)-Yāḫû 'Y's servant', slave (*ardu*) of Nīr(ī)-Yāma and his brothers, and ^{f}Puʿullā 'Achievement', slave woman (*amtu*) of Ṣidq(ī)-Yāma. Mentioned in the Murašû archive from Nippur are the following slaves with Yahwistic names: ^{I}*ia-a-ḫu-lu-ni* (=? Yāḫû-lānû 'Y is for us'), slave (*ardu*) of the Murašûs; Mattan-Yāma 'Y's gift', servant (*ardu*) of queen Parysatis; Barīk-Yāma 'Blessed by Y', servant (*ardu*) of the Iranian official Artabara; and the non-Yahwistic Hebrew ^{f}Barūkā 'Blessed', slave woman (*amtu*) of the Murašûs. The following servant attested in the Murašû archive has a Hebrew patronym: Il-yadīn (West Semitic), son of Yadaʿ-Yāma 'Y knew', servant of prince Artaḫšar. Note that several of these men serving Iranian princes and queens or Iranian noblemen were semi-free servants rather than chattel slaves.

Hybrid Names

Yahwistic names with non-Hebrew predicates are listed here. Nos. 1–3 have Akkadian predicates, nos. 4–7 Aramaic ones. The predicate in no. 8 can be Akkadian or Aramaic.[9]

(1) Three men in Babylonia bore the '*Beamtenname*' Yāḫû-šarru-uṣur 'Y, protect the king!'.
(2) Dagal-Yāma 'Y looked (upon)' is attested in Yāhūdu (unless it is a metathesis of the Hebrew Gadal-Yāma 'Y is/became great').
(3) Yāḫû-aḫu-ēreš 'Y has desired a brother' occurs in an unassigned text from the Nippur area (Zadok 2016, 547).

[9] We consider Yahwistic names containing the root ʿ-Q-B Hebrew, even though its original Canaanite-Amorite denotation 'to protect' seems to have been lost in Hebrew, whereas it was retained in Aramaic (Zadok 2018, 171).

(4) ^{f}Yāḫû-dimr(ī) 'Y's strength/Y is (my) strength' shows up in the Ebabbar temple archive (CT 57 700).
(5) Yāḫû-laqīm 'Y shall raise' is twice recorded in the Murašû archive.
(6) Barīk-Yāma 'Blessed by Y' occurs in the Yāhūdu corpus where it is unambiguously spelled ^{I}*ba-ri-ki-ia-a-ma vel sim.*
(7) Yāḫû-idr 'Y is help' from Yāhūdu, spelled ^{I}*ia-a-ḫu-ú-e-dir* (Zadok 2015b).
(8) Yāḫû-nūr(ī) 'Y's flame/Y is a (my) flame' appears in an unassigned text from a village 'presumably not far from Babylon or Borsippa' (Zadok 2002, 28 no. 9).

One may find hybrid interpretations for several other Yahwistic names, but they are usually highly speculative, based on misreadings, or otherwise unconvincing.

Names with foreign deities and generally West Semitic predicates are excluded from the list, even if the same predicate also appears with YHWH. It concerns names such as Bēl, Nusku, and Adad + *ba-rak-ku /a/i*, Nabû + *-a-qa-bi, -na-tan-na, -ta*$_5$*-ga-bi, -šá-ma-*ˀ, *-si-im-ki-*ˀ, *-ra-pa -*ˀ, Šamaš + *-ḫa-il, -ia-da-*ˀ, and Bēl + *ia-a-da-aḫ*. They need to be thoroughly examined for possible links with Judah or Judean exiles before they can be considered Hebrew. On that account, at least the following two anthroponyms are liable candidates. ^{f}Nanāya-kānat 'Nanāya is reliable', daughter of ^{f}Dibbī (unclear), granddaughter of Dannāya, (son of Šalti-il, West Semitic), and sister of Mušallam (West Semitic) married in Yāhūdu in the presence of several men with Yahwistic/Hebrew names and/or patronyms (Abraham 2005). ˀŪr-Milk(i) 'Milk's light/Milk is (my) light' is explicitly labelled 'the Judean' in the ration lists from Nebuchadnezzar's palace (N1 archive).

Elements in Names

The documented Yahwistic names are compound names (two elements), the non-Yahwistic ones are non-compound (one element, often with hypocoristic endings). Two individuals from Yāhūdu with profane compound names (predicate *yašūb* + subject) test the above general rule. The known Akkadian hybrid names typically consist of three elements.

The sole named deity in Hebrew names is YHWH. In one instance, this theophoric element interchanged with Bēl in the name of the same individual (see section on 'Naming Practices'). If ^{f}Nanāya-kānat, who married a Babylonian man in Yāhūdu, was indeed of Judean descent, which is likely but cannot be proven beyond doubt (Abraham 2005), her name would be the only Hebrew name that refers to a divinity other than YHWH.

The common nominal elements in Yahwistic names are assembled (in Hebrew alphabetic order) in Table 9.2. As can be seen, the nominal elements often express feelings of deliverance, strength, and protection, or are typical kinship and dependence terms.

The nominal elements in non-Yahwistic names were listed earlier in the chapter.

Table 9.2 *Hebrew nominal elements in Yahwistic personal names*

ˀab	'father'	*maq(i)n*	'possession'
ˀuhl (> *ˀohl*)	'tent'	*mattan*	'gift/creation'
**ˀawš* (> **ˀawuš*)[10]	'gift'	*nūr* (Aram./Akk.)	'light, flame'
ˀaḫ	'brother'	*nīr*	'light, lamp'
ˀaṣīl	'noble'	*ˁabd*	'servant'
ˀūr (> *ˀōr*)	'light'	*ˁazz, ˁuzz*	'strong/strength' (or verbal)
baˁl	'lord'	*ˁazr (or ˁizr)*	'help' (of verbal)
gabr	'man'	*ˁidr* (< *ˁiḏr*, Aram.)	'help'
gīr	'client'	*ˁaqb (Aram.?)*	'protection' (or verbal)
dimr (< *ḏimr*, Aram.)	'strength'	*ˁatl*	'prince' (or verbal)
ḫūl	'maternal uncle' (< *ḫāl*, unless < *ḫayl* 'strength')	*pilˀ/pil(l)*[11]	'wonder/ intervention(?)'
ḫinn	'grace'	*palṭ (or pālāṭ)*	'refuge'
ṭūb, ṭīb[12]*/ṭōb*	'goodness/good'	*ṣidq*	'righteousness'
ṭall (> ṭill)	'dew'	*šalm (or šilm)*	'well-being/peace' (or verbal)
yēš (or ˀīš; yišˁ) (wr. ^{I}iš-ši-ˁ)	'present (or: man; salvation)'	*šamr*	'safeguard' (or verbal)
kūl	'everything' (or verbal)	*šūˁ*	'deliverance'
malk (> milk)	'king' (or verbal)	*šūr*	'bulwark'
maˁśēh	'work/deed'		

[10] In ^{I}*a-mu-uš-a-ma*, see Zadok (2015a).

[11] ^{I}*pí-li-ia-a-ma*, ^{I}*pi-il-li-ia-ma, vel sim.* Despite various proposals (Pearce and Wunsch 2014, 76, with literature), the name remains enigmatic.

[12] Jursa and Zadok 2020, 30.

The Hebrew (West Semitic) verbs in personal names attested in Babylonian sources are reproduced in Table 9.3. The verbs are cited according to their root radicals in Hebrew alphabetic order.

Table 9.3 *Hebrew verbs in personal names attested in Babylonian texts*

ʾ-Z-N (G/Hiph.)	'to give ear, hear'	S-M-K	'to support'
ʾ-M-R	'to say'	ʿ-Z-Z	'to be strong'
B-N-Y	'to create'	ʿ-Z-R	'to help'
B-R-K	'to bless'	ʿ-Q-B (Aram.?)	'to protect'
G-D-L	'to be(come) great'	ʿ-T-L	'to be pre-eminent'
G-L-Y	'to redeem'	P-D-Y	'to ransom'
G-M-R	'to accomplish'	P-L-Ṭ	'to bring into security, deliver'
D-L-Y	'to draw out, rescue'	P-L-L	'to intervene'
Z-B-D	'to grant'	P-ʿ-L	'to accomplish'
Z-K-R	'to remember'	Ṣ-P-Y(?)[13]	'to expect for'
Ḥ-W-Y	'to live'	Q-W-Y	'to hope for'
Ḥ-K-Y (G/D)	'to await, hope for'	Q-W/Y-M (G)	'to rise, stand up (vindicate)'
Ḥ-N-N	'to be merciful, show favour, console'	Q-W/Y-M (Hiph.)	'to raise'
Ḥ-P-Y (G/D)[14]	'to cover/protect'	Q-N-Y	'to acquire; create'
Ḥ-Š-B	'to consider, value'	Q-Ṭ-B	(uncl.)
Ḥ-T-Y/ʾ	'to smite'(?)[15]	R-W/Y-M (G)	'to be(come) exalted'
Y-D-ʿ	'to know'	R-W/Y-M (Hiph.)	'to lift up'
Y-P-ʿ	'to appear'	R-P-ʾ	'to heal'
Y-Š-ʿ (G/Hiph.)	'to save'	Ś-G-B	'to be high'
K-W/Y-L	'to contain'	Ś-R-Y	'to persevere; judge'
K-W/Y-N (G)	'to be firm/true'	Š-W-B	'to return'
K-W/Y-N (Hiph.)	'to make firm'	Š-K-N	'to dwell, be manifest'
M-W/Y-Š	'to feel; remove'	Š-L-M (G)	'to be well; to complete'
M-L-K	'to be king, to rule'	Š-L-M (D)	'to keep well, recompense'
N-D-B	'to be generous'	Š-M-ʿ	'to hear'
N-Ḥ-M (G/D)	'to comfort'	Š-M-R	'to keep, preserve'
N-Ṭ-Y	'to bend down'	Š-N-Y/ʾ(?)[16]	'to shine; be exalted'
N-T-N	'to give'	Š-R-B	'to propagate'

[13] Pearce and Wunsch 2014, 80. [14] Jursa and Zadok 2020, 28.
[15] More at PNA 1/I, 10 s.v. Abi-ḫatâ and Abi-ḫiti, and Zadok (1979, 20). [16] Zadok 1988, 44.

Naming Practices

Filiation

Men with Hebrew names in the Babylonian sources all have two-tier filiations, except for those among them who were slaves. They have a given name followed by a patronym, but lack a family name. The use of family names could have been quite convenient as identifier in cases where more than one 'X son of Y' was living in the same locality. This rarely happened in the countryside. In the village Yāhūdu patronyms were sufficient to distinguish between the three ˁAbd(i)-Yāḫ̮ûs who lived there simultaneously (CUSAS 28 15).

Family names were the prerogative of the indigenous Babylonian population and typically borne by its urban elite (see Chapter 4). We do not expect the deportees from Judah or their descendants to have them. Even those who settled in cities or worked for institutional households as merchants and lower administrative clerks remained outside the Babylonian elite group bearing distinct family names. It does not mean that the long-established Babylonian urbanites refrained from developing close business and personal relationships with newcomers from Judah. They even married their daughters, and we wonder whether Gūzānu's future children, from his marriage with the Judean bride ᶠKaššāya, were absorbed into his clan and allowed to use their father's Babylonian family name (Ararru).[17]

'Beamtennamen'

According to the biblical narrative, Daniel and his three friends received Babylonian (lit. 'Chaldean') names by royal decree upon their entry into the palace so that Daniel, for instance, became Belteshazzar (בֵּלְטְשַׁאצַּר). Daniel's new name, meaning 'Bēltu, protect the king!' (Bēltu-šarru-uṣur, in Akkadian), emphasises concern for the Babylonian king's welfare and loyalty to the state. It was typically borne by palace or civil servants. This story reflects a reality well known from Babylonian cuneiform texts (see Chapter 5).

Among the Judean exiles and their descendants living in Yāhūdu, we encounter two men named Yāḫ̮û-šarru-uṣur 'Y, protect the king!'. One was the son of Nubāya, the other the father of Zakar-Yāma 'Y has remembered'. The same name was borne by a man among the foreign residents in

[17] The marriage is discussed by Yigal (Bloch 2014, 127–35).

Susa. His father had the Akkadian name Šamaš-iddin (OECT 10 152, 493 BCE).

These men act as creditors and witnesses in private transactions. We do not know whether they also worked in the service of the state or were dependents of the palace household, but it is certainly possible given their name. Upon entering the palace household or assuming administrative duties, they changed their name (or had it changed) to names that expressed their loyalty to the king. However, it is not entirely impossible that these are birth names. In that case, they are an expression of the parents' loyalty to the Babylonian king, and we do not know if the children eventually became court officials or civil servants as adults.

Double Names, Nicknames, and Name Changes

Babylonian scribes had a fixed formula to describe individuals with double names: 'PN$_1$ whose (other) name is PN$_2$' (PN$_1$ *ša šumšu* PN$_2$). Explicit cases of Judeans in Babylonia with double names are at present not attested. Yet, several men with Yahwistic names in Yāhūdu are attested under their full and short name (for examples, see the section 'Abbreviated Yahwistic Names'). In addition, we encounter among the Judean exiles and their descendants at least one man who changed or had his name changed. Bēl-šarru-uṣur became Yāḫû-šarru-uṣur, in all likelihood for reasons of etiquette against the backdrop of governmental changes (Pearce 2015, 24–7).

Finally, there is Banā-Yāma 'Y created', son of Nubāya, who is also called, or became, Bānia in the course of his life. In 532 BCE, and again in 528 BCE, the scribe Arad-Gula had to write down this man's name. At first he wrote ^{I}*ba-ni-ia*, which is a common orthography for the non-compound Babylonian name Bānia, from the Akkadian noun *bānû* 'creator' + hypocoristic suffix *-ia*. Had he not recognised the theophoric element, invented a unique orthography for it (*-ia*), or did he Babylonise the Hebrew name? Or, did Banā-Yāma, when asked for his name, abbreviate it to Bānia to make it sound more Babylonian (and perhaps even obliterate his Judean identity?). Four years later, when writing ^{I}*ba-na-a-ma* Arad-Gula clearly understood it as a compound name composed of the root B-N-Y in the G *qatal*-perf. (// Biblical Hebrew *bānāh*) 'he created' + the divine name, now spelled in one of the conventional orthographies *-a-ma*. Alternatively, Banā-Yāma had two names simultaneously: a long theophoric one (formal?), and an abbreviated one (nickname?) which happened to sound very Babylonian.

Programmatic or Symbolic Names

^{I}*ia-a-šu-bu*, son of ^{I}*ḫa-ka-a* (PBS 2/1 85:2–3), are short(ened) Hebrew names, the first one similar to biblical Yāšûb (יָשׁוּב) 'He will return', from the root Š-W/Y-B, the second one probably a hypocoristic form of biblical Ḥăkalyāh (חֲכַלְיָה) 'Wait for Y!', from the root Ḥ-K-Y. This being the case, 'these names may express the expectations of the exiles for their repatriation' (Zadok 1979, 18). The same hopes are expressed in the imperative Yahwistic names Šūbnā-Yāma (^{I}*šu-bu-nu-ia-a-ma*) 'Y, return (urgently)!', Qī-lā-Yāma 'Hope for Y!' (Q-W-Y), and perhaps also ^{I}*si-pa-ʾ-ia-a-ma* (<? Ṣ-P-Y) 'Expect (for) Y!'.[18]

Biblical Names

Almost all Yahwistic/Hebrew names in cuneiform texts from first-millennium BCE Babylonia surface in the Bible in one form or another. The same verbs and nouns are productive in biblical name-giving, a few exceptions notwithstanding (e.g., M-W/Y-Š, N-Ṭ-Y, Š-N-Yʾ, Ś-G-B, *ḥūl*, *ʾaškōl*, *šūr*).

With the help of the handy list by Laurie E. Pearce and Cornelia Wunsch (2014, 308–11), similarities and differences become easily apparent, although the lack of vocalisation for the biblical names hinders the comparison. Moreover, it is limited to Yahwistic names and sets out from attestation in Yāhūdu, or in Yāhūdu and Murašû, so that names attested in Murašû alone or in other sources (e.g., the ration lists from Babylon's N1 archive) remain unnoticed.

Additional useful tools for comparative research are available in Zadok 1988, such as the list of roots productive in biblical name-giving (pp. 350–5) and the list of biblical names in cuneiform sources from the first millennium BCE (both Neo-Assyrian and Neo-/Late Babylonian; pp. 459–64).

The most common differences between the biblical names and their cuneiform parallels regard sequence, vowel pattern, and predicate typology. Two examples from among many are: cuneiform Yāḫû-ʿaz 'Y is strong/strength' (G perf. or *qatl* noun) vs. biblical ʿUzzīyāh(û) עֻזִּיָּה(וּ) 'My strength is Y' (*qutl* noun); and ʿAqab-Yāma or Yāma-ʿaqab 'Y protected' (G perf.) and ʿAqb(ī)-Yāma '(My) protection is Y' (*qatl* noun) vs. Yaʿăqōb יַעֲקֹב 'He will protect' (G impf., without YHWH). Further note that the comparison sometimes requires either replacing the Yahwistic theophoric

[18] For these names, see Zadok (1988, 306) (§ 721435); CUSAS 28 20, 22, 23; TMH 2/3 123:9 (Pearce and Wunsch 2014, 80). Interestingly, the Aramaic-speaking Jewish community in Elephantine had similar aspirations (*ṣplyh*, *šbnyh*, and *yšwb*, Schwiderski 2008, 377, 712, 766).

element in the cuneiform name with ʾEl or ʾab, or omitting it altogether, so that cuneiform ʾUhl(ī)-Yāma 'A (My) tent is Y/Y's tent' can be compared with biblical ʾOhŏlîʾāb אָהֳלִיאָב 'My tent is the father', Qanā-Yāma 'Y acquired' with ʾElqānāh אֶלְקָנָה 'El acquired', and Yāḫû-ḫīn 'Y is grace' with Ḥēn חֵן 'Grace'.

Socio-Onomastics

Socio-Economic Profile

Bearers of Yahwistic/Hebrew names in Babylonia in the long sixth century constituted a heterogeneous socio-economic group. The majority was linked in one way or another to the palatial sector, mostly implicitly, though sometimes explicitly. Upon arrival in Babylonia, they were integrated in the state's land-for-service development programme. They received a plot of land in underdeveloped areas against the payment of various imposts and the performance of military and civil service. In this manner, they could invest in their own livelihood, and at the same time provide the state with staple crops, cash income, and cheap labour. This was the destiny of the Judeans living in the environs of Yāhūdu in the sixth and early fifth centuries BCE. A similar type of semi-dependent Judean landholders shows up in the Murašû archive of the late fifth century, but new types emerge. Judeans are now also attested as owners of private land, as minor officials in the service of royalty and high officials, and probably even as entrepreneurs in the land-for-service sector, like the Murašûs, or as their business partner.

In the capital Babylon deportees from Judah were detained in official custody. Among them we find king Jehoiachin, his five sons (without their names), seven men with Yahwistic names, and a group of unnamed courtiers (*ša rēši*) from Judah. They received oil rations from the storerooms in Nebuchadnezzar's palace or assisted in their distribution.

About 60 km north of Babylon, in the port city of Sippar, Judeans with Yahwistic/Hebrew names or patronyms were active members of the local merchant community (Alstola 2017). The better known are the descendants of Ariḫ: his four sons, of whom two had Yahwistic names, and his five grandchildren, children of his son Hawšiʿ, with Babylonian names. They traded in gold with the local temple and, in their function of 'royal merchants', most likely partook in international, long-distance trade. Their social network consisted of fellow Judeans and merchants, but also of members of long-established Babylonian priestly families.

A few Judeans were dependants of Babylonian temples or were hired by the temples to farm its lands.

For many of the recorded Judeans we remain in the dark as to their socio-economic whereabouts, because they appear among the witnesses of contracts and thus played no more than a passive role in the transactions.

Almost all the recorded Judeans are freemen, or at least belonged to the class of the semi-free population in Babylonia. Attached to the land-for-service system, the state and its representatives controlled them and exploited their labour quite extensively, but they were not chattel slaves (Bloch 2017). Some of them served the local or state administration as minor officials and 'as such they were responsible for collecting taxes, organising work and military service, and ensuring the efficient cultivation of royal lands' (Alstola 2020, 261).

Courtiers (*ša rēš šarri*) and scribes trained in the Aramaic language and script (*sēpiru*) were recruited from among the Judean deportees to work in Nebuchadnezzar's palace. Later, we also find such scribes among the Judeans in Nippur. Bloch (2018, 291–2, 379–97) identified five men with Yahwistic names and two with Yahwistic patronyms bearing the title *sēpiru* among the Murašû tablets. Other professions occupied by Judeans, such as fishermen and herdsmen, are adduced by Zadok in his various studies (mainly Zadok 1979 and 2002).

Names As Carriers of Identity

Family trees contain valuable information on acculturation among the Judean exiles and their descendants. The family of Samak-Yāma in Yāhūdu stuck to the tradition of its ancestors, and over three generations all recorded members received Hebrew names: Samak-Yāma → Rapaˀ-Yāma → ˀAḥīqam (West Semitic) → Nīr(ī)-Yāma, Ḥaggay, Yāḫû-ˁaz, Yāḫû-ˁizrī, and Yāḫû-šūˁ. The family tree of the bride ᶠKaššāya in Sippar reveals a different situation (Bloch 2014). She and her four siblings had Babylonian names, but going up the tree we see a mixture of Yahwistic/Hebrew and Babylonian names. Her father was Hawšīˁ, her mother ᶠGudādītu (Hebrew–Aramaic). Hawšīˁ had three brothers, two with Babylonian names, one with a Yahwistic name. Their father, ᶠKaššāya's grandfather, went by the name Ariḫ (Hebrew–Aramaic). The family tree of ˀAḥīqar bears witness to still another tendency – namely, to return to Yahwistic names after two generations bearing Akkadian and West Semitic names (Alstola 2020, 120).

Further Reading

A treasure trove, and an indispensable tool for the study of cuneiform parallels of biblical names, is Ran Zadok's monumental study *The Pre-Hellenistic Israelite Anthroponymy and Prosopography* (1988). The rich onomastic material from the Yāhūdu corpus is conveniently summarised in Laurie E. Pearce and Cornelia Wunsch (2014, 33–93). They use the siglum B to highlight biblical counterparts. Their index on pp. 308–11 lists 'Yahwistic Names Appearing in the Āl-Yāḫūdu, Murašû, and Biblical Corpus'. Earlier comparative lists are by Michael D. Coogan (1976) and Alan Millard (2013, 843–4).

Paper editions of texts mentioning Judeans are offered by Abraham (2005 and 2007), Yigal Bloch (2014), Guillaume Cardascia (1951), Veysel Donbaz and Matthew W. Stolper (1997), Francis Joannès and André Lemaire (1999), Laurie E. Pearce and Cornelia Wunsch (2014), Matthew W. Stolper (1985), and Ernst F. Weidner (1939). See also the new edition by C. Wunsch (BaAr 6). Several digital platforms offer online access to the text corpora and the prosopographical data:

- *Achemenet*, www.achemenet.com/
- *CTIJ* = Cuneiform Texts mentioning Israelites, Judeans, and related population groups, http://oracc.museum.upenn.edu/ctij/
- *NaBuCCo* = The Neo-Babylonian Cuneiform Corpus, https://nabucco.acdh.oeaw.ac.at/
- *Prosobab* = Prosopography of Babylonia (c. 620–330 BCE), https://prosobab.leidenuniv.nl/
- *Prosopographical Database of Judeans in the Murašû Archive*, https://researchportal.helsinki.fi/en/datasets/prosopographical-database-of-judeans-in-the-murašû-archive/projects/
- *Prosopographical Database of Yahudu and Its Surroundings*, https://researchportal.helsinki.fi/en/datasets/prosopographical-database-of-yahudu-and-its-surroundings

Corrigenda et addenda to CUSAS 28 (Pearce and Wunsch 2014), the major source for Hebrew names:

- Abraham, K., M. Jursa, and Y. Levavi 2018. 'Further Collations to CUSAS 28', *Nouvelles Assyriologiques Brèves et Utilitaires* 2018/53.
- Pearce L. E. and C. Wunsch, Additions and Correction section in CUSAS 28's webpage, http://cuneiform.library.cornell.edu/publications/documents-judean-exiles-and-west-semites-babylonia-collection-david-sofer-cusas-28
- Pearce, L. E. Corrigenda to CUSAS 28, https://www.academia.edu/10981661/_2015_Corrigenda_to_CUSAS_28._appearing_in_second_press_run

- Waerzeggers, C. 2015. 'Review of L. E. Pearce and C. Wunsch 2014. Documents of Judean Exiles and West Semites in Babylonia in the Collection of David', *STRATA. Bulletin of the Anglo-Israel Archaeological Society* 33, 179–94.
- Waerzeggers, C. 2017. 'Collations of CUSAS 28', *Nouvelles Assyriologiques Brèves et Utilitaires* 2017/86.

References

Abraham, K. 2005. 'West Semitic and Judean brides in cuneiform sources from the sixth century BCE: new evidence from a marriage contract from Āl-Yahudu', *Archiv für Orientforschung* 51, 198–219.

Abraham, K. 2007. 'An inheritance division among Judeans in Babylonia from the Early Persian period' in M. Lubetski (ed.), *New Seals and Inscriptions, Hebrew, Idumean, and Cuneiform*. Hebrew Bible Monographs 8. Sheffield: Sheffield Phoenix, pp. 206–21.

Al-Qananweh, E. 2004. 'Transjordanische Personennamen in der eisenzeitlichen Periode und ihre semitischen Entsprechungen'. PhD dissertation: Freie Universität Berlin, available at https://refubium.fu-berlin.de/handle/fub188/13806 (accessed March 2021).

Alstola, T. 2017. 'Judean merchants in Babylonia and their participation in long-distance trade', *Die Welt des Orients* 47, 25–51.

Alstola, T. 2020. *Judeans in Babylonia: A Study of Deportees in the Sixth and Fifth Centuries BCE*, Culture and History of the Ancient Near East 109. Leiden: Brill.

Bloch, Y. 2014. 'Judeans in Sippar and Susa during the first century of the Babylonian exile: assimilation and perseverance under Neo-Babylonian and Achaemenid rule', *Journal of Ancient Near Eastern History* 1/2, 119–72.

Bloch, Y. 2017. 'From horse trainers to dependent workers: the šušānu class in the Late Babylonian period, with a special focus on Āl-Yāhūdu tablets', *KASKAL* 14, 91–118.

Bloch, Y. 2018. *Alphabet Scribes in the Land of Cuneiform: sēpiru Professionals in Mesopotamia in the Neo-Babylonian and Achaemenid Periods*, Gorgias Studies in the Ancient Near East 11. Piscataway: Gorgias Press.

Cardascia, G. 1951. *Les archives du Murašû: Une famille d'hommes d'affaires de Babylonie à l'époque perse (455–403 av. J.-C.)*. Paris: Imprimerie Nationale.

Coogan, M. D. 1976. *West Semitic Personal Names in the Murašû Documents*. Missoula: Scholars Press for Harvard Semitic Museum.

Donbaz V. and M. W. Stolper 1997. *Istanbul Murašû Texts*, Publications de l'Institut Historique-Archéologique Néerlandais de Stamboul 79. Istanbul: Nederlands Historisch-Archaeologisch Instituut.

Hackl, J., M. Jursa, and M. Schmidl 2014. Spätbabylonische Privatbriefe, Alter Orient und Altes Testament 414/1. Spätbabylonische Briefe 1. Münster: Ugarit-Verlag.

Joannès, F. and A. Lemaire 1999. 'Trois tablettes cunéiformes à onomastique ouest-sémitique (collection S. Moussaïeff)', *Transeuphratène* 17, 17–34.

Jursa, M. and R. Zadok 2020. 'Judeans and other West Semites: another view from the Babylonian countryside', *Hebrew Bible and Ancient Near East* 9, 20–40.

Millard, A. 2013. 'Transcriptions into cuneiform' in G. Khan (ed.), *Encyclopedia of Hebrew Language and Linguistics*, Vol. 3 P–Z. Leiden: Brill, pp. 838–47.

Muraoka, T. and B. Porten 1998. *A Grammar of Egyptian Aramaic*, Handbuch der Orientalistik I/32. Leiden: Brill.

Pearce, L. E. 2015. 'Identifying Judeans and Judean identity in the Babylonian evidence' in J. Stökl and C. Waerzeggers (eds.), *Exile and Return: The Babylonian Context*, Beihefte zur Zeitschrift für alttestamentliche Wissenschaft 478. Berlin: De Gruyter, pp. 7–32.

Pearce L. E. and C. Wunsch 2014. *Documents of Judean Exiles and West Semites in Babylonia in the Collection of David Sofer*, Cornell University Studies in Assyrioloy and Sumerology 28. Bethesda: CDL Press.

Radner, K. (ed.) 1998. *The Prosopography of the Neo-Assyrian Empire*, 1/I: A. Helsinki: The Neo-Assyrian Text Corpus Project.

Schwiderski, D. 2008. *Die alt- und reichsaramäischen Inschriften. The Old and Imperial Aramaic Inscriptions*, Bd 1: *Konkordanz*; Bd. 2: *Texte und Bibliographie*. Berlin: De Gruyter.

Stolper, M.W. 1985. *Entrepreneurs and Empire: The Murašû Archive, the Murašû Firm, and Persian Rule in Babylonia*, Publications de l'Institut Historique-Archéologique Néerlandais de Stamboul 54. Istanbul: Nederlands Historisch-Archaeologisch Instituut.

Van der Merwe, C. H. J., J. A. Naude, and J. H. Krauze 1999, 2017. *A Biblical Hebrew Reference Grammar* (2nd ed.). Sheffield: Sheffield Academic Press.

Weidner, E. F. 1939. 'Jojachin, König von Juda' in Babylonischen Keilschrifttexten' in *Mélanges syriens offerts à Monsieur René Dussaud par ses amis et ses élèves*. Paris: Geuthner, pp. 923–35, pls I–V.

Zadok, R. 1977. *On West Semites in Babylonia During Chaldean and Achaemenian Periods: An Onomastic Study*. Jerusalem: Wanaarta.

Zadok, R. 1979. *The Jews in Babylonia During the Chaldean and Achaemenian Periods According to the Babylonian Sources*. Haifa: University of Haifa.

Zadok, R. 1988. *The Pre-Hellenistic Israelite Anthroponymy and Prosopography*, Orientalia Lovaniensia Analecta 28. Leuven: Peeters.

Zadok, R. 2002. *The Earliest Diaspora: Israelites and Judeans in Pre-Hellenistic Mesopotamia*. Tel Aviv: Tel Aviv University.

Zadok, R. 2014. 'Judeans in Babylonia – Updating the dossier' in U. Gabbay and S. Secunda (eds.), *Encounters by the Rivers of Babylon: Scholarly Conversations Between Jews, Iranians and Babylonians in Antiquity*, Texts and Studies in Ancient Judaism 160. Tübingen: Mohr Siebeck, pp. 109–29.

Zadok, R. 2015a. 'Notes on the onomastics from Yahūdu', *Nouvelles Assyriologiques Brèves et Utilitaires* 2015/85.

Zadok, R. 2015b. 'Yamu-iziri the summoner of Yahūdu and Aramaic linguistic interference', *Nouvelles Assyriologiques Brèves et Utilitaires* 2015/86.
Zadok, R. 2016. 'Neo- and Late-Babylonian notes' in I. Finkelstein, C. Robin, and T. Römer (eds.), *Alphabets, Texts and Artifacts in the Ancient Near East. Studies Presented to Benjamin Sass*. Paris: Van Dieren, pp. 520–64.
Zadok, R. 2018. *A Prosopography of the Israelites in Old Testament Traditions: A Contextualized Handbook*. Tel Aviv: Archaeological Center Publications.

CHAPTER 10

Phoenician and Related Canaanite Names

Ran Zadok

Introduction

There is a very restricted number of anthroponyms which can be defined as Phoenician and fringe Canaanite (practically, Moabite and Ammonite) in Neo-Babylonian and Late Babylonian sources. [1] No more than twenty-three individuals bore Phoenician names, with various degrees of plausibility. There is only one individual among them whose name is not strictly speaking purely Phoenician, as it ends with the Akkado-Aramaic gentilic suffix (Ṣūrāya 'Tyrian', a man of undoubtedly Phoenician extraction; see [33]). In addition, there are two Moabites and one Ammonite.

The sample is not only very small but also very dispersed, as it covers over 300 years and originates from almost all the Babylonian regions and documentation centres.[2] Relying on such a limited sample, which is almost entirely reconstructed (the only person explicitly said to be Phoenician is the aforementioned Tyrian), necessitates maximum contextualisation – namely, thorough analysis and evaluation of the pertinent prosopographical pool.

The main criteria for distinguishing Phoenician names from other Canaanite corpora, in the first place the onomasticon of the Old Testament, are (1) phonological, viz. the shift of *á* to *ó*, and (2) theological: the Phoenician onomasticon preserved the old Canaanite theophoric elements (with several individual modifications), whereas most of the theophoric anthroponyms of the Old Testament contain Yhw and kinship terms. Like Hebrew, the residual onomastica of Moab and Ammon lack the shift of *á* to *ó*, whereas their main theophoric elements differ from the other Canaanite onomastica due to the popularity of their main local gods,

[1] All the names discussed in this chapter are Neo-Babylonian or Late Babylonian unless otherwise stated. Numbers in square brackets refer to the personal names discussed in the chapter.

[2] One individual is recorded in a deed from Susa outside Babylonia [36], but he might have been based in Babylon, as the contract belongs to the archive of the Egibi family from Babylon.

viz. Moabite Kemosh and Ammonite Milkom. Of course, the distinction and delimitation among the various Canaanite dialects, as well as between Phoenician and Aramaic, is not always clear-cut. Cases where disambiguation is not possible are discussed where applicable.

Phoenicians in Babylonian Sources

The earliest Phoenician person attested in Babylonian sources is Ašid-rummu (^{I}*a-šid-ru-um-mu*, [9]). His three sons, viz. Nūr$^{?}$-gumê, Iqīšāya, and Šūzubu, sold a palm grove in the Bīt-Dakkūri region at the end of 624 BCE.[3] It is not explicitly stated that the three sellers were his sons, but this is implied by the fact that they belonged to the 'house' (*bītu*) of Ašid-rummu and Kaššâ (^{I}*kaš-šá-*$^{?}$) < Kaššāya. The latter is preceded by a '*Personenkeil*', which defines male names, but Kaššāya was a common female name in Babylonia. Therefore it is very likely that she was Ašid-rummu's wife. From the fact that the alienation of the property was by his sons, it stands to reason that he had passed away some time before late 624 BCE. He or his ancestors were very probably deported to Babylonia by the Assyrians.

The next person with a Phoenician name, Ḫaru-Ṣapūnu (^{Id}*ḫa-ru-ṣa-pu-nu*, [15]), is recorded in 617 BCE (i.e., more than a decade before the campaigns of Nebuchadnezzar II to the Levant). The Akkadian name of his brother, Nabê-ṣīru, may be an indication that the family was established for at least two generations in Babylonia. Therefore, it can be hypothesised that his ancestors were deported to Babylonia by the Assyrians.

As is expected, most Phoenician individuals are recorded in the long sixth century BCE, which has an abundant documentation, whereas only three are attested in the late-Achaemenid period, with its more restricted textual corpus [4, 5, 23], and just two in the dwindling documentation from the beginning of the Hellenistic period [28 and his brother].

Unfortunately, almost all the numerous Phoenician prisoners of war (mostly sailors) of Nebuchadnezzar II's campaigns are recorded anonymously at the beginning of the sixth century BCE.[4] They are mentioned in the N1 archive which was unearthed in the Southern Fortress of Babylon and concerns the palatial sector.[5]

[3] San Nicolò 1951, 26–7 *ad* AnOr 9 4 ii 44–iii 44.

[4] Zadok 2018, 117.

[5] Pedersén 2005, 111–27.

Several of the few Phoenicians, who are recorded by name in later sources from the sixth century, belong to that same, palatial sector. One of them, Yatūnu (^{I}*ia-a-tu-nu*, [17]), held the prominent position of royal resident (*qīpu*) of a Babylonian temple about 50 to 60 years later – that is, no more than two generations after the military campaigns which resulted in the deportation and resettlement of Phoenicians and other Levantines in Babylonia.[6] The Neo-Babylonian rulers and their Persian successors generally nominated individuals who were not members of the urban elite for inspecting the temples. This is a unique case where a person of foreign extraction was nominated to this office by the native rulers.

Itti-šarri-īnīa, who is mentioned a decade earlier, bore an anthroponym which is typical of members of the palatial sector (see Chapter 5). He was probably born in Babylonia to a father bearing the very common Phoenician name *bʿlytn* [1]. Itti-šarri-īnīa was a business partner of a royal courtier (*ša rēš šarri*).

Five to six individuals belonged to, or had links with, Babylonian temples rather than with the palace.[7] They might initially have been donated to the temples by the Neo-Babylonian rulers. On the whole, foreigners and outsiders were absorbed in the public rather than in the private sector in first-millennium Babylonia.

None of the very few named inhabitants of the Tyrian colony near Nippur bore a Phoenician anthroponym.[8] Even the only explicitly Tyrian filiation from there consists of an Akkadian paternal name and a common West Semitic given name (Zadok 2015, 107–8).

The three (or four) named 'carpenters of Lebanon', who are mentioned in the archive of the Ebabbar temple, were sent from there to Mt. Lebanon in order to hew cedar wood and transport it to Sippar. Since they had Akkadian filiations as early as 582 BCE,[9] they were very probably Babylonians and not Phoenicians: if they were Phoenicians, one would

[6] The deed recording his name (*Nbn.* 33) concerns the receipt of silver, barley, and dates, probably from the Ebabbar temple of Sippar in 16th year of Nabonidus (540/39 BCE). The deed itself was written on the 14th day of *Abu* (fifth month) of the first year of '[. . .], king of Babylon', in all probability Cambyses as viceroy of Babylon – that is, the first year of Cyrus (538 BCE). The silver and commodities were given by order of the chief administrator (*šatammu*) of the Eigikalamma temple of Marad to the oblates of the god Lugal-Marada. It is therefore very likely that Yatūnu was the royal resident of the Eigikalamma temple.

[7] These are individuals [2, 3, 6, 7, 11, 27] and perhaps [12, 28].

[8] The Tyrian colony (Bīt-Ṣūrāyi) is mentioned in the Murašû archive; see the discussion in Zadok (1978b, 60).

[9] Bongenaar 1997, 131, 392–3, 395, 400–3, 407.

expect their fathers, who lived around 600 BCE, when the Phoenician deportees arrived in Babylonia, to bear Phoenician names.

Ammonites and Moabites in Babylonian Sources

The only person with an Ammonite filiation and one of the two individuals with Moabite filiations were probably linked to the palatial sector in view of the predicative element of their names, viz. DN-šarru-uṣur, referring to an earthly king, in all likelihood their ultimate employer [35, 37; see Chapter 5 on this type of name]. Strictly speaking, both names are not purely Ammonite–Moabite but hybrid – that is, Ammonite/Moabite–Akkadian. Their characterisation as such is due to the fact that their theophoric elements are Ammonite (Milkom) and Moabite (Kemosh). Settlements named after Philistines are recorded in Neo- and Late Babylonian sources (Ḫazatu and Išqillūnu; i.e., Gaza and Ashkelon),[10] but no named Philistines appear in these texts.

Classification of the Phoenician Anthroponyms

Due to the limited number of Phoenician names attested in the Babylonian text corpus, we offer only a very basic classification of their structure here, viz. twenty-two compound and non-compound names (respectively, thirteen and nine names each). This sample represents the names with a high degree of plausibility; the maximum is thirty-four names, which are all classified herein. One of the simplex names can be regarded an isolated predicate [17]. Both members of the only purely Phoenician filiation (father and son [12, 13]) have the same initial component.

Compound Names

Verbal Sentence Names

The pattern subject + predicate (G perfect 3.sg. m.) is represented by [1] Bēl-yatūnu (^{Id}EN-*ia-a-tu-nu*), father of Itti-šarri-īnīa, which renders the Phoenician name *bʿlytn* 'Baal has given'.[11] The Akkadian scribe had no difficulty in identifying Akkadian Bēl (^{d}EN) with his Phoenician divine

[10] Zadok 1985, 158, 183 s.vv. (see Zadok 1978b, 61b and add ^{uru}*ḫa-za-tu*$_4$ in Pearce and Wunsch 2014 no. 101:6, 11). The settlement ^{uru}*pal(-la)-áš-ti* was named after Philistia (see Zadok and Zadok 2003).

[11] *Nbn.* 282:3 (Babylon, 548 BCE); see Benz (1972, 94–6, 328–9).

cognate, seeing that the latter is transcribed not only *ba-al* (/*baˁl*/) but also *ba-ˀ-il*, even in the name of one and the same individual (see [8]).

Another instance of the same name pattern is possibly **[2]** Ab-ḫalalu (^{I}*ab-ḫa-la-lu*$_4$), recorded in the archive of the Eanna temple of Uruk, possibly at the end of the seventh or the beginning of the sixth century BCE.[12] His name is apparently identical to the Phoenician anthroponym *ˀbḥll*. The latter seems to consist of *ˀb-* '(divine) father' and a form, apparently *qatal* (G perfect 3.sg. m.), deriving from Ḥ-L-L (eventually 'to fear').[13] However, doubt is cast on Ab-ḫalalu's Phoenician descent in view of his milieu, viz. that of shepherds, who generally bore Akkadian and Arameo-Arabian names in first-millennium BCE Babylonia. Therefore, an identification with Safaitic *ˀbˁll* (two occurrences) is an alternative (Harding 1971, 14).

The pattern predicate + subject is presumably represented by **[3]** Azabtī-il (^{I}*a-zab-tì-ìl*), father of Gūsāya,[14] which ends with the theophoric element *ˀl* 'god, El' and begins with a G perfect 1.sg. of ˁ-Z-B, viz. **azab-tī-* (i.e., 'I have entrusted to god').[15] Alternatively, this name may be Hebrew or Transjordanian. Another instance of this name pattern is **[4]** Ḫašb-ilīm, rendering Phoenician **ḥšb-ˀlm*, contained in the toponym *Bīt* (É) ^{I}*ḫaš-bi-il-li-im-ma* in the Nippur region:[16] 'The gods have thought, reckoned' (Ḥ-Š-B with *qátal-* > *qatl-*; the subject is morphologically plural but syntactically singular, as it is a *pluralis maiestatis*).[17]

The following name, borne by a slave of the Murašû firm of Nippur, is of the same pattern but uses a D short-imperfect 3.sg. m.: **[5]** Yāḫû-lūnu (^{I}*ia-a-ḫu-lu-ni*/*nu*).[18] This name renders *yḥw*(*ˀ*)*ln*, extant in Punic,[19] 'May god keep alive'.[20] The spelling *ia-a-* does not indicate a long /*a*/, as its *-a* is inserted in order to confirm the reading /*ia*/ of the polyphonic sign IA. This is the only attestation of *ˀln* outside Punic, and actually its earliest

12 Gehlken 1996, 57–8 *ad* no. 221:2, r. 2; Zadok 2003, 494.

13 Benz (1972, 310 *ad* 54) compares Bibl. Heb. (*lby*) *ḥll* (*bqrby*, Psalms 109, 22) and quotes Kaddary (1963). The latter was of the opinion that *ḥll* in this verse is a case of interchange between Ḥ-L-L and Ḥ-W/Y-L (< Ḫ-W/Y-L) 'to tremble from fear' > 'to fear' (Phoen., Heb., Ugar.) – namely, 'The father has feared (god)'.

14 Tarasewicz and Zawadzki 2018, 643 no. 349 r. 12′ (archive of the Ebabbar temple of Sippar; 547 BCE).

15 Cf. Bibl. Heb. *ˁzb byd* and for the suffix of 1.sg.; see Friedrich et al. (1999, 75–6: 128).

16 BE 10 126:5 (417 BCE). 17 See Zadok (1978b, 60b); cf. Friedrich et al. (1999, 169: 241, b).

18 BE 9 55:1, 14 (Nippur, 427 BCE); EE 28:1, r.: *-l*[*u-nu*] (same place and year). Note that in the last text, the slave uses a stamp seal (Bregstein 1993, 479 no. 87).

19 Benz 1972, 127, 308.

20 Zadok 1978b, 61a. Friedrich et al. 1999, 117–18: 174bis classify the Late Babylonian name as G-stem without justification, while they aptly consider the Punic name as D-stem.

occurrence. Hence, Yāḫû-lūnu is a rendering of the Phoenician forerunner of the Punic anthroponym.

Nominal Sentence Names

Two names possibly display the pattern substantive + substantive. **[6]** Milki-izirî (ᴵ*mil-ki-i-zi-ri*) 'Milki is (my) support' corresponds with the Phoenician name *mlqrtˁzr*.[21] The latter, like other names of the type DN-*ˁzr*, may alternatively be a verbal sentence name with a G perfect 3.sg. m. of ˁ-Z-R: 'Milqart has helped'.[22] The Phoenician name *mlkyˁzr* consists of *Mlk* and an imperfect verb;[23] *-y-* as a plene spelling of a connecting vowel (*-i-*, the equivalent of Bibl. Heb. *hiriq compaginis*) is not recorded in the Phoenician onomasticon. The name is explicable also in Hebrew or fringe Canaanite – that is, Moabite or Ammonite, but not in Aramaic.

In the female name [7] ᶠNīr-ˀimmî (ᶠ*ni-ri-ˀ-im-mi-ˀ*),[24] the theophoric element is originally an epithet 'light' which is exclusively Canaanite–Hebrew (*nyr*). Its Aramaic equivalent *nr* (*nūr*) is paired with the sun god in the Sefire inscription (*šmš wnr*).[25] The second member of each preserved divine pair in that inscription from northern Syria (there are four such pairs in addition to damaged ones) is a female deity (at least in this Aramaic milieu). This accords well with the predicative element *-im-mi -ˀ*. Hence, this female name would denote 'Nyr is my mother'. The predicative element *ˀm* 'mother' is recorded as the first component in Phoenician names.[26] A seemingly alternative interpretation, viz. 'Nyr is with me', is less likely if the name is Phoenician, as the preposition *ˁm* 'with' is not recorded in Phoenician–Punic.[27] This alternative interpretation is possible if the name refers to a Judean or a Transjordanian woman.

[21] The name is recorded in a tablet from the Ebabbar temple of Sippar (549 BCE) published by Tarasewicz and Zawadzki 2018, 641 no. 348:17; the final sign is mistakenly written *-ḫu*. The predicative element of this name is with anaptyxis /*ˁizr*/ > /*ˁizir*/. For anaptyctic forms in Phoenician, see, for instance, Σεδεκ/Συδεκ/Συδυκ < **Ṣidq* (Friedrich et al. 1999, 26: 45; their opinion that *q*V*tl* in Phoenician is retained [6: viii] should be relativised).

[22] For this ambiguity of DN-*ˁzr*, see Benz (1972, 214), who cautiously states 'with possible preference for the latter' (i.e., the nominal predicative element). This statement is unfounded not only due to the negligible number of pertinent unambiguous examples, but also in view of the fact that DN + perfect verb is more common than the inverted order (like in the Aramaic onomasticon).

[23] Benz 1972, 139, 344–5, 375–6.

[24] The name is attested in CT 57 26 (Zawadzki 2018, 203 no. 40:5; c. sixth century BCE).

[25] Donner 1957–8 and Fitzmyer 1961, 191. [26] Benz 1972, 269.

[27] The predicative element (*ˁm*) is found in Aramaic (including Samalian) and Hebrew. The Aramaic name type DN + *ˁm* + *-y* is extant in, for example, *Nusku-im-mi-ˀ* (AnOr 9 19:35) and *Nabê-ḫi-im-mì-i* (BIN 1 177:15), 'Nusku/Nabû is with me'.

The pattern substantive + adjective is represented by at least two names. **[8]** Baal-rūm (^{I}*ba-al-ru-um*) 'Baal is exalted', referring to a Tyrian boatman (var. ^{I}*ba-ˀ-i*[*l-r*]*u-um-mu*),[28] is the same name as Phoenician *bˁlrm*.[29] Comparable is **[9]** Ašid-rummu (^{I}*a-šid-ru-um-mu*) 'Aš(a)d is exalted'.[30] The theophoric element *ˀšd* 'lion' is recorded in Punic.[31] **[10]** Milki-rām 'Milki is exalted', the name of a boatman recorded in the Ebabbar archive from Sippar in the early Neo-Babylonian period,[32] can be either Phoenician or Aramaic.

Interrogative Sentence

[11] Ayy-mitūnu (^{I}*a-a-mi-tu-nu*) 'Where is Mitōn?', a shepherd of the Eanna temple, is recorded in Uruk in the fourteenth year of an unknown ruler – that is, either Nabopolassar, Nebuchadnezzar II, or Nabonidus (612, 591, or 542 BCE).[33] This name is recorded as ^{I}*a-a-mì-tu-nu* in the Neo-Assyrian text corpus.[34]

Genitive Compound

[12] Abdu-Ḫmūnu (^{I}*ab-du-uḫ-mu-nu*), son of **[13]** Abdu-Milki (^{I}*ab-du-mi-lik*), acted as the second witness in a deed of Sîn-qitri, son of a Moabite father [35], which was issued in Babylon in the sixth year of Cambyses (524 BCE).[35] ^{I}*ab-du-uḫ-mu-nu* renders Phoenician *ˁbdḥmn* 'Servant of Ḥamōn' with dropping of the short unstressed vowel of the theophoric element. The father's name renders Phoenician–Punic *ˁbdmlk* 'Servant of Milki'.[36] It is not necessarily an anaptyctic form, as the CVC-sign LIK is indifferent to vowel quality and may render CøC (i.e., <*mi-lik*> = /*milk*/).

The name spelled **[14]** Aḫ-ˀabi (^{I}ŠEŠ-*ˀ-bu*; i.e., *ˀḫˀb* 'The father's brother') is not recorded in Phoenician–Punic, but it is explicable in Phoenician terms; cf. Phoen. *ˀḫˀm* 'The mother's brother' (Pun. *ḫˀm* with aphaeresis).[37] This man is mentioned as the father of Nidintu, the fourth of six

[28] Zadok 2018, 117 *ad* VAT 16284+16285:21′ and Weidner 1939, pl. iii opposite p. 928 no. B r. i 12′, respectively.

[29] Benz 1972, 98, 408–9; Friedrich et al. 1999, 38–9:75.

[30] See Friedrich et al. (1999, 106:166). CVC-signs like ŠID are indifferent to vowel quality.

[31] Lipiński 1995, 357–60. The theophoric element is common in Arabic and is productive in the Arabian onomasticon, but in view of the predicative element the Neo-Babylonian name is more likely Phoenician (cf. Zadok 1979, 154 *ad* 110 and Zadok 2000, 643, n. 21).

[32] Da Riva 2002, 436b, BM 78907:3 (transcription only).

[33] Kozuh 2014, 49–50 no. 7 (= NCBT 673):49, 56.

[34] PNA 1/I, 91, s.v. Aia-Mitūnu, and Zadok 1978a, 351; cf. NA ^{I}*mi-tu-nu* (PNA 2/II, 758, s.v. Mitūnu).

[35] De Clercq and Ménant 1903, pl. C opposite p. 160.

[36] Benz 1972, 154–5, 369–72; Zadok 1978b, 60.

[37] Benz 1972, 61, 109, 263, 269; for Hebrew and Aramaic equivalents, see Stamm (1980, 76).

debtors in a receipt of 55 *kors* of barley delivered at Duqulān in the reign of Darius I (496 BCE).[38] The fifth debtor mentioned in this text is Aštartu-šēzib, son of Šillimu ([I]*šil-li-mu*), who was very probably of Phoenician extraction [26]. The second debtor bore a hybrid Akkadian–Aramean paternal name Rammān-šarru-uṣur – that is, with the Aramaic theophoric element Rammān (spelled ^{d}KUR^{an}) and an Akkadian predicative element linking him with some probability to the palatial sector (see Chapter 5). The guarantor bore a similar Akkadian–Aramaic paternal name: Rammān-(mu)kīn-apli. The creditor, a courtier who acted via his slave as proxy, belonged to the palatial sector. Three of the six debtors and two out of the six witnesses have Akkadian filiations. The fourth witness bears the paternal name Munaššê ([I]*mu-na-še-e*) which is common in Canaanite (Phoenician)–Hebrew [29]. It seems more likely that its bearer was a Phoenician, in view of the absence of recognisable Judeans in this deed. This is stated with all due reserve in view of the very restricted statistical pool of this isolated document. The remaining three witnesses have mixed Aramaic–Akkadian filiations. The fifth witness, Sūqāya, son of Iddin-Nabû, who follows Iddin-Nabû, son of Munaššê, was perhaps a son of the preceding witness. The place of issue, Duqulān (*du-qu-la-an*), is not recorded elsewhere and its location is unknown. It is apparently a rural settlement, whose name (written without a determinative) is explicable in Aramaic terms. As is typical of rural settlements, the only individual who bears a family name is the scribe. Hence, he was not necessarily a resident of this village, but originated from a town. He might have been brought by the creditor, who was in all probability external to the village.

Toponym

The name [15] Ḫaru-Ṣapūnu ([Id]*ḫa-ru-ṣa-pu-nu*) is an oronym, viz. 'Mt. Zaphon' (**Harr-Ṣapōn*, on the north Syrian coast where Phoenician colonies were located), used as an anthroponym.[39] The interpretation of Lipiński (1995, 247, n. 184) – namely, that this anthroponym consists of two theophoric elements (Horus and Zaphon) – seems less likely. Ḫaru-Ṣapūnu belonged, together with his father Uggâ ([I]*ug-ga-a*) and brother Nabê-ṣīru, to a group of nine individuals of the same profession (presumably ^{lú}MUŠEN.[DÙ.MEŠ] 'bird-catchers'). They are subsumed as ten individuals and probably formed a decury, a unit which by definition consisted of ten people, but exceptionally it may include slightly fewer or more individuals. In addition to Uggâ and his sons, the decury included two more

38 NBC 4611:6.

39 VS 6 6. See Zadok 1978b, 59b; cf. Benz 1972, 303, 401–2; Friedrich et al. 1999, 14:17, 131:192 *bis*.

individuals with two-tier filiations and two individuals without filiations. Six out of the nine individuals, including Nabê-ṣīru, bear Akkadian names, and one has an Aramaic anthroponym (Reḫīm-Adad). Ḫaru-Ṣapūnu's paternal name (Uggâ) is explicable in West Semitic terms,[40] but is not exclusively Phoenician. Still, in view of his son's name there is no doubt about the father's Phoenician connection. The document was issued in the ninth year of Nabopolassar (617 BCE). The place of issue is not indicated, but from the format of this administrative record it may be surmised that it belongs to the archive of the Ebabbar temple of Sippar. However, so far, no prosopographical links with the rich documentation of this archive can be demonstrated.

Compound or Simplex Names

[16] Šalūma-x ([. . .] ^{I}*šá-lu-ma*-x-([. . .]) was in charge of sailors from Maḫazīn on the North Syrian coast, where some Phoenician colonies and outposts were located.[41] It is based on Canaanite *šlm* 'peace'; cf. Phoenician–Punic *šlm*.[42] The context strongly suggests that he was a Phoenician.

Simplex Names

Isolated Predicate

[17] A man named Yatūnu served as the royal resident (*qīpu*) of a Babylonian temple.[43] His name renders Phoenician *ytn* 'He has given'. This is a short version of names of the type DN-*ytn*,[44] as seen in name [1].

qatl *(optional)*

[18] Abdūnu (^{I}AD-*du-ú-un*, ^{I}*ab-du-ú-nu*) 'Little slave, servant', son of Abī-râm, was either a Phoenician/Philistine or a Judean.[45] He collected the annual rent of a house, apparently acting as co-agent of an Assyrian house owner (Kīnāya, son of Tarībi-Iššar or Erība-Aššur). The first witness of the deed is Šalam-aḫi, son of Dūrāya, perhaps originally from Dor (or the patronym may be understood as a gentilic based on *Dūru*, which is common in Mesopotamian toponymy). A homonymous individual (^{I}*ab-du-nu*) is the father of a certain Nabû-nāṣir from Ālu-ša-^{lú}xx[x].MEŠ.[46]

[40] Zadok 1984, 45 with n. 23.
[41] Zadok 2018, 117 *ad* VAT 16284+16285:2′.
[42] Cf. Benz 1972, 180, 417–18.
[43] *Nbn.* 33:5; and see the Introduction to this chapter.
[44] Benz 1972, 129, 328–9.
[45] Pearce and Wunsch 2014 no. 98:9 and no. 99:8 (Ālu-ša-Našar, 525 BCE); see Abraham et al. (2018) for collations.
[46] BaAr 6 16:23; 512 BCE.

qitl *(optional)*

[19] The name Izirî (^{I}*i-zi-ri-ʾ*, son of ^{I}*bi-ʾ-ú-e*),[47] which ends in the hypocoristic suffix *-ī*, derives from Canaanite–Hebrew ʿ-Z-R 'to help, to support'; cf. OT *ʿzry* and related names.[48] ^{I}*i-zi-ri-ʾ* is with anaptyxis; its bearer may alternatively be a Judean or a Transjordanian.

[20] A woman named ^{f}Ḫilb/punnu (^{f}*ḫi-il-b/pu-un-nu*), whose father bore the Egyptian name ^{I}PA-TAR-^{d}e-si, adopted a three-month-old female baby ^{f}Lillidu (^{f}*lil-li-di*) in the city of Borsippa in 489 BCE.[49] The baby's mother had died and she was given up for adoption by her grandmother, ^{f}Amtia, who belonged to the Borsippean clan of Bāʾiru. The adoptive mother ^{f}Ḫilb/punnu was married to Bēl-ēṭir, a member of the Itinnu family and likewise an urbanite Borsippean, as can be inferred from his family name. ^{f}Ḫilb/punnu herself bore in all probability a West Semitic name which is explicable in Phoenician, Transjordanian, or Levantine Aramaic terms, since it ends with *-ōn* < *-ān* and is based on Ḫ-L-P 'to substitute' (common West Semitic).[50] Typically, a woman of foreign extraction, married to an urbanite Borsippean, was of lower status. This impression is strengthened by the fact that two of the five witnesses to the deed are oblates of Nabû (i.e., of the Ezida temple of Borsippa), including one with an Egyptian name like that of ^{f}Ḫilb/punnu's father. As is well-known, Babylonian urbanites married foreign women, but did not give their daughters in marriage to men who did not belong to their constituency.

qatal *(optional)*

[21] A man called Amanūnu (^{I}*am-ma-nu-nu*), son of Marduk-ibni, is attested as a witness in the time of Nabonidus.[51] His name, ending in the adjectival suffix *-ōn* < *-ān*, derives from ʾ-M-N,[52] in which case it is related to OT *ʾmnwn* 'faithful' (based on a *qatl*-formation; Zadok 1988, 75). He might alternatively be a Judean or a Transjordanian.

47 Durand 1982, 602:12 (Nippur, 521 BCE). 48 Zadok 1988, 79–80.

49 Wunsch 2003–4, 243–4 no. 23 (BM 26506:5, 7, 11). The terms of the adoption are thoroughly discussed by Wunsch, who aptly suggests that ^{f}*ḫi-il-bu/pu-un-nu* was of lower status; there is no need to identify her father with the witness ^{I}*pa-ṭe-*^{d}*e-si*. Both bore names with the Egyptian theophoric element Esi (Isis), but the predicative elements are different: *pa-ṭe-* is very common, while *pa-tar-* is very rare.

50 A derivation from *ḥlb* 'milk' does not seem likely, as this lexeme does not produce West Semitic anthroponyms.

51 Wunsch 1993 no. 254a r. 5′.

52 The doubling of *m* is merely graphic, in order to avoid a reading of <V*m*V> as /*w*/.

The same applies to **[22]** Ḫaraṣīnu (^{I}*ḫa-ra-ṣi-nu*), son of Gūzūnu (^{I}*gu-zu-nu*), who is mentioned in the archive of the Ebabbar temple from Sippar.[53] His name may consist of Ḫ-R-Ṣ 'to cut in, carve' (Phoen., Heb.) and a rare suffix *-īn*,[54] while the paternal name, which ends in *-ōn* < *-ān*, is based on a *qūl*-formation of G-W/Y-Z 'to pass' (Heb., Aram.).

qatál > qatól

The name **[23]** Adūmê (^{I}*a-du-me-e*), father of Ṣiḫā (^{I}*ṣi-ḫa-ˀ*),[55] is based on *ˀdm* 'man'[56] and ends with the suffix *-ē* < *-ī* < *-iy*,[57] which can be either adjectivising ('man-like, human'), a gentilic (*nisbe* 'belonging to Adam'),[58] or a hypocorism (short for a compound name with the theophoric element *ˀdm*). His son's name is Egyptian.

qatīl *(optional)*

[24] Arīšu (^{I}*a-ri-iš-šú*), father of Abdia, a witness in the Egibi archive from Babylon,[59] may render the common Phoenician–Punic name *ˀrš* 'desired, requested' (Latin *Arisus*).[60] For an alternative (Arabian) interpretation, see Zadok 1981, 70 (no. 15).

qātil > qōtil *(G active participle)*

The name of **[25]** Sūkinni (^{I}*su-ki-in-ni*), son of Bēl-uballiṭ, who acted as a witness in a deed from Uruk,[61] renders */Sōkin/* 'inspector, prefect, steward'.[62] The doubling of the *n* is unexpected, but is also recorded in Middle Babylonian transcriptions of this title from Ugarit.[63]

qittīl

The name of **[26]** Šillimu, who is attested as the father of Aštartu-šēzib [34] in the text from Duqulān discussed earlier [14],[64] renders Phoenician–Punic *šlm*,[65] which is either a substantive ('Recompense') or an isolated

[53] Tarasewicz and Zawadzki 2018, 650 no. 354 r. 5′ (511 BCE).

[54] This suffix (cf., e.g., Littmann 1953, 195) is also found in the name Ḫamadinnu (^{I}*ḫa-ma-din-nu*) in a ration list from Tel Keisan in a Phoenician-speaking region; see Horowitz et al. (2018, 101–2:6′).

[55] BE 10 66:13 (Nippur, 421 BCE). This person appears as a witness and uses a ring seal (Bregstein 1993, 518 no. 124).

[56] Friedrich et al. 1999, 134: 196.

[57] Benz 1972, 260; Zadok 1978b, 60b.

[58] Friedrich et al. 1999, 139: 204.

[59] *Dar.* 474:18 (503 BCE).

[60] Benz 1972, 64–8, 276–7; Friedrich et al. 1999, 135: 197b.

[61] YOS 6 2:21 (556 BCE).

[62] The title attained an honorific dimension; cf. Phoen. *skn bs<k>nm* after *mlk bmlkm*, quoted in Hoftijzer and Jongeling 1995, 2: 785–6, s.v. skn_2.

[63] Cf. CAD S 76.

[64] NBC 4611:7 (496 BCE).

[65] Benz 1972, 180, 417–18; cf. Heb. *šlm* (Septuagint Σε/υλλημ).

predicate, viz. D perfect 3 sg. m. of Š-L-M ('He has paid').[66] It is a substitute name (i.e., an anthroponym whose bearer is named after a deceased family member).[67]

maqtal

Two names of this type are attested in the Babylonian text corpus:[68] **[27]** Mattanu (*ᴵma-at-ta-nu*) and **[28]** Mattannāya (*ᴵma-tan-na-a-a*).[69] Both names have the same base (*mtn* 'gift'), the second one ending in the hypocoristic suffix *-ay*.[70] They are explicable in any Northwest Semitic dialect and therefore not necessarily Phoenician.[71] The second vowel of the first name is *-a-* conforming to the rendering of the initial component of the name of the king of Arwad in an inscription of Esarhaddon (*ᴵma-ta-an-ba-ˀ-al*)[72] and the second vowel of the defective spelling Μαθαν in Josephus (both Phoenician names).[73] On the other hand, the CVC-sign TAN in *ᴵma-tan-na-a-a* is indifferent to vowel quality and can render either *á* or *ó* < *á*, like most of the *comparanda*.[74]

muqattil *(optional)*

The name of **[29]** Munaššê (*ᴵmu-na-še-e*), father of Iddin-Nabû,[75] can render Phoenician *mnšy*.[76] Similarly, with attenuation *u* > *i*, **[30]** Minaššê (*ᴵmi-na-áš-še-e*), father of Dādia.[77] This anthroponym, which is also common in Hebrew, is a substitute name (D active participle of N-Š-Y 'to forget', cf. *ad* **[26]**).

qūl

The name of **[31]** Ṣūlūa (*ᴵṣu-lu-ú-a*), father of [11]), apparently ending in –*ūa*, may be based on a cognate of Biblical Hebrew *ṣwlh* 'ocean-deep' (possibly a numen).

66 Cf. the Phoenician compound anthroponyms DN + *šlm* (-σελημ-, defective) which are discussed in Friedrich et al. 1999, 88: 143.
67 See Stamm (1980, 46, 52, 73, 78, 118), cf. Zadok (1988, 115).
68 Friedrich et al. 1999, 136–7: 200.
69 *Nbn.* 450:7 (Ebabbar archive; 546 BCE) and the 'Bellino text' BM 68610:23, lo.e. (308/7 BCE; van der Spek 1986, 202–9). In the latter text, Mattannāya is mentioned alongside his brother, who was named after Izalla, an Aramaic-speaking region in the northern Jazirah. Their father bore an Akkadian name, Ina-ṣilli-Nanāya 'In the shade of Nanāya'.
70 Friedrich et al. 1999, 140: 205.
71 Zadok 1978b, 60a with n. 10.
72 PNA 2/II, 746, s.v. Mattan-Baˀal 3.
73 Friedrich et al. 1999, 137: 201.
74 For a discussion of the *comparanda*, see Benz (1972, 356–7) (cf. 143–6).
75 NBC 4611:17 (Duqulān, 496 BCE).
76 Benz 1972, 142, 363–4.
77 Zadok 2014, 119 (no. 1); 558 BCE.

qill *(optional)*
[32] Giddâ (^{I}*gi-id-da-a*), father of a messenger of an alphabet scribe,[78] is a hypocorism of **gadd* (variants: **gedd*, **gidd*) 'fortune, good fortune', which is also extant in Phoenician.[79] Alternatively, the name can be an Aramaic dialectal form.

Gentilic
[33] Ṣūrāya (^{I}*ṣu-ra-a-a*) 'Tyrian' is the name of a Phoenician inhabitant of Yāhūdu, a colony of Judeans in or near the Nippur region. In a similar vein, the Tyrian colony of Bīt-Ṣūrāyi near Nippur had Judean inhabitants.[80] He is mentioned in a list of sixteen holders of fractions of bow-fiefs whose names are preserved.[81] The majority of the names (eleven) contain the theophoric element Yhw, hence referring to Judeans. The remaining four names are all explicable in Canaanite–Hebrew terms. It can be surmised that few Tyrians were settled by the Babylonians in the Judean settlement after the conquest of Tyre, which had taken place just a few years after the earliest occurrence of Yāhūdu. It is well known that Judeans and Lycians lived in the settlement of the Tyrians (Bīt-Ṣūrāyi) in the Nippur region during the late-Achaemenid period.

Hybrid Names

A hybrid Phoenician name is [34] Aštartu-šēzib (^{Id}*áš-tar-tu$_4$-še-zib*), borne by the son of [26] Šillimu.[82] Anthroponyms with the theophoric element ʿAštart are common in Phoenician and Punic, where all their predicative elements are explicable in Phoenician-Canaanite terms.[83] However, here the predicative element is Aramaic–Akkadian ("ʿAštart save!") due to the Babylonian–Aramaic milieu. The predicative element is masculine because the name-bearer is male, despite the fact that the subject is a female deity (see also Chapter 3 n. 1 on this practice).

Moabite Anthroponyms

Only two Moabite personal names are attested in the Babylonian text corpus so far. In a deed concerning an Egyptian slave woman, two brothers (Sîn-qitri and Itti-Nabû-balāṭu) bear the Moabite patronym [35] Kamuš-šarru-uṣur

78 Pearce and Wunsch 2014 no. 1 (Ālu-ša-Yāḫūdāyi, 572 BCE).
79 Friedrich et al. 1999, 131: 192 *bis*. 80 Zadok 2002, 41:113.
81 Pearce and Wunsch 2014 no. 15 (517 BCE). 82 NBC 4611:7 (Duqulān, 496 BCE).
83 Benz 1972, 386–7.

(^{Id}*ka-mu-šú*-šarru-uṣur) 'Kemosh protect the king!'.[84] The same text mentions the Phoenician Abdu-Ḫmūnu, discussed earlier [12]. The second Moabite anthroponym is **[36]** Kamuš-il 'Kemosh is god' (^{I}*ka-mu-šu-i-lu*, ^{I}*ka-am-mu-šú*-DINGIR.MEŠ). The person bearing this name is recorded as the father of Ḫanṭušu, a witness in Susa in 505 BCE.[85]

An Ammonite Anthroponym

The only Ammonite name attested in the Babylonian text corpus so far is **[37]** Milkūmu-šarru-uṣur (^{I}*mil-≪ki≫ku-mu-* . . .) 'Milkom protect the king', who is recorded in a text dated to Nabonidus.[86] This person's presence in Babylonia accords well with the assumption that Ammon was transformed from a vassal kingdom to a Babylonian province in c. 582 BCE[87] (i.e., one generation earlier). The Neo-Babylonian Empire pursued the Assyrian policy of deporting members of the local elite as well as experts following such an administrative transformation.

Statistical Evaluation and Some Conclusions

The percentage of bearers of names deriving from Phoenician and fringe Canaanite in the abundant prosopographical record from first-millennium Babylonia is negligible. Almost half of the thirty-four Phoenician names are undoubtedly such, the other half is optional – that is, either Phoenician or belonging to other Northwest Semitic dialects, mostly fringe Canaanite or Hebrew; two are alternatively Arabian.

Most individuals bearing these names have filiations. All the filiations are two-tier: a son's and a father's name are combined. Two-tier filiation is typical of foreigners in the Babylonian documentation, where only Babylonian urbanites bore three-tier filiations (son, father, and remote ancestor). This is an indication that the Phoenicians did not marry members of the segregated urbanite elite. Like other foreigners, they assimilated to the less prestigious classes of the Babylonian society. However, members of these classes did not necessarily form a poorer layer of the Babylonian society: a clear case in point are prominent members of the palatial sectors and entrepreneurs lacking family names.

84 De Clercq and Ménant 1903, pl. C opposite p. 160 (Babylon, 524 BCE); cf. Zadok 1978b, 60 and Stol 1977.

85 TCL 13 193:33 and *Dar.* 435 r. 3′; Zadok 1978b, 62a; Abraham 1997, 56 with n. 7; Stolper 1996, 520 with n. 22.

86 VS 3 53:5 (Babylon, 545 BCE); Zadok 2003, 502.

87 Lipschits 2004, 39–41 with literature.

Eleven individuals are recorded without filiations. There are several reasons for this omission. One anthroponym [4] is derived from a toponym, where no patronyms are expected. Slaves or people having a title (as in [5, 17]) bear an identifier and therefore do not need to be presented with a paternal name which is an additional, superfluous, identifier. Filiations are not required in non-legal documents, which supplies the context of several attestations [6, 8, 16]. Ṣūrāya [33] is mentioned in a deed where only recurrent and homonymous individuals are listed with their paternal names. Another one is recorded in a deed without witnesses [2].

Only one purely Phoenician filiation is attested [12, 13]. All the other filiations are mixed – that is, with members bearing Akkadian or West Semitic, mostly Aramaic, names. This is expected in first-millennium Babylonia where people bearing Akkadian and Aramaic names belonged to the local scene. Cases where the father bore a Phoenician name but the son had a local (Akkadian or Aramaic) anthroponym are recorded in the earliest occurrences (624 and 617 BCE [9, 15]) and in 548 BCE [1] (i.e., about one generation after the deportations of the Phoenicians by Nebuchadnezzar II). These are clear cases of acculturation that, to some extent, hint at assimilation. The earliest inverted case – a father with an Akkadian name and a son with an undoubtedly Phoenician anthroponym – is from 556 BCE [25]. Such cases are also encountered slightly later in the reign of Nabonidus [21], one or two generations after these deportations. The Akkadian names are either typical of members of the palatial sector or very common.

As stated earlier, there are also cases where the other member of the filiation has a West Semitic name. Such cases are recorded in 547 and 503 BCE [3, 24]. The paternal name of [19] (^{I}*bi-*$^{?}$*-ú-e*) is too short for an unambiguous linguistic affiliation; it may be common West Semitic. The last-recorded filiation has members with Akkadian and Aramaic names [28].

Exceptionally, an individual with an Egyptian name has a Phoenician paternal name (421 BCE [23]). An analogous case from 489 BCE is [20], where a common Canaanite anthroponym is combined with an Egyptian paternal name. Two waves of Egyptian deportees arrived in Babylonia, notably due to Nebuchadnezzar II's western campaigns around 600 BCE and the conquest of Egypt by Cambyses about 80 years later. An influx of Egyptians into Babylonia continued in the late-Achaemenid period. Phoenicia itself, like the whole coast of the southern Levant, was under Egyptian cultural influence. The purely Phoenician filiation from 524 BCE

[12–13], slightly less than forty years after Nebuchadnezzar II conquered Tyre, is a remarkable but isolated case of keeping Phoenician identity during two generations. However, there is no telling when their ancestors arrived in Babylonia. Still, there is a possibility that both members enjoyed a long life-span, in which case the father arrived as early as 600 BCE. Like in their motherland, several Phoenicians in Babylonia are related to individuals with Egyptian names. On the whole, within few generations the Phoenicians intermarried with non-urbanite Babylonians and assimilated.

Very few Phoenicians occupied prominent positions (at least two [1, 17]), but most of them are recorded in a rural milieu, notably the earliest ones: the individuals from Duqulān [14, 26, 29, 34], the Tyrian from Yāhūdu [33], and the shepherds [2, 11]. Several Phoenicians were absorbed by the temples. As expected, some played the passive role of witnesses, like most individuals who are recorded in deeds from the Neo-Babylonian and Late Babylonian periods.

The Ammonite person [37] has an Aramaic paternal name ('Hammatean'; i.e., North Syrian). One of the Moabites has an Aramaic given name [35]. The other Moabite has a West Semitic anthroponym common in first-millennium BCE Babylonia [36].

Further Reading

In addition to Frank L. Benz (1972), who lists most of the Phoenician anthroponyms (with their references) and succinctly analyses and classifies them, Felice Israel (1991) can be consulted with benefit as he offers a synthetic treatment. Johannes Friedrich et al. (1999) provides a linguistic analysis of most of the predicative elements, while Edward Lipiński (1995) discusses most of the pertinent theophoric elements. Since the names of the Moabites and the only Ammonite name discussed herein are linguistically Akkadian (with Moabite and Ammonite theophoric elements) and Aramaic, there is no point in referring to the bibliography on Ammonite–Moabite onomastica; consult any recent and updated Old Testament comprehensive dictionary or encyclopaedia where the deities Kemosh and Milkom are amply discussed.

References

Abraham, K. 1997. 'Šušan in the Egibi texts from the time of Marduk-nāṣir-apli', *Orientalia Lovaniensia Periodica* 28, 55–85.

Abraham, K., M. Jursa, and Y. Levavi 2018. 'Further Collations to CUSAS 28', *Nouvelles Assyriologiques Brèves et Utilitaires 2018*/53.

Baker, H. D. (ed.) 2001. *The Prosopography of the Neo-Assyrian Empire*, 2/II: L–N. Helsinki: The Neo-Assyrian Text Corpus Project.

Benz, F. L. 1972. *Personal Names in Phoenician and Punic Inscriptions*, Studia Pohl 8. Rome: Pontificium Institutum Biblicum.

Bongenaar, A. C. V. M. 1997. *The Neo-Babylonian Ebabbar Temple at Sippar: Its Administration and its Prosopography*, Publications de l'Institut historique-archéologique néerlandais de Stamboul 80. Leiden: Nederlands Historisch-Archaeologisch Instituut te Istanbul.

Bregstein, L. B. 1993. Seal Use in Fifth Century BC Nippur, Iraq: A Study of Seal Selection and Sealing Practices in the Murašû Archive. PhD dissertation: University of Pennsylvania, Philadelphia.

de Clercq, L. and J. Ménant 1903. *Collection de Clercq: Catalogue méthodique et raisonné*, Vol. 2. Paris: Leroux.

Da Riva, R. 2002. *Der Ebabbar-Tempel von Sippar in frühneubabylonischer Zeit (640–580 v.Chr.)*, Alter Orient und Altes Testament 291. Münster: Ugarit-Verlag.

Donner, H. 1957–8. 'Zur Inschrift von Sudschīn Aa 9', *Archiv für Orientforschung* 18, 390–2.

Durand, J.-M. 1982. *Documents cunéiformes de la IVe section de l'École Pratique des Hautes Études. Tome I: Catalogue et copies cunéiformes*. Geneva: Droz.

Fitzmyer, J. A. 1961. 'The Aramaic inscriptions of Sefire I and II', *Journal of the American Oriental Society* 81, 178–222.

Friedrich, J., W. Röllig, M. G. Amadasi Guzzo, and W. Mayer 1999. *Phönizisch-Punische Grammatik*, 3rd ed., Analecta Orientalia 55. Rome: Pontificium Institutum Biblicum.

Gehlken, E. 1996. *Uruk: Spätbabylonische Wirtschaftstexte aus dem Eanna-Archiv, Tl. 2: Texte verschiedenen Inhalts*, Ausgrabungen in Uruk-Warka Endberichte 11. Mainz: Philipp von Zabern.

Harding, G. L. 1971. *An Index and Concordance of Pre-Islamic Arabian Names and Inscriptions*, Near and Middle East Series 8. Toronto: University of Toronto Press.

Hoftijzer, J. and K. Jongeling 1995. *Dictionary of the North-West Semitic Inscriptions*, 2 Vols, Handbuch der Orientalistik I/21. Leiden: Brill.

Horowitz, W., T. Oshima, and S. L. Sanders 2018. *Cuneiform in Canaan: The Next Generation*, 2nd ed. University Park: Eisenbrauns.

Israel, F. 1991. 'Note di onomastica semitica IV: rassegna critica sull'onomastica fenicio-punica' in *Atti del II congresso internazionale di studi fenici e punici, Roma, 9–14 novembre 1987*. Rome: Consiglio Nazionale delle Ricerche: Istituto per la Civiltà Fenicia e Punica, pp. 511–22.

Kaddary, M. Z. 1963. 'Ḥll = "bore", "pierce"?', *Vetus Testamentum* 13, 486–9.

Kozuh, M. 2014. *The Sacrificial Economy: Assessors, Contractors, and Thieves in the Management of Sacrificial Sheep at the Eanna Temple of Uruk (ca. 625–520 BC)*, Explorations in Ancient Near Eastern Civilizations 2. Winona Lake: Eisenbrauns.

Lipiński, E. 1995. *Dieux et deésses de l'univers phénicien et punique*, Orientalia Lovaniensia Analecta 64. Leuven: Peeters.

Lipschits, O. 2004. 'Ammon in transition from vassal kingdom to Babylonian province', *Bulletin of the American Schools of Oriental Research* 335, 38–52.

Littmann, E. 1953. 'Arabische Hypokoristika' in F. F. Hvidberg (ed.), *Studia Orientalia Ioanni Pedersen Septuagenario AD VII id. Nov. anno MCMLIII a collegis discipulis amicis dicata*. Copenhagen: Munskaard, pp. 193–9.

Pearce, L. E. and C. Wunsch 2014. *Documents of Judean Exiles and West Semites in Babylonia in the Collection of David Sofer*, Cornell University Studies in Assyriology and Sumerology 28. Bethesda: CDL Press.

Pedersén, O. 2005. *Archive und Bibliotheken in Babylon: Die Tontafeln der Grabung Robert Koldeweys 1899–1917*, Abhandlungen der Deutschen Orient-Gesellschaft 25 Saarbrücken: Saarländische Druckerei und Verlag.

Radner, K. (ed.) 1998. *The Prosopography of the Neo-Assyrian Empire*, 1/I: A. Helsinki: The Neo-Assyrian Text Corpus Project.

San Nicolò, M. 1951. *Babylonische Rechtsurkunden des ausgehenden 8. und des 7. Jahrhunderts v. Chr.*, Abhandlungen der Bayerischen Akademie der Wissenschaften, Philologisch-historische Klasse, Neue Folge 34. München: Verlag der Bayerischen Akademie der Wissenschaften.

van der Spek, R. J. 1986. *Grondbezit in het Seleucidische Rijk*. Amsterdam: Vrije Universiteit Uitgeverij.

Stamm, J. J. 1980. *Beiträge zur hebräischen und altorientalischen Namenkunde. Zu seinem 70. Geburtstag herausgegeben von Ernst Jenni und Martin A. Klopfenstein*, Orbis Biblicus et Orientalis 30. Freiburg/Göttingen: Universitätsverlag/ Vandenhoeck & Ruprecht.

Stol, M. 1977. 'Un texte oublié', *Revue d'assyriologie et d'archéologie orientale* 71, 96.

Stolper, M. W. 1985. *Entrepreneurs and Empire: The Murašû Archive, the Murašû Firm, and Persian Rule in Babylonia*, Uitgaven van het Nederlands Historisch-Archaeologisch Instituut te Istanbul 54. Istanbul: Nederlands Historisch-Archaeologisch Instituut.

Stolper, M. W. 1996. 'A paper chase after the Aramaic on TCL 13 193', *Journal of the American Oriental Society* 116, 517–21.

Tarasewicz, R. and S. Zawadzki 2018. *Animal Offerings and Cultic Calendar in the Neo-Babylonian Sippar*, Alter Orient und Altes Testament 451. Münster: Ugarit-Verlag.

Weidner, E. F. 1939. 'Jojachin, König von Juda, in babylonischen Keilschrifttexten' in *Mélanges Syriens offerts à M. René Dussaud, secrétaire perpétuel de l'Académie des inscriptions et belles-lettres, par ses amis et ses élèves* II, Bibliothèque archéologique et historique 30. Paris: Geuthner, 923–35, pls I–V.

Wunsch, C. 1993. *Die Urkunden des babylonischen Geschäftsmannes Iddin-Marduk: Zum Handel mit Naturalien im 6. Jahrhundert v. Chr.*, Vol. 2, Cuneiform Monographs 3b. Groningen: Styx.

Wunsch, C. 2003–4. 'Findelkinder und Adoption nach neubabylonischen Quellen', *Archiv für Orientforschung* 50, 172–244.

Zadok, R. 1978a. *On West Semites in Babylonia during the Chaldean and Achaemenian Periods: An Onomastic Study*, revised version. Jerusalem: Wanaarta/Tel Aviv University.

Zadok, R. 1978b. 'Phoenicians, Philistines and Moabites in Mesopotamia in the first millennium BC', *Bulletin of the American Schools of Oriental Research* 230, 57–65.

Zadok, R. 1979. *The Jews in Babylonia during the Chaldean and Achaemenian Periods According to Babylonian Sources*, Studies in the History of the Jewish People and the Land of Israel Monograph Series 3. Haifa: University of Haifa.

Zadok, R. 1981. 'Arabians in Mesopotamia during the Late-Assyrian, Chaldean, Achaemenian and Hellenistic Periods', *Zeitschrift der Deutschen Morgenländischen Gesellschaft* 131, 42–84.

Zadok, R. 1984. 'Assyro-Babylonian lexical and onomastic notes', *Bibliotheca Orientalis* 41, 33–46.

Zadok, R. 1985. *Geographical Names according to Neo- and Late-Babylonian Texts*, Répertoire Géographique des Textes Cunéiformes 8. Wiesbaden: Reichert.

Zadok, R. 1988. *The Pre-Hellenistic Israelite Anthroponymy and Prosopography*, Orientalia Lovaniensia Analecta 28. Leuven: Peeters.

Zadok, R. 2000. 'On the prosopography and onomastics of Syria–Palestine and adjacent regions', *Ugarit Forschungen* 32, 599–674.

Zadok, R. 2002. *The Earliest Diaspora: Israelites and Judeans in Pre-Hellenistic Mesopotamia*, Publications of the Diaspora Research Institute 151. Tel Aviv: Tel Aviv University.

Zadok, R. 2003. 'The representation of foreigners in Neo- and Late Babylonian legal documents (eighth through second centuries BCE)' in O. Lipschits and J. Blenkinsopp (eds.), *Judah and the Judeans in the Neo-Babylonian Period.* Winona Lake: Eisenbrauns, pp. 471–589.

Zadok, R. 2014. 'Judeans in Babylonia: Updating the Dossier' in U. Gabbay and S. Secunda (eds.), *Encounters by the Rivers of Babylon: Scholarly Conversations between Jews, Iranians and Babylonians in Antiquity*, Texts and Studies in Ancient Judaism 160. Tübingen: Mohr Siebeck, pp. 109–29.

Zadok, R. 2015. 'West Semitic groups in the Nippur region between c. 750 and 330 BCE' in J. Stökl and C. Waerzeggers (eds.), *Exile and Return: The Babylonian Contexts*, Beihefte zur Zeitschrift für die alttestamentliche Wissenschaft 478. Berlin: De Gruyter, pp. 94–156.

Zadok, R. 2018. 'People from countries west and north of Babylonia in Babylon during the reign of Nebuchadnezzar II', *Hebrew Bible and Ancient Israel* 7, 112–29.

Zadok, R and T. Zadok 2003. 'Neo/Late-Babylonian geography and documentation', *Nouvelles Assyriologiques Brèves et Utilitaires* 2003/35.

Zawadzki, S. 2018. *The Rental of Houses in the Neo-Babylonian Period (VI–V Centuries BC)*. Warsaw: Agade Bis.

CHAPTER 11

Arabian Names

Ahmad al-Jallad

Introduction

The term 'Arabian' in cuneiform sources is primarily geographic, covering a range of toponyms, ethnonyms, and anthroponyms ultimately stemming from the arid regions to the west and south of Mesopotamia. As such, the term encompasses a wide array of languages, some known and attested independently in the Arabian epigraphic record, such as Sabaic and Taymanitic. In other cases, the cuneiform sources constitute our only evidence for the shadowy vernaculars of North Arabia and the Syrian Desert in the first millennium BCE. During this period, Arabia was home to several independent writing traditions that made use of variants of the South Semitic alphabet, a sister script to the Phoenico–Aramaic script. There thrived a rich writing culture in the south-western corner of the Peninsula, in what is today Yemen. Four principal languages are encountered in the epigraphic record: Sabaic, Minaic, Qatabanic, and Hadramitic (Stein 2011). The oases of North and West Arabia also boasted their own scripts and dialects: Dadanitic (at Dadān, mod. al-ˁUlā), Taymanitic (at Taymāˀ), and Dumaitic (at Dūmat, mod. Dūmat al-Jandal) (Macdonald 2000). These materials provide important comparanda when trying to identify Arabian names in cuneiform transcription and in trying to locate their source.

Historical Background

Beginning in the Neo-Assyrian period, contacts between Arabians and Mesopotamian states begin to increase. The Neo-Assyrians carried out several military campaigns against the inhabitants of northern Arabia, specifically targeting the oasis city of Adummatu, mod. Dūmat al-Jandal (Eph'al 1984, 20–53). At the same time, these sources record a growing presence of Arabians in Babylonia (Eph'al 1974). A number of inscriptions in the South Semitic alphabet – written on seals and clay tablets – have also been discovered in the environs of Babylonia, independently attesting to the presence of Arabian groups in the region (Sass 1991, 43–68).

Principles for Distinguishing Arabian Names in Babylonian Sources

Arabian names in Babylonian sources are usually identified on the basis of linguistic features that distinguish them from Northwest and East Semitic. One of the most salient isoglosses is the preservation of word-initial *w*, which has merged with *y* in the Northwest Semitic languages, and the presence of a non-etymological word-final *u* – what is termed *wawation* (Al-Jallad 2022). Arabian names are also identified based on their association with groups of people labelled 'Arabian' in the sources, as well as on the basis of etymology (Zadok 1981, §1). The number of Arabian anthroponyms, tribal names, and toponyms in first millennium BCE Babylonian sources is comparatively small but nevertheless attests to the growing presence of Arabians in southern Babylonia and the importance of Arabia in trade and other external affairs of the country.

Toponyms

In 552 BCE, Nabonidus, the last king of the Neo-Babylonian Empire, campaigned in North Arabia and conquered several oasis settlements. The Harran stele (Schaudig 2001, 486–99; Weiershäuser and Novotny 2020 no. 47) furnishes us with the longest list of Arabian toponyms:

^{uru}*te-ma-a*: This refers to the North Arabian oasis town of Taymāˀ, attested in the local Taymanitic inscriptions as *tmˀ* (Eskoubi 1999, 239–41; Hayajneh 2001, 81–95). It is mentioned in the Hebrew Bible as תֵּימָא (Jeremiah 25:23).

^{uru}*da-da-(nu)*: Dadān was an important oasis to the southwest of Taymāˀ, also mentioned in Jeremiah 25:23 as דְּדָן. The town boasted its own script and writing tradition (Macdonald 2000; Kootstra 2023). The name is attested both in the inscriptions of Taymāˀ and Dadān as *ddn*.

^{uru}*pa-dak-ku*: This renders *fadak*, an Arabian oasis southwest of Dadān, located near the modern site of al-Ḥāˀiṭ, and which carries the same name today (Hausleiter and Schaudig 2016, 236–7). It is unclear whether the plosive *p* in cuneiform transcription is a faithful representation of the town's name or whether the use of *pa-* was simply an approximation of the spirantised *f*, characteristic of Arabic today. A cuneiform inscription of Nabonidus has been discovered at this site, possibly mentioning the name of the settlement as *p*[*a-dak-ku*] (Hausleiter and Schaudig 2016).

^{uru}*ḫi-ib-ra-a*: This appears to render the name of the oasis of Khaybar, which is about 60 kilometres as the bird flies southwest of Fadak. The spelling, however, does not match its current name, which goes back at least to the seventh century CE. Like *te-ma-a*, it appears that the oasis' name in the middle of the first millennium BCE was Ḫibrāʾ.

^{uru}*iá-di-ḫu*: This oasis lies about sixty kilometres south of *pa-dak-ku* and is known today as al-Ḥuwayyiṭ, but locals apparently still know the uninhabited site as *yadīˁ* (Hausleiter and Schaudig, *forthcoming*). The anthroponym *ydˁ* is common in the Ancient North Arabian inscriptions and may suggest that the town bore the name of a person (Harding 1971, 663).

^{uru}*iá-at-ri-bu*: The final site on Nabonidus' campaign is today the most well-known and important of these settlements, *yaṯrib*, the capital of Mohammad's state and the site of his burial. The cuneiform spelling is a faithful transcription of the Arabian name. It is next attested in an undated Nabataean inscription from the area of al-ˁUlā (Al-Theeb 2002 no. 163), and finally in Islamic-period sources, where its name was officially changed to al-Madīnah.

Ethnonyms

The Arabians mentioned in cuneiform sources belong to several social groups, ranging from the macro-identity, *arab*, to tribes and smaller clans and families.

$^{\text{lú/kur}}$*a-ra-bi*: The term 'Arab', which first appears in Neo-Assyrian documents, is an umbrella label covering the inhabitants of the 'distant desert' of North Arabia, and sometimes elsewhere. Not all whom this title encompasses identified as a self-conscious community or were necessarily speakers of a language we would call Arabic (Macdonald 2009). By the eighth century BCE, Arabian groups had settled in southern Babylonia, in the territories of Bīt-Dakkūri and Bīt-Amukāni (Eph'al 1974). A settlement called Ālu-ša-Arbāyi 'City of the Arabians' was located near Nippur (Zadok 1977, 224–7). It seems clear that *arab* was a macro-label encompassing several ethnic/social groups, as evidenced by the compound name *te-mu-da-a ar-ba-a-a*, which could refer to an Arabian, belonging to the tribe/clan of Thamūd (Zadok 1977, 224–7).

^{uru}*qi-da-ri*: Zadok (1981, 66) suggests a connection between this toponym, which is attested in a Neo-Babylonian document from Nippur (BE 8/1 65), with Neo-Assyrian *qid-ri-na*, an Arabian settlement in Bīt-Dakkūri possibly named after the large Arabian confederacy of Qedar. The name is attested in the Bible (Gen 25:13; 1 Chron 1:29), and a Qedarite king, Gušam son of ʕAmru, offered a votive bowl to the deity *hnʔlt* 'the Goddess' at Tell al-Maskhūṭah in the Nile Delta (Rabinowitz 1956). The vocalisation in cuneiform transcription – alongside the spelling of the name in the Tell al-Maskhūṭah bowl as *qdr* – suggests an original pronunciation of *qidar* rather than *qaydar*.

^{lú}*sa-ba-ʔ*, ^{lú}*ša-ba-ʔ-a-a*: This term transcribes the name of one of the four principal states of South Arabia, *sabaʔ*, mentioned in the Bible as שְׁבָא (e.g., Gen 25:3). Some have suggested that the references to the Sabaeans in cuneiform texts are in fact to a trading outpost in the Ḥigāz, perhaps near Dadān, rather than to the kingdom itself (Macdonald 1997; Retsö 2003, 135). The spelling of the name with *sa* in a Neo-Babylonian fragment in contrast to *ša-* in the southern Babylonian inscriptions from Sūḫu (Zadok 2013, 317; Dietrich 2003, 4) may suggest that the initial sibilant was not identical to either sound and was therefore approximated in different ways depending on the scribe.

^{lú}*ta-am-da-a-a*: Ran Zadok has connected this name with the famous Arabian tribe Thamūd (Zadok 2013, 317), attested already in Neo-Assyrian records. A close linguistic match may be found in the Jordanian toponym *wādī ṯamad*, in the area of Madaba. The form *ṯmdn* is attested once in Safaitic (KRS 2271) and would correspond to the anthroponym ^{I}*tam-da-nu*, which Zadok suspects is linguistically related to the tribal name (Zadok 2013, 317). The Arabic meaning of the root *ṯmd* is 'to dig a well or channel', and is comparable to the meaning of *nbṭ*, which later gives rise to the ethnonym *nbṭ* 'Nabataean'.

Anthroponyms

One-Word Names with Wawation

^{I}*gu-da-du-u* (Gudādû): This name appears to be formed with the *qutāl* noun pattern, which is quite common in the Arabic onomasticon (Zadok 2013, 318; 2004, 205). It may be compared to Safaitic *gdd* or

Nabataean *gdw* (Negev 1991, 18), although the latter appears to belong to a different noun pattern. The basic sense of this root is 'to cut', but also gives rise to words meaning 'lot' and 'fate'.

^{I}*kal-li-lu-ú* (Kallilû): Zadok (2013, 318) connects it with Aramaic *klylʾ* and Arabic *iklīl* 'crown'. A similar name is attested in Safaitic as *kll*, but the vocalisation is unclear. G. Lankester Harding suggests a connection with Arabic *kālilun* 'weary' (Harding 1971, 504). *Kll* may be a divine name, if it is to be connected with the South Arabian *ʿbdkllm* 'worshipper of *kll*' (Harding 1971, 400) and the Arabic theophoric name ʿAbd-kulāl, preserved in Islamic-period sources.

^{I}*bal-ta$_5$-mu-ʾ* (Baltam(mu); Zadok (2013, 319)): The root *bśm* is common to Arabic and Northwest Semitic, but *wawation* suggests that this name has an Arabic source. The name *bśm* is attested at Taymāʾ, and Palmyra *bsm* (Stark 1971, 11). The word seems ultimately to come from a Northwest Semitic source meaning 'spice', 'perfume', Aramaic *besmā*.

^{I}*s/šam-šu-ʾ* (Šamšu; Zadok 2003, 532): This name is derived from the common Semitic word for 'sun'. The name *śms* is common in Safaitic (Harding 1971, 258), and may be a shortened form of the theophoric name ʿAbd-śams 'worshipper of Shams', which is common in the Arabic onomasticon until the rise of Islam (Caskell 1966, 131), of which this name could be a hypocoristic form.

^{I}*šab-pu-ú* (Šabbû): Zadok connects this name with the Arabic root *šbb* 'to cut' (Zadok 2013, 308), but it is also possible to see in it the sense of 'youth'. The name is common in Ancient North Arabian, attested as *śb* in Safaitic and Hismaic, and a possible diminutive form in Dadanitic, *śbb* (Harding 1971, 337). The name *šby* is attested in Nabataean (Negev 1991, 61), as well as in Palmyrene (Stark 1971, 50), perhaps with a hypocoristic *y*.

^{I}*zu-uḫ-ru-ʾ* (Zuḫru): This *wawated* name is given in Aramaic transcription as *zʿrʾ*, which Zadok interprets as the replacement of *wawation* with an Aramaic hypocoristic ending ʾ (Zadok 2013, 318). The Aramaic spelling may further suggest that its original vocalisation was *zuġru* 'small'. This spelling does not find any parallels in the Ancient North Arabian onomasticon, but note that the root for 'small' is in fact *zġr* in many modern Arabic vernaculars. One can rule out late Aramaic influence as the phoneme *ġayn* is preserved; thus, it seems to be a native Arabic biform of the root.

^{I}*ia-ʾ-lu-u/ú* (Yālû): Zadok (2013, 318) identifies this as a form of the name *wʾlw*, which is widely attested in the Ancient North Arabian onomasticon (Harding 1971, 645). This connection posits a change of *w* > *y*, which is typical of the Northwest Semitic languages and in the local vernacular of Taymāʾ (Kootstra 2016, 84–5), and may suggest that the name was drawn from that area. On the other hand, one might see in this name a prefix-conjugated verb, *yaʿlu* 'to go up'. The personal name *yʿly*, which reflects a confusion of the *w* and *y* in the root *ʿlw*, is common in Ancient North Arabian (Harding 1971, 677) and Nabataean (Negev 1991, 34). A similar confusion of roots is encountered in the Arabian name *ia-u-ta-ʾ*, attested in Neo-Assyrian sources (Eph'al 1974, 111), which appears to correspond with Safaitic *yṯʿ*, attested in Greek transcription as ιαιθεου (Winnett and Harding 1978 no. 3562 and Greek 2).

One-Word Names Derived from Verbs

ᴵ*ia-a-šu-pi*: Zadok (2013, 319) connects this name with Arabic Yasūf, from *swf* 'to endure'. While such a name is not attested in the Ancient North Arabian onomasticon, the name *yśf* is found once in Safaitic (CEDSQM 15) and attested in Sabaic and Qatabanic (DASI, s.v.). The name would appear to be a prefix-conjugated form of the root *śwf* 'to adorn'. The representation of Arabian s^2, a lateral sibilant, with *šu* rather than *lt*, as in *baltam* (see 'One-Word Names with *Wawation*'), may suggest inconsistency in the representation of this foreign sound, similar to the representation of Sabaic s^1 in the name *sabaʾ*.

One-Word Names With the ān Termination

The final *-ān* termination appears to be a hypocoristic suffix commonly used in Arabic names. Names of this sort do not take *wawation* in Nabataean and the same rule appears to be observed in cuneiform sources.

ᴵ*ḫa-ir-a-nu* (Ḫairān): Zadok (2013, 319) takes this as an Arabian name, contra Michael P. Streck (1999, 289). The name is attested in Ancient North Arabian as *ḫrn* (Harding 1971, 220) and *ḥyrw* in Nabataean (Negev 1991, 29). The name also appears in Greek transcriptions from the Roman period in southern Syria, Χαιρανης (PAES III.a 793.9), Χαιρανο (PAES III.a 793).

ᴵ*a-tu-ba/ma-nu* (Zadok 2013, 319): This name likely renders Arabic *ʿ-t-b* 'to scold, reproach', which gives rise to the name *ʿtb* in Hismaic and Dadanitic (Harding 1971, 404). The name, in its diminutive form, is that of the large tribal confederacy *ˁutaybah*, pl. *ˁutbān*, in Saudi Arabia today. The present vocalisation appears to combine the hypocoristic *-ān* with a passive participial form *ˁatūb*, thus *ˁatūbān*.

Theophoric Names

The commonest theophoric element in Arabian names in pre-Islamic times is *ˀil* 'god'; this holds true in both South Arabian and in the Ancient North Arabian inscriptions. Other elements like *ˀab* 'father', *ˀaḫ* 'brother' are attested as well. Arabian names in Neo-Babylonian sources reflect these trends.

[I]*ad-bi-i-lu* (Adbi-il; Zadok 2013, 319): A theophoric name with *ˀil* as a divine name. Such names are common in Ancient North Arabian and Ancient South Arabian. The name *ˀdbˀl* is attested in Safaitic and Hismaic (Harding 1971, 31). The element *ˀdb* is also attested independently (Harding 1971, 31). The name would seem to mean 'Guest of ˀil'.

[I]*abi-ḫa-zu-mu* (Abī-ḫazumu): Zadok (2013, 319) takes this as 'My father is firm', connecting it to Arabic *ḥazuma*, which is attested as a one-word name in Ancient North Arabian and Arabic (Harding 1971, 187).

[I]*da-ḫir-ri-ˀil* (Daḫīr-il): Zadok (2013, 319) connects the first element with Arabic *daḫīrah* 'treasure'. *Dḫr* and *dḫrt* are attested in Safaitic and Hismaic but never as a component of a theophoric name (Harding 1971, 236). The basic sense of this root is 'to be contemptible, despicable'.

Further Reading

For an overview of Arabs in cuneiform sources, see Israel Eph'al (1984) and Jan Retsö (2003). On Arabs in Babylonia during the eighth century BCE, see Israel Eph'al (1974). The works of Ran Zadok on the Arabian onomasticon in cuneiform sources are indispensable; for the latest summary, see Zadok (2013) and the bibliography there. See Benjamin Sass (1991) on Arabian inscriptions in Babylonia.

References

Al-Jallad, A. 2022. 'One wāw to rule them all: the origin and fate of wawation in Arabic' in F. M. Donner and R. Hasselbach-Andee (eds.), *Scripts and Scripture: Writing and Religion in Arabia circa 500–700 CE*. Chicago: The Oriental Institute of the University of Chicago.

Al-Theeb, S. 2002. *Nuqūsh Jabal Umm Jadhāyidh al-Nabaṭiyyah*. Riyadh: Maktabat al- Malik Fahd al-Waṭaniyya.

Caskell, W. 1966. *Ǧamharat an-nasab. Das genealogische Werk des Hišām ibn Muḥammad al-Kalbī*, Vol. 2. Leiden: Brill.

Dietrich M. 2003. *The Babylonian Correspondence of Sargon and Sennacherib*. Helsinki: Helsinki University Press.

Eph'al, I. 1974. '"Arabs" in Babylonia in the 8th century BC', *Journal of the American Oriental Society* 94/1: 108–15.

Eph'al, I. 1984. *The Ancient Arabs: Nomads on the Borders of the Fertile Crescent, 9th–5th Centuries BC*. Jerusalem: Magnes Press/Hebrew University.

Eskoubi, Ḫ. M. 1999. *Dirāsah taḥlīliyyah muqāranah li-nuqūš min minṭaqah (rum) ǧanūb ġarb taymāʾ*. Riyāḍ: wazīrat al-maʿārif.

Harding, G. L. 1971. *An Index and Concordance of Pre-Islamic Arabian Names and Inscriptions*. Toronto: University of Toronto Press.

Hausleiter, A. and H. Schaudig 2016. 'Rock relief and cuneiform inscriptions of king Nabonidus at al-Ḥāʾiṭ (province of Ḥāʾil, Saudi Arabia), ancient Padakku', *Zeitschrift für Orient-Archäologie* 9, 224–40.

Hayajneh, H. 2001. 'First evidence of Nabonidus in the ancient North Arabian inscriptions from the region of Taymāʾ', *Proceedings of the Seminar for Arabian Studies* 31, 81–95.

Kootstra, F. 2016. 'The language of the Taymanitic inscriptions and its classification', *Arabian Epigraphic Notes* 2, 67–140.

Kootstra, F. 2023. *The Writing Culture of Ancient Dadan*. Leiden: Brill.

Macdonald, M. C. A. 1997. 'Trade routes and trade goods at the northern end of the "Incense Road" in the first millennium BC' in A. Avanzini (ed.), *Profumi d'Arabia: atti del convegno, Saggi di storia antica 11*. Rome: L' "Erma" di Bretschneider, pp. 333–49.

Macdonald, M. C. A. 2000. 'Reflections on the linguistic map of pre-Islamic Arabia', *Arabian Archaeology and Epigraphy* 11, 39–79.

Macdonald, M. C. A. 2009. 'Arabs, Arabias, and Arabic before late antiquity', *Topoi* 16, 277–332.

Negev, A. 1991. *Personal Names in the Nabatean Realm*. Jerusalem: Institute of Archaeology, Hebrew University.

Rabinowitz, A. 1956. 'Aramaic inscriptions of the fifth century BCE from a North-Arab shrine in Egypt', *Journal of Near Eastern Studies* 15/1, 1–9.

Retsö, J. 2003. *The Arabs in Antiquity: Their History from the Assyrians to the Umayyads*. New York: Routledge.

Sass, B. 1991. *Studia Alphabetica: On the Origin and Early History of the Northwest Semitic, South Semitic and Greek Alphabets*, Orbis Biblicus et Orientalis 102. Freiburg/Göttingen: Universitätsverlag/Vandenhoeck & Ruprecht.

Schaudig, H. 2001. *Die Inschriften Nabonids von Babylon und Kyros' des Großen, samt den in ihrem Umfeld entstandenen Tendenzschriften. Textausgabe und Grammatik*, Alter Orient und Altes Testament 256. Münster: Ugarit-Verlag.

Stark, J. K. 1971. *Personal Names in Palmyrene Inscriptions*. Oxford: Clarendon.

Stein, P. 2011. 'Ancient South Arabian' in S. Weninger, G. Khan, M. P. Streck, and J. C. E. Watson (eds.), *The Semitic Languages: An International Handbook*. Handbücher zur Sprach- und Kommunikationswissenschaft 36. Berlin/Boston: De Gruyter Mouton, pp. 1042–72.

Streck, M. P. 1999. 'Review of S. W. Cole 1996. The Early Neo-Babylonian Governor's Archive from Nippur', *Zeitschrift für Assyriologie und Vorderasiatische Archäologie* 89, 286–95.

Weiershäuser, F. and J. Novotny 2020. *The Royal Inscriptions of Amēl-Marduk (561–560 BC), Neriglissar (559–556 BC), and Nabonidus (555–539 BC), Kings of Babylon*, Royal Inscriptions of the Neo-Babylonian Empire 2. University Park: Eisenbrauns.

Winnett, F. V. and G. L. Harding 1978. *Inscriptions from Fifty Safaitic Cairns*. Toronto: University of Toronto Press.

Zadok, R. 1977. *On West Semites in Babylonia During the Chaldean and Achaemenian Periods. An Onomastic Study*. Jerusalem: Wanaarta.

Zadok, R. 1981. 'Arabians in Mesopotamia during the Late-Assyrian, Chaldean, Achaemenian and Hellenistic periods chiefly according to the cuneiform sources', *Zeitschrift der Deutsschen Morgenländischen Gesellschaft* 131/1, 42–84.

Zadok, R. 2003. 'The representation of foreigners in Neo- and Late Babylonian legal documents (eighth through second centuries BCE)' in O. Lipschits and J. Blenkinsopp (eds.), *Judah and the Judeans in the Neo-Babylonian Period*. Winona Lake: Eisenbrauns, pp. 471–589.

Zadok, R. 2013. 'The onomastics of the Chaldean, Aramean, and Arabian tribes in Babylonia during the first millennium' in A. Berlejung and M. P. Streck (eds.), *Arameans, Chaldeans, and Arabs in Babylonia and Palestine in the First Millennium BC*, Leipziger Altorientalistische Studien 3. Wiesbaden: Harrassowitz, pp. 261–336.

CHAPTER 12

Egyptian Names

Steffie van Gompel

Introduction

Ancient Egyptian is an autonomous branch of the Afroasiatic language family.[1] The Egyptian language shares a common origin with cognate Afroasiatic languages in Proto-Afroasiatic. Yet certain aspects of Egyptian vocabulary, phonology, and morphology differ from those of the other Afroasiatic languages (Semitic, Berber, Chadic, Cushitic, and Omotic). The exact position of Egyptian within the Afroasiatic language family is still being determined – Egyptian shares a number of characteristics with Chadic in particular.[2]

The time period considered in this chapter (750–100 BCE) was a tumultuous time in Ancient Egyptian history. During this period, Egypt maintained trade relations and diplomatic contacts with foreign powers, and was also involved in inter-regional military conflicts. The country was incorporated into the Persian Empire by Cambyses. This first Persian period was followed by a brief rule of indigenous dynasties and a second Persian conquest before Alexander the Great invaded, and Egypt passed into the hands of the Ptolemaic dynasty after his death. This resulted in a higher number of free and unfree Egyptians living abroad than in earlier periods of Egyptian history.

Aside from significant political upheaval, this period also featured new developments in Egyptian writing. All forms of the Egyptian script reflect one underlying language – Ancient Egyptian – although the relationship that each form bears to the spoken language differs (see the section on 'Spelling and Normalisation'). While hieroglyphs on temple or tomb walls are the iconic representations of Ancient Egyptian writing in modern popular culture, in reality information about mundane and practical

[1] Also referred to as the Hamito-Semitic language family in some publications.
[2] Takács 1999, 35–6.

elements of Egyptian life was usually recorded on papyrus documents or ostraca (limestone flakes or pottery sherds). In earlier periods of Egyptian history forms of the 'hieratic' script were used for cursive writing. But from the end of the 26th dynasty (664–526 BCE) onwards a script called 'Demotic' became the dominant cursive script, used particularly in (private) legal and administrative documentation. Demotic was eventually replaced by a script called 'Coptic', which became dominant from the third century CE onwards. Coptic uses the Greek alphabet, with a number of additional letters that reflect Egyptian phonemes not found in Greek. It is the only form of the Egyptian script that consistently shows vowels.

Egyptian Names in Babylonian Sources

Text Corpora

Egyptians living in Babylonia, and by extension the names they bore, are the subject of a number of dedicated studies (see 'Further Reading' section). Egyptian names occur in different contexts in cuneiform sources from Babylonia, often in those with multiple actors bearing Egyptian or other non-Babylonian names. Most sources in which Egyptian names appear come from urban environments.

The total number of Egyptian names that is attested is not indicative of the total number of Egyptians in Babylonia at any given time, as Egyptians and their descendants could bear non-Egyptian names. Thus, a chamberlain from Babylon, who is referred to as 'the Egyptian', Bagazuštu son of Marḫarpu,[3] bore an Iranian name but an Egyptian patronym. In the case of Egyptian slaves, their master might choose to change their name. As acculturation to Babylonian society took place, descendants of Egyptians took on Babylonian names, although Egyptian names could re-appear down the family line (see section on 'Social and Historical Context').

Text corpora and types of sources that feature persons with Egyptian names are the following:

- *The Murašû archive.* The more than 800 texts and fragments from the archive of the Murašû business firm, dated to the second half of the fifth century BCE and located in Nippur, feature various people with non-Babylonian names, including Egyptians.[4]

[3] Joannès and Lemaire 1996, 48 no. 6. The name [I]*ma-ar-ḫa-ár-pu* seems Egyptian in origin but has not been conclusively identified.

[4] Stolper (1985, 14) notes that there are 'somewhat fewer than 868 texts'.

- *Ration lists for oblates belonging to the Ebabbar temple in Sippar.* Several tablets from the Ebabbar temple, dated predominantly to the reign of Nebuchadnezzar II, feature lists of rations of barley, flour, and garments that are given to a group of Egyptian oblates (*širku*), many of whom bear Egyptian names.[5] The overseers of these men reoccur in several texts. No female names are recorded in these lists. The quantity of the rations the men received seems to indicate that they did not perform highly skilled labour.[6]
- *Transactions and alliances taking place in a predominantly non-Babylonian environment.* In some documents, most or all of the actors involved seem to be of foreign extraction. Notable is the marriage document *Dar.* 301 from Babylon,[7] wherein both the acting parties and many of the witnesses bear Egyptian and other non-Babylonian names. In the apprenticeship contract BM 40743 a man is apprenticed to an Egyptian slave for six years, and the majority of the actors in the contract, as well as the witnesses, bear Egyptian names.[8] A slave sale from Nippur (belonging to the Murašû archive) takes place between Egyptian (descendants), as both the seller and the previous owner have Egyptian patronyms, and a slave woman and her brother bear Egyptian names.[9] CT 4 34d documents a loan of dates between men bearing Egyptian names and patronyms.[10]
- *Singular texts that mention people bearing Egyptian names in various capacities.* Sometimes people with Egyptian names pop up in texts with otherwise very little context. Thus, we find a Ḫar-maṣu who was a judge in charge of a prison (ROMCT 2 37:24), but we know little else about him. Some of these texts are linked to archives.[11]

Social and Historical Context

People bearing Egyptian names appear in different strata of Babylonian society.[12] Among the free population, they seem to include people ranging from a modest to an average socio-economic status. People with Egyptian

[5] Spar et al. (2006, 444) give an overview of all relevant texts. [6] Huber 2006, 321.
[7] Roth 1989, 81–4 no. 23. [8] Hackl 2011, 86–7 no. 8.
[9] PBS 2/1 65; and see Dandamayev (1992, 322).
[10] CT 4 34d:2–5, and see Dandamayev (1992, 323).
[11] Some Egyptian names occur in the Kasr archive from Babylon and the Tattannu archive from Borsippa (Hackl and Jursa 2015, 157.)
[12] For overviews of contexts in which Egyptians appear, see Hackl and Jursa (2015), Huber (2006), and Dandamayev (1992).

names who function as high-ranking officials, or who belong to the highest socio-economic spheres, are much rarer. Some Egyptians seem to have entered Babylonia as prisoners of war. There may have been two waves of incoming Egyptians from military confrontations: the first during the reign of Nabopolassar and early in the reign of Nebuchadnezzar II, and the second in the later reign of Cambyses and onwards, as these were times of Egypto-Babylonian/Persian clashes.[13] The former was the origin of the male temple slaves appearing in the Ebabbar ration lists. However, Egyptians also served as free soldiers in the Persian army and may have relocated themselves and their families this way. The presence of Egyptian merchants who settled abroad permanently should also not be excluded.

Slaves with Egyptian names also appear in private contracts. The Nippur slave sale mentioned earlier notably shows some social stratification, as both the contracting parties and some of the slaves sold bear Egyptian names or patronyms. Other private documents show free persons with Egyptian names acting as contracting parties (as buyers, sellers, and tenants) or witnesses. It is not always clear if these people were acting fully independently or if they were representatives or agents of another person or institution.[14]

Many Egyptians attested in Babylonian sources seem to have been integrated into existing structures in Babylonian society, particularly the royal administration.[15] This institution appears to have been tolerant towards professionals with a suitable intellectual or cultural background who were not native Babylonians. Not all of these people were necessarily of low rank, as is evident from men such as Ḫar-maṣu, the prison judge, the chamberlain Bagazuštu with his Egyptian patronym (mentioned earlier), and the significant number of bearers of Egyptian names who belonged to the middle strata of administration. Hackl and Jursa suggest that because in the fourth and fifth centuries a higher number of Egyptians were affiliated with the royal administration, and these people represented a large share of the total number of attested Egyptians, this may indicate an increase in absolute numbers of Egyptians present in Babylonia, and of those involved in administrative tasks in particular.[16]

Egyptian names sometimes re-appear in families, even after a generation bore Babylonian names due to their assimilation to the Babylonian

[13] Hackl and Jursa 2015, 159, 166.

[14] Hackl and Jursa (2015, 165, 171, n. 34) suggest that Egyptians appearing in the Murašû archive likely had links to the royal establishment, even when this is not explicitly indicated in the sources.

[15] Hackl and Jursa 2015, 165–72 section 5, and see n. 14 (this chapter).

[16] Hackl and Jursa 2015, 170–1.

society.[17] One important Babylonian family gave an Egyptian name to at least one of their children,[18] suggesting that bearing an Egyptian name did not carry overtly negative connotations.

Typology of Egyptian Names

The following discussion pertains to characteristics of Egyptian names and naming practices that are relevant for the time period covered in this chapter. In Babylonian sources we encounter Egyptian names that can be classified into several types. Broadly speaking, there are 'complex' names that form (verbal or non-verbal) clauses and 'simple' names that do not.

Common Elements in Egyptian Names

Articles

Many Egyptian names start with articles: the definite article *pꜣ* (*tꜣ* for female, *nꜣ* for plural) and the 'belonging' article *pa* (*ta* for female, *na* for plural). These articles look similar in transliteration, but differ in meaning. The definite article reflects simply 'the' (*Pꜣ-whr* 'The hound'). The 'belonging' article, on the other hand, evolved out of a combination of the definite article with a following genitive *-n(.t)* in Late Egyptian (for example, in the names *Pꜣ-n-Divinity* and *Tꜣ-n.t-Divinity* for 'The (male/female) one 'of' *Divinity*', 'The (male/female) one belonging to *Divinity*')[19] that resulted in a special orthographic form in Demotic that is distinguished from the definite article in transliteration convention. Thus, the name *Ta-Ỉs.t* means 'She/the female one of Isis'.

Babylonian scribes do not consistently distinguish between these two types of articles in writing; the articles may have sounded very similar or even identical to a foreign listener when pronounced.[20] In Egyptian name collections, however, these articles are listed under separate sections in indexes (*pꜣ* is listed before *pa*, and *tꜣ* before *ta*, etc.).

Divinities

Names that show or express a relationship to an Egyptian divinity are common among Egyptian names found in Babylonian texts. Our

17 Hackl and Jursa 2015, 171–2; Zadok 1992, 144.
18 Hackl and Jursa 2015, 172.
19 'Being of' or 'belonging' in the sense of being a servant, devotee, etc. of the divinity.
20 Coptic does show some differences in vocalisation between the definite articles *pꜣ*/*tꜣ*/*nꜣ*, the possessive articles *pa*/*ta*/*na*, and the demonstratives *pꜣỉ*/*tꜣỉ*/*nꜣỉ*: *pꜣ* is expressed as /p/ or /p(e)/, *pa* as /pa/, and *pꜣỉ* as /p(e)i/.

perception of exactly how common is likely a little skewed: names including an Egyptian divinity are generally easier to recognise than names without one. However, even in Egyptian sources names with a divinity – theophoric names – are numerous. The gender of a divinity included in a name is not an indicator of the gender of the name-bearer: both male and female names can show male and female divinities.

The distribution of divinities in Egyptian names found in cuneiform material is somewhat uneven: some occur quite often, while some are completely absent, even though they are relatively common in native Egyptian sources.

The Egyptian divinities that occur regularly in the Neo- and Late Babylonian material are *Ỉmn* 'Amun' (m), *Ỉs.t* 'Isis' (f), and *Ḥr* 'Horus' (m). Divinities that are attested multiple times include *Ỉtm* 'Atum' (m), *Wn-nfr* 'Onnophris' (m), *Wsỉr* 'Osiris' (m), *Bꜣst.t* 'Bastet' (f), and *Ḥp* 'Apis' (m). Rarer occurrences are *Ptḥ* 'Ptah' (m), *Mḥy.t* 'Mehyt' (f), *Nfr-tm* 'Nefertem' (m), *Rᶜ* 'Ra' (m), *Ḥᶜpy* 'Hapy' (m), *Ḫnsw* 'Khonsu' (m), and *Ḏḥwty* 'Thoth' (m). Divinities that seem to be unattested in Egyptian names in Babylonian texts so far, but who appear somewhat regularly in Egyptian sources, are *Ỉnp(w)* 'Anubis' (m), *Bs* 'Bes' (m), *Mn(w)* 'Min' (m), *Nỉ.t* 'Neith' (f), *Ḫnm(w)* 'Khnum' (m), and *Sbk* 'Sobek' (m). This section does not include all Egyptian divinities.

The absence of certain divinities could be due to the fact that names with these divinities were indeed not used by people appearing in cuneiform sources. But it could also be an indication that names with these divinities have not yet been recognised or identified. A name with the divine name *Ḏḥwty* is instantly recognisable due to its unusual construction *t-h-u-t-(possible vowel), reflected in the name Tiḫut-arṭēsi (^{I}*ti-ḫu-ut-ar-ṭe-e-si*), Egyptian *Ḏḥwty-ỉ.ỉr-dỉ.t=s*, 'Thoth is the one who gave him' (BE 9 82:12). By contrast, in earlier Babylonian writings of *Ptḥ*, the initial -p is usually unwritten, leaving only the phonemes -th for identification (e.g., MB Taḫ-māya, ^{I}*ta-aḫ-ma-ia*, *Ptḥ-my*).[21] From Greek writings of the divine name *Sbk* it can be deduced that this name was actually vocalised as something akin to 'Sōk', the middle -b disappearing in pronunciation (cf. *DN* 914ff.). And due to variations in vowel use in cuneiform writings of Egyptian names, the difference between *Mn(w)* and *Ỉmn* might be impossible to tell in certain cases, due to their parallel consonants.

21 Ranke 1910–11, 18.

In some cases, Babylonian scribes recognised the name of an Egyptian divinity in a personal name and indicated this by giving it a divine determinative. This predominantly happened with the name of the goddess Isis: for example, Pati-Esi (^{I}*pa-at-*^{d}*e-si-*$^{?}$, PBS 2/1 65:23), for Egyptian *Pꜣ-di͗-I͗s.t*, 'The one whom Isis has given' (see also section on 'Hybrid Names').

Common Words in Egyptian Names

Nouns and adjectives that occur regularly in Egyptian names include *wḏꜣ* 'healthy, hale', *ꜥnḫ* 'life, live', *nfr* 'good, beautiful; goodness, beauty', *nṯr, nṯr.w* 'god, gods', *nḫ̂t* 'strong; strength', *ḥꜣ.t* 'front', *ḥr* 'face' (not to be confused with *Ḥr*, 'Horus'), *ḥtp* 'peace(ful)', *ḫl*/*ḫr* 'servant, slave', and *šr, šr.t* 'child (m/f)'.

Verbs that occur regularly in Egyptian names include *i͗r* 'to do', *i͗w*/*i͗y* 'to come', *ꜥr*/*ꜥl* 'to bring', *nḥm* 'to save', *ms* 'to be born', *rḫ* 'to know', *ḫꜣꜥ* 'to leave/place', *ṯꜣy* 'to grab/take', *di͗(.t)* 'to give', and *ḏd* 'to say'.

Non-Clausal Names

These name types include names with an unclear structure and meaning (e.g., Abāya, ^{I}*a-ba-a*, possibly Egyptian *I͗by(?)*;[22] Ukkāya, ^{I}*uk-ka-a*, perhaps Egyptian *I͗ky(?)*[23]); names that are simply the name of a deity or person and thus essentially a noun (e.g., Ḫūru, ^{I}*ḫu-ú-ru*, Egyptian *Ḥr*, 'Horus'); and names that consist of nouns (and pronouns) or nominal constructions (e.g., Paḫatarê, ^{I}*pa-ḫa-ta-re-e*, Egyptian *Pꜣ-ḥtr*, 'The twin', and Ḫarsisi, ^{I}*ḫar-si-si*, Egyptian *Ḥr-sꜣ-I͗s.t*, 'Horus son (of) Isis').[24]

[22] Bongenaar and Haring 1994, 65, refer to Schneider (1992, 16–17) for a possible Semitic origin: *ab(i͗)ja* , meaning 'My father (is divinity X)'. But note that the names *I͗by*, *I͗bw*, and derivatives occur as early as the Old Kingdom in Egypt and were in use until the end of the first millennium BCE (ÄPN I 20:5–10, 13–18, and cf. pp. 19, 21; *DN* 61). This might rather support a native origin of the name, while being a homophone to Semitic *abija*. Vittmann (2013b, 1, 7) considers the name untranslatable and possibly a pet name.

[23] A tentative suggestion by Spar et al. (2006, 454); see also 457. Names with an unclear structure are liable to multiple interpretations, however, and their Egyptian origin is speculative rather than certain. Since Ukkāya is mentioned in a list of foreign workers with a great number of Egyptian names, its classification as an Egyptian name is supported by the context. A homophonous name Ukkāya can be interpreted as meaning '(Man) from Ukku'; see Chapter 18 in this volume.

[24] These five examples are taken from: BM 56348:1 in Wiseman 1966, pl. XLIV and BM 59410 r. 12 in Bongenaar and Haring 1994, 62, but cf. Spar et al. 2006, 457; MMA 86.11.110+ iii 21 in Spar et al. 2006, 448, 454; MMA 86.11.110+ iii 27 in Spar et al. 2006, 448; BM 59410:5 in Bongenaar and Haring 1994, 59; BM 59410:11 in Bongenaar and Haring 1994, 59.

Clausal Names

Some clausal name types consist of a non-verbal clause. An example is the name Amnapi (^{I}*am-na-pi-*$^{?}$), Egyptian *Ỉmn-m-Ỉp.t*, 'Amun (is) in Ipet'.[25] Notable non-verbal clause names are those formed with 'belonging' articles that indicate a person belonging to someone or something: Tamūnu (^{I}*ta-mu-ú-nu*), Egyptian *Ta-Ỉmn*, 'She (who is) of Amun'.[26]

Names consisting of a verbal clause include names formed with statives and names with conjugated verbs. A stative name can look like this: Amutu (^{I}*a-mu-tú*), Egyptian *Ỉy-m-ḥtp*, '(He) has come in peace'.[27] Verbal clause names with conjugated verbs are relatively common in the Babylonian source material. This is not surprising, as these names are some of the more easily recognisable Egyptian names. Notable patterns include:[28]

- *Pꜣ/Tꜣ-dỉ-Divinity* 'The one (male/female) whom *Divinity* has given'; for example, Paṭumunu (^{I}*pa-ṭu-mu-nu*), Egyptian *Pꜣ-dỉ-Ỉmn*, 'The one whom Amun has given'.
- *Divinity-ỉ.ỉr-dỉ.t=s* '*Divinity* is the one who gave him/her'; Atam-artais (^{I}*a-ta-mar-ṭa-*$^{?}$*-is*), Egyptian *Ỉtm-ỉ.ỉr-dỉ.t=s*, 'Atum is the one who gave him'.
- *Ḏd-Divinity-ỉw=f-ꜥnḫ* '*Divinity* says: "He will live!"'. No full version of the name is attested yet in Babylonian texts, but a shortened version of the name occurs: Ṣī-Ḫūru (^{I}*ṣi-i-ḫu-ú-ru*), Egyptian *Ḏd-Ḥr-(ỉw=f-ꜥnḫ)*, 'Horus says ("He will live!")'.

Non-Egyptian Names

Names with a 'Libyan' origin were regularly used as personal names by Egyptians in the first millennium BCE, as an influx of people from territories to the west of Egypt took place during this time.[29] A number of pharaohs and local rulers of Libyan descent bore Libyan names during the 22nd, 23rd and 26th dynasties (c. 945–750, 664–526 BCE). The names of these rulers became somewhat popular personal names for Egyptians,

[25] MMA 86.11.110+ iii 18 in Spar et al. 2006, 448. [26] Stol 1977, 96.

[27] MMA 86.11.110+ iii 23 in Spar et al. 2006, 448.

[28] The following three examples are taken from: MMA 86.11.110+ iii 28 in Spar et al. 2006, 448; BM 59410:14 in Bongenaar and Haring 1994, 59; BM 59410:21 in Bongenaar and Haring 1994, 59.

[29] North-African (semi)-nomadic tribes living in the territory west of Egypt are commonly referred to as 'Libyan', following the ancient Greek designation of the entire region as Λιβύη. These people did not record their language(s) in writing. While 'Libyan' names are recorded in Egyptian texts, their origin and meaning in their language of origin remains unknown (Winnicki 2009, 378–425, esp. 393, 401–2).

and appear in Babylonian texts in this capacity. The meaning of Libyan names is unknown.[30]

Notable Libyan names that appear in Babylonian sources are Ḫalabesu (Egyptian *Ḥrbs*, in cuneiform, e.g., ^{I}*ḫa-la-bé-su*),[31] Takelot (Egyptian, e.g., *Ṯkrt*/*Ṯkrṯ*; in cuneiform, e.g., ^{I}*tak-la-a-ta*, ^{I}*tak-la-ta*), and Psamtek (Egyptian *Psmṯk*; e.g., ^{I}*pu-sa-mi-is-ki* in cuneiform).[32] Basilophorous Egyptian names may also feature the names of these kings (e.g., *ꜥnḫ-Ššnḳ* 'May (king) Shoshenq live!', *DN* 105).

Hybrid Names

Hybrid names that include an Egyptian divinity are attested in the Babylonian sources, but they seem to be limited to the goddess Isis. We find, for example, ^{f}Amat-Esi (^{f}*am-mat-*^{d}*e-si-ʾ* or ^{f}*a-mat-*^{d}*e-si-ʾ*) 'Maidservant of Isis' and Abdi-Esi (^{I}*ab-di-*^{d}*e-si-ʾ*) 'Slave of Isis'.[33] Ran Zadok (1992, 142) argues that these people were not necessarily of Egyptian origin, but rather that these names indicated the international popularity of the Isis cult.

There is a single attestation of a hybrid name with a Babylonian divinity along with an Egyptian verbal element, namely Bēl-paṭēsu (^{Id}EN-*pa-ṭe-e-su*), Egyptian *Bēl-pꜣ-di͗-s(w)*, 'Bēl has given him'.[34]

Naming Practices

In Egyptian texts from the first millennium BCE, filiation is commonly indicated by the construction 'X, son (of) Y, his mother (is) Z' and 'X, daughter (of) Y, her mother (is) Z'. In cuneiform texts the mother's name is omitted.

Two further aspects of Egyptian naming practices may be relevant to the identification of Egyptian names. First, Egyptians often bore 'family names' that skipped a generation. 'Papponymy' – naming a child after the grandfather (or grandmother) – was common, which complicates the identification of individuals in texts with multiple family members. In

30 Winnicki 2009 (see n. 29). Some names were given an Egyptian 'reinterpretation'; for example, *Psmṯk* is also written as *Pꜣ-s-(n)-mṯk*, meaning 'The mixed wine seller' (Ray 1990, 197; Winnicki 2009, 394).

31 For the Libyan origin of this name, see Leahy (1980, 43–63), and, recently, Draper (2015, 1–15), who discusses 'Libyan' names borne by Egyptians in a Neo-Assyrian text.

32 BM 57701 r. iii 1 in Bongenaar and Haring 1994, 63, 66; BM 59410:15, r. 20 in Bongenaar and Haring 1994, 59, 62; BM 59410:4 in Bongenaar and Haring 1994, 59, 70.

33 These three examples are from PBS 2/1 17:2, 13; PBS 2/1 65:4, 9; ROMCT 2 48:2.

34 MMA 86.11.117:3 in Spar et al. 2006, 456.

Egyptian texts, like-named relatives could be distinguished by the addition of a descriptor such as '(the) elder' (*ꜥꜣ* or *pꜣ ꜥꜣ*) or '(the) younger' (*ḫm* or *pꜣ ḫm*) that followed directly after the name: for instance, **Pꜣ-dỉ-Ḫnsw pꜣ ꜥꜣ sꜣ Pꜣ-msḥ*, '**Pꜣ-dỉ-Ḫnsw* ("The one whom Khonsu has given") the elder, son of *Pꜣ-msḥ* ("The crocodile")'. One can wonder how *(pꜣ) ꜥꜣ*, which includes the enigmatic phonemes *ayin* and *aleph*, would be realised in cuneiform writing. To my knowledge these descriptors are not yet attested along with Egyptian names in Babylonian sources, but there are examples of Greek renderings of Egyptian names, where descriptors were interpreted as a part of the name.[35]

Second, in Egyptian sources Egyptians are seen bearing nicknames or shortened names, as well as multiple names. An example of the former is *Rwrw*, derived from *Ỉr.t=w-r-r=w* and similar name patterns, which has its own entry in name collections.[36] Bearing multiple or secondary names was an old Egyptian practice that was revived during the first millennium, when people could take on a 'beautiful name' in addition to their first name. These names were often basilophorous,[37] and could be completely different from a person's first name: for example, a man *Ḥr-sꜣ-Ỉs.t* 'Horus, son (of) Isis' also bore the 'beautiful' name *Psmṯk-m-ꜣḫ.t* 'Psamtek (is) in the *ꜣḫ.t*'.[38] Under Ptolemaic rule in Egypt, Egyptian people involved in the Ptolemaic administration or army could take on a Greek name in addition to their given name. Some used their double names in different circumstances: the Greek name or both the Greek and Egyptian name in contexts of administration and bureaucracy, and in formal legal documents; the Egyptian name in informal and personal contexts.[39] A similar practice may underlie the two names of the man Pati-Esi 'The one whom Isis has given', who also bore the Iranian name Bagadāta.[40]

Spelling and Normalisation

Identifying possibly Egyptian names in cuneiform material and linking them to known Egyptian names is not an easy task. This has three causes. First, the exact conversion rules of some Egyptian phonemes are

35 Vittmann 2013b, 8; for example, *DN* 582, 677, 805. 36 *DN* 712; ÄPN I 221: 8.

37 Vittmann 2013a, 3. 38 ÄPN I 136: 11; II 6–8.

39 Conversely, Graeco–Egyptian double names have been interpreted as an indication of Greek integration in Egyptian society – for example, when children of Greek-Egyptian mixed marriages bore a double name. On this complex social practice of double names, see Vandorpe and Vleeming (2017, 173–4) and Broux and Coussement (2014); the papyri of the lady Senmonthis (also called Apollonia) offer a notable case study of how people used one or the other name in different social contexts (Broux and Coussement 2014, 127–9).

40 See text IMT 43:2 ([^{I}*pa-ti-*^{d}]⌈*e*⌉*-si*). Cf. Hackl and Jursa (2015, 168, 172), who suggest that the choice of an Iranian name indicated an aspiration to integrate into the administrative elite of the Persian Empire.

not entirely clear. An overview of established correspondents of Egyptian signs to cuneiform writings can be found in the section on 'Tools for Identifying Egyptian Names in Babylonian Cuneiform Texts'. The Egyptian signs *ꜣ* and *ỉ/j* are enigmatic and the discussion about their interpretation is ongoing. They seem to reflect different phonemes or glottal stops, or remain unrealised, depending on their position in a word or name. Second, while cuneiform writing shows vowels, the Egyptian script does not do so as a rule, although some phonemes such as *w*, *ỉ/j*, and *y* function as semi-vowels or indicate the presence of a vowel of unknown quality. It is thus prudent to first focus on discerning consonants when trying to identify an Egyptian name. Third, the Egyptian script is archaising. Even in the cursive scripts, which were closer to the spoken language than monumental hieroglyphs, scribes often tended to maintain the traditional writing of a word even when consonants had undergone a sound change or were lost altogether.

Egyptian vocalisation can in part be reconstructed with the aid of spellings of Egyptian words in other scripts. In the first millennium BCE, these are found in Greek texts from Egypt and in the Assyrian and Babylonian cuneiform material. An additional source used for the reconstruction is Coptic, the version of the Egyptian language and script that follows Demotic. However, Coptic texts appear centuries later than the Greek and Akkadian ones and must be used with some caution when reconstructing earlier phonemes.

Egyptology uses a transliteration system to transliterate both hieroglyphic and cursive scripts. Because the Egyptian script does not reflect vowels and is archaising, this transliteration also does not directly reflect the pronunciation of words. It is rather an artificial tool and 'code' to indicate how a researcher reads and interprets the signs that also allows those who are not specialised in a particular language phase to understand the reading.

Egyptological transliteration generally follows the archaising writings of names in Egyptian sources. Thus, the Egyptian name element meaning 'belonging to', both written and transliterated as *Ns*-, was in reality vocalised as **Es*/*Is*- or **S*- at the end of the first millennium BCE. This can be deduced from Greek writings of, for example, the name *Ns-Mn* as Ἐσμινις or even Σμιν (*DN* 674).[41] The Babylonian rendering ^{I}*sa-man-na-pi-ir* (*Dar.* 301:2, 9),

[41] In Aramaic too, Egyptian *ns* is recorded as ᶜ+*s*; cf. Vittmann 1989, 213; for example, *Ns-Mn* written ᶜ*smn*.

transcribed Samannapir, thus reflects the Egyptian name *Ns-Wn-nfr* 'He who belongs to Onnophris',[42] which had become *(Ỉ)s-Wn-nfr* in pronunciation (in Greek Σοννωφρις), also showing the correspondence of Egyptian *-w* with Babylonian intervocalic *-m*(*a*) (which was realised as [w] in pronunciation).

The common name *Ỉr.t-n.t-Ḥr-r.r=w* 'The eye of Horus (is) against them' presents a similar difficulty. It appears as Ἰναρως in Greek, and has been identified as Babylonian Inaḫarû, written ^I^*i-na-ḫa-ru-ú*.[43] In pronunciation, *Ỉr.t-n.t* had apparently been reduced to only 'ina-'. An alternative writing of the name in Egyptian exists: *Ỉn-ỉr.t-Ḥr-r.r=w* (*DN* 72). The additional element *Ỉn* perhaps reflects an attempt to show the real vocalisation.

Egyptological name collections and text publications list names in transliteration which reflect the writing of the name in Egyptian. Thus, a conversion of the syllables recorded in the cuneiform version of the name to the equivalent graphemes in the Egyptological transliteration must be made in order to identify a name. The *DN* provides some assistance here: when known, the Greek and Coptic writing of a name are given (Fig. 12.1).

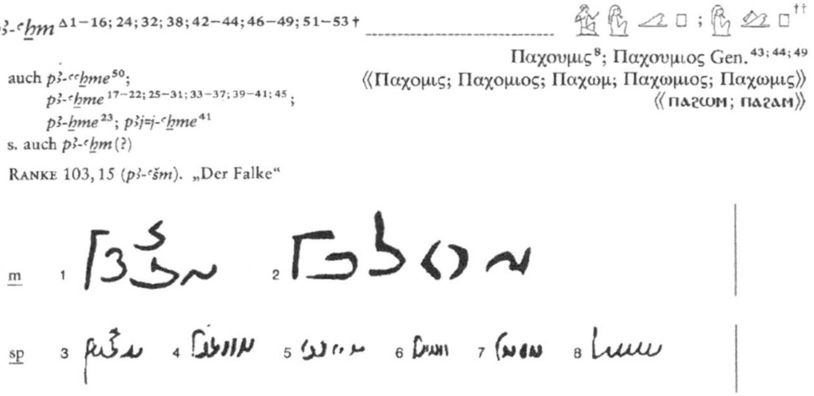

Figure 12.1 Example of an Egyptian name with additional Greek and Coptic writings (*DN* 165; reproduced with the kind permission of Dr. Ludwig Reichert Verlag).

[42] *DN* 660; ÄPN I 174: 10. [43] MMA 86.11.110+ ii 25 in Spar et al. 2006, 447, 453.

The Egyptological transliteration of the name in the entry of the *DN* is *P3-ʿḫm*, with alternate writing as *P3-ʿḫme*, etc. We can see that the name is also included in Ranke's ÄPN under *P3-ʿšm* (Bd. I 103: 15).[44] To the right of the name in transliteration, there are examples of the name in Greek and Coptic. Combining the three writings in Egyptian, Greek, and Coptic, we can deduce that the defining phonemes of the name are *p-ḫ/ḫ-m*. The vowel *o* is not written in Egyptian, but it is clearly realised in pronunciation, as it appears in the Greek and Coptic writings. The Greek and Coptic writings also consistently show a vowel *a* at the start of the word, which suggests that this vowel was also pronounced (and was not a ∅ as *aleph* and *ayin* may sometimes be; see Table 12.2). It is the defining phonemes, and secondarily the vowels, that should be considered when comparing cuneiform writings of Egyptian names for identification.

Tools for Identifying Egyptian Names in Babylonian Cuneiform Texts

Table 12.2 gives an overview of Egyptian graphemes, their corresponding (reconstructed) phoneme(s), and the known correspondents of these phonemes in Neo- and Late Babylonian. The information in this chart is based on correspondences between Egyptian and Akkadian that have been established in the literature (for this, see the 'Further Reading' section).

Additional suggestions for reconstructions of phonological values and correspondents by James P. Allen (2013) and Gabor Takács (1999) are included in the table notes.[45] For further study of correspondents between Egyptian and Akkadian and other Semitic languages, these works are recommended.[46]

Further Reading

The standard collection of Egyptian names in Demotic is the *Demotisches Namenbuch* (*DN*) (Lüddeckens et al. 1980–2000). Birgit Jordan created a search-list (*Demotisches*

[44] A consonant shift between *ḫ* and *š* occasionally occurs; cf. Table 12.2.

[45] The following abbreviations are used: JPA = Allen 2013, esp. chps. 4 and 5.; GT = Takács 1999, 263–78. Additional symbols in the table are: ∅ = non-realised sound or null-value; [] = encloses symbols of pronunciation.

[46] James P. Allen's work is a diachronic study of the phonology and grammar of the Egyptian language, while Gabor Tacáks offers a linguistic comparison of the ancient Egyptian lexical material with other Afroasiatic languages and Proto-Afroasiatic. Takács predominantly bases his analyses on older phases of the Egyptian language (Old/Middle Egyptian), but he investigates Egyptian phonology compared to that of languages within the same language family, as well as to the proto-language underlying these languages. Thus, his analysis of Egyptian phonemes is worth considering in comparative perspective.

Table 12.2 *Egyptian graphemes, their corresponding phonemes, and their known correspondents in Neo- and Late Babylonian*

Egyptian graphemes in transliteration	Reconstructed phonological values in Egyptian	Correspondents to phonological values in Neo- and Late Babylonian
ȝ (aleph)	The value of this sign is debated.[a]	Exact correspondent(s) in Neo- and Late Babylonian are unknown, likely representing different values depending on the place in the word. Alternatively, these different values can be explained by *ȝ* actually being realised as ∅ everywhere.[b]
ỉ or *j* (yod)	Semi-vowel. The value of this sign is debated.[c]	Indicates the presence of a vowel, or ∅.[d] E.g., ᴵ*am-na-pi-ʾ*, Amnapi, for *Ỉmn-m-Ỉp.t* 'Amun (is) in Ipet' E.g., ᴵ*ab-di-*ᵈ*e-si-ʾ*, Abdi-Esi, for *abdi-Ỉs.t* 'Slave of Isis'
y	Semi-vowel, [y]	Indicates a long vowel. E.g., ᴵ*se-e-pí*, Sēpi, for *Syf* '(Divine) child'
ᶜ (ayin)	[ˤ]	ˤ (ayin) or ∅ E.g., ᴵ*an-ḫa-pu*, Anḫapu, for *ᶜnḫ-Ḥp* 'Apis lives'
w (waw)	Semi-vowel, [w][e]	u, intervocalic -m(a) or -b(a) (pronounced [w]) ᴵ*ḫar-ma-ṣu*, Ḫar-maṣu, for *Ḥr-wḏȝ* 'Horus (is) hale'
e	Indicates the presence of an indeterminate vowel.	Indeterminate vowel.
b	[p] or [b]	b, u E.g., ᴵ*pa-aṭ-ú-as-tú*, Paṭuastu, for *Pȝ-dỉ-Bȝst.t*, 'The one whom Bastet has given'
p; *f*	[p], [pʰ], [f]	p, b, or ∅ in initial position E.g., ᴵ*a-mu-nu-ta-bu-na-aḫ-ti*, Amunu-tabunaḫti, for *Ỉmn-tȝy=f-nḫt* 'Amun (is) his strength'

Table 12.2 (*cont.*)

Egyptian graphemes in transliteration	Reconstructed phonological values in Egyptian	Correspondents to phonological values in Neo- and Late Babylonian
		E.g., ^{I}*ta-aḫ-ma-ia* (MB), Taḫ-māya, for *Ptḥ-my* (full mng. unknown)
m	[m]	m
n	[n], or [l] in some words.	n, l, or ∅
r; *l*	[r],[f] [l]	r, l, or ∅ at the end of words E.g., ^{I}*ú-sa-mu-nu*, Usamunu, for *Wsr-Ỉmn* 'Amun (is) strong'
h	[h]	ḫ or ∅
ḥ	[ħ]	ḫ or ∅ E.g., ^{I}*si-ip-ta-$^{?}$-$^{?}$*, Sipta$^{?}$, and ^{I}*si-ip-ta-ḫu*, Siptaḫu, for *Sꜣ-Ptḥ* 'Son of Ptah'
ḫ	[x]	ḫ, or k, q, g
ẖ; *h̭*	A consonant shift between *ḫ* and *š* occasionally occurs. E.g., the word 'arm' is written as *ḫpš* and *špš*; 'enemy' written as *ḫft* and *šft*.	
s	[s]	s or š
š	[ʃ] A consonant shift between *ḫ* and *š* occasionally occurs.	š, s
k; *ḳ*/*q*; *g*	[k], [k^{h}], [q], [g]	k, q, or g
t; *d*	[t] or less often [t^{h}]; and ∅ in case of a feminine marker '.t' at the end of a word.	t, ṭ, or ∅ at the end of a word E.g., ^{I}*pa-aṭ-im-ḫa-$^{?}$*, Patimḫa, for *Pꜣ-dỉ-Mḥy.t* 'The one whom Mehyt has given'. The Egyptian feminine marker '.t' is reduced to ∅.
ṯ; *ṱ*	[ṯ/t^{h}] or ∅ at the end of word.	s, ṣ, possibly š E.g., ^{I}*pi-sa-mi-is-ki*, Pisamiski, for *Psmṯk*

Table 12.2 (*cont.*)

Egyptian graphemes in transliteration	Reconstructed phonological values in Egyptian	Correspondents to phonological values in Neo- and Late Babylonian
		E.g., ^I^*šá-am-mu-ú*, Šammû, for *Ṯꜣy-n-ỉm=w* 'May (god) take them!'[g]
ḏ	[ṯ][h]	ṣ E.g., ^I^*ḫar-ma-ṣu*, Ḫar-maṣu, for *Ḥr-wḏꜣ* 'Horus (is) hale'

[a] JPA, 53: realised as [ʔ], [y], or ∅. GT, 273–5: originally a 'strong liquid' [r]/[l], gradually weakened and disappeared, becoming a glottal stop [ʔ], but retaining its liquid pronunciation under certain conditions.

[b] JPA, 36: Realised as [l], [r], or ∅. GT, 263, 273–5: [r], [l], and/or [ʔ], or ∅.

[c] JPA, 53: Realised as both [ʔ] and ∅. Can also represent a vowel (incl. y) at the beginning or end of words, and a gap between two vowels.

[d] JPA, 36: Realised as [ʔ], with cognates [ʔ], [y], and [l]. GT, 263: [w], [y], and/or [ʔ], and/ or [r], [l].

[e] JPA, 53: Realised as [w] and a vowel; can also represent a final vowel.

[f] JPA, 53: Realised as [ɾ] and [l] in some words.

[g] Suggested by Zadok (1992, 142 no. 33), who notes the name appears as *Šmw* in Aramaic (Vittmann, 1989, 229). For this name, see *DN* 1348.

[h] JPA, 54: perhaps also [ḏ] in some dialects.

Namenbuch: Suchliste) for the *DN* that allows for searching by name element (available online as pdf). While the *DN* is limited to names occurring in Demotic texts, the three volumes of Hermann Ranke's *Ägyptische Personennamen* (1935, 1952, 1976), in short ÄPN, deal with names from the entire span of Egyptian history. Michelle Thirion's articles (beginning with 1979) add missing names and corrections to Ranke's ÄPN. Burkhard Backes and Guido Dresbach (2007) created an index to Thirion's articles. Additionally, Günter Vittmann's overviews of Egyptian names and naming practices in the *UCLA Encyclopedia of Egyptology* (2013a–b) are useful introductions to the subject of Egyptian names.

Notable publications that discuss and interpret Egyptian names in (Babylonian) cuneiform texts are (in alphabetic order): Arminius C. V. M. Bongenaar and Ben J. J. Haring (1994), Muhammad A. Dandamayev (1992), Elmar Edel (1980), Johannes Hackl and Michael Jursa (2015), Hermann Ranke (1910–11), Ira Spar et al. (2006), Ernst Weidner (1939), Donald J. Wiseman (1966), and Ran Zadok (1989–90, 1992). Note also the discussions in Göttinger Miszellen by Jürgen Osing (1978), Helmut Satzinger (1984), Günter Vittmann (1984), and Ran Zadok (1977, 1983). Recent publications often include corrections to earlier publications.

References

Allen, J. P. 2013. *The Ancient Egyptian Language. An Historical Study*. Cambridge: Cambridge University Press.

Backes, B. and G. Dresbach 2007. 'Index zu Michelle Thirion, "Notes d'onomastique. Contribution à une révision du Ranke PN", 1–14e série', *British Museum Studies in Ancient Egypt and Sudan* 8, 1–48.

Bongenaar, A. C. V. M. and B. J. J. Haring 1994. 'Egyptians in Neo-Babylonian Sippar', *Journal of Cuneiform Studies* 46, 59–72.

Broux, Y. and S. Coussement 2014. 'Double Names as Indicators of Social Stratification in Graeco-Roman Egypt' in M. Depauw and S. Coussement (eds.), *Identifiers and Identification Methods in the Ancient World*, Orientalia Lovaniensia Analecta 229. Leuven: Peeters, pp. 119–39.

Dandamayev, M. A. 1992. 'Egyptians in Babylonia in the 6th–5th centuries BC' in D. Charpin and F. Joannès (eds.), *La circulation des biens, des personnes et des idées dans le Proche-Orient ancien. Actes de la XXXVIIIe Rencontre Assyriologique Internationale (Paris, 8–10 juillet 1991)*. Paris: Éditions Recherche sur les Civilisations, pp. 321–5.

Draper, C. 2015. 'Two Libyan names in a seventh century sale document from Assur', *Journal of Ancient Egyptian Interconnections* 7/2, 1–15.

Edel, E. 1980. *Neue Deutungen keilschriftlicher Umschreibungen ägyptischer Wörter und Personennamen*, Sitzungsberichte der österreichischen Akademie der Wissenschaften 375. Vienna: Österreichische Akademie der Wissenschaften.

Hackl, J. 2011. 'Neue spätbabylonische Lehrverträge aus dem British Museum und der Yale Babylonian Collection', *Archiv für Orientforschung* 52, 77–97.

Hackl, J. and M. Jursa 2015. 'Egyptians in Babylonia in the Neo-Babylonian and Achaemenid Periods' in J. Stökl and C. Waerzeggers (eds.), *Exile and Return: The Babylonian Context*, Beihefte zur Zeitschrift für die alttestamentliche Wissenschaft 478. Berlin: De Gruyter, pp. 157–80.

Huber, I. 2006. 'Von Affenwärtern, Schlangenbeschwörern und Palastmanagern: Ägypter im Mesopotamien des ersten vorchristlichen Jahrtausends' in R. Rollinger and B. Truschnegg (eds.), *Altertum und Mittelmeerraum: die antike Welt diesseits und jenseits der Levante. Festschrift für Peter W. Haider zum 60. Geburtstag*, Oriens and Occidens 12. Stuttgart: Franz Steiner, pp. 303–29.

Joannès, F. and A. Lemaire 1996. 'Contrats babyloniens d'époque achéménide du Bît-Abî râm avec une épigraphe Araméenne', *Revue d'Assyriologie et d'Archéologie Orientale* 90, 41–60.

Jordan, B., with the assistance of S. Specht, since 2017. *Demotisches Namenbuch: Suchliste*. www.aegyptologie.unimuenchen.de/download/jordan_demot_nb_suchliste_2017.pdf.

Leahy, A. 1980. '"Ḥarwa" and "Ḥarbes"', *Chronique d'Égypte* 55, 43–63.

Lüddeckens, E. and W. Brunch. 1980–2000. *Demotisches Namenbuch*. Wiesbaden: Dr. Ludwig Reichert.

Osing, J. 1978. 'Zu einigen ägyptischen Namen in keilschriftlicher Umschreibung', *Göttinger Miszellen* 27, 37–41.

Ranke, H. 1910–11. *Keilschriftliches Material zur altägyptischen Vokalisation*, Abhandlungen der Königlich Preussischen Akademie der Wissenschaften, Philosophisch-historische Klasse 2. Berlin: Königliche Akademie der Wissenschaften.

Ranke, H. 1935, 1952, 1976. *Die Ägyptische Personennamen.* 1935. Bd. I: *Verzeichnis von Namen*; 1952. Bd. II: *Einleitung. Form und Inhalt der Namen. Geschichte der Namen. Vergleiche mit andren Namen. Nachträge und Zusätze zu Bd I. Umschreibungslisten*; 1976. Bd. III: *Verzeichnis der Bestandteile.* Glückstadt: J. J. Augustin.

Ray, J. D. 1990. 'The names Psammetichus and Takheta', *Journal of Egyptian Archaeology* 76, 196–9.

Roth, M. T. 1989. *Babylonian Marriage Agreements: 7th–3rd centuries BC*, Alter Orient und Altes Testament 222. Kevelaer/Neukirchen-Vluyn: Butzon & Bercker/Neukirchener Verlag.

Satzinger, H. 1984. 'Zu den neubabylonischen Transkriptionen ägyptischer Personennamen', *Göttinger Miszellen* 73, 89.

Schneider, T. 1992. *Asiatische Personennamen in ägyptischen Quellen des Neuen Reiches*, Orbis Biblicus et Orientalis 114. Freiburg/Göttingen: Universitätsverlag/ Vandenhoeck & Ruprecht.

Spar, I., T. J. Logan, and J. P. Allen 2006. 'Two Neo-Babylonian texts of foreign workmen' in A. K. Guinan, M. deJ. Ellis, A. J. Ferrara, et al. (eds.), *If a Man Builds a Joyful House. Assyriological Studies in Honor of Erle Verdun Leichty*, Cuneiform Monographs 31. Leiden: Brill, pp. 443–61.

Stol, M. 1977. 'Un texte oublié', *Revue d'Assyriologie et d'Archéologie Orientale* 71, 96.

Stolper, M. W. 1985. *Entrepreneurs and Empire: the Murašû Archive, the Murašû Firm, and Persian Rule in Babylonia*, Uitgaven van het Nederlands Historisch-Archaeologisch Instituut te Istanbul 54. Istanbul: Nederlands Historisch-Archaeologisch Instituut.

Takács, G. 1999. Etymological Dictionary of Egypt, Vol. 1: *A Phonological Introduction*, Handbuch der Orientalistik 84. Leiden: Brill.

Thirion, M. 1979–2001. 'Notes d'onomastique. Contribution à une revision du Ranke PN', *Revue d'Égyptologie* 31 (1979), 81–96; 33 (1981), 79–87; 34 (1982–3), 125–43; 36 (1985), 125–43; 37 (1986), 131–7; 39 (1988), 131–46; 42 (1991), 213–30; 43 (1992), 163–8; 45 (1994), 175–88; 46 (1995), 171–80; 52 (2001), 265–76.

Vandorpe, K. and S. P. Vleeming 2017. The Erbstreit Papyri: A Bilingual Dossier from Pathyris of the Second Century BC, Studia Demotica 13. Leuven: Peeters.

Vittmann, G. 1984. 'Zu einigen keilschriftlichen Umschreibungen ägyptischer Personennamen', *Göttinger Miszellen* 70, 65–6.

Vittmann, G. 1989. 'Zu den ägyptischen Entsprechungen aramäisch überlieferter Personennamen', *Orientalia Nova Series* 58/2, 213–29.

Vittmann, G. 2013a. 'Personal names: function and significance' in E. Frood and W. Wendrich (eds.), *UCLA Encyclopedia of Egyptology*. Los Angeles. https://es cholarship.org/uc/item/7t12z11t.

Vittmann, G. 2013b. 'Personal names: structures and patterns' in E. Frood and W. Wendrich (eds.), *UCLA Encyclopedia of Egyptology*. Los Angeles. https://es cholarship.org/uc/item/42v9x6xp.

Weidner, E. F. 1939. 'Jojachin, König von Juda, in babylonischen Keilschrifttexten' in *Mélanges Syriens offerts à M. René Dussaud, secrétaire perpétuel de l'Académie des inscriptions et belles-lettres, par ses amis et ses élèves* II, Bibliothèque archéologique et historique 30. Paris: Geuthner, 923–35.

Winnicki, J. K. 2009. Late Egypt and Her Neighbours. Foreign Population in Egypt in the First Millennium BC, The Journal of Juristic Papyrology Supplements 12. Warsaw: Drukarnia Duo Studio.

Wiseman, D. J. 1966. 'Some Egyptians in Babylonia', *Iraq* 28, 154–8.

Zadok, R. 1977. 'On some Egyptians in first millennium Mesopotamia', *Göttinger Miszellen* 26, 63–8.

Zadok, R. 1983. 'On some Egyptians in Babylonian documents', *Göttinger Miszellen* 64, 73–5.

Zadok, R. 1989–90. 'Review of M. W. Stolper 1985. *Entrepreneurs and Empire: The Murašû Archive, the Murašû Firm, and Persian Rule in Babylonia*', *Die Welt des Orients* 20–1, 273–6.

Zadok, R. 1992. 'Egyptians in Babylonia and Elam during the 1st Millennium BC', *Lingua Aegyptia: Journal of Egyptian Language Studies* 2, 139–46.

CHAPTER 13

Anatolian Names

Zsolt Simon

Introduction

The terms 'Anatolian' and 'Anatolian languages' have two different meanings in the present context: a genetic one and a geographical one. Anatolian as a genetic term refers to a branch of the Indo-European language family consisting of the following nine languages (the dates in brackets show the range of their attestation): Hittite (20th–early 12th c.), Palaic (16th–13th c.), Luwian (20th–early 7th c.), Lydian (end 8th/early 7th–3rd c.), Carian (8th–4th/3rd c.), Lycian (Lycian A) (5th–4th c.), Lycian B (Milyan) (5th/4th c.), Sidetic (5th–3rd c.), and Pisidian (1st–3rd c. CE). Hittite, Palaic, and Luwian were written in the Hittite version of cuneiform writing; Luwian was also written in a locally developed hieroglyphic writing. All other languages were written in locally adapted forms of the Greek alphabet. Anatolian as a geographical term refers to all languages once spoken in Anatolia, many of which either belonged to other branches of the Indo-European family (Phrygian, Thracian, Armenian) or were not Indo-European at all (Hattian, Kaškean, Hurrian, Urartean, and the Kartvelian languages). These languages are not treated here.[1] Accordingly, throughout this chapter 'Anatolian (languages)' refers to this specific branch of Indo-European.

It is important to note that some of these languages were more closely related to each other within the Anatolian branch and are subsumed under the term 'Luwic': these languages are Luwian, Lycian A, Lycian B, Carian, Sidetic, and Pisidian.[2] The term 'Luwic' is also used when the material cannot be unambiguously classified within these languages, typically in case of widespread onomastic elements, isolated words, or references to local, otherwise unknown languages; this affects the evaluation of the name

[1] For possible occurrence of such names in Babylonian sources, see Chapter 18 in this volume.
[2] The position of Lydian inside or outside of this subgroup is disputed.

material in Babylonian sources, too.[3]

The aforementioned date ranges give an impression of the disappearance of these languages and a preliminary answer to the question of which languages should be taken into consideration when evaluating names attested in Babylonian sources. Nevertheless, this is partly misleading, for two reasons. First, the dates refer to the end of the textual transmission of these languages. However, onomastic material and references to local spoken languages continue, occasionally even up to the sixth century CE. Due to a lack of investigations, it is hard to tell whether these names reflect living languages. From a Babylonian point of view, the most important issue is that one can still expect Luwian names well after the early seventh century BCE.[4]

Second, as will be discussed, Anatolia is a distinct onomastic area with strict rules that hardly changed throughout the millennia, and since the languages in cuneiform and hieroglyphic transmission are much better attested than those in alphabetic transmission, it is these languages that frequently provide the missing comparanda to the Anatolian names in Babylonian transmission.[5]

Anatolian Name Material in Babylonian Sources

The Problems of Transmission

Due to the contacts of the Neo-Babylonian and Achaemenid Empires with regions of Anatolian speakers,[6] Anatolian names are expected and do appear in both Babylonian historical sources and administrative texts.

[3] For instance, the female name ᶠMulâ (*ᶠmu-la-a-ʾ*), recorded in the Babylonian text UET 4 129:4 and identified as Anatolian by Zadok (1979, 168), is known not only in Lycian (Melchert 2004, 99; Neumann 2007, 225), but also in Pamphylia and Pisidia (Houwink ten Cate 1961, 153–4) as well as in Luwian (Laroche 1966, 120 no. 817 and perhaps no. 816; cf. also Zehnder 2010, 225).

[4] An example is Appuwašu (*ᴵap-pu-ú-a-šú*), king of Pirindu, who is mentioned in a Babylonian source in 557 BCE (ABC 6:1). Although the first member of this compound name is unclear, the second member is without doubt the Luwian word *wašu-* 'good' (cf. Laroche 1966, 60 no. 294 with references). This type of name is further discussed in the section 'The Structure of the Anatolian Names: A Short Overview'.

[5] For instance, the toponym Bīt-Kikê (*ᴵki-ki-e*), identified as Anatolian by Zadok (1979, 167), is based on the Anatolian personal name *Ki(ya)k(k)i(ya)* attested in Old Assyrian, Hittite, and Hieroglyphic Luwian transmission (Laroche 1966, 92 no. 569 and ACLT s.v.); for Neo-Assyrian spellings of this name, see PNA 2/II, 615 s.v. Kikkia.

[6] Besides in Anatolia proper, such contacts occurred in Egypt where a sizeable Carian-speaking community was present. It is unclear whether Luwian speakers in northern Syria survived until the Neo-Babylonian period.

The main problem is their identification, due to the history of research and the nature of the transmission.

Unfortunately, the history of research consists only of scattered investigations. Furthermore, Anatolian linguistics progressed dramatically in the last few decades, which necessitates the re-evaluation of earlier analyses, a task still to be accomplished.

As for the nature of the transmission, one can distinguish two groups of names. The first group consists of names recorded without any ethnic labels. Such names can be identified as Anatolian only by linguistic investigation, which necessarily reflects our defective contemporary knowledge. The second group consists of names recorded with ethnic labels. Although this seems to be the easier group, this is not necessarily the case. First, the Babylonian terminology slightly differs from ours. Although the terminology is straightforward, it is easy to miss Anatolian names if these differences are not taken into account. Specifically, the ethnonym *ḫilikāya* (Cilicians) refers to 'Luwians', both *karšāya* and *bannēšāya* refer to 'Carians' (the origin of the latter term is disputed), *sapardāya* (Sardeans) refers to 'Lydians', and *tarmilāya* refers to 'Lycians'. Second, these labels do not necessarily refer only to these languages, for these regions were linguistically heterogenous. Hence, persons labelled 'Lydian', 'Carian', 'Lycian', and 'Cilician' may actually bear Greek names; some 'Lydians' and 'Lycians' may bear Carian names; 'Carians' may bear Egyptian, Akkadian, and Aramaic names; and it should cause no surprise that even Phrygian and Iranian names resort under these labels.[7] In other words, a linguistic investigation is inevitable in all of these cases.

One must also take language-specific problems into account, especially in the case of the languages in alphabetic transmission. First, some of these languages have phonemes without any equivalent in Babylonian. Second, there are some signs in the writing systems of these languages that are not fully deciphered. It is currently unclear if the relatively high number of names in Babylonian texts with or without the aforementioned ethnic labels that are still unidentified in the local language(s) is due to these problems.[8] A specific case is Carian, where Carian and foreign spellings

[7] See, for instance, the Babylonian texts published in Waerzeggers (2006) and Zadok (2005, 84–95), where persons labelled by the ancient scribe as 'Carian' in fact bear Carian, Egyptian, Akkadian, as well as Aramaic names. Another example is the investigation by Vernet Pons (2016), who demonstrated that the widespread Anatolian name known in Babylonian transmission as ^{f}Artim (Zadok 1979, 168 with references) is etymologically Iranian. The Babylonian text IMT 3:3 mentions ^{I}*mi-da-*$^{?}$, a 'Sardean' bearing a Phrygian name.

[8] See, for instance, the examples in Eilers (1940, 206–14) and in Zadok (1979).

grossly differ: while the names in non-Carian transmission are always fully vocalised (except, of course, in Egyptian hieroglyphs), the vowels are hardly ever noted in Carian transmission (of which the rules still elude us). This obviously poses a serious problem in identifying and analysing Carian names in Babylonian transmission.[9]

Having said that, Anatolian names have a specific typology with name elements typical only for this region, both of which are conducive to their identification in the Babylonian material. The specific structure of Anatolian names will be elucidated later in the chapter.

Texts and Socio-Historical Contexts

Attempts at analysing the Anatolian onomastic material in Babylonian texts are valuable since the Babylonian transmission offers important insights into Anatolian languages, both linguistically and historically. In the linguistic sense, Babylonian spellings provide independent evidence for discussions of Anatolian onomastic materials preserved, for instance, in Neo-Assyrian or Egyptian transcriptions. From a historical point of view the Babylonian material contributes to a better understanding of Anatolian history as well as of the history of communities speaking (at least originally) Anatolian languages.

Unsurprisingly, Anatolian names appear in two types of Babylonian texts: historical and administrative. Historical texts deal with Anatolian events and, accordingly, their number is very low. A typical and instructive example is the aforementioned king of Pirindu, Appuwašu (^{I}*ap-pu-ú-a-šú*), who is mentioned in a Babylonian chronicle (ABC 6:1). The chronicle dates from a period (mid-sixth century) when we do not (yet) have local, Anatolian historical sources. The fact that the ruler of a Neo-Hittite state still carries a Luwian name (cf. n. 4), demonstrated by the Babylonian transmission more than a century after the disappearance of Hieroglyphic Luwian texts, has important repercussions regarding the history and linguistic landscape of sixth century Anatolia.

The bulk of the attestations are provided by administrative texts. Anatolian names typically appear in Babylonian texts after the Persian conquest of Anatolia and Egypt, which led to the occasional relocation of individuals and communities speaking Anatolian languages. Nevertheless, due to the problems mentioned earlier, the informative value of these texts

[9] See the most recent attempt in Simon (2016). The claims of Dees (2021) (who frequently misrepresents Simon 2016) are linguistically untenable.

and the details of the historical processes they document are limited to specific cases. For instance, the linguistic identification of most of the 'Lydians' with bow-fiefs in Bīt-Tabalāyi in the region of Nippur, who appear in the archive of the agricultural firm of the Murašû family in the last quarter of the fifth century, is still problematic.[10] The names of most of the 'Lycians', protagonists of a receipt from the same archive, are equally unidentifiable.[11] Even less understood is the presence of Luwian speakers from Central Anatolia ('Tabal') implied by the aforementioned toponyms Bīt-Tabalāyi and Bīt-Kikê ([I]*ki-ki-e*), from the same region and period, which is based on a Luwian (Tabalite) personal name.[12] Currently, the only case where the linguistic identification is sufficiently advanced and the historical context instructive is that of the texts mentioning Carians.[13] These texts originate from Borsippa and most of them are receipts for provision of food rations to Carians stationed in Borsippa by local citizens in the reign of Cambyses and the early years of Darius I. These Carians arrived with their families from Egypt after its conquest by Cambyses, presumably as part of their military service or, alternatively, as prisoners of war. From an onomastic point of view, their Caro–Egyptian origin is evident as most of their names are either Carian or Egyptian in roughly equal proportion, although new (i.e., Babylonian and Aramaic) names are not unknown, if still very limited.[14]

All in all, very few Anatolian names have been found in Babylonian texts until now, and they are mostly known from Borsippa and Nippur, while isolated examples appear all around Babylonia (e.g., Babylon, Ur, Uruk).

The Structure of the Anatolian Names: A Short Overview

Independently from the specific languages, Anatolia had its own, typically local naming practices, quite different from the other regions of the Ancient Near East and continuous through the millennia without notable changes. The latter feature is especially helpful in identifying Anatolian names since we can use the far-better-attested cuneiform and hieroglyphic material too. Noteworthy features specific to the Anatolian naming area

[10] Cf. Zadok 1979, 167 with references, but also n. 5 in this chapter. [11] Eilers 1940, 206–14.

[12] Although Luwian was the most widespread language in both regions of Tabal and Cilicia, [I]*ki-ki-e* is not a Cilician name, contra Zadok (1979, 167); cf. n. 5 this chapter. For Cilicians and Tabalites in Babylonia in general, see Zadok (1979, 167–8) and Zadok (2005, 76–9), both with references.

[13] For the following, see the detailed historical evaluation of these texts by Waerzeggers (2006); cf. also Zadok (2005, 80–4).

[14] Cf. most recently Simon (2016), with references and discussions.

include the complex system of the so-called '*Lallnamen*' ('elementary names') and the compound names with some standard elements that are extremely widespread. In general, Anatolian names other than the '*Lallnamen*' are transparent, meaningful names built on Anatolian material, which obviously makes their identification easier.

Anatolian names fall into two categories: '*Lallnamen*' and non-elementary names. '*Lallnamen*' are 'elementary names' since they are not built on meaningful words but on syllables of the simplest shapes.[15] These syllables are not completely freely chosen, as Table 13.1 illustrates.[16]

There are five types of non-elementary names: non-compound names (known in German as '*einstämmige Vollnamen*'), compound names ('*zweistämmige Vollnamen*'), abbreviated names ('*Kurznamen*'), sentence names ('*Satznamen*'), and hypocoristic names ('*Kosenamen*').

Non-compound names are built on appellatives, toponyms, and divine names. In the case of the appellatives, stems and their derivatives are equally attested. Typical examples include Muwa 'Might' / Muwattalli 'Mighty', Piḫa 'Splendour' / Piḫammi 'Resplendent', Ḫantili 'First', *Imrassa/i-/(I)βrsi '(the one) Of the open country'. Names built on toponyms and ethnic names are derived by language-specific suffixes, for

Table 13.1 *Anatolian Lallname types*

	Structure	Example
1.	CV (monosyllables)	Tā, Pā, Tū
2.	CV$_i$-CV$_i$ (the reduplication of Type 1)	Lala, Nana, Kikki
3.	aCa	Aba, Ada, Ana
4.	aC$_i$aC$_i$a(/i/u) (the reduplication of Type 3)	Ababa, Anana(/i/u)
5.	[CVCV]$_i$-[CVCV]$_i$ (full reduplication, also with syncope)	Waliwali, Murmura
6.	[CV]$_i$-[CV]$_i$CV (disyllabic base with reduplicated first syllable)	Kukkunni, Pupuli
7.	(C)V[CV]$_i$-[CV]$_i$ (disyllabic base with reduplicated last syllable)	Mulili, Palulu
8.	Ci/u+(glide)+a (monosyllabic base)	Niya, Puwa

[15] Note that Anatolian '*Lallnamen*' never serve as hypocoristic names.

[16] Here and in the following, most of the names will be quoted from the languages attested in cuneiform writing since they provide the richest material.

instance *-ili-* (e.g., Ḫattušili '(the one) Of (the city of) Ḫattuša', Nerikkaili '(the one) Of (the city of) Nerik'), *-uman-* / *-umna-* (Ḫupišnuman '(the one) From (the city of) Ḫupišna'), and *-wann(i)-* (Urawanni '(the one) From (the city of) Ura').[17] Names built on divine names can include a single divine name (e.g., Kuruntiya), a suffixed divine name, and even a double divine name (e.g., Arma-Tarḫunta). A specific group of divinities is especially popular in first-millennium names, including Arma, Iya, Runtiya, Šanda, and Tarḫunta (with regional phonological variants).[18]

Compound names are created from nouns, adjectives, and adverbs. Recurring, typical elements include kinship terms and divine names. Several types of compound names exist, the two most important ones being determinative compounds and possessive compounds (also known as bahuvrihis). The relation between the composing elements, the first member (M_1), and the second member (M_2) – the meaning of a determinative compound – is varied. One possibility is 'M_2 is for M_1', as in the name Tarḫunta-warri 'Help to Tarḫunta' with the typical element *warra/i-* 'help'. Another possibility is 'M_2 of/has the quality of M_1', as in the name Arma-nāni 'Brother of (the moon god) Arma'. A typical element is *zida/i-* 'man', especially in combination with divine names and toponyms; for example, Arma-ziti 'Man of (the moon god) Arma' and Ḫalpa-ziti 'Man of (the storm god of) Aleppo'.[19] The second member is frequently a divine name: for example, Ḫalpa-runtiya '(belonging to) Runtiya of Aleppo'. A typical adverb is *šr* 'up, above', as, for instance, in the name *Šr-quq* 'Super-/Hyper-grandfather'. In a further typical construction M_2 is a past participle; a frequent version is X-*piyamma/i-* 'Given by X'.

The meaning of the possessive compounds is 'Having the M_2 of M_1' (thus the meaning is not 'Having M_1 and M_2'). An extremely widespread type has *muwa-* as its second member, with the meaning 'Having the might of M_1': the first member can be a divine name, toponym, appellative, adjective, or even an adverb. Some examples are Šauška-muwa 'Having the might of Šauška', Ḫalpa-muwa 'Having the might of (the storm god of) Aleppo', and Piḫa-muwa or Pariya-muwa 'Having might beyond

[17] The Carian name known as Lukšu (*ᴵlu-uk-šu*) in Babylonian transmission (BRM 1 71:7) probably means 'Lycian' with a Carian ethnic suffix (Simon 2016, 276–7).

[18] The name Sarmâ (*ᴵsa-ar-ma-ʾ*) in Babylonian transmission (GC 2 351:3) is generally held to be a by-form of *Šarruma* since its identification by Zadok (1979, 168). However, as Simon (2020) demonstrated, this is not possible on formal grounds and *ᴵsa-ar-ma-ʾ* (together with some Anatolian names) originates in a Luwian word of unknown meaning.

[19] Yakubovich (2013, 101–2) plausibly suggests that some of the names built on toponyms are in fact elliptic theophoric names referring to the (main) deity of the settlement. This possibility applies also to the names quoted herein.

(surpassing might)'. Yet another widespread type has *wasu-* as its second member, with the meaning 'Having the favour of M_1': for example, Ḫalpa-wasu 'Having the favour of (the storm god of) Aleppo'.[20]

Abbreviating names represents a widespread practice among the elder Indo-European languages. In fact, abbreviated names are a subtype of the compound names since they are created by the abbreviation of the second member of a compound name. The abbreviation is limited only by the constraint that the first consonant (group) must be preserved (see the well-known example Hera-kles vs. Patro-kl-os [abbreviated from Patro-kles]). This immediately shows that the abbreviation does not change the meaning of the name and does not turn it into a hypocoristic name. There are reasons to assume that the practice of abbreviation was known in Anatolia, too: names with the 'shortening' *muwa-* > *mu-* (e.g., Ḫalpa-mu) are well attested, although further investigation is needed as to whether they represent contracted forms (then with a long vowel, i.e., *mū-* [for a possible case in Babylonian transmission see n. 20]) or abbreviated names (then with a short vowel). The names with *-piya-* have a debated morphology, but as M_2 from the participle *piyammal i-* 'given' (e.g., Tarḫunta-piya 'Given by Tarḫunta'), they might also belong here.

As for the sentence names, although their precise meaning and origin are quite debated (they are supposed to be created after Hurrian and/or Akkadian models), this does not influence their identification, as they are built from the usual elements as well as from verbs; thus, their Anatolian origin is easily recognisable. A typical example is Aza-tiwada 'The sun god favours' or 'Favour (him), sun god!'.

Finally, the relatively rarely attested hypocoristic names require a language-specific diminutive suffix, such as Luwian *-annal i-* (e.g., Zidanna/i 'Little Man', ^{d}U-*ni* /*Tarḫunni- 'Little Storm-god').

Further Reading

The available overviews on Anatolian languages vary in terms of up-to-dateness and trustworthiness; H. Craig Melchert (2017), Christian Zinko (2017), and Elisabeth Rieken (2017) can serve as a starting point. Anatolian names in Babylonian transmission have been investigated by several scholars; the most important papers include those of Wilhelm Eilers (1940), Albrecht Goetze

20 For a name with *wasu-* in Babylonian transmission, see earlier in chapter. For a name with *muwa-*, see Šandamû (^{I}*šá-an-da-mu-ú*, CT 57 135:4′, identified as Anatolian by Zadok 1994, 16 with references), the equivalent of Sanda-mu attested in the Hieroglyphic Luwian inscription of CEKKE (ACLT s.v.).

(1962), Ran Zadok (1979 and 2005), Caroline Waerzeggers (2006), and Zsolt Simon (2016). The most useful overviews of Anatolian naming practices are Emmanuel Laroche (1966) and Thomas Zehnder (2010), and, from a 'Western Anatolian' point of view, H. Craig Melchert (2013). Note that the articles of Johann Tischler (1995 and 2002) are superficial and the entry of Harry A. Hoffner (1998) in the standard lexicon of Ancient Near Eastern Studies is confusing.

The standard handbook of Anatolian names in cuneiform and hieroglyphic transmission is from Emmanuel Laroche (1966). It has several supplements (Laroche 1981; Tischler 1982; Beckman 1983; Trémouille n.d.), but no complete and up-to-date version exists. Nevertheless, several handbooks offer updated versions of specific sub-corpora. Female names are treated by Thomas Zehnder (2010), and Hittite names in Old Assyrian sources by Alwin Kloekhorst (2019). Although the latter book contains a chapter on Luwian names, Ilya Yakubovich's discussion (2010) of the Luwian names is still indispensable (on Old Assyrian material, see also Dercksen 2014). The digital platform ACLT (Annotated Corpus of Luwian Texts; http://web-corpora.net/LuwianCorpus) provides an updated list of attestations of Hieroglyphic Luwian names in the Iron Age.

The standard handbook of Anatolian names in alphabetic transmission is by Ladislav Zgusta (1964), which is outdated from every possible point of view. It is generally supplemented by the relevant volumes of the LGPN, especially vol. A (Coastal Asia Minor from Pontos to Ionia) and vol. B (Coastal Asia Minor from Caria to Cilicia); vol. C (Inland Asia Minor) is forthcoming. For more in-depth investigations one must consult the handbooks of the relevant languages: for Carian, see Ignacio J. Adiego (2007); for the Lycian varieties, see H. Craig Melchert (2004) and Günter Neumann (2007); for Lydian, see Roberto Gusmani (1964 and 1980–6); for Sidetic, see Santiago Pérez Orozco (2007); and for Pisidian, see Claude Brixhe (2016). The book of Philo H. J. Houwink ten Cate (1961) is a classical treatment of the regions of Lycia and Cilicia Aspera (and their environs), although outdated from many points of view.

Finally, the continuously expanding eDiAna platform (Digital Philological-Etymological Dictionary of the Minor Ancient Anatolian Corpus Languages; www.ediana.gwi.uni-muenchen.de/) discusses many personal names from different periods, especially those from the alphabetic languages and the Luwian names in Old Assyrian transmission.

References

Adiego, I. J. 2007. *The Carian Language*, Handbuch der Orientalistik 86. Leiden/Boston: Brill.

Baker, H. D. (ed.) 2001. *The Prosopography of the Neo-Assyrian Empire*, 2/II: L–N. Helsinki: The Neo-Assyrian Text Corpus Project.

Beckman, G. 1983. 'A contribution to Hittite onomastic studies', *Journal of the American Oriental Society* 103, 623–7.

Brixhe, C. 2016. *Stèles et langue de Pisidie*. Nancy: Association pour la Diffusion de la Recherche sur l'Anitquité.

Dees, L. C. 2021. 'Carian names in Babylonian records: some new analyses', *Nouvelles Assyriologiques Brèves et Utilitaires 2021/23*.

Dercksen, J. G. 2014. 'Review of T. Zehnder 2010. Die hethitischen Frauennamen: Katalog und Interpretation', *Orientalistische Literaturzeitung* 109, 196–9.

Eilers, W. 1940. 'Kleinasiatisches', *Zeitschrift der Deutschen Morgenländischen Gesellschaft* 94, 189–233.

Goetze, A. 1962. 'Cilicians', *Journal of Cuneiform Studies* 16, 48–58.

Gusmani, R. 1964 and 1980–6. *Lydisches Wörterbuch. Mit grammatischer Skizze und Inschriftensammlung und Ergänzungsband*. Heidelberg: Winter Verlag.

Hoffner, H. A. 1998. 'Name, Namengebung. C. Bei den Hethitern', *Reallexikon der Assyriologie und der Vorderasiatischen Archäologie* 9, 116–21.

Houwink ten Cate, P. H. J. 1961. *The Luwian Population Groups of Lycia and Cilicia Aspera during the Hellenistic Period*, Documenta et Monumenta Orientis Antiqui 10. Leiden: Brill.

Kloekhorst, A. 2019. *Kanišite Hittite. The Earliest Attested Record of Indo-European*, Handbuch der Orientalistik 132. Leiden/Boston: Brill.

Laroche, E. 1966. *Les noms des hittites*. Paris: Klincksieck.

Laroche, E. 1981. 'Les noms des hittites. Supplément', *Hethitica* 4, 3–58.

Melchert, H. C. 2004. *A Dictionary of the Lycian Language*. Ann Arbor: Beech Stave.

Melchert, H. C. 2013. 'Naming practices in second- and first-millennium western Anatolia' in R. Parker (ed.), *Personal Names in Ancient Anatolia*, Proceedings of the British Academy 191. Oxford: Oxford University Press, pp. 31–49.

Melchert, H. C. 2017. 'Anatolian' in M. Kapović (ed.), *The Indo-European Languages*, 2nd ed. London/New York: Routledge, pp. 171–201.

Neumann, G. 2007. Glossar des Lykischen. *Überarbeitet und zum Druck gebracht von Johann Tischler*, Dresdner Beiträge zur Hethitologie 21. Wiesbaden: Harrassowitz.

Pérez Orozco, S. 2007. 'La lengua sidética. Ensayo de síntesis', *Kadmos* 46, 125–42.

Rieken, E. 2017. 'The dialectology of Anatolian' in J. S. Klein, B. D. Joseph, and M. Fritz (eds.), *Handbook of Comparative and Historical Indo-European Linguistics*, Handbücher zur Sprach- und Kommunikationswissenschaft 41.1. Berlin: De Gruyter, pp. 298–309.

Simon, Zs. 2016. 'Bemerkungen zu den karischen Namen aus Borsippa', *Res Antiquae* 13, 273–80.

Simon, Zs. 2020. 'On some central Anatolian Neo-Hittite ruler names with Šarruma', *Nouvelles Assyriologiques Brèves et Utilitaires* 2020/92.

Tischler, J. 1982. 'Beiträge zur hethitischen Anthroponymie' in J. Tischler (ed.), *Serta indogermanica. Festschrift für Günter Neumann zum 60. Geburtstag*, Innsbrucker Beiträge zur Sprachwissenschaft 40. Innsbruck: Institut für Sprachwissenschaft der Universität, pp. 439–53.

Tischler, J. 1995. 'Kleinasiatische Onomastik (Hethitisch)' in E. Eichler (ed.), *Namenforschung. Ein internationales Handbuch zur Onomastik*, Handbücher zur Sprach- und Kommunikationswissenschaft 11.1. Berlin: De Gruyter, pp. 636–44.

Tischler, J. 2002. 'Zur Morphologie und Semantik der hethitischen Personen- und Götternamen' in M. P. Streck and S. Weninger (eds.), *Altorientalische und Semitische Onomastik*, Alter Orient und Altes Testament 296. Münster: Ugarit-Verlag, pp. 75–84.

Trémouille, M.-C. n.d. *Répertoire onomastique*. www.hethport.uni-wuerzburg.de /hetonom/ONOMASTIdata.html.

Vernet Pons, M. 2016. 'The Lycian PN Artimas and Arteimas: a new proposal for an Iranian and epichoric etymology', *Glotta* 92, 280–94.

Waerzeggers, C. 2006. 'The Carians of Borsippa', *Iraq* 68, 1–22.

Yakubovich, I. 2010. *Sociolinguistics of the Luvian Language*, Brill's Studies in Indo-European Languages and Linguistics 2. Leiden: Brill.

Yakubovich, I. 2013. 'Anatolian names in -wiya and the structure of Empire Luwian onomastics' in A. Mouton, I. Rutherford, and I. Yakubovich (eds.), *Luwian Identities. Culture, Language and Religion Between Anatolia and the Aegean*, Culture and History of the Ancient Near East 64. Leiden: Brill, pp. 87–123.

Zadok, R. 1979. 'On some foreign population groups in first millennium Babylonia', *Tel Aviv* 6, 164–81.

Zadok, R. 1994. 'On some anthroponyms and toponyms', *Nouvelles Assyriologiques Brèves et Utilitaires 1994*/14.

Zadok, R. 2005. 'On Anatolians, Greeks and Egyptians in "Chaldean" and Achaemenid Babylonia', *Tel Aviv* 32, 76–106.

Zehnder, T. 2010. *Die hethitischen Frauennamen. Katalog und Interpretation*, Dresdner Beiträge zur Hethitologie 29. Wiesbaden: Harrassowitz.

Zgusta, L. 1964. *Kleinasiatische Personennamen*. Prag: Verlag der Tschechoslowakischen Akademie der Wissenschaften.

Zinko, C. 2017. 'The documentation of Anatolian' in J. S. Klein, B. D. Joseph, and M. Fritz (eds.), *Handbook of Comparative and Historical Indo-European Linguistics*, Handbücher zur Sprach- und Kommunikationswissenschaft 41.1. Berlin: De Gruyter, pp. 239–49.

CHAPTER 14

Greek Names

Paola Corò

Introduction to the Language and Its Background

The Greek language belongs to the Indo-European linguistic family. It is attested from the second half of the second millennium BCE to the present day. Conventionally, it is divided into three main phases: the ancient period, from the first attestations to the end of the Roman Empire; the Byzantine period, from the end of the Roman Empire to the conquest of Constantinople in 1453 CE; and the modern period, from 1453 CE to date. For our purposes only the ancient phase will be taken into consideration.

The earliest attested dialect is Mycenean Greek, written on clay tablets using a syllabary known as 'Linear B', adapted from the syllabary (Linear A) used to express the language of Minoan Crete, which is still undeciphered. With the collapse of the Mycenean civilisation (c. 1200 BCE), the Linear B script disappeared during the so-called Greek 'Dark Age', from which writing was not preserved. Writing was re-introduced between the end of the ninth and the beginning of the eighth centuries BCE, now using an alphabetic system derived from the Phoenician alphabet.

The new alphabetic writing was used until the Hellenistic period on a number of different writing materials (wood, marble, bronze, and lead, as well as clay, ostraca, wooden boards, parchment, and papyrus scrolls) to express different dialects of the Greek language (Ionic and Attic, Arcado–Cypriot, Pamphylian, Macedonian, the Doric group of dialects, the Aeolic group, and literary dialects; e.g., that of Homeric poetry). Following the conquests of Alexander the Great, a new supra-regional dialect – the *koiné* – evolved from Attic as the lingua franca of the empire. The ancient phase of the Greek language is conventionally said to end in the year 394 CE, at the time of the division of the Roman Empire.

All along its mature phase, the Greek alphabet includes twenty-four discrete letters. The Greek language is inflectional, like Akkadian, and includes five cases: the nominative (for the subject), the genitive (for the possessive relationship), the dative (for the indirect object, plus other syntactic functions; e.g., instrument and cause), the accusative (for the direct object), and the vocative (for addressing people). Greek personal names are usually transliterated into Babylonian in the nominative. Although Greek names are in general rendered into Babylonian with their own Greek nominative endings, Babylonian nominative case endings may sometimes replace the equivalent (masculine or feminine) Greek ones.

The Name Material in the Babylonian Sources

The Corpus

The appearance of Greek names in the onomastic corpus from Babylonia is directly connected to the more general matter of Greek presence in Mesopotamia, which is treated in more detail in 'Socio-Onomastics'. Suffice it to note here that with the Hellenistic period the number of Greek names attested in Babylonian sources noticeably increases, reaching a total of about 130 distinct entries. The largest portion of Greek names occurs in the legal tablets from the southern Mesopotamian city of Uruk dated to the Hellenistic period,[1] but Greek names are also recorded in the Astronomical Diaries, the Babylonian chronicles, and some royal inscriptions, as well as in legal and administrative documents from the cities of Babylon and Borsippa.[2]

The corpus includes both male and female names, the second group consisting of about ten names only. This comes as no surprise as male individuals are in general much more frequently represented in the Babylonian sources than women (see 'Female Names').

Types

Following Ina J. Hartmann's classification, Greek names may be divided into monothematic and dithematic names.[3] Monothematic names are non-compound names, consisting of one grammatical element such as an

[1] The estimation is based on Monerie (2014); single name entries are considered here, irrespective of the number of different individuals who may have borne the same name, and of the attested spellings for each of them.

[2] For a complete listing the reader is referred to the entries of each personal name in Monerie (2014); see also the index of sources in the same volume, pp. 213–21. For the Astronomical Diaries, see Sachs and Hunger (1988, 1989, and 1996) as well as Van der Spek, Finkel, Pirngruber and Stevens (forthcoming) (incl. the chronicles). Royal inscriptions referring to Greek personal names are the Antiochos Cylinder (VR 66), the Nikarchos Cylinder (YOS 1 52), and the stamped brick of Anu-uballiṭ/Kephalon (WVDOG 51, pl. 58).

[3] We follow here the simplest classification of Greek names into two main groups, as suggested by Hartmann (2002). One should, however, note that according to Hartmann, Greek non-compound

adjective, a verb, a substantive, or a proper noun (with or without the addition of a suffix): this is the case with personal names such as Κεφάλων (Kephalōn, with suffix; from κεφαλή 'head'). Dithematic names are compounds, usually made up of two complete and recognisable lexical elements, such as adjectives, verbs, substantives, and proper nouns: a typical example is the name Τιμοκράτης (Timokratēs; from τιμάω 'to honour' + κράτος 'strength').

The corpus of Greek names in cuneiform likewise consists of both non-compound/simplex and compound names. Theophoric elements are frequently used in the formation of names, both non-compound/simplex, for example, the name of the god Apollo in Ἀπολλωνίδης (Apōllonidēs) or Ἀπολλώνιος (Apollōnios), and compound, as in the case of the divine name Artemis in Ἀρτεμίδωρος (Artemidōros). Theophoric elements used in the representation of Greek names in the cuneiform corpus include the names of the gods Athena (e.g., Ἀθηνόδωρος, Athēnodōros), Zeus (e.g., Διοφάνης, Diophanēs; Διόφαντος, Diophantos), Herakles (e.g., Ἡρακλείδης, Herakleidēs), and Poseidon (e.g., Ποσειδώνιος, Poseidōnios). A full list is presented in Table 14.1.[4]

Lexical items such as 'strength' (κράτος, *kratos*), 'gift' (δῶρον, *dōron*), 'to rule' (ἄρχω, *archō*), 'renown' (κλέος, *kleos*), 'horse' (ἵππος, *hippos*), 'head'

Table 14.1 *Greek theophoric names*

God name	Non-compound names	Compound names
Apollo	Apōllonidēs (2); Apollōnios (5)	Apollodōros (1)
Artemis	–	Artemidōros (3)
Athena	–	Athēnodōros (1); Athēnophilos (1)
Demetra	Demetrios (3)[5]	
Dionysus	Dionysia (1)	
Helios	–	Heliodōros (1)
Hephaestus	Hephaistiōn (1)	
Herakles	Herakleidēs (4)	–
Heros		Herotheos (1)
Isis		Isidōros (2); Isitheos (1)
Poseidon	Poseidōnios (2)	
Zeus	–	Diophanēs (2); Diophantos (7)

names can be further sub-divided into monothematic names with or without suffixes. Furthermore, compound names are dithematic names falling into three different sub-groups: full dithematic (two elements fully recognisable), extended dithematic (two elements + suffix), and abbreviated dithematic (two elements, one of which shortened). Such a refined distinction is, however, not productive for the purposes of the present analysis.

[4] In Tables 14.1 and 14.2, digits between round brackets refer to the number of discrete individuals bearing the name, as recorded in Monerie (2014).

[5] Royal names are excluded here.

(κεφαλή, *kephalē*), 'man' (ἀνήρ, *anēr*), 'victory' (νίκη, *nikē*), 'army' (στρατός, *stratos*),[6] 'god' (θεός, *theos*), and 'to honour' (τιμάω, *timaō*), 'friend' (φίλος, *philos*), 'lineage' (γένος, *genos*), 'father' (πατήρ, *patēr*), and 'better' (ἄριστος, *aristos*) are productive in the corpus in the formation of names, especially (but not exclusively) compound ones, as can be seen in Table 14.2.[7]

Also common in the corpus are royal names, of both Argead and Seleucid rulers (as, e.g., Seleucos, Antiochos, Demetrios etc.):[8] there is one case where a royal name is used in the feminine, in the female name Antiochis. No restrictions apply to the use of royal names in the onomastics of ordinary people, a situation which differs from what we know from Mesopotamia in other periods (see Chapter 1, and section 'Royal Names' in this chapter).

Table 14.2 *Greek names according to lexical items*

anēr	Alexandros (5); Menandros (1); Sōsandros (1)
archō	Archelaos (1); Archias (1)
aristos	Aristeus (1); Aristoklēs (1); Aristokratēs (2); Aristōn (3)
dōron	Artemidōros (3); Athenodōros (1); Diodōros (2); Heliodōros (1); Isidōros (2); Menodōros; Theodōros (2)
genos	Antigenēs; Diogenēs (2)
hippos	Alexippos (1); Hipponikos; Philippos (1)
kephalē	Kephalōn (9)
kleos	Agathoklēs (1); Dioklēs (1); Patroklēs (1)
kratos	Aristokratēs (2); Dēmokratēs (5); Timokratēs (5)
nikē	Andronikos (2); Nikanōr (12); Nikarchos (1); Nikēratos (1); Nikolaos (3)
patēr	Antipatros (3)
philos	Athenophilos (1); Menophilos (1); Philinos (1); Philippos (1); Philos (1); Zenophilos (1)
stratos	Stratōn (5)
theos	Herotheos (2); Isitheos (1); Theoboulos (1); Theodōros (2); Theodosios (1); Theogenēs (1); Theomelēs (2); Timotheos (2)
timaō	Timokratēs (5); Timotheos (2)

6 According to Julien Monerie the popularity of the name Στράτων (Stratōn) in Uruk at the end of the third century BCE might be due to a phenomenon of assonance with the common divine name Ištar, assimilated to Astarte. See Monerie (2014, 76–7) and Del Monte (1997, 41–2), both with bibliography.

7 The table only covers compound names built with the elements listed here and does not pretend to include all names attested in the corpus and their components. Occurrences referring to royal names are excluded from the total considered here.

8 Representing approximately 10 per cent of the individuals with a Greek name according to Monerie 2014, 75.

Naming Practices

In Greek sources, individuals are identified by a personal name and the patronym (i.e., the father's name), which can either be expressed in the genitive or as an adjective (usually ending in -ιδης). The use of the patronym is crucial for identification. The demotic (i.e., the name of the *dēmos* the individual belongs to) and/or the ethnicon are commonly added to the patronym when the individual is referred to in documents stemming from a place other than the one from which he originates.[9]

In the Hellenistic sources from Uruk, which make up the bulk of the material under consideration here, Greek names transliterated into Babylonian may occur as single names or as part of a full onomastic chain. Kings are usually identified by their first name only (see 'Royal Names' section of this chapter). Conversely, ordinary individuals are seldomly identified by their first name only. This may happen in exceptional circumstances, such as the identification of the neighbours in a property description or in the captions of seal impressions (but in this last case, full names are commonly preserved in the witness list of the same document).

Commonly, a complete onomastic chain is recorded. The following options are possible:

a. Greek name/Greek patronym/(Greek grandfather's name)
b. Greek name/Greek patronym/(Babylonian grandfather's name)/ Babylonian family name
c. Greek name/Babylonian patronym/(Babylonian grandfather's name)/ Babylonian family name
d. Greek name/Babylonian patronym/Babylonian grandfather's name/ (Babylonian great-grandfather's name).

It is generally believed that type a. identifies individuals who are 'ethnically' Greek. It is, however, difficult to ascertain the ethnic identity of the individuals with Greek names, as the sources only specify it in two cases: Poseidōnios, son of Metrodōros (or Myrtolos?), is labelled 'the Greek' (in YOS 20 70:8′), while Diophanēs, son of Stratōn, grandson of Kidin-Anu, is called 'the Urukean' (in BRM 2 55:15–16).[10]

Acculturation is frequently invoked as the reason for the choice of a Greek name within traditional Babylonian families. Stephanie M. Langin-Hooper

[9] Thompson 2001, 678–9.

[10] The name of the son of Poseidōnios is interpreted as Metrodōros (reading the name as ^I^*me-te-du-ur-su*) in YOS 20; it is tentatively read Myrtolos (i.e., ^I^*me-èr-ṭù-lu-su*) by Monerie (2014, 152, s.v).

and Laurie E. Pearce (2014) recently demonstrated that, at least in some cases, the attribution of a Greek name to the offspring of Babylonian families may result from maternal-line papponymy naming practices; that is, a mother would preserve her own family's cultural heritage by naming one of her sons after his maternal grandfather (who, in this case, bore a Greek name).

Spelling and Normalisation

Rendering Greek names with the Babylonian script was not an easy task. Babylonian scribes were confronted with two interconnected challenges: first, rendering a name whose spelling was designed for an alphabetic script by means of a mixed logo-syllabic system; second, adapting phonemes specific to the Greek language to the Babylonian phonetic system – for example, the vowel *o*, which does not exist in Babylonian, was usually replaced by *u*. Moreover, in the *koiné*, some of the phonemes of the Greek language (e.g., the diphthongs) were no longer pronounced as they were written.[11]

According to Julien Monerie,[12] when writing Greek names with the Babylonian script, the scribes, who always rendered them syllabically, more frequently resorted to the names' pronunciation rather than faithfully transcribing their standard written form. Furthermore, the more a name came into use, the more the scribes became familiar with it and tended to harmonise its spelling, also adapting it to Babylonian. These processes and the constraints, inherent to the differences between the two systems, explain why various spellings often occur for one and the same name.

It is thus difficult, if not impossible, to establish a full and mechanical set of conversion rules for Greek names into the Babylonian writing system. The most comprehensive and recent attempt in this regard is that by Julien Monerie (2014), to which the reader is referred for details. Suffice it here to lay out the most important correspondences generally applied to the reconstruction (see Table 14.3).

In order to identify Greek names in Babylonian writing, it also proves useful to list their most typical endings or second elements (see Table 14.4).

Socio-Onomastics

As we have observed, the diffusion of Greek names in Babylonian is linked to the more general matter of the contacts between the Greek world and Mesopotamia, and the debate on the significance of the

[11] See Horrocks (2010, esp. chp 4), and also Monerie (2015, 350–4). [12] Monerie 2015, 350.

Table 14.3 *Conversion rules for Greek names into the Babylonian writing system*[13]

Babylonian	Greek	Babylonian	Greek
a/–/(e in Neo-Assyrian)/ia	α	–/intervocalic *m*=*w*	Ϝ (*digamma*)
b	β	*u* but also *a*/*i*	ο
g	γ	*p*	π
d	δ	*r*/(*l*)	ρ
e/*i*	ε	*s*/(*š* in Neo-Assyrian)	σ, ς (in final position)
z	ζ	*ṭ*	τ
a-e/*e-e*/*i-e*/*e-ʾe*/*e-ʾa-a*	η	*i*/–	υ
t	θ	*p*	φ
i/*ʾi-i*	ι	*k*	χ
q	κ	*p*V-*s*V(?)	ψ
l	λ	*u* but also *a*/*i*	ω
m	μ	$v_1C_1C_2/C_1vC_2$-	C_1C_2-
n/–(before dentals)/ assimilated to following	ν	$v_1C_1C3/v_1C_1v_2C_2/v_1C_1C_2v_2C_3$	$C_1C_2C_3$
v_1 *k*-v_1*s*	ξ	*ḫ*/–	ʽ (rough breathing)

Greek presence in Babylonia in the first millennium BCE. While early contacts are already attested in the sources at the time of the Assyrian expansion to the west in the eighth century BCE, it is with the annexation of Babylonia by Cyrus in 539 BCE, and especially following Alexander III's conquest, that the Greek presence in the region becomes more than intermittent.[14]

Greek individuals (kings, officials, and ordinary men) as well as Babylonians bearing a Greek name begin to appear in the sources. The corpus consists primarily of masculine names; among them are royal names, used to identify the ruling kings and as part of the common onomastic repertoire. A very small percentage of the Greek onomasticon is represented by feminine names. It is in the Hellenistic period that an official of the city of Uruk is known to have received another, Greek name next to his Babylonian one, directly from the king. More and more Greek

[13] In Tables 14.3 and 14.4, 'C' stands for any consonant and 'v' for any vowel.

[14] On these topics, see, for example, Rollinger (2001) as well as Monerie (2012 and 2014), with earlier bibliography.

Table 14.4 *Typical endings and second elements of Greek names in Babylonian writing*

Babylonian rendering of name ending	Equivalent in transcription	Equivalent in Greek
C*u-su*	-C-os	-C-ος
V-*su*	-Vs	-V-ς
C*u-ú-ru*	-C-or	C-ωρ
C*u-ú-nu*/C*u-nu*/C*i-nu*	-Con	C-ων
an-dar/*an-da-ri*/*an-dar-ri-is*/*and-dar-su*/*an-der*/*a-dar*	-andros	-ανδρος
ar-ku-su/*ar-qu-ra-su*/*ar-qu-su*/*ar-qu-ú-su*/(C)*ar-su*	-archos	-αρχος
e-du-su	-ades	-αδης
du-ru-us/*du-ur-su*/*du-ur*/*du-ru*/*ˀu-du-ru*(?)	-doros	-δωρος
ig-nu-us/*ig-nu-su*/*ig-nu-us-su*/*ig-is-su*	-V-gonos	-V-γονος
gi-ra-te/*gu-ra-te*/*uq-ra-te*	-krates	-κρατης
uq-la-e/*uq-ra-la-e*	-V-kles	-V-κλης
ni-qé-e/*ni-qé*	-nikes	-νικης
pa-lu-su/*pa-lu-ú-*[*su*?]	-philos	-φιλος
C*i-de-e*/C*i-di-e*	-Cides/-Ceides	-ιδης/ειδης
pa-tu-su	-phantos	-φαντος
i-si/*ip-su*/*lìp-su*/*pi-is-su*/*pi-li-su*/*pi-su*/*pi-is*/*lìp-i-si*/*lip-pu-us*/*lip-is*/*lìp-us*/*lip-su*/*li-pi-su*	-(l)ippos	-ιππος
C*i-ia*/C*i-su*/C*i-e-su*/C*i-si*	-Cios	-C-ιος

names are incorporated in the corpus of personal names in Uruk alongside traditional Babylonian ones, identifying both individuals of likely Greek origin and Babylonians.[15]

Royal Names

Kings are usually referred to by their first name, with no onomastic chain following. Their names typically (though not exclusively) occur in the date formulas of the documents and in the payment sections of the contracts to specify the currency used to pay the price of the commodity that is the object of a transaction. Thus, for example, according to STUBM 45-RE Lâbâši, son of Anu-zēru-iddin, from the Ekur-zakir

[15] On double names in Hellenistic Uruk, see Bowman (1939), Doty (1988), and Boiy (2005), with bibliography. Recently also Pearce and Corò (2023).

family, buys a house and an unbuilt plot located in the Šamaš Gate district in Uruk. The document is dated to the early regnal years of Seleucos II and the formula reads 'Uruk. Ṭebēt, (day broken), year 69, Seleucos (^{I}*se-lu-ku*), the king'. Lâbâši pays a total price of 8 shekels of silver in good-quality staters of Antiochos (*is-ta-tir-ri*.MEŠ *šá* ^{I}*an-ti-'i-ku-su bab-ba-nu-ú-tú*) for the property. Although the document is issued in the reign of Seleucos II, the currency used is still that of his predecessor, Antiochos II.

Partial exception to the use of the first name for kings is represented by date formulas indicating co-regencies, where the parental relationship between the reigning kings may be mentioned. An example is provided by STUBM 74-RE which, according to its date formula, was issued in year 109 'of Antiochos and Antiochos, his son, the kings' (^{I}*an-ti-'i-ku-su u* ^{I}*an-ti-'i-ku-su* DUMU-*šu* LUGAL.MEŠ).

Abbreviations for the king names are sometimes used, especially in the Astronomical Diaries. A list of abbreviated royal names is presented in Table 14.5.

No restriction apparently applied to the use of Greek royal names for ordinary people in the Hellenistic period. A large number of individuals in the corpus exhibit names such as Alexandros (^{I}*a-lek*, ^{I}*a-lek-si-an-dar*, and ^{I}*a-lek-sa-an-dar*), Antiochos (^{I}*an-ti-ʾi-i-ku-su*, ^{I}*an-ti-i-ku-su*, ^{I}*an-ti-ʾu-ku-su*, and ^{I}*an-ti-ʾu-uk-su*), Demetrios (^{I}*de-e-meṭ-ri-su*, ^{I}*de-meṭ-ri*, and maybe also ^{I}*di-i-meṭ-ri:ti-ia*), Philippos (^{I}*pi-il-pi-li-su* and ^{I}*pi-il-pi-su*), and Seleucos (^{I}*se-lu*, ^{I}*se-lu-ku*, and ^{I}*se-lu-uk-ku*).[17]

Table 14.5 *Abbreviations of Greek royal names*

Akkadian rendering	Reading	Full name
^{I}*a-lek-sa*[16]	Alexa	Alexandros
^{I}*an*; ^{I}*an-ti*	An; Anti	Antiochos
^{I}*de*	De	Demetrios
^{I}*pi*	Pi	Philippos
^{I}*se*	Se	Seleucos

[16] Note also the exceptional use of KI.MIN (= 'ditto'), preceded by the determinative for masculine personal names, as patronym for the king Alexander mentioned in the date formula of OECT 9 75:6′ from Kish. I thank Laurie Pearce for drawing my attention to this case.

[17] Only the spellings of royal names used to identify ordinary people are recorded here. For a complete list of spellings of each royal name, see Monerie, (2014 s.vv). See also the website HBTIN, s.vv: http://oracc.museum.upenn.edu/hbtin/index.html.

Female Names

Only a few Greek female names occur in the corpus, three of which identify queens and four of which identify ordinary women.[18] Queen names include Laodice 'People's justice' (Λαοδίκη, spelled ^I^*lam-ú-di-qé-ʾa-a*, ^I^*lu-da-qé*, ^I^*lu-di-qé-e*, and ^f^*la-ú-di-qé-e*),[19] identifying the two Seleucid queens married to Antiochos II and Antiochos III, respectively; Stratonice 'Army's victory', the wife of Seleucos I and Antiochos I (Στρατονίκη, spelled ^I^*as-ta-ar-ta-ni-iq-qú*, ^I^*as-ta-rat-ni-qé*, and ^I^*as-ta-rat-ni-qé-e*); and Thalassia 'From the sea' (Θαλασσία spelled ^I^*ta-la-si-ʾa-a-ṣu-u*), the wife of Hyspaosines of Charax.

Among ordinary women mentioned in the corpus from Hellenistic Uruk, both Antiochis 'Against support' (Ἀντιοχίς spelled ^f^*an-ti-ʾi-i-ki-su*), the daughter of Diophantos, and Dionysia (mng. unknown) (Διονύσια spelled ^f^*di-ni-ʾi-i-si-ʾa*), the daughter of Herakleidēs, are likely of Greek origins and married into Babylonian families. The name Antiochis confirms the diffusion of royal names among common people, including women, and Dionysia preserves a clear theophoric name. Phanaia 'One who brings light' (Φάναια spelled ^f^*pa-na-a*) is a slave who probably got her Greek name from her mistress, a certain ^f^Šamê-ramât, also known with the Greek name Kratō 'Strength' (Κρατώ spelled ^f^*ka-ra-ṭu-ú*), the daughter of a certain Artemidōros. It is uncertain whether ^f^Šamê-ramât *alias* Kratō stemmed from a Greek family;[20] however, she probably married a Greek man whose name is tentatively reconstructed as Tatedidos (mng. uncertain).

Double Names

Greek names may also occur in combination with a Babylonian name to identify an individual bearing two names. The typical Babylonian formula is 'PN_1 whose other name is PN_2'. Only about twenty double Greek/Babylonian names occur in the corpus. The use of polyonomy is not limited to Greek/Babylonian names; it also appears in names that pair Babylonian/Babylonian and Babylonian/other languages. The order of the two names is apparently irrelevant, and in many instances only one of the two was used in the documents.[21] In the well-known case of the high official Anu-uballiṭ alias

18 On women in the sources from Hellenistic Uruk, see Corò (2014; Corò 2021), with earlier bibliography.
19 On the spellings of the name of Laodice, see Corò (2020).
20 According to Oelsner (1992, 343) she was Greek; for a different hypothesis, see Monerie (2014, 73–4).
21 We have no clear idea of what is the rationale behind the use of one or the other; see Boiy (2005). See also Sherwin-White (1983) and, recently, Monerie (2014). On the use of his Greek name by Nikolaos alias Riḫat-Anu, see Pearce and Corò (2023).

Nikarchos, his Greek name was apparently entrusted to him by the king, but one cannot generalise from it and the rationale behind this practice still escapes our full understanding.[22]

Further Reading

As an introduction to the history of the Greek language and its dialects, the main reference is the book by Geoffrey Horrocks (2010). A classical reference for Greek grammar is by Herbert W. Smyth (1956). The most recent grammar of the Greek language in English, offering a new linguistically oriented approach, is by Evert van Emde Boas, Albert Rijksbaron, Luuk Huitink, and Mathieu de Bakker (2019). The Lexicon of Greek Personal Names (LGPN) is an essential tool for Greek names, listing the attestations of names, showing their geographical distribution, and providing the total of attestations. It features an online version (www.lgpn.ox.ac.uk) and a paper version (both still incomplete as for their geographical coverage since it is an ongoing project). It is a very useful tool for our purposes, as it offers the possibility to check the original spellings of Greek names and to look for names that might not be recorded in Julian Monerie's prosopographic dictionary. The reader is referred to the publications page of the LGPN website for details on the published volumes.

The first systematic study of Greek names attested in Babylonian sources is by Wolfgang Röllig (1960). The most recent and important reference book for Greek names in Babylonian sources is the prosopographic dictionary compiled by Julien Monerie (2014), where all Greek personal names occurring in Babylonian sources are recorded. Two reviews to this volume are published so far: one by Zsolt Simon (2017), the other by Reinhard Pirngruber (2015). Also useful is the synthesis in English by Julien Monerie (2015) on the principles governing the transcription of Greek in cuneiform. Another useful tool is the name glossary on the website HBTIN 'Hellenistic Babylonia: Text, Images, and Names' (http://oracc.museum.upenn.edu/hbtin/index.html) directed by Laurie Pearce. Here, the occurrences of Greek personal names attested in the corpus of texts from Hellenistic Babylonia are recorded alongside the Babylonian ones.

Other literature one might also want to consult includes:

Clancier, P. and J. Monerie 2014. 'Les sanctuaires babyloniens à l'époque hellénistique. Évolution d'un relais de pouvoir', *Topoi* 18, 181–237.

Heller, A. 2018. 'Review of J. Monerie 2014: D'Alexandre à Zoilos. Dictionnaire prosopographique des porteurs de nom grec dans les sources cunéiformes', *Klio* 100/2, 544–9.

[22] The inscription in question is the so-called Nikarchos Cylinder (YOS 1 52). According to Langin-Hooper and Pearce (2014, 195–9) it is possible that double names were used at least in some cases to preserve both the maternal and paternal onomastic heritage.

Karali, M. 2007. 'The classification of the ancient Greek dialects' in A. F. Christidis (ed.), *A History of Ancient Greek. From the Beginnings to Late Antiquity*. Cambridge: Cambridge University Press, pp. 387–94.

Masson, E. 2007. 'Greek and Semitic languages: early contacts' in A. F. Christidis (ed.), *A History of Ancient Greek. A History of Ancient Greek. From the Beginnings to Late Antiquity*. Cambridge: Cambridge University Press, pp. 733–7.

Petrounias, E. B. 2007. 'Development in pronunciation during the Hellenistic period' in A. F. Christidis (ed.), *A History of Ancient Greek. From the Beginnings to Late Antiquity*. Cambridge: Cambridge University Press, pp. 599–609.

Pirngruber, R. 2014. 'A new Greek from Seleucid Babylonia', *Nouvelles Assyriologiques brèves et utilitaires 2014/35*.

Sarkisian, G. 1974. 'Greek personal names in Uruk and the Graeco-Babyloniaca problem', *Acta Antiqua* 22, 495–503.

Sarkisian, G. 2000. 'Zu einigen Besonderheiten der Wiedergabe der griechischen Namen in Keilschrift' in J. Marzahn and H. Neumann (eds.), *Assyriologica et Semitica. Festschrift für Joachim Oelsner anlässlich seines 65. Geburtstages am 18. Februar 1997*, Alter Orient und Altes Testament 252. Münster: Ugarit-Verlag, pp. 401–6.

References

Boiy, T. 2005. 'Akkadian Greek double names in Hellenistic Babylonia' in W. H. van Soldt and D. Katz (eds.), *Ethnicity in Ancient Mesopotamia. Papers Read at the 48th Rencontre Assyriologique Internationale Leiden, 1–4 July 2002*, Uitgaven van het Nederlands Instituut voor het Nabije Oosten te Leiden 102. Leiden: Nederlands Instituut voor het Nabije Oosten, pp. 47–60.

Bowman, R. 1939. 'Anu-uballit-Kefalon', *American Journal of Semitic Languages and Literatures* 56/3, 231–43.

Corò, P. 2014. 'Identifying women in Hellenistic Uruk: a matter of perspective?', *KASKAL* 11, 183–92.

Corò, P. 2020. 'A new spelling for the name of Laodice in cuneiform: a matter of literacy?', *Nouvelles Assyriologiques Brèves et Utilitaires* 2020/79.

Corò, P. 2021. 'Between a queen and an ordinary woman: on Laodice and the representation of women in cuneiform sources in the Hellenistic period' in K. Droß-Krüpe and S. Fink (eds.), *Powerful Women in the Ancient World Perception and (Self)Presentation. Proceedings of the 8th Melammu Workshop, Kassel, 30 January–1 February 2019*, Melammu Workshops and Monographs 4. Münster: Zaphon, pp. 201–10.

Del Monte, G. F. 1997. *Testi dalla Babilonia ellenistica, Vol. 1: Testi cronografici, Studi Ellenistici 9*. Pisa: Istituti editoriali e poligrafici internazionali.

Doty, L. T. 1988. 'Nicharchos and Kephalon' in E. Leichty, M. deJ. Ellis, and P. Gerardi (eds.), *A Scientific Humanist. Studies in Memory of Abraham Sachs*, Occasional Publications of the Samuel Noah Kramer Fund 9. Philadelphia: University Museum, University of Pennsylvania, pp. 95–118.

van Emde Boas, E., A. Rijksbaron, L. Huitink, and M. de Bakker 2019. *The Cambridge Grammar of Classical Greek*. Cambridge: Cambridge University Press.

Finkel, I. L., R. J. van der Spek, and R. Pirngruber forthcoming. *Babylonian Chronographic Texts from the Hellenistic Period*. Atlanta: SBL.

Hartmann, I. J. 2002. 'What name, what parentage? The classification of Greek names and the Elean corpus', *Oxford University Working Papers in Linguistics, Philology & Phonetics* 7, 55–81.

Horrocks, G. 2010. *A History of Greek Language and its Speakers*, 2nd ed. Chichester: Wiley-Blackwell.

Langin-Hooper, S. M. and L. E. Pearce 2014. 'Mammonymy, maternal-line names and cultural identification: clues from the onomasticon of Hellenistic Uruk', *Journal of the American Oriental Society* 134, 185–202.

Monerie, J. 2012. 'Les communautés grecques en Babylonie (VIIe – IIIe s. av. J.-C.)', *Pallas* 89, 345–65.

Monerie, J. 2014. *D'Alexandre à Zoilos. Dictionnaire prosopographique des porteurs de nom grec dans les sources cuneiforms*, Oriens et Occidens 23. Stuttgart: Franz Steiner.

Monerie, J. 2015. 'Writing Greek with weapons singularly ill-designed for the purpose: the transcription of Greek in cuneiform' in R. Rollinger and E. van Dongen (eds.), *Mesopotamia in the Ancient World. Impact, Continuities, Parallels. Proceedings of the Seventh Symposium of the Melammu Project held in Obergurgl, Austria, November 4–8, 2013*, Melammu Symposia 7. Münster: Ugarit-Verlag, pp. 349–64.

Oelsner, J. 1992. 'Griechen in Babylonien und die einheimischen Tempel in hellenistischer Zeit' in D. Charpin and F. Joannès (eds.), *La circulation des biens, des personnes et des idées dans le Proche-Orient Ancien, Actes de la XXXVIIIe Rencontre Assyriologique Internationale, Paris, 8–10 juillet 1991*. Paris: Editions Recherche sur les civilisations, pp. 341–7.

Pearce, L. E. and P. Corò 2023. 'Constructing identities: Greek names as a marker of Hellenizing identity', *Studia Orientalia Electronica* 11/2, 72–108.

Pirngruber, R. 2015. 'Review of J. Monerie 2014. D'Alexandre à Zoilos: Dictionnaire prosopographique des porteurs de nom grec dans les sources cunéiformes', *H-Soz-u-Kult, H-Net Reviews*, 1–2.

Röllig, W. 1960. 'Griechische Eigennamen in Texten der babylonischen Spätzeit', *Orientalia* 29, 376–91.

Rollinger, R. 2001. 'The ancient Greeks and the impact of the Ancient Near East: textual evidence and historical perspective' in R. Whiting (ed.), *Mythology and Mythologies*, Melammu Symposia 2. Helsinki: The Neo-Assyrian Text Corpus Project, pp. 233–64.

Sachs, A. and H. Hunger 1988, 1989, 1996. *Astronomical Diaries and Related Texts from Babylonia*, 3 Vols. Vienna: Austrian Academy of Sciences.

Sherwin-White, S. 1983. 'Aristeas Ardibelteios. Some aspects of the use of double names in Seleucid Babylonia', *Zeitschrift für Papyrologie und Epigraphik* 50, 209–21.

Simon, Zs. 2017. 'Review of J. Monerie 2014. *D'Alexandre à Zoilos. Dictionnaire prosopographique des porteurs de nom grec dans les sources cuneiforms*', *Ancient West and East* 16, 437–9.

Smyth, H. W. 1956. *Greek Grammar.* Revised by G. M. Messing. Cambridge: Harvard University Press.

Thompson, A. 2001. 'Ancient Greek personal names' in A. F. Christidis (ed.), *A History of Ancient Greek. From the Beginnings to Late Antiquity*. Cambridge: Cambridge University Press, pp. 677–92.

CHAPTER 15

Old Iranian Names

Jan Tavernier

Introduction

When the Teispid king Cyrus conquered Babylonia in 539 BCE, Mesopotamia found itself governed by two Iranian dynasties (Teispids and Achaemenids) for more than two centuries. This foreign rule has led to the presence of many Iranian names in texts drafted in the local vernacular, Babylonian.

The new rulers spoke Old Persian, a language belonging to the Old Iranian family. In fact, Old Iranian is the global name for a group of languages, of which Old Persian and Avestan are the best-known ones, others being Median and Old Eastern Iranian (Avestan). Avestan is the language in which the sacred books of the Zoroastrian religion were written. Accordingly, the textual corpus of this language is relatively extended, but, despite the large number of Avestan texts, the language itself has no importance for the current article, as there are practically no Avestan names and/or elements in Babylonian texts.

Old Persian is a southwest Iranian language (Schmitt 2004, 739; Isebaert and Tavernier 2012, 299) and most likely the mother tongue of the Achaemenid elite. It is the principal language of the Achaemenid royal inscriptions, the other languages being Babylonian, Elamite, Egyptian, and Aramaic. Accordingly, Old Persian was the royal Achaemenid language par excellence. It was written by means of a deliberately designed cuneiform writing system, containing thirty-six phonemic signs, eight logograms, two-word-dividers, and various number symbols (Schmitt 2004, 719; Isebaert and Tavernier 2012, 304).

Finally, the Median dialect is a northwest Iranian language (Schmitt 2004, 717). It is exclusively attested in the Achaemenid royal inscriptions and in the reconstructed Old Iranian material from the '*Nebenüberlieferung*' (i.e., reconstructed Iranian proper names and loanwords; Tavernier 2007, 4). There are no extant Median texts, so it remains impossible to know with which writing system it would have been written. Interestingly, most Iranian names in Babylonian appear in a Median shape (e.g., *Bṛziya- and not Old Persian Bṛdiya-, *Miθrapāta- and not Old Persian *Miçapāta-). An explanation for this may be that the Babylonians adopted the Assyrian manner of rendering Iranian names. This Assyrian manner was the direct result of the contacts between Median people and the Neo-Assyrian Empire which had no linguistic contacts with the Persian-speaking tribes situated more to the south (Brandenstein and Mayrhofer 1964, 12).

This chapter will discuss the Old Iranian names in Babylonian texts from the Neo-Babylonian, Achaemenid, and post-Achaemenid periods. Quite expectedly, the major part of Old Iranian names occurs in texts dated to the Achaemenid period, when Babylonia was in Iranian hands. Currently, the chronological distribution of the names is as follows, though we must bear in mind that new texts will reveal more Iranian names and, because of this, the numbers presented herein will certainly be modified in the future.

- In pre-Achaemenid Babylonian texts a total of fifteen Old Iranian names are attested, two of which are Median (Cyaxares, Astyages) and two Teispid (Teispes, Cambyses I). Most names are recorded in tablets written under the Neo-Babylonian Empire; only one name is attested in the period when Babylonia was under Neo-Assyrian rule.
- In Achaemenid Babylonian texts, we find 393 complete Old Iranian names and four hybrid names.
- In post-Achaemenid Babylonian texts, a total of sixty-one Old Iranian names are attested, of which twenty-three date to the Alexandrine and Seleucid period and thirty-eight to the Arsacid period.

From a methodological point of view, this chapter will use Tavernier's categorisation of Old Iranian personal names in Babylonian documents (Tavernier 2007, 3–5). This categorisation divides the names into five groups, of which the most important ones are:

- Directly attested names: this category consists of anthroponyms attested in the Babylonian versions of the Achaemenid royal inscriptions. As we know the Old Iranian original name through the Old Persian version of these inscriptions, it is easy to compare the original form of the name and its rendering in Babylonian. An example of a directly attested name is Dādṛšiš, a derivation from *darš-* 'to dare', which is written *d-a-d-r-š-i-š* in Old Persian and ᴵ*da-da-ar-šú* in Babylonian.[1]

- Semi-directly attested names: this category is closely connected with the previous one and contains two sub-groups. The first group appears in texts other than the Babylonian versions of the Achaemenid royal inscriptions (e.g., documentary texts) and thus lacks a direct Old Iranian equivalent. The Achaemenid royal names, occurring on many documentary texts and written in one of the target languages, are a good example of this category. Accordingly, it is possible that the same name or word belongs to both categories one and two. The second group consists of anthroponyms, of which an Iranian original is attested in the Achaemenid royal inscriptions, but which show slight differences with that original. Such a difference is mostly a dialectal one (e.g., Old Persian Ṛtavardiya- [category 1] vs. Median *Ṛtavarziya- [category 2]), but also contracted equivalents of forms of category 1 are attested (e.g., OP Vahyazdāta- [category 1] vs. *Vēzdāta- [category 2]).

The directly and semi-directly transmitted Iranica provide the key to the transpositional systems between the source language (Old Iranian) and the target language (Babylonian). The largest group, however, are the indirectly attested Iranica ('*Nebenüberlieferung*') – that is, personal names that are reconstructed based on their reflections in Babylonian. As they are reconstructed names, the semi-directly and indirectly attested anthroponyms are marked conventionally with an asterisk (*). In this chapter the names are rendered in their Old Iranian shape, not in their Babylonian denotation. In general, Old Iranian names appear in their 'naked' form (without any case endings), but sometimes it is necessary to list them in their nominative form, as this nominative is what the Babylonian spellings render and is different from the 'naked' form. For instance, *Suxra- is the 'naked' form of *Suxra; Cincaxriš and *Ṛtā(h)umanā are the nominative forms of, respectively, Cincaxri- and *Ṛtā(h)umanah-. 'Naked' forms are always accompanied by a hyphen, whereas nominative forms appear without a hyphen. Unless otherwise stated, text references to the name attestations can be found in Tavernier 2007.

[1] Tavernier 2007, 15 no. 1.2.13; Zadok 2009, 188 no. 240. For the sake of completeness, we should also mention the Aramaic rendering of this name (*ddrš*) and the Elamite rendering (*da-tur-ši-iš*).

Iranian Name Material in the Babylonian Sources

Text Corpora

The Iranian names occur in two large text corpora. First, there are the Babylonian versions of the Achaemenid royal inscriptions (containing names of categories 1 and 2, discussed earlier). The majority of the Iranian names, however, can be found in the numerous Babylonian documentary texts. In that context, one must mention the Murašû archive, an archive of a Babylonian family that had business relations with the Persian overlords. Not surprisingly, their texts contain many Iranian names (cf. Zadok 2009, 66). Only a few names, such as Ištumegu (Astyages), are attested in literary texts (e.g., chronicles).

Typology of Names

The large number of Iranian names in Babylonian sources enables us to draw a detailed typology of these names. This is what Ran Zadok did in his study of Iranian names in Babylonian texts (Zadok 2009, 54–63). Nevertheless, it seems useful to present a simpler typology of the names under discussion. The Iranian names are either single-stem full names (58 names), two-stem full names (168 names), prefixed names (26 names), full names composed of three elements (6 names), patronymic names (19 names), or hypocoristic names (shortened names; 116 names).

Single-Stem Full Names (58 Names)

This category consists mainly of nominal forms (55 names). These names morphologically belong to the various stem classes attested in Old Iranian. The largest group is the *a*-stems (42 names), where one finds, inter alia, animal names (e.g., *Varāza- 'Boar'), relationship names (*Kāka- 'Uncle'), colour names (e.g., *Suxra- 'Red'), adjectival names (e.g., Vivāna- 'Brilliant'), and superlatives (e.g., *Masišta- 'The greatest'). The second largest group is the *u*-stems, with five names, one of which is again an animal name (*Kṛgu- 'Cock'). The other four names are basic substantives and adjectives: *Bāmu- 'Lustre', *Mṛdu- 'Soft', *Parnu- 'Old', and *Xratu- 'Wisdom'. Next to that, there are names belonging to *i*-stems (three names, e.g., Dādṛši- 'Brave'), *h*-stems (two names, e.g., *Aujah- 'Strong'), and *n*-stems (two names, e.g.,

*Ṛšan- 'Hero').[2] This group also contains three verbal forms as personal names: *Dāraya- 'He who holds', Frāda- 'He who furthers', and *Fradāta- 'Furthered'.

Two-Stem Full Names (168 Names)

The names belonging to this very productive name type have two elements: for example, *Bagapāta- 'Protected by God', where *baga-* means 'God' and *pāta-* means 'Protected' (past participle of **pā-*). The elements themselves may belong to various classes, such as divine names (e.g., Baga, Miθra-, etc.), adjectives (e.g., **arba-* 'Swift', **haθya-* 'Truthful', etc.), substantives (e.g., *aspa-* 'Horse', *farnah-* 'Divine glory'), and verbal forms (e.g., *jāma-* 'Leading', *vinda-* 'Finding', etc.).

It may be interesting to have a closer look at the names with divine elements. Divine names occur in no fewer than sixty-nine cases[3] and function preferably as the first element. They occur in the following constellations:

- Adjective + divine name (3 names): *Arbamihra- 'Young through Mithra', *Arbamiθra-, *Haθēbaga- 'Truthful through Baga'.
- Divine name + divine name (1 name): *Bagamihra- 'Baga-Mithra'.
- Divine name + adjective (9 names): *Bagāma- 'Strong through Ama', *Ṛtarēva- 'Rich through Arta', *Tīryāvauš 'Good through Tirya', etc.
- Divine name + non-participial verbal form (11 names): Bagabuxša- 'Rejoicing Baga', *Miθravasa- 'Mithra willing', *Ṛtaviša- 'He who is occupied with Arta', etc.
- Divine name + past participle (13 names): *Amadāta- 'Given by Ama', *Bagadāta- 'Given by Baga', *Miθradāta- 'Given by Mithra', *Rauxšnapāta- 'Protected by Rauxšna', etc.
- Divine name + substantive (31 names): *Agnifarnah- 'Glory of Agni' (in Neo-Assyrian sources), *Miθrapāna- 'Having the protection of Mithra', *Ṛtabānu- 'Having the splendour of Arta', etc.
- Substantive + divine name (1 name): *Bāzubaga- 'Baga's arm'.

[2] The Old Iranian names often appear in their nominative form in Babylonian: ^{I}*ši-in-šá-aḫ-ri-iš* renders the nominative Cincaxriš (of Cincaxri-), the name of Xerxes (Xšayaršan-) appears in its nominative form Xšayaršā, etc.

[3] Adjectives occur in 48 names, substantives in 114 names (the most productive category) and verbal forms in 67 names. Note also the unique Old Persian name Cincaxri- 'Effectuating something', composed of a pronoun and a verbal form.

The other classes (adjectives, substantives, and verbal forms) are easily combinable with each other. The most frequent constellations are:

- Adjective + substantive (18 names): *Āsuraθa- 'Having a fast chariot', Vahyazdāta- 'Having the better law', Vaumisa- 'Longing for the good', etc.
- Verbal form + substantive (11 names): *Jāmāspa- 'Leading the horses', *Vindafarnah- 'Finding glory', Xšayaršan- 'Ruling over heroes', etc.
- Substantive + substantive (26 names): Aspacanah- 'Delighting in horses', Haxāmani- 'Having the mind of someone allegiant', Ṛšāma- 'Having a hero's strength', etc.
- Substantive + verbal form (18 names): *Ciθrabṛzana- 'Exalting his lineage', Gaubar(u)va- 'Devouring cattle', *Uštapāna- 'Protecting happiness', etc.

Prefixed Names (38 Names)

A smaller category of Iranian names in Babylonian texts also consists of two-element names, but here the first element is a prefix. Although various prefixes are used in anthroponyms, the adjectival prefix *hu-/u-* is overwhelmingly dominant in this respect. No fewer than twenty-seven names begin with this element. Some examples are *(H)ufrata- 'Good and excellent', *Humāta- 'Good thoughts', *(H)urāna- 'The good warrior', and Utāna- 'Having a good offspring'. Mostly, this prefix is followed by a substantive; only three times is **(h)u-* constructed with an adjective, and two times with a participle.

The other prefixes occurring in this group of names are *ā-* 'to, towards' (2 names: *Āmṛda- 'He who crushes' and *Ārāšta- 'Equipped with truth'), *abi-* 'to' (1 name: *Abisaukā- 'Shining'), *ati-* 'beyond' (1 name: *Atikāma- 'Beyond wish'), *hadā-* 'with' (1 name: *Hadābāga- 'With a share', i.e., 'Wealthy'), *ham-/han-* 'co-' (2 names: *Hambāzu- 'Co-arm', i.e., 'Embracer' and *Hantu(h)ma- 'Co-exerting', i.e., 'Striving'), *pati-* 'to, towards, thereto; against' (3 names, e.g., *Patināša- 'He who supports'), and *upa-* 'under' (1 name: Upadarma- 'He who is under right conduct').

Names Composed of Three Elements (5 Names)

This small category is composed of only five names, three of which contain the infix *-(h)u-* 'good': *Bagā(h)uvīra- 'A good man through God', *Razmahuarga- 'Well-worthy in battle', and *Ṛtā(h)umanā 'Having a good mind through Arta'. The only name of this type without this element is *Astašēbarva- 'Cherishing his homestead'.

Patronymic Names (19 Names)

Nineteen anthroponyms take a patronymic suffix, either *-āna-* (15 names, e.g., *Haθyāna- 'Son of *Haθya-', *Vištāna-, *Zangāna-) or *-i-* (4 names: *Farnaini-, *Gausūri-, *Gundaini-, and *Xšēti-).

Hypocoristic Names (116 Names)

One of the larger groups consists of names that take a hypocoristic suffix:

- On -a (6 names; especially used with names having a divine element): *Amâ-, *Aspâ-, *Bagâ-, *Miθrâ-, *R̥tâ-, *Tīrâ-
- On -aica-/-ēca- (8 names): *Humēca-, *Mazdaica-, *Zātaica-, etc.
- On -aina-/-ēna- (18 names): *Bagaina-, *Nāfēna-, *Xaraina-, etc.
- On -āta- (8 names): Gaumāta-, *Miθrāta-, *Vanāta-, etc.
- On -ca- (1 name): *R̥tapātacā-
- On -ima- (1 name): *R̥tima-
- On -ina- (1 name): *Āθrina-
- On -ita- (3 names): *R̥šita-, *Sakita-, Xšaθrita-
- On -(i)ya- (26 names): *Br̥ziya-, *Kr̥gaya-, *Miθraya-, etc.
- On -ka- (36 names): *Aspaka-, *Jīvaka-, *Raudaka-, etc.
- On -uka- (2 names): *R̥tuka-, *Zānuka-
- On -va- (3 names): *(H)uvārava-, *Paršava-, *Šībava-
- Two-stem hypocoristics (4 names): *Baga-x-aya-, *R̥ta-b-a-, *R̥ta-xš-ara-, *R̥ta-xš-ī- (< *R̥taxšiya-)

Hybrid Names

The Babylonian textual material has four hybrid names. It should, however, be noted that there is no certainty on the language behind the Sumerograms. It is probably Babylonian, but the possibility that the Sumerograms conceal an Iranian lexeme cannot be excluded.

- ^{I}AD-*ar-ta-*$^{?}$: rendering of *Abr̥ta- 'Having Arta as father', a hybrid form of Babylonian *abu* 'father' and Iranian **r̥ta-* 'Arta' (Tavernier 2007, 472 no. 5.2.1.2; cf. Zadok 2009, 127 no. 120)
- ^{I}*a-te-*$^{?}$-^{d}EN, ^{I}*a-ti-*$^{?}$-^{d}EN, ^{I}*ḫa-ti-*^{d}EN: most likely a rendering of *Haθya-Bēl 'True through Bēl' (Tavernier 2007, 512 no. 5.4.2.10; Zadok 2009, 128 no. 126a–c)
- ^{I}DINGIR.MEŠ-*da-a-ta*: this may be a rendering of *Ildāta- or of *Bagadāta-. In the latter case, it is not a real hybrid name (Tavernier 2007, 472 no. 5.2.1.6; Zadok 2009, 193 no. 251)
- ^{Id}*mi-it-ri-*AD*-u-a*: *Miθra-abūa- 'Mithra is my father' (Tavernier 2007, 472 no. 5.2.1.6; Zadok 2009, 270 no. 367)

Elements in Names

Old Iranian names contain various elements, both theophoric and others. In this section, the most frequent ones will be presented.

Theophoric Elements

Not surprisingly, several deities occur in the names discussed here. Note that they do not automatically reflect purely Zoroastrian divinities and/or concepts. The first deity, Agni-, is only attested in one name from the Neo-Assyrian period, *Agnifarnah- 'Having the glory of Agni'. Interestingly, this deity is not an Iranian one, but an Indian one, more precisely the Vedic fire god. His Iranian equivalent, Ātṛ-, occurs in seven names (e.g., *Ātṛbānu- 'Having the lustre of Ātṛ', *Ātṛciθra- 'Originating from Ātṛ' and *Ātṛfarnah- 'Having the glory of Ātṛ').

The most frequent divine element is *Baga- 'God', which occurs in thirty names. Examples are Bagābigna- 'Having the attacking power of Baga', Bagabuxša- 'To whom Baga bestows benefit', *Bagadāta- 'Given by Baga', and *Bagavinda- 'Finding Baga' (only in Neo-Babylonian sources). The names with the element Ṛta- 'Truth' (e.g., *Ṛtabāna- 'Having the lustre of Arta' [in Arsacid texts] and the royal name Ṛtaxšaça- 'Whose kingdom is based on Arta') are only one less than those with Baga. Sixteen names have an element Mithra (e.g., *Miθradāta- 'Given by Mithra' and *Miθrapāna- 'Having the protection of Mithra'). The other deities occurring in anthroponyms are A(h)ura- 'Lord' (1 name), Ama- 'Strength' (3 names), Ārmati- 'Piety, Devotion' (1 name), Hauma- 'The divine *haoma*-plant' (1 name), (H)uvar- / Xvar- 'Sun' (6 names), Māhi- 'Moon' (1 name), Mazdā- 'Wisdom' (4 names), Rauxšna- 'Light' (2 names), and Tīra-/Tīrī-/Tīrya-, the god of rain and writing (10 names). The latter element is nearly exclusively attested in names belonging to the Aramaic and Babylonian '*Nebenüberlieferung*' that usually transliterate Median names. This could indicate a Median origin for this divinity.

Iranian names prefer to have the divine name as first element, contrary to Babylonian names where the place of the divine element is not fixed. There are only six exceptions to this rule: *Arbamihra- 'Young through Mithra', *Bagamihra- 'Baga-Mithra', *Bāzubaga- 'Arm of Baga', *Farnahuvara- 'Having the glory of Huvar' (in Seleucid texts), *Haθyabaga- 'Truthful through Baga', and *Raznamiθra- 'Following Mithra's command' (in Seleucid texts).

Toponyms
The toponyms, as they occur in the corpus of names, are all ethnonyms and they all refer to lands rather than to cities. Most of them are hypocoristics. The only non-Iranian region is India. The land names are Arya- 'Iranian' (e.g., Aryāramna- 'Who creates peace for the Aryans' and *Aryaušta- 'Iranian happiness'), Daha- 'Dahian' (e.g., *Dahaka-), Hindu- 'Indian' (e.g., *Hinduka-), Kr̥māna- 'Carmanian' (*Kr̥māniya- [in Seleucid texts]), Māda- 'Median' (^{f}Mādumītu, the Babylonian feminised form of *Māda-), Pārsa- 'Persian' (*Badrapārsa- 'The happy Persian'), Parθava- 'Parthian' (*Parθava-), and Skudra- 'Skudra' (*Skudrava-).

Frequent Elements
Clearly, Iranian name-giving practices preferred some elements more than others. What follows is a list of the most frequent elements in Iranian names attested in Babylonian sources.

- Aspa- 'horse' (16 names): Aspacanah-, *Aspastāna- (in Arsacid texts), Vištāspa-, etc.
- Dāta- 'given' (14 names): this element is usually combined with a divine name (e.g., Baga-, Miθra-) or a divine concept (e.g., *farnah-*, **hauma-*)
- *Farnah- 'divine glory' (15 names): *Ātr̥farnah- 'Having the glory of Ātr̥', *Farnaka-, Vindafarnah- 'Finding glory' (also in Seleucid and Arsacid texts), etc. This element appears in its nominative singular *farnā* in the Babylonian records
- Gau-/gu- 'cattle' (9 names): Gaubar(u)va- 'Devouring cattle', Gaumāta-, *Īsgu-, etc.
- Kāma- 'desire, wish' (8 names): *Bagakāma-, *Kāmaka-, *Tīrakāma-, etc.
- R̥šan- 'hero' (7 names): R̥šāma-, *R̥šita-, Xšayaršā, etc.
- Šāta- 'prosperous' / šāti- 'prosperity' (7 names): *Paurušāti-, *Šātaka-, *Šātibara-, etc.

Spelling and Normalisation

Generally, the Babylonian scribes rendered the (in their eyes) foreign Iranian names quite accurately; they wrote what they heard. Only final vowels can appear as (C)u in Babylonian, due to the tendency to use the Babylonian final nominative vowel.[4] The use of *u*, however, is probably

[4] See also the Appendix to this chapter.

a scribal convention, since Babylonian final vowels were no longer pronounced in the Achaemenid period, just like their Iranian counterparts.

Vowels

Most inaccurate writings occur when Babylonians noted down Iranian vowels, especially short vowels, although in general a renders /a/, i /i/, and u /u/. Vowel harmony is rare in Babylonian renderings of Iranian names.

Long vowels may be rendered by explicit vowel signs, for example, ^{I}*ḫu-ú-ma-a-ta-*$^{?}$ for *Humāta- 'Having good thoughts' or the element data- 'Given by', which nearly always appears as *da-a-tV* in Babylonian cuneiform texts. However, these vowel signs can also denote a short vowel, which has led some scholars (Justeson and Stephens 1991–3, 32) to believe that the cuneiform writing system was developing into an alphabetic system. There are only four examples of this phenomenon, three of which are renderings of the divine element *Miθra-, suggesting that scribal convention played a role here.[5] The fourth one, in reality the best example, is not a name but a loanword: **hamārakara-* 'accountant', spelled *am-ma-ri-a-kal*, *am-ma-ri-a-ka-ri*, and *am-ma-ru-a-kal*. This is the nicest example, as one could argue that the signs RI and RU function as a rendering of the consonant /r/, not of the syllables /ri/ and /ru/. Nonetheless, the extremely low number of such cases strongly pleads against any alphabetic features in the Mesopotamian cuneiform writing system.

Consonants

One can only admire the Babylonian scribes for their accuracy in noting down the Old Iranian consonants. Only a couple of errors occur, such as mistakes against the distinction between voiced and voiceless consonants, a distinction that is nevertheless present in both Babylonian and Old Persian/Median. Here follows an overview of these errors:

- /b/ = *-p-* (2 examples): *Bagakāna- (^{I}*pa-ga-ka-an-na*) and *Ṛtabānu- (^{I}*ar-ta-ap-pa-nu*)
- /d/ = *-t-* (2 examples): *Tīhūpardaisa- (^{I}*ti-ḫu-par*^{ar}*-ta-*$^{?}$*-is*) and Vindafarnā (^{I}*ú-mi-in-ta-pa-ar-na-*$^{?}$ and ^{I}*ú-mi-in-ta-par-na-*$^{?}$)

[5] *Miθradāta-, spelled ^{I}*mi-tir-ri-a-da-da-*$^{?}$ (note also the scribal error against the distinction between voiceless and voiced stop); *Miθrāta-, spelled ^{I}*mi-ti-ri-a-ta*; *Miθravasa-, spelled ^{I}*mi-tir-ri-a-ma-a-su*.

- /g/ = *-k-* (2 examples): *Bagasravā (^{I}*ba-ak-ka-su-ru-ú*) and Gaubar(u)va- (^{I}*ku-bar-ra*).
- /k/ = *-g-* (2 examples): *Jīvaka- (^{I}*zi-ma-ga-*ˀ and ^{I}*zi-ma-ga*) and *Zabrakāna- (^{I}*za-ab-ra-ga-nu*)
- /t/ = *-d-* (10 examples): *Aspazanta- (^{I}*as-pa-za-an-da-*ˀ), *Bagadāta- (^{I}*ba-ga-da-du* and ^{I}*bag-da-da*), *Bagapāta- (^{I}*ba-ga-*ˀ *-pa-da* and ^{I}*ba-ga-pa-da*), *Bagapitā (^{I}*ba-ga-pi-du*), *Bagavanta- (^{I}*ba-ga-*ˀ*-un-du*, ^{I}*ba-ga-un-du*, and ^{I}*ba-gu-un-du*), *Dātafarnā (^{I}*da-da-a-pa-ar-na-*ˀ and ^{I}*da-da-par-na-*ˀ), *Davantāna- (^{I}*du-un-da-na-*ˀ), *Miθradāta- (^{I}*mi-tir-ri-a-da-da-*ˀ), *Sravanta- (^{I}*su-ru-un-du*) and *Šātaina- (^{I}*šad-da-a-a-nu*)

These errors occur in both royal inscriptions and documentary texts. The stops most sensitive for abandoning the distinction voiced/voiceless are the dentals, while velars and labials appear more accurately. The explanation for the higher number of errors when dentals are involved is not hard to find, as Babylonian itself contains some rare equivalent variations: for example, *ba-aḫ-ma-a-du* and [*ba-a*]*r-ma-tú*, plurals of *barumtu* 'coloured wool' (Zadok 1976, 217 no. 1.51), *galādu* and *galātu* 'to tremble', *dudittu* and *tudittu* 'dress-pin' (GAG, 35). The direction of error is mostly that Iranian voiceless consonants are rendered by their Babylonian voiced equivalent (twelve out of eighteen examples), except for the labials. Remarkably, of the ten examples where Babylonian d renders Iranian /t/, four have the error after /n/ (*Aspazanta-, *Bagavanta-, *Davantāna-, and *Sravanta-). Three are errors in the rendering of the element **data-*. As a last remark on the rendering of Iranian stops in Babylonian, one can point to the increased use of signs with ṭ in the denotations of an Iranian voiceless dental /t/, for example, ^{I}*mi-it-ra-a-ṭu* for *Miθrāta- (a name always written with T-signs in Achaemenid texts).

Old Iranian fricatives did not pose a problem for the Babylonian scribes, despite the lack of specific graphemes in the Mesopotamian cuneiform writing system that could express Old Iranian /f/ and /θ/. The first phoneme (a voiceless labial glide) is expressed using the signs otherwise indicating the Babylonian voiceless labial stop /p/. The Old Iranian voiceless interdental glide /θ/ is expressed by signs which render the Babylonian dental stops. The Babylonian scribes mostly wrote the Iranian voiceless velar glide /x/ with a sign feathering ḫ used to render its Babylonian equivalent. The only exception to this transposition rule is the cluster /xš/, where the glide /x/ can also be rendered by a K-sign (Zadok 1976, 217 no. 1.45).

The Old Iranian sibilants are rendered in a logical way in Babylonian and only a few exceptional transpositions exist. One of them appears just one time: Iranian /š/ is rendered by an S-sign in *Šātibaxša- (^{I}*šá-ta-ba-ak-su*). Once, a Z-sign renders Old Iranian /s/ (*Satamēša-, ^{I}*za-at-tu-me-e-šú*). In another name (*Mazduka-, ^{I}*maš-du-ku*), /z/ is rendered by a Š-sign.

Iranian glides did not pose a problem for the Babylonian scribes either. The glide /w/ may be expressed in three ways: by M-signs, by U-signs, or not at all. The last manner is only attested in expressions beginning with /wi/-. The choice for M- and U-signs is not surprising. In Babylonian, /m/ and /w/ are relatively close to each other, as a result of which Babylonian /w/ is expressed by M-signs from the mid-second millennium onwards. The use of U-signs (e.g., U, Ú, and UN) may be the result of Aramaic influence, where *wāw* has a double function as an indication of /w/ and as a mater lectionis for /u/.

For the rendering of Iranian /y/, Babylonian generally uses its sign for the glide /y/. In some cases, /y/ is not explicitly indicated but is implied by the sequence of two vowels.

Consonant Clusters

In general, there are four systems used by the Babylonian scribes to denote Old Iranian clusters of two consonants. These systems are listed here. The first one is the most frequent one, the last one the least frequent.

- Ir. C_1C_2 = Bab. VC_1-C_2 V: ^{I}*as-pa-ši-ni* = Aspacanā, ^{I}*ši-in-šá-aḫ-ri-iš* = Cincaxriš, ^{I}*ip-ra-da-a-ta* = *Fradāta-, etc.
- Ir. C_1C_2 = Bab. C_1 V-C_2 V: ^{I}*si-ṭu-nu* = *Stūnā-, ^{I}*šá-ta-ri-ta* = *Xšaθrita-, ^{I}*ú-ru-da-a-tú* = *(H)uvardāta-
- Ir. C_1C_2 = Bab. C_1 V-VC_2: ^{I}*pa-ar-mar-ti-iš* = Fravarti-, ^{I}*ra-za-am-ár-ma* = *Razmārva-
- Ir. C_1C_2 = Bab. C_1VC_2: ^{I}*par-ta-am-mu* = *Fratama-, ^{I}*ši-tir-an-taḫ-mu* = *Ciθrantaxma-

Two personal names show a more complicated system: Ir. C_1C_2 = VC_1-VC_2-C_2 V (^{I}*u-pa-da-ar-am-ma-*^{ʔ} = Upadarma-) and Ir. C_1C_2 = VC_1-C_1 V-C_2 V (^{I}*is-si-pi-ta-am-ma* = *Spitāma-).

Socio-Onomastics of Iranian Names in Babylonian Sources

One of the most conspicuous aspects of Iranian names in Late Babylonian sources is that the functions of persons bearing Iranian names reflect the political situation of that time. This pattern can be traced in cuneiform documents from the Neo-Babylonian, Achaemenid, Alexandrinian, Seleucid, and Arsacid periods.

The oldest attestation of an Iranian non-royal name in a Babylonian document is that of *Agnifarnah- who, in the middle of the seventh century, was an official of the Neo-Assyrian king Assurbanipal (PNA 1/I, 56). Unfortunately, no more information is available on this person. In the Neo-Babylonian period, not that many individuals bearing Iranian names are attested. In addition, not much is known of them. Ethnographically interesting is that *Bagadēna- 'Possessing the religion of Baga' is called an Elamite (Babylon 28178 B r. ii 7, 592/591 BCE; in Weidner 1939, 929 and Pl. 3). The same goes for *Marza- 'Frontier area' (Babylon 28178 B r. ii 14). The unfortunately broken name *[. . .]zāta- is also interesting, as this person, attested in a text from c. 595/594–569/568 BCE (reign of Nebuchadnezzar II), is called an 'envoy of Parsumaš' (VAT 16287:28′). Finally, in 539 BCE, not long before Cyrus' conquest of Babylon, *Bagayāza- (name for a child born during the *bagayāza*-feast) is a royal official of Nabonidus (YOS 6 169:20, 231:24). A female slave named *Amatavāta- 'Having the strength of Ama' is sold by Rakal to Iltabiya, two persons with Semitic names, in a document from 561 BCE (ROMCT 2 3:2; reign of Amīl-Marduk).

With the arrival of Iranian dominance in Mesopotamia, this pattern continues and the attested persons with Iranian names reflect the society of that time. For instance, several Achaemenid princes appear in the archive of the Murašû family with whom they did business, including *Haxiyabānu- (420–419 BCE), *Arbarēva- (419 BCE), *Ṛšita- (421–417 BCE), and the well-known prince Ṛšāma-, who was satrap of Egypt during the reign of Darius II and who also appears in Aramaic and Egyptian texts (Stolper 1985, 64–7). Most Iranians attested in Babylonian sources belong to the higher social strata and could also own slaves, as demonstrated by *Ārmati-, the owner of a slave named Nabû-ikṣur (TMH 2/3 171:6). Many Iranians are only known because they are mentioned as the father of a contracting party or of a witness. Some servants or slaves with Iranian names are also mentioned: *Arbamiθra- (FuB 14 17–18 no. 7:3, u.e. 2), servant of *Šātibṛzana- (Iranian name); *Īsgu- (BE 9 13:4), slave (*qallu*) of *Ṛtabara- (Iranian name); *Armaka- (AMI NF 23 175:2), servant of Tattannu (Babylonian name).

Some of the high-ranking individuals with an Iranian name attested in cuneiform texts from the Achaemenid period can be identified with people figuring in Greek classical works. For instance, Ctesias (*apud* Photios, §§ 38, 39, 46, and 48) tells us about Menostanes, son of Artarios. This Artarios was satrap of Babylon and brother of Artaxerxes I. When Artaxerxes I died,

Menostanes, who had served the late king, became commander for the throne claimant Sogdianus, but when Darius II finally took power, Menostanes died shortly afterwards. This Menostanes can easily be identified with *Manuštāna- from the Babylonian Murašû archive; his father Artarios appears as Artareme (*Ṛtarēva-) in the same archive (Stolper 1985, 90–1).

An interesting case is *Ṛtaxšara-, who occurs in thirteen texts (443–418 BCE) of the Murašû archive (Stolper 1985, 91–92) and who is probably identical to the Paphlagonian eunuch Ἀρτοξάρης, who supported Darius II and became an influential person at his court. That he occupied a high rank within Babylonian society is clear from the fact that eight subordinates of him occur in the Murašû archive: Bazuzu (son of Bēl-bullissu), Bēl-ittannu, Il-yadīn (son of Yadaˁ-Yāma), Lâbâši (son of [. . . -it]tannu), Marduk-ibni, Nergal-aḫu-ittannu, Nidinti-Šamaš (son of *Kṛtaka-), and Pamūnu. Mostly these persons are called *ardu* of *Ṛtaxšara-, but some of them also have other titles. Two were foremen (*šaknu*) of a so-called *ḫaṭru*: Bazuzu was foreman of the 'scouts of the left flank' and possessed a seal as well as a golden signet ring, whereas Pamūnu was foreman of the '*šušānu*s of the storehouse/treasury'. He too owned a seal and a golden signet ring. Marduk-ibni was an accountant of *Ṛtaxšara-. In two instances Nidinti-Šamaš is called a *paqdu* (bailiff). In any case, all but one of the subordinates of this high-ranked official also bore the title *ardu* 'servant, subordinate'. Only Itti-Bēl-abni, attested in a text from 443 BCE (BE 9 4), was a slave (*qallu*). Nevertheless, they nearly all had a seal, which again corroborates their rather high social position.

Within one family, people could have names belonging to different languages. In BE 10 59, a certain Bēlšunu (Babylonian), son of *Dēfrāda- (Iranian), appears. The inverse direction is found in BE 9 39, where *Hadābāga- is the son of Iddin-Nabû. In the text *Camb.* 384 a person with an Iranian name, *Naryābigna- 'Having the attacking power of a hero', is described with an Elamite gentilic (^{lú}*e-la-mu-ú*).

One late-Achaemenid, imprecisely dated document (K 8133; in Stolper 1994, 627) has a very large concentration of individuals bearing Iranian names who did not make up an isolated community but who engaged in transactions with Babylonians (or, at least, people with a Babylonian name). Not fewer than twelve Iranian names occur in this lease of oxen to a person named Iddin-Nabû. The lessor has an Iranian name. The other Iranians are witnesses, together with at least two Babylonians. It is interesting to see that one witness with a Babylonian name (Nidinti-Bēl) has a father with an Iranian name (*Gauniya-, a hypocoristic of *Gauna- 'Hairy'). Possibly the father had adopted an Iranian name in the hope of a career in the Achaemenid administration.

As can be expected, the number of Iranian names drops significantly after the conquest of Babylonia by Alexander the Great in 331 BCE. In the Alexandrinian Empire as well as in the following Seleucid period, Greco-Macedonian political power reduces the number of officials with Iranian names. Some officials are attested: for example, *Nababṛzana- 'Furthering his family', a chiliarch (CT 49 6:2; 327 BCE); *Vindafarnah- 'Finding divine glory', a governor (308–307 BCE); *Aryapā- 'Protecting the Aryans', a commander (AD -144:16′; 145 BCE). A high military commander – a general, in fact – was *Ṛtaya-, who organised a census in Babylon and Seleucia in 145 BCE (AD -144:36′).

People with an Iranian name and a Babylonian patronym also appear in the Seleucid period. In 262 BCE, *Kṛmāniya-, son of Iddināya, appears in a letter from Bēl-ibni, the chief administrator (*šatammu*) of the Esagil temple in Babylon (CT 49 118:6).

In the Arsacid period the number of Iranian names attested in cuneiform Babylonian texts rises again, when the Iranian-speaking Arsacids take control in Babylonia. Many of the Iranian names, however, are names of kings or members of the royal family. Interestingly, the son of the king of Elymais also bears an Iranian name: *Varya- (spelled ^{I}*ur-*$^{?}$*-a* and ^{I}*ur-ri-*$^{?}$*-a*; AD -124 B:21′; 132–125/124 BCE). Military officials appear sometimes – for example, three generals: *Miθradāta-, 'Given by Mithra' (AD -107 r. 15′; 107 BCE), *Miθrāta- (AD -90:15′, 32′; 91 BCE), and *Aspastāna- 'He whose place is with horses' (AD -87 C r. 32′; 87 BCE). Interesting also is the high priest *(H)urauda- 'Having a beautiful growth', who appears in a document dated to 107 BCE (LBAT 1445:2–3).

In the post-Achaemenid period, contrary to the Achaemenid period, various double names are attested. An example is *Bagâ, 'whose other name is Nikanōr' (BaM 15 274:12; Zadok 2009, 137 no. 167).

Appendix: Transposition Tables

The following tables offer an overview of how Babylonian scribes rendered the sounds of the Old Iranian language in their script.

1. Vowels

Old Ir.	Babylonian	Old Ir.	Babylonian
/a/-	(C)a	-/i/-	(C)a
/a/-	(C)u	-/i/-	(C)e
-/a/-	(C)a	-/i/-	(C)i
-/a/-	(C)i	-/ī/-	(C)e
-/a/-	(C)u	-/ī/-	(C)i
/ā/-	(C)a	/u/-	(C)u
-/ā/-	(C)a	-/u/-	(C)a
-/ā/-	(C)u	-/u/-	(C)i
-/ē/-	(C)e	-/u/-	(C)u
-/ē/-	(C)i	-/ū/-	(C)u

2. Consonants

2.1 Stops

Old Ir.	Babylonian	Old Ir.	Babylonian
/b/-	b	/k/-	k
/b/-	p	-/k/-	g
-/b/-	b	-/k/-	k
/d/-	d	/p/-	p
/d/-	t	-/p/-	p
-/d/-	d	/t/-	d
-/d/-	t	/t/-	t
/g/-	g	-/t/-	d
/g/-	k	-/t/-	t
-/g/-	g	-/t/-	ṭ
-/g/-	k		

2.2 *Fricatives*

Old Ir.	Babylonian	Old Ir.	Babylonian
/f/-	p	/x/-	ḫ
-/f/-	p	-/x/-	ḫ
/θ/-	t	-/x/-	k
-/θ/-	t		

2.3 *Laryngeals*

Old Ir.	Babylonian
/h/-	Ø
/h/-	ḫ
-h-	Ø
-h-	ʾ
-h-	ḫ

2.4 *Sibilants (Dental and Palato-Alveolar Fricatives)*

Old Ir.	Babylonian	Old Ir.	Babylonian
-/ç/-	ḫs	-/š/-	š
-/ç/-	s, ss	-/š/	s
-/ç/-	š	-/š/	š
-/ç/-	ts	/z/-	z
/s/-	š	-/z/-	š
-/s-	s	-/z/-	z
-/s/-	z	-[ž]-	š
/š/-	š		

2.5 *Affricates*

Old Ir.	Babylonian	Old Ir.	Babylonian
/c/-	š	-/c/-	z
-/c/-	s	/j/-	z
-/c/-	š	-/j/-	z

3 Sonorants

3.1 *Glides*

Old Ir.	Babylonian	Old Ir.	Babylonian
/w/-	m	-/y/-	(C)e-a(C)
/w/-	u	-/y/-	(C)e-a-a(C)
-/w/-	Ø	-/y/-	(C)e-e-a(C)
-/w/-	m	-/y/-	(C)i-ʾ-a(C)
-/w/-	(C)u(C)	-/y/-	(C)i-a(C)
/y/-	i(a)	-/y/-	(C)i-e(C)
-/y/-	ʾ	-/y/-	(C)i-i-a(C)
-/y/-	(C)a-e(C)	-/y/-	i(a)
-/y/-	(C)a-i(C)	-/y/-	Ø
-/y/-	i(C)-ʾ-a(C)		

3.2 *Liquids*

Old Ir.	Babylonian	Old Ir.	Babylonian
-/l/-	l	-[r̥]-	AR
/r/-	r	-[r̥]-	RA
-/r/-	l	-[r̥]-	RE/RI
-/r/-	r	-[r̥]-	RU
[r̥]-	AR		

3.3 *Nasals*

Old Ir.	Babylonian	Old Ir.	Babylonian
/m/-	m	/n/-	n
-/m/-	m	-/n/-	n

Further Reading

Grammatical overviews of the Old Persian language are numerous. The most important ones are those from Roland G. Kent (1953), Wilhem Brandenstein and Manfred Mayrhofer (1964), Rüdiger Schmitt (2004), and Lambert Isebaert and Jan Tavernier (2012). The Old Iranian names as attested in Old Iranian (i.e., Avestan and Old Persian) sources were collected and analysed by Manfred Mayrhofer in the prestigious series *Iranisches Personennamenbuch* (1979). One later publication also discussed the Old Persian anthroponyms, but for the Avestan names Mayrhofer's volume remains indispensable. This later publication is the Old Persian dictionary by Rüdiger Schmitt (2014). An onomastic study of the Old Iranian names in general (including those attested in Greek sources) has not yet been undertaken.

The Old Iranian name material in Babylonian documents was brought together for the first time by Walther Hinz (1975; review by Ran Zadok 1976). As many new texts came to light after the publication of this volume, new studies were quickly needed. This lacuna was tackled by the author, who collected all Old Iranian names in non-Iranian texts from the Achaemenid period (Tavernier 2007), leaving out the pre- and post-Achaemenid periods. In his 2009 volume on Iranian anthroponyms in Babylonian sources, Ran Zadok did include both periods. This volume (published in the *Iranisches Personennamenbuch* series) should be consulted together with the review by Jan Tavernier (2015). Ran Zadok (1976) offers the first study of the renderings of Iranian sounds in Babylonian orthography.

Finally, for historical aspects concerning the better-known individuals bearing Iranian names in Babylonian sources, the reader is referred to Matthew W. Stolper (1985) and Pierre Briant (1996).

References

Brandenstein, W. and M. Mayrhofer 1964. *Handbuch des Altpersischen*, Wiesbaden: Harrassowitz.

Briant, P. 1996. *Histoire de l'empire perse de Cyrus à Alexandre*. Paris: Fayard.

Hinz, W. 1975. *Altiranisches Sprachgut der Nebenüberlieferungen*, Göttinger Orientforschungen III/3. Wiesbaden: Harrassowitz.

Isebaert, L. and J. Tavernier 2012. 'Le vieux-perse', *Res Antiquae* 9, 299–346.

Justeson, J. S. and L. D. Stephens 1991–3. 'Evolution of syllabaries from alphabets: transmission, language contrast, and script typology', *Die Sprache* 35, 2–46.

Kent, R. G. 1953. *Old Persian: Grammar, Texts, Lexikon*, 2nd ed., American Oriental Series 33. New Haven: American Oriental Society.

Mayrhofer, M. 1979. *Die altiranischen Namen*, Iranisches Personennamenbuch 1. Vienna: Verlag der Österreichischen Akademie der Wissenschaften.

Sachs, A. and H. Hunger 1988, 1989, 1996. *Astronomical Diaries and Related Texts from Babylonia*, 3 Vols. Vienna: Austrian Academy of Sciences.

Schmitt, R. 2004. 'Old Persian' in R. D. Woodard (ed.), *The Cambridge Encyclopedia of the World's Ancient Languages*. Cambridge: Cambridge University Press, pp. 717–41.

Schmitt, R. 2014. *Wörterbuch der altpersischen Königsinschriften*. Wiesbaden: Reichert.

Stolper, M. W. 1985. *Entrepreneurs and Empire: the Murašû archive, the Murašû Firm, and Persian Rule in Babylonia*. Istanbul: Nederlands Historisch-Archaeologisch Instituut.

Stolper, M. W. 1994. 'A Late-Achaemenid lease from the Rich collection', *Journal of the American Oriental Society* 114, 625–7.

Tavernier, J. 2007. *Iranica in the Achaemenid period (c. 550–330 BC): Lexicon of Old Iranian Proper Names and Loanwords, Attested in Non-Iranian Texts*, Orientalia Lovaniensia Analecta 158. Leuven: Peeters.

Tavernier, J. 2015. 'Review of R. Zadok 2009. *Iranische Personennamen in der neu- und spätbabylonischen Nebenüberlieferung*', *Archiv für Orientforschung* 53, 472–4.

Weidner, E. F. 1939. 'Jojachin, König von Juda in babylonischen Keilschrifttexten' in *Mélanges syriens offerts à Monsieur René Dussaud*, Vol. 2. Paris: Librairie Orientaliste Paul Geuthner, 923–35.

Zadok, R. 1976. 'Review of W. Hinz 1975. *Altiranisches Sprachgut der Nebenüberlieferungen*', *Bibliotheca Orientalis* 33, 213–19.

Zadok, R. 2009. *Iranische Personennamen in der neu- und spätbabylonischen Nebenüberlieferung*, Iranisches Personennamenbuch 7/1B. Vienna: Verlag der Österreichischen Akademie der Wissenschaften.

CHAPTER 16

Elamite Names

Elynn Gorris

Introduction to the Language and Its Background

Elamite was the main language of south-western Iran between approximately the twenty-third and fourth century BCE and developed more or less contemporaneously with neighbouring Sumerian and later with Akkadian. Elamite remains, to our current knowledge, an isolated language that is not fully understood (Tavernier 2018; Stolper 2004). Since we are dealing in this chapter with a language that has no linguistic ties with the Mesopotamian languages, one should highlight the fact that Elamite onomastic conversions into Babylonian texts are actually transcriptions of Elamite personal names into Akkadian. Even though this chapter will treat mainly Elamite names deriving from Neo-Babylonian sources, the general outlines for the conversion of Elamite names into Akkadian do not only apply to Neo-Babylonian texts, but also to Neo-Assyrian texts.

Due to the limited amount of Elamite textual sources, we are not always able to fully reconstruct the Elamite anthroponyms attested in Neo-Babylonian texts. Even if we can identify an Elamite variant, there are still numerous lacunas in our understanding of Elamite phonology and grammar. Jan Tavernier (2010, 1059–60) has given four main reasons for this lack of knowledge:

(1) First, Elamite was written in a Sumero–Akkadian cuneiform script that was not designed for the Elamite language. This means that the script lacks characters to express specific Elamite phonemes. The Elamites either simplified the orthography of their words or used a combination of cuneiform characters to write down their language as correctly as possible.

(2) Second, due to the isolated status of the Elamite language, comparative linguistic material for the study of Elamite is nearly absent. This restricted text corpus, including the lack of bilinguals (Elamite–Akkadian) for the early to mid-first millennium BCE, is partly the

result of limited archaeological exploration in the Iranian provinces Khuzestan and Fars.

(3) Third, there might have existed several Elamite dialects of which we are not aware. The territory of the Elamite kingdom was a long strip divided into the lowlands of Susiana, the highlands of Fars, and some more isolated mountainous Zagros regions, such as Izeh, which bordered areas that were inhabited by other language groups (e.g., Indo-Iranians, Arameans, etc.). These other languages doubtlessly had an influence on Elamite phonology.

(4) Fourth, there is a diachronic development in the phonological system. The transcriptions of Elamite proper names and words in non-Elamite texts, mostly Akkadian texts, can therefore be quite useful to get a better understanding of Elamite phonology.

The Elamite Name Material in the Babylonian Sources

Text Corpora

Neo-Elamite personal names that occur in the Neo- and Late Babylonian text corpus (c. 750–100 BCE) are extremely limited and dispersed over several text genres:[1]

1. Literary texts: Since the Babylonian Chronicle (ABC 1) informs us on the Elamite dynastic succession from 743 to 664 BCE, this text contains a significant amount of Elamite royal names. A Babylonian scribe copied this historical document in 499 BCE.
2. Official correspondence: Bēl-ibni, a Babylonian official in service of the Neo-Assyrian king Assurbanipal as the governor of the Sealand, reported on Elamite political and military activities in the Babylonian–Elamite border region between 650 and 645 BCE (de Vaan 1995). Due to the geographical proximity and the content of the letters, the Bēl-ibni correspondence contains transcriptions of the names of several Elamite officials.
3. Private archives: During the Neo-Babylonian and early Achaemenid period, several business men trading with the Susiana region encountered individuals with Elamite names who occasionally appear in their written documents.

[1] The author could identify about sixty-six different Elamite names in the Neo-Babylonian text corpus. This figure excludes the various orthographies of the same name/individual.

Typology of Elamite Names Rendered in Neo-Babylonian

Ran Zadok already stated in his *Elamite Onomasticon* (1984, 49–50) that, since the Elamite language is not yet fully known, a typology of Elamite personal names will remain preliminary as well. With our current knowledge of Elamite onomastics, the composition of Elamite names seems very similar to Babylonian names, or more generally Akkadian names.

Typically, Elamite names are compound names consisting of two elements (Zadok 1984, 49–59; 1991, 231). The most common typologies of Neo-Babylonian renderings of Elamite names are:

1, Substantive + substantive: Imba-dara? 'Helper of Huban(?)' (*ᴵim-ba-da-ra-?*, YOS 7 30:11); Ištar-ḫundu ~ Neo-Elamite Šutur-Nahhunte 'The justifier Nahhunte' (*iš-tar-ḫu-un-du*, ABC 1 ii 32)
2, Substantive + adjective: Šutar-šarḫu 'The proud righteous one' (*ᴵšu-tar-šar-ḫu*, BRM 1 82:17)
3, Substantive + pres. active participle: Adda-ten 'Father being favourable' (*ᵇᵉad-da-te-na*, MDP 9 110 r. 4, MDP 9 167:4, MDP 9 172 r. 11, MDP 9 181:3; *ᵇᵉad-da-te-en*, MDP 9 73:2–3)[2]
4, Substantive + verb: Atta-luš 'Father [. . .]' (*at-ta-lu-uš*; *-š*: first conj. 3. sg.; Zadok 1984, 26 nr. 132)

Elamite names consisting of three elements are, like in Semitic onomastics, also attested but they occur more rarely. As for the Neo-Babylonian renderings, one has, for instance, the Elamite name Huban-haltaš 'Huban received the land' (*ḫum-ba-ḫal-da-šu*, ABC 1 iii 27, 33), consisting of a divine name + substantive + verb. The first element is the god Huban, the second element is the noun *hal* 'land', and the third element *taš* is a verbal form *ta+š* 'he installed' in the first conjugation 3.sg. (*-š*), meaning 'Huban installed the land'. Or *taš* could be read *tuš* 'he received' with the system of vowel changes, and then the name translates 'Huban received the land'. The final *-u* is an Akkadian nominative marker.

Neo-Babylonian renderings of Elamite names consisting of one element, other than hypocoristica, are to our knowledge not attested.

[2] These examples are taken from Neo-Elamite texts, where the determinative ᵇᵉ ⁽ᴮᴬᴰ⁾ is used as a marker of personal names. On the '*Personenkeil*' used with Elamite names, see later in chapter.

Hypocoristica

If we look at the examples attested in the Neo-Babylonian sources, the most common renderings are hypocoristica with a reduplication of the final syllable (Zadok 1983). The Elamite origin of these names is not always certain.

Of all Elamite personal names in the Neo-Babylonian corpus, hypocoristica are by far the largest group. In fact, almost a third of the Elamite anthroponyms (33 per cent) in the Neo-Babylonian renderings belong to the hypocoristic type with a reduplication of the final syllable. In the Susa Acropole Archive, a large Elamite administrative archive of the Susa region from the late seventh century BCE, only about 15 per cent of the Elamite names are hypocoristica.[3] Adding the other types of hypocoristica (Zadok 1983, 107–20), Elamite hypocoristica rendered in Babylonian are at least twice as numerous as the hypocoristica in Elamite archives of the same

Table 16.1 *Elamite hypocoristica in Neo-Babylonian sources*

Neo-Babylonian renderings	References
a-mur-ki-ki	Zadok 1983, nr. 351, n. 351
^{f}*bu-sa-sa*	Tallqvist 1905, 51; ElW 237
^{I}*e-zi-li-li*	Tallqvist 1905, 62; ElW 403
^{I}*ki-ru-ru*	Tallqvist 1905, 91; ElW 484
^{I}*ḫa-am-nu-nu*	ElW 577
^{I}*ḫa-lu-lu*	Tallqvist 1905, 66; ElW 611
^{I}*ḫa-ni-ni*	Tallqvist 1905, 66; ElW 618
^{I}*ḫa-nu-nu*	Tallqvist 1905, 66; ElW 618
^{I}*in-da-bi-bi*	De Vaan 1995, 352–3
^{I}*me-na-na*	Zadok 1983, nr. 76, n. 229
šag-di-di / *šak-ti-ti*	Tallqvist 1905, 179; ElW 1120, Zadok 1984, 38
^{I}*ur-ki-ki* (or *lik-ki-ki*?)	Zadok 1983, nr. 147, n. 350
^{I}*zu-zu-zu*	Zadok 1983, nr. 1150, n. 70

3 ^{be}*mu-me-me* (MDP 9 95:4), ^{be}*am-pi-pi* (MDP 9 137:2), ^{f}*um-pu-pu* (MDP 9 182:4), *hu-ud-da-da* (MDP 9 178:6), ^{be}*ud-da-da* (MDP 9 29:5), ^{f}*i-du-du* (MDP 9 240 r. 3), *li-pi-pa* (MDP 9 132 r. 14), ^{be}*me-na-na* (MDP 9 104:11), ^{f}*mi-ti-ti* (MDP 9 49:8), ^{f}*mu-ti-ti* (MDP 9 81:2), ^{be}*na-is-su-su* (MDP 9 4:1), ^{f}*par-ri-ri* (MDP 9 169 r. 15), ^{I}*pu-uh-ha-ha* (MDP 11 299:3), ^{be}*rap-pi-pi* (MDP 9 190:2), ^{be}*ras-ma-nu-nu* (MDP 9 259:12), ^{be}*si-ki-ki* (MDP 9 56:4), ^{be}*si-ik-ka-ka* (MDP 9 116:2), ^{be}*si-ni-ni* (MDP 9 30:7), ^{f}*sà-ma -ma* (MDP 9 282 r. 1), ^{be}*šu-pi-pi* (MDP 9 7:9), ^{be}*tak-ku-ku* (MDP 9 32:8), *tan-nu-nu* (MDP 9 294:4), *te-ri-ri* (MDP 9 74 r. 1), ^{be}*tuh-ha-ha* (MDP 9 146:11), ^{be}*ú-ki-ik-ki* (MDP 9 240:6), and ^{f}*za-ni-ni* (MDP 9 90:8).

period. Moreover, to our knowledge, all the Elamite names with a single compound rendering in Babylonian are in general presented as hypocoristica. An explication for this phenomenon could be that the Babylonian scribes used the hypocoristicon as a method for abbreviating Elamite compound anthroponyms.

Hybrid Names

Several persons attested in the Neo-Babylonian sources have hybrid names. The typology of these names is first, Elamite deity/substantive + Akkadian verb or, second, Elamite substantive + Akkadian adjective.

An example of the first category is the name Šadi-redû (*^{I}šá-di-re-e-du*), which consists of an Elamite deity, Šadi respectively Šati, and an Akkadian stative of the verb *redû* 'Šadi is accompanying'. Ran Zadok (1984, 36, n. 199), on the contrary, classifies this name as an Elamite name and translates the cuneiform combination *ri*/*e-e-du* as the Elamite component *riti* 'spouse' based on the onomastic conversion rule in which the voiced consonant /d/ is shifting to a voiceless consonant /t/. However, the vowel sign /e/ clearly indicates that the preceding sign /ri/ has the value /re/, meaning that the word is actually the Akkadian *redû* and not the Elamite *riti*. Šadi-redû is subsequently a hybrid name. On the other hand, an Elamite personal name that looks at first glance very similar to Šadi-redû is the personal name *te-em-ti-ri-di*. In this case, *ri-di* is a Neo-Babylonian rendering of the Neo-Elamite *riti* (Neo-Babylonian *d* ~ Neo-Elamite *t*) which is a linguistic evolution of the word *rutu* (see section on 'Vowel Changes').

In the second category of Elamite hybrid names, Šutar-šarḫu (*^{I}šu-tar-šar-ḫu*) is a combination of an Elamite noun *šutur* with an Akkadian adjective *šarḫu*. The Neo-Babylonian rendering of *šutu+r* (delocutive) has undergone a vowel modification (Neo-Babylonian *a* ~ Neo-Elamite *u*), while the adjective *šarḫu* 'proud' is attested with the Akkadian nominative case ending *-u*.

Babylonian Orthography of Elamite Names

The Theophoric Element

Since most Elamite names have a compound composition with two or three elements, one of these elements is often the name of a deity (Zadok 1991, 231). However, since the names of the Elamite gods were not similar to those of the

Table 16.2 *Neo-Elamite gods occurring in Neo-Babylonian personal names*

Neo-Elamite gods	Babylonian variants
Huban	*ḫum-ba*
	um-man
	um-ma
	am-ba
	im-ba
	im-ma
	Ø
Inšušinak	Ø
Nahhunte	*ḫu-un-du*
	Ø
Šati	*ša-di*
Tepti	*te-im-ti*

Babylonian gods, the theophoric element was not perceived as highly relevant by the Babylonian scribes. When Elamite personal names were transcribed into Babylonian, the theophoric element was either omitted or converted in Akkadian.

Omission of the Theophoric Element

Most Neo-Elamite royal names are known through Mesopotamian or Akkadian sources in which their regnal name is modified to a Babylonian or Assyrian dialect. A typical phenomenon is the omission of the theophoric element. As a matter of fact, the deity Inšušinak as second element of the Elamite name is never written in Babylonian sources (e.g., Ḫallušu-<Inšušinak> (reigned 699–693 BCE) 'Inšušinak made the country rich', ABC 1 iii 7). The deities Huban and Nahhunte are mostly attested in a variety of writings; Huban is often written as first particle and Nahhunte as last particle of a compound name. However, these deities could occasionally be absent as well (e.g., <Huban>-menanu (692–688 BCE) 'Huban is authority', ABC 1 iii 26; Kutur-<Nahhunte> (693–692 BCE) 'The lord Nahhunte', RINAP 3/1 22 v 14–16; Grayson 1963, 90 l. 19).

The Elamite royal name Urtak, witten *ur-ta-gu* (675–664 BCE; ABC 1 iv 13) in Babylonian, is a special case. The name Urtak/Urtagu only occurs in Akkadian sources and has no corresponding Neo-Elamite attestation yet. Urtak consists of two parts, *ur.ta+k*, in the Babylonian sources: *ur* is a sandhi writing of *u+ir* (personal pronoun 1.sg. 'I, me') and *ta+k* is a verbal form (passive participle 'is placed, installed'), meaning 'I, who is installed (by x)'. Based on the typology of Elamite names, one can assume that Urtak was followed by a noun, most likely a theophoric element. Within the group of theophoric elements, Nahhunte or Inšušinak are the most plausible candidates, because these divine names are generally positioned as the last element in a compound construction and are almost always omitted in Babylonian renderings. However, since no Elamite inscription is known that mentions this king, the reconstruction of Urtak's full name remains hypothetical.

Conversion of the Theophoric Element

If one takes into consideration that the Elamite pronunciation may have sounded foreign to Babylonian and Assyrian ears, one must accept that Elamite names may have been written similarly to, but not necessarily identically with, a Neo-Assyrian or Neo-Babylonian anthroponym. An example of such a Babylonian confusion is the conversion of the Elamite royal name Šutur-Nahhunte/Šutruk-Nahhunte 'The justifier, Nahhunte' into Ištar-ḫundu (717–699 BCE; ABC 1 ii 32). At first glance, one would expect that the Babylonians changed an Elamite theophoric element into the equivalent deity of the Babylonian pantheon – that is, from *šutur* to *Ištar*. However, *šutur*/*šutruk* is not an Elamite god, but a noun (-r delocutive), meaning 'the justifier, the righteous'. The Babylonian scribe probably used the Babylonian deity *Ištar* for the rendering of *šutur* because of the Semitic principle: as the three consonants *š-t-r* of *šutur* and *Ištar* are identical, *šutur* sounded like *Ištar* for the Babylonians.

The conversion of the other theophoric particles, namely Huban, Tepti, Nahhunte, and Šati, can be clustered in a number of Elamite–Babylonian onomastic conversion rules.

Sumerograms

Although rarely attested, Elamite names can be transferred in Neo-Babylonian renderings by the use of Sumerograms. One example is the Elamite royal name Kutur-Nahhunte. As we have seen, the Babylonians omitted the theophoric element Nahhunte. Kutur, the Elamite word for 'lord', is rendered as *kuduru* in Neo-Babylonian according to the onomastic conversion rules explained in 'Elamite–Babylonian Onomastic Conversion Rules' (*t* ~ *d*; Akk. case ending *-u*). This conversion subsequently sounded like the Babylonian word *kudurru* 'son' (CAD K 497), a meaning quite different from the Elamite 'lord'. Subsequently, for Akkadian *kudurru* the Sumerogram

NÍG.DU was used by the Babylonians to express the Elamite royal name Kutur-Nahhunte (693–692 BCE; ABC 1 iii 14′).

The 'Personenkeil'

In Neo-Babylonian texts, male anthroponyms are indicated with the determinative DIŠ (the '*Personenkeil*'; see Chapters 1 and 2), while male names in Neo-Elamite texts are preceded by the determinative $^{\text{be (BAD)}}$. Due to this discrepancy in traditions, the personal determinative before an Elamite name is often missing in a Babylonian text, while in that same text the Akkadian names are accompanied by a determinative (e.g., in ABC 1). The addition of a personal determinative to Elamite names probably depended on the onomastic knowledge of the scribe writing or copying the tablet. If the scribe or copyist did not recognise the foreign word as an Elamite personal name, then he was incapable of adding the correct determinatives as well. Perhaps this is the reason why the Akkadian determinative DIŠ for Elamite anthroponyms is correctly applied in the Bēl-ibni archive and is lacking in the Babylonian Chronicle.

Elamite–Babylonian Onomastic Conversion Rules

When looking for Elamite personal names in the Mesopotamian textual records, three features of Neo-Elamite phonology and orthography that may influence the Akkadian rendering of Elamite words should be kept in mind: the reduction of consonants, consonant shifts, and vowel alterations.

Reduction of Consonants

When Elamite personal names occur in Babylonian texts (or more widely in Akkadian texts) several consonants tend to be omitted. In the Neo-Babylonian renderings of the theophoric element 'Hu(m)ban' (Gorris 2020b, 164–77), for instance, the consonants /h/, /n/, and /m/ are altered.

The Consonant /h/

In the theophoric element the initial consonant /h/ is predominantly omitted. In this case, the Babylonian spellings adopt an evolution known from Elamite. During the Neo-Elamite period /h/ gradually disappeared in Elamite words, a development that continued in Achaemenid Elamite

(Stolper 2004, 71; Tavernier 2018, 425). Although the god Huban continued to be written with an /h/ in Neo-Elamite spellings, the /h/ was probably not pronounced anymore. Therefore, the Mesopotamian spelling reflects the common pronunciation of Huban in the first millennium BCE.

In the Babylonian Chronicle (ABC 1), one can find the only Neo-Babylonian attestation of the theophoric element 'Huban' written with an initial /h/ in the royal name Huban-haltaš[4] 'Huban received the land' (*ḫum-ba-ḫal-da-šu*). The Babylonian Chronicle is, however, not consistent in the use of the initial /h/ since the royal name Huban-nikaš[5] 'Huban has blessed' is attested in the more common Neo-Babylonian orthography *um-ma-ni-gaš*. Based on the Babylonian attestations (e.g., ^I^*um-man-ši-bar*, ^I^*um-ma-ḫal-da-šú*, ^I^*um-man-al-da-šú*, and ^I^*im-ba-da-ra-*?) the rendering *um-ma*(*n*) for the theophoric element is indeed most frequently used.

The Consonant /m/

The Neo-Babylonian attestations of Huban and Tepti are consistently written with a medial /m/ (*hum-ba, um-ma*(*n*), *i*/*am-ba*, *im-ma*, and *te-im-ti*), whereas the Neo-Elamite renderings *hu-ban* and *te-ip-ti* omit the middle /m/.[6] The /m/ in the Babylonian attestations is an indication of the Elamite nasalised vowels (Tavernier 2018, 424). In the Huban element, the reduplication of the /m/ is the result of the assimilation of /m/ with the consonant /b/ or /p/, which is also the case for the Babylonian attestation of the Elamite god Tepti (*te-im-ti*).

The Consonant /n/

In Neo-Elamite orthography, the final consonant *-n* is not consistently written. Françoise Grillot-Susini and Claude Roche (1987, 11; also Grillot-Susini 1994, 15; Khačikjan 1998, 10; Stolper 2004, 73) argue that the neutralisation of some final vowels and the elision of some medial vowels suggests that the stress was not final, but probably initial. This would suggest that the

[4] Three kings are known by the name Huban-haltaš during the Neo-Elamite period: (1) Huban-haltaš I (688–681 BCE), the founder of the second Neo-Elamite dynasty (i.e., the Hubanids); (2) his successor Huban-haltaš II (681–675 BCE); (3) Huban-haltaš III (648–647 BCE; 647–645 BCE), one of the Elamite Rebel Kings, who came into power twice during a period of Assyrian-induced political turmoil marking the downfall of the Hubanid dynasty (Gorris 2020a, 55–60). For more information on the division of the Neo-Elamite kings into dynasties and their genealogy, see Gorris (2020a, 37–8).

[5] The name Huban-nikaš is attributed to two Neo-Elamite kings. Huban-nikaš I (743–717 BCE) is the first known king of the first Neo-Elamite dynasty (Gorris 2020a, 20–22), while nearly a century later the Assyrian ruler Assurbanipal installed Huban-nikaš II (653–652/1 BCE) as Elamite king over the Susa territory (Gorris 2020a, 45–6).

[6] The only royal Elamite inscriptions (IRS 22; IRS 24–30) attested with a *hu-um-ban* orthography are those of the Middle Elamite king Untaš-Napiriša (1345–1305 BCE); see Gorris (2020b).

stress was put on the initial syllable of the word and that the pronunciation of the final consonant /n/ was rather weak, which resulted in the omission of the final /n/ in Neo-Babylonian renderings. This omission of the final /n/ is frequently attested in Neo-Babylonian renderings of Elamite toponyms (Gorris 2018, 324–5), but the same conversion rule counts for Elamite anthroponyms (e.g., Huban ~ *um-ma*; *im-ba*).

The Consonant /t/

Due to a weakening of /t/ in Neo-Elamite, the middle or final /t/ may occasionally disappear in Neo-Babylonian onomastic renderings (Tavernier 2014, 62); for example, Ḫallušu ~ Ḫallutuš-Inšušinak and Ḫallušu ~ Ḫallutuš-Inšušinak (ABC 1 iii 7; PTS 2713; VS 4 1; 1 N 297).[7]

Consonant Shifts

Voiced vs. Voiceless

According to Tavernier (2018, 425), there is no difference in Elamite between voiceless and voiced consonants. In general, Babylonian renderings of Elamite personal names are written with the voiced consonant, while the Elamite version uses the voiceless consonant. Hence, Neo-Elamite /k/ is rendered /g/ in Neo-Babylonian (e.g., *ur-ta-ak* ~ *ur-ta-gu*; *šak-ti-ti* ~ *šag-di-di*) and Neo-Elamite /t/ is rendered /d/ (e.g., *ḫu-ban-te-na* ~ *im-ba-de-en-na*; *ḫu-un-du* ~ *nah-hu-un-te*).

Sibilants

The Elamite language has more sibilants than Akkadian (Tavernier 2010, 1067–70) which is the reason why Elamite words converted into Akkadian reveal a variety of orthographies. It is commonly known that the sibilants /s/ and /š/ switched places in the Neo-Assyrian and Neo-Babylonian dialects (GAG § 30d; Hämeen-Anttila 2000, 9–10) and thus the writers of these dialects opted to express the Elamite sibilants differently. Whereas the Neo-Assyrian variations often use an /s/ sound for rendering an

[7] The royal name Ḫallutuš-Inšušinak is attributed to two Neo-Elamite kings. The Babylonian Chronicle (ABC 1 iii 7) refers to Ḫallutuš-Inšušinak I (699–693 BCE), who belonged to the first Neo-Elamite dynasty (Gorris 2020a, 33–5). Ḫallutuš-Inšušinak II (c. 598/93–583/78 BCE) was one of the late Neo-Elamite kings, whose reign is attested in Elamite as well as Neo-Babylonian documents (Gorris 2020a, 73–80). For the most plausible orthography of Ḫallutuš-Inšušinak, see Tavernier (2014).

Elamite /š/, the Neo-Babylonian renderings are much closer to the original and also use /š/ (e.g., Neo-Elamite ^{be}*hal-lu-iš* = Neo-Assyrian ^{I}*ḫal-lu-su/i* = Neo-Babylonian ^{I}*ḫal-lu-šú/i*). The geographical proximity of the Neo-Babylonian kingdom may have been the reason for a more accurate vocal transition.

Babylonian Consonant Modification

Although rarely attested, Babylonian renderings of Elamite names undergo even further changes when they are submitted to the Neo-Babylonian assimilation rules. One example is the royal name Urtak. Elamite Urtak, with the onomastic conversion rules, become *ur-ta-gu* in Babylonian, but in the latter dialect the -rt- consonant combination is modified into -št-. Therefore, a common Neo-Babylonian rendering of Urtak is ^{I}*uš-ta-gu* (Zadok 1984, 42).

Vowel Changes

Vowel changes regularly occur in Babylonian renderings of Elamite names. The Akkadian nominative case ending *-u* replaces in general the last vowel of the Neo-Elamite name or it is added to a Neo-Elamite name ending on a consonant. Since the vowel in Elamite anthroponyms written with /CvC/ signs is uncertain, the Babylonian renderings of Elamite names may exhibit various orthographies; for example, Neo-Elamite ^{be}*hu-ban-šu-pír* ~ Neo-Babylonian ^{I}*um-man-ši-pár* or ^{I}*um-man -ši-pír* 'Huban, the worshipper'. It is much harder to find a system behind the vowel changes at the beginning and in the middle of the personal name with /Cv/ or /vC/ signs. Sometimes the Neo-Babylonian rendering undergoes a vowel change, sometimes it reflects the conventional Elamite vowel. Therefore, the overview of the vowel changes presented in Table 16.3 is a non-exhaustive list, which may be extended after further research on the topic.

According to Jan Tavernier (2007, 278–9), signs of the type /Cu/ can be pronounced as /Ci/. In late Elamite sources not only the sound but also the orthography of the vowel /u/ is evolving into /i/ (Tavernier 2007, 278–9; 2018, 424). This also has an impact on the Neo-Babylonian renderings of Elamite names such as *te-em-ti-ri-di*. The element *riti* 'wife' is attested in a Neo-Elamite source (Ururu bronze plaque), but traditionally the word is written *rutu* in Elamite.

Table 16.3 *Neo-Babylonian renderings of Neo-Elamite vowels*

Neo-Elamite vowel	Neo-Babylonian rendering	Example
a	a	*ḫu-ban-nu-kaš* ~ *um-man-ni-gaš*
a	i	*ḫal-taš* ~ *il-da-šú*
u	u	*ḫu-ban* ~ *um-ba, um-ma*
u	i	*ḫu-ban* ~ *im-ba*
		šu-pir ~ *ši-pir*
		nu-kaš ~ *ni-gaš*
u	a	*ḫu-ban* ~ *am-ba* (in [I]*am-ba-zi-ni-za*, Ambaziniza, mng. uncertain)

Socio-Onomastics

This brings us to the ethno-sociological context of Elamite names that were written in the Neo-Babylonian texts. Who were the Elamites mentioned in those Neo-Babylonian texts? To which social class did they belong, and what were their professions? Only a few clusters of Neo-Babylonian documents, such as the Babylonian chronicles or the Bēl-ibni archive, contain multiple Elamite personal names and can give us some insight in the ethno-sociological context.

Since the Babylonian chronicles record specifically the regnal years and succession of the Babylonian kings and their royal neighbours, only names of Elamite kings from the reign of Huban-nikaš I (743–717 BCE) to the accession of Urtak (675–664 BCE) are described. The chronicles target a specific group within the Elamite upper class of the population, namely the king as the highest political authority within the Neo-Elamite kingdom.

Since the governor Bēl-ibni was positioned in southern Babylonia to monitor Elamite political activities at the Elamite–Babylonian border (de Vaan 1995), his archive mentions several Elamite kings: Indabibi (mng. unknown), Huban-nikaš II 'Huban has blessed', Tammaritu (mng. unknown), and Huban-ḫaltaš III; additionally, various Elamite royal officials concerned with foreign policies are noted, including the palace herald Ummanšibar 'Huban, the worshipper', the chief of the *šarnuppu*-officials Umḫuluma? 'Huban is connecting(?)', Huban-nikaš, son of Amedirra (a West Semitic name), and the borderland sheikhs Undadu (hypocorism of (Huban)-untaš '(Huban) installed me(?)') of the zilliru-people and Atmanu (possibly from Atta-menu 'Father is authority') of B/Manānu.[8] So, based on the official governmental character of the Bēl-ibni archive, it seems that the individuals with Elamite names occurring in these Babylonian texts were either highly ranked Elamite officials or specialised professionals, and Babylonian–Elamite borderland sheikhs with a mixed identity (Elamite–Aramean–Babylonian).

Interestingly, three seemingly unrelated Neo-Babylonian documents (an adoption contract and two loans of silver) give a rather exceptional insight in Babylonian–Elamite social relations. This adoption contract of a girl (OIP 122 1), drafted in Sumuntunaš (Western Elam) and found in Nippur, was dated to the 15th regnal year of Ḫallutuš-Inšušinak II. A loan of silver (VS 4 1), drafted in Elam and presumably found in Babylon, is linked to the archive of Iqīša, son of Bēl-nāṣir, of which all contracts are dated to the reign of Nebuchadnezzar II (605–562 BCE). Another loan of silver (PTS 2713) was drafted during the first regnal year of Ḫallutuš-Inšušinak II at Bīt-Hullumu (i.e., in the vicinity of the Sumuntunaš). What is special about these Neo-Babylonian documents is that the date formula referred to an Elamite place of writing and used the reign of the Elamite king Ḫallutuš-Inšušinak II (c. 598/93–583/78 BCE) as the year reference. Hence, these contracts must have been drawn up by a Babylonian community living (in the case of the adoption contract) or trading extensively in the western border region of the Neo-Elamite kingdom.[9]

As for the ethno-sociological profile of Elamite names in the Neo-Babylonian texts, we can thus roughly distinguish two groups. One group of Elamite kings and high officials active in Elamite–Babylonian bilateral relations was mentioned in official Neo-Babylonian state documentation. Another group are Elamites (including the hybrid and hypocoristic names) occasionally mentioned in dispersed Neo-Babylonian private archives, generally in connection with Babylonian trading activities or communities in the western Elamite Susiana region.

8 The latter occurs in the correspondence of Bēl-ibni, governor of the Sealand, and Assurbanipal with the Elders of Elam (Gorris 2020a, 180), aka the southern Mesopotamian–Elamite border zone. Whereas Joop M. C. T. De Vaan (1995) reads Banānu, Ran Zadok (1985) reads Manānu; thus with almost identical signs, either BA or MA.

9 For a detailed study of these documents (including further references) and their relation to the history of Elam, see Gorris (2020a, 73–7).

Further Reading

For Elamite, there is only one sign list, the *Syllabaire Elamite* by Marie-Joseph Stève (1992), and one dictionary, the *Elamisches Wörterbuch* (ElW) by Walther Hinz and Heidemarie Koch (1987). In the ElW lexicon, the word entries are catalogued by the occurrence in the texts rather than by their root, and translations are often very tentative. The most recent grammars, with references to preceding grammatical, morphological, and phonological studies, are by the hand of Jan Tavernier (2018) and Matthew W. Stolper (2004). Ran Zadok (1983; 1984; 1991) has especially contributed to our knowledge of Elamite onomastics.

References

Gorris, E. 2018. 'Crossing the Elamite borderlands: a study of interregional contacts between Elam and the "kingdom" of Hara(n)' in J. Tavernier, E. Gorris, K. Abraham, and V. Boschloos (eds.), *Topography and Toponymy in the Ancient Near East. Perspectives and Prospects*, Publications de l'Institut Orientaliste de Louvain 71. Leuven: Peeters, pp. 313–44.

Gorris, E. 2020a. *Power and Politics in the Neo-Elamite Kingdom*, Acta Iranica 60. Leuven: Peeters.

Gorris, E. 2020b. 'When God is forgotten . . . The orthography of the theophoric element Hu(m)ban in Elamite and Mesopotamian onomastics', *Les Études classiques* 88, 163–80.

Grayson. 1963. 'The Walters Art Gallery Sennacherib inscription', *Archiv für Orientforschung* 20, 83–96.

Hinz, W. and H. Koch 1987. *Elamisches Wörterbuch*, Archäologische Mitteilungen aus Iran, Ergänzungsband 17. Berlin: Dietrich Reimer.

Khačikjan, M. 1998. *The Elamite Language*, Documenta Asiana 4. Rome: Consiglio nazionale delle ricerche/Istituto per gli studi Micenei ed Egeo-Anatolici.

Grillot-Susini, F. 1994. 'Une nouvelle approche de la morphologie élamite: racines, bases et familles de mots', *Journal asiatique* 1, 1–18.

Grillot-Susini, F. and C. Roche 1987. *Éléments de grammaire Élamite*. Paris: Geuthner.

Hämeen-Anttila, J. 2000. *A Sketch of Neo-Assyrian Grammar*, State Archives of Assyria Studies 13. Helsinki: The Neo-Assyrian Text Corpus Project.

Stève, M.-J. 1992. *Syllabaire Elamite: Histoire et paléographie*, Civilisations du Proche Orient, Série 2, Philologie I. Neuchâtel/Paris: Recherches et Publications.

Stolper, M. W. 2004. 'Elamite' in R. D. Woodard (ed.), *The Cambridge Encyclopedia of the World's Ancient Languages*. Cambridge: Cambridge University Press, pp. 60–94.

Tallqvist, K. L. 1905. *Neubabylonisches Namenbuch zu den Geschäftsurkunden aus der Zeit des Shamash-shum-ukîn bis Xerxes*, Acta Societatis Scientarium Fennicae 32/2. Helsinki: Societas Litteraria Fennica.

Tavernier, J. 2007. 'On some Elamite signs and sounds', *Zeitschrift der Deutschen Morgenländischen Gesellschaft* 157, 265–91.

Tavernier, J. 2010. 'On the sounds rendered by the s-, š-, and ṣ/z- series in Elamite' in L. Kogan (ed.), *Proceedings of the 53e Rencontre Assyriologique Internationale, Vol. 1: Language in the Ancient Near East*, Winona Lake: Eisenbrauns, pp. 1059–78.

Tavernier, J. 2014. 'What's in a name: Hallušu, Hallutaš, or Hallutuš', *Revue d'Assyriologie et d'archéologie orientale* 108/1, 61–6.

Tavernier, J. 2018. 'The Elamite language' in J. Álvarez-Mon, G. P. Basello, and Y. Wicks (eds.), *The Elamite World*. London: Routledge, pp. 416–49.

de Vaan, J. M. C. T. 1995. *'Ich bin eine Schwertklinge des Königs'. Die Sprache des Bēl-ibni*, Alter Orient und Altes Testament 242. Kevelaer/Neukirchen-Vluyn: Butzon & Bercker/ Neukirchener Verlag.

Zadok, R. 1983. 'A tentative structural analysis of Elamite hypocoristica', *Beiträge zur Namenforschung NF* 18, 93–120.

Zadok, R. 1984. *The Elamite Onomasticon*, Supplemento n. 40 agli Annali vol. 44.3. Naples: Istituto Universitario orientale.

Zadok, R. 1985. *Geographical Names According to New- and Late-Babylonian Texts*, Répertoire Géographique des Textes Cunéiformes 8. Wiesbaden: Dr. Ludwig Reichert.

Zadok, R. 1991. 'Elamite Onomastics', *Studi Epigrafici e Linguistici* 8, 225–37.

CHAPTER 17

Sumerian Names

Uri Gabbay

Introduction

Sumerian, which most scholars treat as an isolated language, is the first identifiable language written in cuneiform.[1] By the end of the third millennium BCE it was no longer used as a vernacular language, but it continued to be used for the next two millennia, until the end of cuneiform culture, as a scholarly, literary, and religious language. This does not imply that the 'real', 'living' Sumerian tongue of the third millennium BCE perished and was replaced by an 'artificial', 'dead' language. Sumerian remained 'alive' and 'real' for another 2,000 years, perhaps not as a mother tongue but certainly as a language with a crucial and defining importance for the Mesopotamian scholarly and religious milieu. Many (perhaps even most) of the verbal religious performances in Mesopotamia in the second and first millennia BCE were conducted in Sumerian, whether they were based on the *kalûtu* corpus of Sumerian lamentations that constituted the regular temple cult or on the many Sumerian incantations included in the *āšipūtu* corpus which consisted of the purification and therapeutic rituals for temples and individuals. These corpora were not only performed but also studied. The scribal curriculum of the second and first millennia BCE began with lexical lists consisting of Sumerian or Sumero-Akkadian correspondences, and Sumerian remained an important part of scribal education and scholarly lore during advanced study.[2]

Therefore, although the number of Sumerian personal and family names recorded in Babylonia in the first millennium BCE is tiny, their

[1] I would like to thank Prof. Ran Zadok for discussing with me some of the materials in this chapter, and for reading and commenting on an earlier version.

[2] For the second millennium BCE, see, recently, Crisostomo (2019) (Old Babylonian period) and Bartelmus (2016) (Middle Babylonian period). For the curriculum of the first millennium BCE, see Gesche (2001).

existence points to the cultural importance Sumerian held for the bearers of these names, especially if they were priests or scholars. Sumerian in the first millennium BCE was not only a language that scholars and priests knew from their training and liturgical repertoire, but also a source of identity for its users.

Sumerian Onomastic Material in Babylonian Sources

Although Akkadian names in Babylonia during the first millennium BCE extensively use logograms that originate in the Sumerian language, actual Sumerian names in this period are practically non-existent. In fact, only one Sumerian personal name is attested in first-millennium BCE Babylonia: the ceremonial name of the daughter of Nabonidus, whom he dedicated as a priestess in Ur.[3] Otherwise, there are a few Sumerian family names in first-millennium BCE Babylonia.

Personal Names

Priests in the first millennium BCE, although sometimes writing their names in an orthography reflecting a pseudo-Sumerian origin, were usually given Akkadian (Babylonian) names (unlike Old Babylonian priests, who often had Sumerian names such as Ur-Utu). There is one exception to this: according to several inscriptions of Nabonidus, he installed his daughter as *en*-priestess of the god Nanna in Ur and gave her the ceremonial name en-níĝ-al-di-^{d}nanna (En-nigaldi-Nanna), '*En*-priestess, the request of Nanna' (Schaudig 2001, 708). This case (which has no historical anchor besides the passages in the royal inscriptions) is exceptional, just as the whole cultic act described in the passage is exceptional, and thus this use of a Sumerian

[3] Excluded are Sumerian personal names that are found in literary and scholarly texts composed or transmitted in the first millennium BCE but not otherwise attested as actual personal names or family names in Babylonia in the first millennium BCE. These include various names in VR 44 (Lambert 1957; some of these names, however, are known as family names in the first millennium BCE, see section on 'Family Names'), some of which also appear in other literary texts. For example, ^{I}làl-úr-alim-ma (interpreted in antiquity as Ṭāb-utul-Enlil 'Enlil's lap is sweet'), listed in VR 44 ii 17 (Lambert 1957, 12) appears in the dream of the protagonist of the composition Ludlul (III 25–6, see Oshima 2014, 279; note that ^{I}làl-úr-alim-ma is attested as a personal name in Kassite Nippur, see Hölscher 1996, 130). Other examples are the fanciful Sumerian names in the humoristic scribal composition 'Ninurta-pāqidat's Dog Bite' (George 1993). Also excluded from the discussion are the Sumerian names ^{I}ka-áš-du$_{11}$-ga (perhaps 'The decision is instructed'; see Jursa 2001–2, 83) and ^{I}lugal-šìr-ra ('Lord of the song/lament'), known from a list from Sippar of divine or mythological cultic functionaries, which clearly do not relate to actual contemporary persons (Jursa 2001–2, 77–9, BM 54725+ i 10′, iii 6′, 19′).

name similar to those given to priestesses in the third millennium BCE should be understood in the context of the antiquarian values promoted by Nabonidus himself.

Family Names

A few Sumerian family names are attested in the first millennium BCE, usually associated with scholars and priests.[4] These include:

(1) Ur-(Divine name)

Two family names are formed on the pattern Ur-(Divine name), meaning 'The one of (Divine name)', which is attested already in personal names of the third and second millennia BCE: Ur-Nanna 'The one of Nanna' and Ur-Nintinuga 'The one of Nintinuga'. The name Ur-Nintinuga was interpreted in antiquity as 'The one (= man) of Gula' (Amīl-Gula) (VR 44 ii 9; Lambert 1957, 12). The family name Ur-Nanna is already attested in archival texts from Babylon dating to the thirteenth and twelfth centuries BCE.[5] Since there is no evidence of Akkadian renderings of these names, it is assumed that these names were indeed Sumerian.[6]

(2) (Diving name)-ma-an-sum

A few family names, mostly from Babylon and Borsippa, are formed on the pattern (Divine name, or: temple name)-ma-an-SUM,[7] meaning '(Divine name, or: temple name) gave me (this son)', which is attested already in personal names of the third and second millennia BCE: ^{I}urudu(^{d}ùru-dù)-mansum, Esagil-mansum, and Asarluḫi-mansum. The first name was interpreted in antiquity as 'Nusku gave me' (Nusku-iddin) (VR 44 ii 16; Lambert 1957, 12). Since syllabic spellings of the first two names are

[4] Not included in the list are the following family names which may seem Sumerian but are probably not: ^{I}sag-di-di/ti (cf. Zadok 2003, 482, n. 8), ^{I}ARAD-^{d}(é-)gir$_4$-kù (probably a writing for Arad-Nergal, cf. Lambert 1957, 6, n. 23a), ^{I}ga-ḫúl-^{d}tu-tu (probably the same name as Gaḫal, and not likely to be of Sumerian origin, contra Wunsch 2014, 297, 305, n. 48), and ^{I}aš-gan-du$_7$ (probably of non-Sumerian origin, contra Sandowicz 2018, 58, n. 77). Also excluded are family names ending with *-akku* (e.g., Iššakku, Kassidakku) which are based on Sumerian loanwords in Akkadian.

[5] Nielsen 2011, 175; Wunsch 2014, 290–1; Jiménez 2017, 213.

[6] Sandowicz 2018, 57–8; Wunsch 2014, 296. Note the syllabic spelling of the divine name Nanna in Ur-Nanna in one text, indicating that it was rendered in Sumerian and not as Akkadian Sîn, see Wunsch (2014, 310, n. 77).

[7] The sign SUM is usually rendered 'sum' or 'šúm', but there are syllabic writings that may indicate 'sì'; see Wunsch (2014, 297 with nos. 29, 31).

attested, the names indeed seem to have been originally Sumerian and rendered in Sumerian form (although they may have been reinterpreted as near-homonymic Akkadian names; Wunsch 2014, 297).

(3) (Divine name)-ù-tu

A few family names, mostly from Babylon and Sippar, are formed on the pattern (Divine name)-ù-tu, in which the element ù-tu may be interpreted as the Sumerian verb meaning 'to give birth, create': Baba-utu 'Baba created', Zababa-utu 'Zababa created', and Nanna-utu (Nannûtu) 'Sîn created' (Wunsch 2014, 301). The name ^{Id}nanna-ù-tu was interpreted in antiquity as Akkadian Sîn-ibni 'Sîn created' in VR 44 ii 13 (Lambert 1957, 12). It is not clear, however, whether 'ù-tu' is indeed the Sumerian verb ù-tu 'create', or whether this is a reinterpretation of the suffix *-ūtu* (or *-iaūtu*) that is found with other names (e.g., Zērūtu; see Wunsch 2014, 301), especially since there are also syllabic renderings of the name Nanna-utu (Tallqvist 1902, 159; Baker 2004, 356).

(4) Lú-dumu-nun-na

The Lú-dumu-nun-na (Lu-dumununna) family, whose name literally means 'The one (= man) of the princely son', is attested in colophons from Achaemenid Nippur and in Late Babylonian archival texts from Ur.[8] The family name Lú-dumu-nun-na is already attested in a late Old Babylonian text dealing with a legal case in the area of Nippur and Dūr-Abiešuḫ, known from three unprovenanced tablets (George 2010 no. 17). Although the 'Princely Son' probably refers to Sîn,[9] there is no indication that Lú-dumu-nun-na was a writing for an Akkadian name such as Amīl-Sîn (so Wunsch 2014, 290), and it is likely that the name was pronounced in Sumerian (Lu-dumununna; Charpin 2019).

(5) $(E_{(4)})$-$gi_{(3/7)}$-ba-ti-la (E-gi-bi)

The name of the ^{I}($e_{(4)}$)-$gi_{(3/7)}$-ba-ti-la (E-gi-bi) family from Babylon was interpreted in antiquity as 'Sîn, you granted, may he live' (Sîn-taqīša-libluṭ) in VR 44 iii 53 (Lambert 1957, 13). It should be noted that e_4-gi_7 (A-KU) is not a regular name or epithet in Sumerian, and the interpretation of the element ba as *taqīša*, 'you granted', although lexically anchored, looks like a fanciful rendering. Such an interpretation of the name Egibatila would seem to be in line with learned pseudo-Sumerian writings of Akkadian

8 George 2010, 135; Wunsch 2014, 290, n. 8; Gabbay 2014, 258.

9 Compare An-Anu III 15: ^{d}dumu-nun-na = MIN (= ^{d}Sîn) (Litke 1998, 118).

names, especially since the Akkadian interpretation of the name agrees with Akkadian name patterns (Wunsch 2014, 297). Nevertheless, the name Egibatila may be a genuine Sumerian name, albeit of late, scholarly origin, that is based on an Akkadian pattern. It is also possible that, despite the Akkadian interpretation, the sign ba is to be understood as part of the verbal chain (ba-ti-la), perhaps with the meaning 'Sîn gave life' (cf. Tallqvist 1902, 57). In any case, the shortened form Egibi indicates that the name was indeed pronounced in Sumerian. Still, one cannot exclude the possibility of a name Egibi, of uncertain origin,[10] that was reinterpreted as a short form of a supposedly Sumerian Egibatila.

(6) Ab-sum-mu

The interpretation of the name Ab-sum-mu (Absummu), a family name attested in Nippur, is uncertain, although the writing sum-mu seems to indicate a Sumerian name containing the verb 'to give'. The element 'ab' could mean 'father' in some Sumerian contexts, or it may be a Sumerian verbal prefix; alternatively, the sign AB could be read as 'èš', with the meaning 'shrine'. None of these interpretations of the name are certain. In any case, there is no indication that this is a Sumerian orthography that masks an Akkadian name.

(7) A-ba-$^{(d)}$ninnu-da-ri

^{I}a-ba-$^{(d)}$ninnu-da-ri, perhaps to be rendered Aba-Enlil-da-ri, is interpreted as 'Who (else) is a protector like Enlil?' (Mannu-kīma-Enlil-ḫātin) in VR 44 iii 42 (Lambert 1957, 13), where da-ri stands for *ḫatānu* 'to protect' (an attested but rare lexical equation), and *kīma* 'like' is not reflected in the Sumerian name. However, contrary to the interpretation given in VR 44, the original meaning of the name may have been 'Who leads (ri) with (-da) Enlil?' (i.e., 'Who leads but Enlil?'; cf. Oshima 2017, 149, n. 44). In addition, while Ninnu surely refers to Enlil, it is not clear whether it was pronounced as Ninnu or as Enlil. The name is known from a colophon from Nineveh, referring to the 'house' of this family, as well as from archival texts from Late Babylonian Nippur (Oshima 2017, 152). There is no indication, nor reason to assume, that the writing stands for an Akkadian name, especially since one text writes the last element as -r[a] rather than -ri (colophon of K 2757:7′; collated).

Although, as seen earlier, there are some problems with the interpretation of some of the Sumerian family names, it is important to realise that

[10] It is in any case not West Semitic; see Tallqvist (1902, 57) with previous literature; Wunsch 2000, 1–2, n. 3; Abraham 2004, 9, n. 13.

almost all of these names belonged to families of a high social status whose members usually included priests or scholars. Besides the high social prestige that a Sumerian name conveys, it is important to remember that the religious and scholarly training and repertoire of many of the bearers of these names included much Sumerian, and a name in that language thus attests to their identity as the transmitters of the millennia-long Sumerian religious, literary, scholarly, and cultural tradition.

Indeed, according to the ancient Mesopotamian tradition, some of these family names can be traced back to individuals who were considered great priests and scholars (or ancestors of great scholars), adding to the prestige and cultural identity of their bearers.[11] Ur-Nanna, referred to as an exorcist and as a scholar of Babylon, was regarded as the composer of the 'Series of the Poplar'.[12] A son or descendant of Lú-dumu-nun-na, referred to as a scholar of Nippur, was regarded as the composer of the 'Series of the Fox' (Lambert 1962, 66, K 9717+ vi 12; Jiménez 2017, 46, 112). A son or descendant of [... -m]ansum (perhaps Asarluḫi-mansum or Esagil-mansum), referred to as a haruspex and scholar of Babylon, was regarded as the composer of one or more Sumerian texts (Lambert 1962, 66, K 9717+ vii 6–7). Asarluḫi-mansum was regarded as the master scholar at the time of Ḫammurapi, and an ancestor of the well-known scholar Esagil-kīn-apli, who in turn was regarded as the master scholar of the Babylonian king Adad-aplu-iddin in the eleventh century BCE.[13] According to a text from Seleucid Uruk, Aba-Ninnu-da-ri (or: Aba-Enlil-da-ri) was considered the master scholar of Esarhaddon, and was identified with ʾAḥīqar, the composer of an Aramaic proverb collection (Oshima 2017).[14] Finally, Ur-Nintinuga, an *āšipu* from Babylon, is featured in the Babylonian composition Ludlul (Tablet III 40–6), where he appears in the dream of the protagonist, holding a writing board that identifies him as a scholar (Oshima 2014, 285–6; Sandowicz 2018, 57).

The association of a family with a given scholarly ancestor may be correlated with the family's geographical location. The Ur-Nanna family is known from the thirteenth and twelfth centuries BCE from Babylon,

[11] This is also true, of course, for the bearers of some Akkadian family names, such as Sîn-leqe-unninnī, who was regarded as the composer of the Epic of Gilgamesh (Lambert 1962, K 9717+ 66, vi 10).

[12] Lambert 1962, K 9717+ 66, vi 14; Jiménez 2017, 112, 212–13. Note that a colophon of a Late Babylonian tablet states that the text on it is based on a copy of Ur-Nanna, 'scholar of Babylon', indicating the great authority of the text and the scholar (Jiménez 2017, 212–13 with n. 571).

[13] Finkel 1988; Heeßel 2010; Frahm 2018.

[14] Note that a colophon of a tablet from Nineveh probably states that the text on it is based on a copy from the 'house of Aba-Ninnu-da-ra', indicating the great authority of the text and the scholar (K 2757; see Oshima 2017, 152; for the 'houses' of families, see Nielsen 2011, 1).

and Ur-Nanna, as noted earlier, was considered a scholar of Babylon. The Asarluḫi-mansum family is attested especially in Babylon, and as noted, Asarluḫi-mansum himself was considered the scholar of Ḫammurapi, king of Babylon. The Lú-dumu-nun-na family is known especially from colophons from Nippur, and Lú-dumu-nun-na, as seen earlier, was considered a scholar of this city. Two other families are also located in Nippur: Ab-sum-mu and Aba-Ninnu(or: Enlil)-da-ri, although they are not associated with a venerable ancestor. It is probably not a coincidence that three out of the limited number of families bearing Sumerian names are closely associated with Nippur. Scholars from this city, especially those belonging to the Lú-dumu-nun-na and Ab-sum-mu families, occasionally designated themselves as 'Sumerians' (*šumerû*), alluding to the long Sumerian tradition associated with Nippur.[15]

Lastly, some temporal questions may be raised, although they are difficult to answer. Are any of the family names typical of certain periods, and could this information aid in reconstructing the historical origin of those families? For example, family name patterns such as Ur-(Divine name), Lú-(Divine name or epithet) (as in Lú-$^{(d)}$dumu-nun-na), and (Divine name)-ma-an-sum can be found already in the third and early second millennia BCE. However, this does not mean that first-millennium BCE families, whose names share these patterns, should be viewed as members of lineages going back to the third or early second millennium BCE, as such names could have been given later as well.[16] Indeed, the Ur-(Divine name) pattern is known also from the Middle Babylonian period (Hölscher 1996, 229–30). On the other hand, a name such as E_4-gi_7-ba-ti-la, which seems like a late scholarly invention, may reflect the relatively late emergence of this family as *nouveaux riches* in Babylonia (Abraham 2004, 9), though not much can be said more specifically about the date when the name was given to or chosen by the family. In the cases of Lú-dumu-nun-na and Ur-Nanna, however, attestations from the mid- and late second millennium BCE suggest relatively early dates for the emergence of these families (Wunsch 2014, 291–2). Lastly, Aba-Ninnu(or: Enlil)-da-ri was considered a contemporary of Esarhaddon, as seen earlier, which would imply

[15] Oelsner 1982; George 1991, 162; Gabbay and Jiménez 2019, 77.

[16] In this context, note the deliberate archaism found in Nippur colophons, where the title (not the personal name) 'the one of Gula' is written UR $^{(d)}$ME.ME, alluding to such a personal name (and perhaps even alluding to an ancient ancestor); see Gabbay and Jiménez (2019, 71, n. 73).

a very late date for the emergence of this family. However, this tradition is late and ideological in nature (Lenzi 2008), and thus it cannot serve as a basis for speculations regarding the history of this family.

Further Reading

For general surveys and histories of Sumerian and Sumerian literature, see Piotr Michalowski (2004) and Gonzalo Rubio (2009). On late Sumerian of the first millennium BCE, see Thorkild Jacobsen (1991) and Mark Geller (2010). Short discussions on Sumerian family names in the first millennium BCE appear as part of the general discussion of family names in Cornelia Wunsch (2014) and Małgorzata Sandowicz (2018, 57–8, appendix). For a discussion on Sumerian and pseudo-Sumerian family names that are attributed to a supposed scholarly ancestor, see Wilfred G. Lambert (1957). For discussions on fanciful writings of pseudo-Sumerian names, see Andrew R. George (1993) and Uri Gabbay and Enrique Jiménez (2019).

References

Abraham, K. 2004. *Business and Politics under the Persian Empire: The Financial Dealings of Marduk-nāṣir-apli of the House of Egibi (521–487 BCE)*. Bethesda: CDL.

Baker, H. D. 2004. The Archive of the Nappāḫu Family, Archiv für Orientforschung Beiheft 30. Vienna: Institut für Orientalistik.

Bartelmus, A. 2016. *Fragmente einer grossen Sprache: Sumerisch im Kontext der Schreiberausbildung des Kassitenzeitlichen Babylonien*, Untersuchungen zur Assyriologie und Vorderasiatischen Archäologie 12/1–2. Berlin: De Gruyter.

Charpin, D. 2019. 'En marge d'EcritUr, 6: CUSAS 10 17 et l'onomastique théophore de Dumununna', *Nouvelles Assyriologiques Brèves et Utilitaires* 2019/45.

Crisostomo, C. J. 2019. *Translation as Scholarship: Language, Writing, and Bilingual Education in Ancient Babylonia*, Studies in Ancient Near Eastern Records 22. Berlin: De Gruyter.

Finkel, I. L. 1988. 'Adad-apla-iddina, Esagil-kīn-apli, and the Series SA.GIG' in E. Leichty, M. deJ. Ellis, and P. Gerardi (eds.), *A Scientific Humanist: Studies in Memory of Abraham Sachs*, Occasional Publications of the Samuel Noah Kramer Fund 9. Philadelphia: Samuel Noah Kramer Fund, The University Museum, pp. 143–59.

Frahm, E. 2018. 'The exorcist's manual: structure, language, Sitz im Leben' in G. Van Buylaere, M. Luukko, D. Schwemer, and A. Mertens-Wagschal (eds.), *Sources of Evil: Studies in Mesopotamian Exorcistic Lore*, Ancient Magic and Divination 5. Leiden: Brill, pp. 9–47

Gabbay, U. 2014. *Pacifying the Hearts of the Gods: Emesal Prayers of the First Millennium BC*, Heidelberger Emesal-Studien 1. Wiesbaden: Harrassowitz.

Gabbay, U. and E. Jiménez 2019. 'Cultural imports and local products in the commentaries from Uruk: The case of the Gimil-Sîn family' in C. Proust and J. Steele (eds.), *Scholars and Scholarship in Late Babylonian Uruk*, Why the Sciences of the Ancient World Matter 2. Cham: Springer, pp. 53–88.

Geller, M. 2010. 'Late Babylonian Lugal-e' in H. D. Baker, E. Robson, G. Zólyomi (eds.), *Your Praise is Sweet: A Memorial Volume for Jeremy Black from Students, Colleagues and Friends*. London: British Institute for the Study of Iraq, pp. 93–100.

George, A. R. 1991. 'Babylonian Texts from the folios of Sidney Smith. Part Two: Prognostic and Diagnostic Omens, Tablet I', *Revue d'Assyriologie* 85, 137–67.

George, A. R. 1993. 'Ninurta-pāqidāt's dog bite, and notes on other comic tales', *Iraq* 55, 63–75.

George, A. R. 2010. *Babylonian Literary Texts in the Schøyen Collection*, Cornell University Studies in Assyriology and Sumerology 10. Bethesda: CDL.

Gesche, P. D. 2001. *Schulunterricht in Babylonien im ersten Jahrtausend v. Chr.*, Alter Orient und Altes Testament 275. Münster: Ugarit-Verlag.

Heeßel, N. P. 2010. 'Neues von Esagil-kīn-apli: die ältere Version der physiognomischen Omenserie alamdimmû' in S. M. Maul and N. P. Heeßel (eds.), *Assur-Forschungen*. Wiesbaden: Harrassowitz, pp. 139–87.

Hölscher, M. 1996. *Die Personennamen der kassitenzeitlichen Texte aus Nippur*, Imgula 1. Münster: Rhema.

Jacobsen, T. 1991. 'Abstruse Sumerian' in M. Cogan and I. Eph'al (eds.), *Ah, Assyria . . . : Studies in Assyrian History and Ancient Near Eastern Historiography Presented to Hayim Tadmor*. Jerusalem: Magnes Press, pp. 279–91.

Jiménez, E. 2017. *The Babylonian Disputation Poems*, Culture and History of the Ancient Near East 87. Leiden: Brill.

Jursa, M. 2001–2. 'Göttliche Gärtner? Eine bemekenswerte Liste', *Archiv für Orientforschung* 48–9, 76–89.

Lambert, W. G. 1957. 'Ancestors, authors, and canonicity', *Journal of Cuneiform Studies* 11, 1–14, 112.

Lambert, W. G. 1962. 'A catalogue of texts and authors', *Journal of Cuneiform Studies* 16, 59–77.

Lenzi, A. 2008. 'The Uruk list of kings and sages and late Mesopotamian scholarship', *Journal of Ancient Near Eastern Religions* 19, 137–69.

Litke, R. L. 1998. *A Reconstruction of the Assyro-Babylonian God-Lists. AN : da-nu-um and AN : Anu šá amēli*, Texts from the Babylonian Collection 3. New Haven: Yale Babylonian Collection.

Michalowski, P. 2004. 'Sumerian' in R. D. Woodard (ed.), *The Cambridge Encyclopedia of the World's Ancient Languages*. Cambridge: Cambridge University Press, pp. 19–59.

Nielsen, J. P. 2011. *Sons and Descendants: A Social History of Kin Groups and Family Names in the Early Neo-Babylonian Period, 747–626 BC*, Culture and History of the Ancient Near East 43. Leiden/Boston: Brill.

Oelsner, J. 1982. 'Spätachämenidische Texte aus Nippur', *Revue d'Assyriologie* 76, 94–5.

Oshima, T. 2014. *Babylonian Poems of Pious Sufferers: Ludlul Bēl Nēmeqi and the Babylonian Theodicy*, Orientalische Religionen in der Antike 14. Tübingen: Mohr Siebeck.

Oshima, T. 2017. 'How "Mesopotamian" was Ahiqar the Wise? A search for Ahiqar in cuneiform texts' in A. Berlejung, A. M. Maeir, and A. Schüle (eds.), *Wandering Aramaeans: Aramaeans Outside Syria. Textual and Archaeological Perspectives*, Leipziger Altorientalische Studien 5. Wiesbaden: Harrassowitz, pp. 141–67.

Rubio, G. 2009. 'Sumerian Literature' in C. S. Ehrlich (ed.), *From an Antique Land. An Introduction to Ancient Near Eastern Literature*, Lanham: Rowman and Littlefield, pp. 11–75.

Sandowicz, M. 2018. 'Before Xerxes: the role of the governor of Babylonia in the administration of justice under the first Achaemenids' in C. Waerzeggers and M. Seire (eds.), *Xerxes and Babylonia: The Cuneiform Evidence*, Orientalia Lovaniensia Analecta 277. Leuven: Peeters, pp. 35–62.

Schaudig, H. 2001. *Die Inschriften Nabonids von Babylon und Kyros' des Grossen*, Alter Orient und Altes Testament 256. Münster: Ugarit-Verlag.

Tallqvist, K. L. 1902. *Neubabylonisches Namenbuch zu den Geschäftsurkunden aus der Zeit des Šamaššumukîn bis Xerxes*, Acta Societatis Scientiarum Fennicae 32/2. Helsinki: Societas Litteraria Fennica.

Wunsch, C. 2000. *Das Egibi-Archiv: Die Felder und Garten*, Vol. 1, Cuneiform Monographs 20a. Groningen: Styx.

Wunsch, C. 2014. 'Babylonische Familiennamen' in M. Krebernik and H. Neumann (eds.), *Babylonien und seine Nachbarn: Wissenschaftliches Kolloquium aus Anlass des 75. Geburtstages von Joachim Oelsner, Jena, 2. und 3. März 2007*, Alter Orient und Altes Testament 369. Münster: Ugarit-Verlag, pp. 289–314.

Zadok, R. 2003. 'The representation of foreigners in Neo- and Late Babylonian legal documents (eighth through second centuries BCE)' in O. Lipschits and J. Blenkinsopp (eds.), *Judah and the Judeans in the Neo-Babylonian Period*. Winona Lake: Eisenbrauns, pp. 471–589.

CHAPTER 18

Residual, Unaffiliated, and Unexplained Names

Ran Zadok

Introduction

Residual languages, which were productive in the onomasticon of first-millennium Babylonia, are in the first place Kassite and Urartian.[1] Other such languages cannot be identified by name, but it is likely that other dialects, which originated in the central Zagros and the Armenian plateau respectively, also left traces in the pertinent corpus. On the other hand, Elamite, which is an unaffiliated language (like Kassite), cannot be defined as a residual language as it has a rich and variegated corpus lasting for about 2,000 years (see Chapter 16). The Neo-Babylonian anthroponyms from the early first millennium BCE and the period of the Neo-Babylonian Empire originated in the Semitic-speaking core, namely Mesopotamia, the Levant including Egypt, and the Syro-Arabian desert as well as in the neighbouring plateaus of Iran and Anatolia. The pertinent geographical horizon became much wider in the ensuing periods of the Achaemenid, Seleucid, and Parthian Empires and includes also central Asia and the regions east of the Iranian plateau, as far as the Indus, as well as Greece. Nevertheless, the percentage of non-Mesopotamian names in the much smaller Neo-Assyrian corpus is much higher than in the abundant Neo- and Late Babylonian corpus. This is due to two factors. First, the Neo-Assyrian royal inscriptions have a wide geographical scope and enumerate many anthroponyms and toponyms. Second, much of the Neo-Assyrian documentation stems from palatial archives, where lower social strata and deportees are amply represented, whereas most of the Babylonian documentation from the long sixth century BCE belongs to archives of the Babylonian urban elite, with negligible representation of other social strata. In late-Achaemenid and Hellenistic-Parthian Babylonia, the percentage of foreigners is only slightly higher than in the preceding period.

[1] All the names discussed herein are Neo- or Late Babylonian unless stated otherwise.

The special relationship between Babylonia and Assyria is a *longue durée* phenomenon. First, Babylonia and adjacent regions were under a long Assyrian conquest, albeit with various degrees of control. Then, the conquest of most of the eastern Jazirah, including a section of Assyria proper, by Babylonia followed the demise of the Neo-Assyrian Empire. These circumstances compel us to compare the onomasticon of the Neo-Babylonian sources with that of the Neo-Assyrian corpus, which is partially contemporary. This comparative task is greatly facilitated by the completion of the *Prosopography of the Neo-Assyrian Empire* (1–3, Helsinki 1998–2011, henceforth: PNA). On the other hand, the excerption and evaluation of the abundant Neo- and Late Babylonian onomastic material is far from complete and thus far devoid of a comparable and updated *instrumentarium*.

Kassite Names and Related Material

Kassite is an extreme case of a residual language because it is not recorded in any texts. What remains are only a restricted number of names (anthroponyms, theonyms, and toponyms) and very few appellatives. Therefore, the reconstruction of Kassite anthroponymy (practically a list of name elements) is fraught with difficulties and necessarily contains doubtful material. Much of the discussion that follows is inevitably exploratory; an effort will be made to clarify the context that encourages the assignment of anthroponyms to the Kassite language.

The Kassites, whose dynasty exercised the longest rule over Babylonia, in the latter half of the second millennium BCE, became an inseparable part of the Babylonian elite (unlike the Gutians, whose ephemeral rule and partial control of Babylonia perpetuated them as the emblematic 'other'). Hence, the Kassite names in post-Kassite and later Babylonia are, in the first place, family names referring to clans of the elite of the Babylonian temple cities. Commonly attested family names of Kassite origin are Mar/štuk(āta), Tunâ (Zadok 1979, 170), Šabbâ/Šambâ, Gaḫal (cf. Gaḫal-Marduk (in next paragraph)), as well as, perhaps, Ašgandu/Šugandu.[2] The following family names are rarely attested: Šagerīya (^{I}*šá!-ga-e-ri-ia*, UET 4 24:8′, provided that the ZA- of the copy is an error for ŠÁ),[3]

[2] The equation of this name with Amīl-Papsukkal (Powell 1972) may be secondary and homiletic.

[3] This is suggested with all due reservation in view of the occurrence of *šagar* (followed by a resembling suffix) in the MB Kassite onomasticon (Balkan 1954, 78, 179; Hölscher 1996, 200a, s.v. *Šagarē'a*; see Zadok 1979, 170).

presumably Gibindu (^{I}*gi-bi-in-du*, BM 27746:33′, from Borsippa) and Šatarindi (^{I}*šá-ta-ri-in-di*, FLP 1556:14, in Dillard 1975, 253, from Sippar),[4] and perhaps Ḫullunu (^{I}*ḫul-lu-nu*, CTMMA 3 90:20, from Babylon) and Zannētu (^{I}*za-an-né-e-tú*, VS 4 63:10, from Babylon).

Several family names are hybrid, namely Akkado–Kassite, such as Gaḫal-Marduk (^{I}*ga-ḫúl*-^{d}TU.TU, PNA 1/II, 419), Nazi-Enlil (^{I}*na-zi*-^{d}50, Nielsen 2015, 282), and Nazūa (^{I}*na-zu-a*, BE 8/1 112:6). The latter is based on Kassite *nazi* 'shadow, protection' followed by the hypocoristic suffix *-ūa*, similar to Middle Babylonian Nazūtum (^{I}*na-zu-ú-tum*) with *-ūt* (Balkan 1954, 74; cf. UET 7 67 r. 5). The same suffix is attached to *kil-* in the personal name Gilūa.[5]

On the whole, the Kassite family names form no more than 3.33 per cent of the 300 family names referring to the system of Babylonian urbanite clans. These 300 family names were coined during the early first millennium BCE and many of them are archaic (see Chapter 3).[6] Two early Neo-Babylonian family names, which are not attested later, are (if they are not paternal names) Pilamdi (^{I}*pi-lam-di*, NMA 3 i 6, iii 6; see Paulus 2014, 639–40)[7] and Kandar-Šamaš (^{I}*kan-dar-šam-ši*, MZŠ I 2 r. 6; see Paulus 2014, 674).[8] The former is presumably Kassite and the latter is hybrid, as its predicative (initial) element seems to be Kassite while its theophoric element is Akkadian.

Most of the pertinent given names, namely Iddin-Šīḫu (^{I}SUM-*ši-ḫu*), Kadašman-Enlil (^{I}*ka-dáš-man*-^{d}50), and Na'di-Šīḫu (^{I}*na-di-ši-ḫu*), are also hybrid (Akkado–Kassite).[9] Such may also be Nazīya (^{I}*na-zi-ia*, Tallqvist 1905, 160), in view of its hypocoristic suffix which is very common in Akkadian and West Semitic. A hybrid filiation is early Neo-Babylonian

4 Both names end in *-nd-* like Kilandi (Kilamdi), Kunindi, Pilandi (Pilamdi), and Šindi (cf. Šimdi as well as Širinta, Taramdi, and Ziqanta; in Balkan 1954, 63, 65, 76, 81–2, 84, 160–2, 172, 183), as well as, perhaps, Ašgandu.

5 Wunsch 2000, 295, with references. For *kil-* in Kassite names from Babylonia, see Balkan (1954, 160–1). There are hardly any Neo- and Late Babylonian clans whose names are beyond doubt Hurrian; hence, *kil-* is to be kept apart from the homonymous Hurrian element in Nuzi and outside Babylonia (see Richter 2016, 435 with n. 408).

6 For forerunners of these Neo-Babylonian family names, see Brinkman (2006) (mostly on family names denoting professions).

7 Zēria DUMU ^{I}*pi-lam-di*, referring to either the father or the ancestor (i.e., family).

8 Bānia son/descendant (DUMU) of Kandar-Šamaš, scribe, from Sippar. For the initial component cf. perhaps *kandaš-*, *gandaš*, and *gandi* (Balkan 1954, 53, 127–9, 157). Another non-Akkadian family name (or paternal name), which occurs in the same document, is Nana-šuḫi (^{I}*na-na-šu-ḫi*, MZŠ I 2:10); for the initial component cf. *nan-a* (Balkan 1954, 169).

9 Nielsen 2015, 147, 170, 273; Nielsen reads ^{I}SUM-*ši-pak* and ^{I}*na-di-ši-pak*.

Kaššû-šumu-iddin (^{I}*kaš-šú-ú*-MU-SUM.NA), son or descendant (DUMU) of Nazi-Marduk (^{I}*na-zi*-^{d}AMAR.UTU, NMA 1 i 18, vi:1; see Paulus 2014, 624, 629).

Purely Kassite names are only Kurigalzu and Nazi-Maruttaš (Nielsen 2015, 184; Brinkman 1998, 191b), which were originally royal names and therefore survived in the first millennium BCE, like the royal name Ḫammurapi,[10] probably as prestigious anthroponyms. The Kassite character of Kiligug (^{I}*ki-il-li-gu-ug*, *Nbk.* 26:3; cf. NA ^{I}*ki-li-gu-gu*, PNA 2/I, 616) cannot be ascertained.[11] The same applies to ^{f}Inzayītāy > ^{f}Inza'ītâ (^{f}*in-za-*$^{?}$*-id-da* or [^{f}*in-za-*($^{?}$)*-i*]*t-ta-a*), rendered *ʾnzyty* in Aramaic (BE 8/1 53:7, l.e.). Apparently this female name ends in a cluster of feminine hypocoristic suffixes (*-ay-īt-ay*). It seems that it is based on Kassite *inz-*, which is extant in NA ^{I}*in-zi-i* (see, cautiously, PNA 2/I, 559; cf. Balkan 1954, 153), ^{f}*in-zi-a-a* (with a different interpretation, PNA 2/I, 559), and ^{f}*en-zu-u* (provided the reading is not Bēl-lēʾi, PNA 1/II, 397). Similarly, early Neo-Babylonian Pakaštu (^{I}*pa-kaš-tu*, BRM 1 17:12), which has a late Old Babylonian forerunner (^{I}*ba-ka-aš-ti*; cf. Zadok 1999–2000, 355a), might be Kassite.[12]

The bearers of Kassite anthroponyms and family names were an integral part of the Babylonian urban elite. The hybrid names are the product of interference onomastics which is devoid of any ethnic significance, while the purely Kassite names are merely inherited fossils. It is noteworthy that the name of Nebuchadnezzar II's daughter, ^{f}Kaššāya, is based on the designation 'Kassite', another example of this prestigious class of names. The number of Kassite given names dwindles sharply after the end of the post-Kassite period.

The rare family name Lullubāya (^{I}*lul-lu-ba-a-a*, recorded only in Babylon) and Nikkāya (e.g., ^{I}*nik-ka-a-a*, attested in Babylon, Borsippa, and perhaps in Kish; see Wunsch 2014, 306–7) are gentilics of regions in the Zagros and its piedmont respectively.

10 See Zadok (1978, 56) with references. Mut-Dagan (^{I}*mu-ut-*^{d}*da-gan*, BE 8/1 157:12) 'Man of Dagan' might be an Amorite vestige. The pattern *Mut*-DN is common in Amorite (see Streck 2000, 163, 299–300), but has no other occurrences in the abundant onomastic documentation from first millennium BCE Mesopotamia. In view of the occurrence of the given name *mu-ti-e-kur*^{ki} in MB (Hölscher 1996, 144b, s.v. *Muti-Ekur*), it may be surmised that this family name, like other non-Akkadian family names from the first millennium BCE, is an ancient survival: several such family names are recorded as given names in MB.

11 It apparently consists of *kil-* (cf. earlier in chapter) and *-gug*. The latter reminds one of Elamite *kuk*, in which case it would be a hybrid Kassite-Elamite compound name, but such names are very rare.

12 Cf. perhaps *pak-* and -V*št-* (as in ^{I}*ši-ri-iš-ti*, Balkan 1954, 76, 82, 172, 181).

Urartian Names

Urartians are recorded in Babylonia during the early period of the Neo-Babylonian Empire and in the late-Achaemenid period[13] – that is, with a considerable temporal gap. One individual is homonymous with the much earlier Urartian king Menua (c. 810–785/780 BCE; cf. Salvini 1993–7). Minua (^{I}*mi-nu-ú-a*, BE 8/1 101:12) acts as the first out of four witnesses in a deed dated to the first year of Bardia (c. 522 BCE). Unlike the other witnesses, Minua is recorded without a paternal name. Naraggu (^{I}*na-rag-gu*, BE 8/1 87:4, 527 BCE) may be compared with Neo-Assyrian ^{I}*na-ra-ge-e*, an Urartian name (not Elamite, as cautiously suggested in PNA 2/II, 930).

Atypical Names

Atypical names are dubbed 'noms apatrides' by Emmanuel Laroche (1966, 239–46). They may belong to any dialect. In many cases their analysis is not beyond the descriptive-taxonomic level. Such names are Nenê and Nenēa (^{I}*né-né-e*, ^{I}*ne-né-e-a*, PNA 2/II, 940; both variants are (also) borne by people from Babylonia, the latter with a hypocoristic suffix).

The following names have a reduplicated second syllable:[14] Bazizi (^{I}*ba-zi-zi*, Pearce and Wunsch 2014, 44b), Bazuzu (^{I}*ba-zu-zu*, Tallqvist 1905, 23–4), Kiruru (^{I}KI-*ru-ru*, *Cyr.* 360:25),[15] and ^{f}Busasa (^{f}*bu-sa-sa*, *Cyr.* 135:9). The name Qazizi (^{I}*qa-zi-zi*, CUSAS 28 44:18) was borne by a Judean. Ḫubaba (^{I}*ḫu-ba-ba*, CUSAS 28 2:13), also borne by a Judean, may alternatively render the equivalent of OT *Ḥwbb*. Igigi (^{I}*i-gi-gi*, CTMMA 3 6:4) may be Elamite, and Kulūlu (^{I}*ku-lu-lu*) can be either Akkadian 'Headdress' (of deities and kings) or Elamite (see Waerzeggers 2014 no. 175 r. 13).

In early and later Neo-Babylonian texts the female name ^{f}Sinūnu 'Swallow fish' (^{f}*si-nu-nu*, CTMMA 3 52:6; see Nielsen 2015, 335) occurs. Neo-Assyrian ^{I}*su-nu-nu*, which refers to a male person (PNA 3/I, 1159), looks like the same form with vowel harmony.

13 See Zadok (1979, 169; 2018, 113–14). Add ^{lú}*<ú>-ra-áš-ṭa-a-a* (recipient of a ration, probably of oil; Babylon 28122 r. 30, in Weidner 1939, pl. II; cf. Bloch 2018, 229 with n. 13 who recognises it as a gentilic, but does not attempt to identify it). The same text has several omissions of signs; e.g., ^{kur}*ia-<man>-na-a-a* (r. 21) and ^{lú}*ia-<ú>-da-a-a* (r. 28).

14 Cf. the list in Zadok 1981, 60–1 with n. 199. The type, which is based on a reduplicated syllable, might have undergone dissimilation of sibilants if Neo-Assyrian ^{I}*si-zi-i* (PNA 3/I, 1152) originates from ^{I}*zi-zi-i*.

15 Cf. Neo-Assyrian ^{I}KAR-*ru-ru*, in PNA 2/I, 607, with a CVC-sign which is indifferent to vowel quality.

Gigīya (*ᴵgi-gi-ia*), ᶠGigītu (*ᶠgi-gi-i-tu₄*), and ᶠGugûa (*ᶠgu-gu-ú-a*; see Tallqvist 1905, 63–4) consist of a reduplicated syllable and a hypocoristic suffix (cf. Neo-Assyrian Kusisî, spelled *ᴵku-si-si-i*, PNA 2/I, 643). The same applies to ᶠGāgāya (*ᶠga-ga-a*; Tallqvist 1905, 62), Zazāya (*ᴵza-za-a*, CTMMA 4 6:5; cf. Neo-Assyrian *ᴵza-za-a-a* [etc.], PNA 3/II, 1439), Zizīya (*ᴵzi-zi-ia*, CTMMA 4 51:4), and Zuzū (*ᴵzu-zu-ú*, TEBR 6 57:3). They (except for the first name) may derive from Z–W/Y–Z like Zūzâ (*ᴵzu-za-a*, IMT 53:16) and Zūzānu (*ᴵzu-za-nu*, BE 8/1 110:15 and Jursa 1995, 220), in which case their base would be with a long vowel.

Atypical family names are Šalala (*ᴵšá-la-la* or *ᴵšá-a-la-la*) and Sagdidi (*ᴵsag-di-di*, with dissimilation *ᴵsag-di-ti*, Wunsch 2014, 308–9). The former may alternatively be Akkadian (*Ša-alāli*; see Baker 2004, 284 *ad* no. 240:16). The fact that this family name is sometimes preceded by the determinative LÚ is not a decisive argument against the first alternative (as an atypical anthroponym) in view of the fact that LÚ interchanges with the '*Personenkeil*' in Neo- and Late Babylonian family names. Besides, the common spelling of the family name is with *-la*, not *-li*. *ᴵsag-di-di*, with the reading *šak-*, may refer to Elam. *šak-* 'son' (see Zadok 1984, 38:211, 45:251), in which case it would be the only Neo- or Late Babylonian family name of Elamite origin.[16]

Early Neo-Babylonian Baḫiriru or Maḫiriru (*ᴵba/ma-ḫi-ri-ru*, BRM 1 17:7; Nielsen 2015, 195) may end in a reduplicated syllable if the Babylonian scribe adjusted its final vowel to that of the Akkadian nominative. If this practice was applied to early Neo-Babylonian Ḫuḫuḫi (*ᴵḫu-ḫu-ḫi*, Nielsen 2015, 139), then it consists of three identical syllables (**ḫu-ḫu-ḫu*).

A rare type is exemplified by Neo-Assyrian Mesimesi (*ᴵme-si-me-si*), which consists of two reduplicated syllables. The name has nothing to do with Arabic *mišmiš* (> modern Israeli Hebrew 'apricot'), as claimed by Simo Parpola (PNA 2/II, 749), seeing that the latter consists of a single reduplicated syllable. The name can perhaps be compared to the Jewish Babylonian–Aramaic paternal name *mšmš*.[17]

The sequence CV_1-CV_2- (+ hypocoristic suffix) is extant in the following names: Neo-Babylonian Nūnāya (*ᴵnun-na-a*, Nielsen 2015, 301) could be based on *nūnu* 'fish' (cf. Neo-Assyrian *ᴵnu-nu-a*, PNA 2/II, 967). ᶠŠūšāya (*ᶠšu-šá-a-a-ˀ*, BRM 1 5:8; see Nielsen 2015, 380) is perhaps based on *šūšu* 'licorice' as a nickname for a sweet child. Tūtia (*ᴵtu-ti-ia*, Tallqvist 1905, 212) may be based on *tūtu* 'mulberry' (cf. Neo-Assyrian *ᴵtu-ta-ia*, etc., PNA

16 *ᴵsa-ak/ik-ti-ti* in Royal Achaemenid Elamite documents from Persepolis (ElW 1052, s.v.) probably does not belong here in view of the different sibilant.

17 See Shaked, Ford, and Bhayro (2013, 62, 4): 'Maššamaš', without comment about their vocalisation.

3/II, 1337). The sequence tV-tV- is also extant in Neo-Assyrian ^{I}*ti-ti-i*, ^{f}*te-ta-a-a*, and ^{f}*ti-ta-a-a* (PNA 3/II, 1323, 1327). Regarding Nanni, Nannia, and Nannûtu (Waerzeggers 2014, 393a), the last one is based on the divine name Nanna (cf. Nielsen 2015, 279), while the two preceding ones probably do not derive from Luwian *nani* 'brother' (for these names and ^{I}*na-na-te*; cf. PNA 2/II, 925).

Šiu (^{I}*ši-i-ú*, PNA 3/II, 1268, borne by a Babylonian) is based on a single consonant like Neo-Assyrian Buwa (^{I}BU-*u-a*, PNA 1/II, 357), Ṣū'a (^{I}*ṣu-*(*u*)-*a* PNA 3/I, 1177), Nia (^{I}*ni-ia*, PNA 2/II, 959), Agāya (^{I}*a-ga-a-a*, PNA 1/I, 55), Innû (^{I}*i-nu-ú*, PNA 2/I, 544), and (with a hypocoristic suffix which ends with *-t*) ^{f}Kēautu (^{f}*ke-e-a-u-tú*, PNA 2/I, 609–10; cf. ^{I}*ke-e-a-a*, PNA 2/I, 609). Other short names (all with gemmination of the second consonant and a hypocoristic suffix) are Luttûa (^{I}*lu-ut-tu-ú-a*, OIP 122 2:27), Gaggū (^{I}*ga-ag-gu-ú*, EE 77:4; cf. Neo-Assyrian ^{I}*kak-ku-u*; PNA 2/I, 595), Zabāya (^{I}*za-ab-ba-a*, PBS 2/1 188:10), and Pappāya (^{I}*pap-pa-a-a*, a family name; see Wunsch 2014, 307).

Unaffiliated Names

Unaffiliated anthroponyms are mostly unexplained. Unlike the atypical names which can be classified by certain morphological patterns (notably reduplicated syllables), this category has no common denominator even on the purely formal level. Such early Neo-Babylonian names are Ḫušazakmu (^{I}*ḫu-šá-za*-AK-*mu*, Nielsen 2015, 140) which refers to a fugitive, Layyanmua (^{I}*la-a-a*-AN-*mu-a*, BRM 1 6:7), Indēšu (^{I}*in-de-e-šú*, BRM 1 29:11), Paratir? (^{I}*pára-tir-?*, BRM 1 34:8; see Nielsen 2015, 308), ^{f}Ribarmeš (^{f}*ri-bar*(-)meš, BRM 1 7:2), and Tukubenu (^{I}*tu-ku-be-nu*, Nielsen 2015, 386). Aqqunnušu (^{I}*aq-qu-un-nu-šú*) is recorded in an unpublished text (BM 30297 = Bertin 2542:13). ^{f}Manantāya (^{f}*ma-na-an-ta-a*), daughter of ^{f}Bēlessunu (*Nbn.* 75:15, 20), with the reading of the initial sign as *ma-*, looks like a rendering of Old Iranian **Vanantā-* 'victorious',[18] but, unlike Elamite, Neo- and Late Babylonian /*m*/ does not render Old Iranian /*v*/ in initial position, only V*m*V would do.

Other unaffiliated anthroponyms from the long sixth century BCE are, for instance, Ḫaraḫak (^{I}*ḫa-ra-ḫa*-AK, Pearce and Wunsch 2014, 54a), Kilaladia (^{I}⸢*ki*⸣*-la-la-di-iá*, Pearce and Wunsch 2014, 62b), Sinnašu (^{I}*si-in-šú*/⸢*si*?*-in-na-šu*⸣, Pearce and Wunsch 2014, 80a), and Rappari (^{I}*rap-pa-ri*), son of Gultam (^{I}*gu-ul-ta-mu*, BE 8/1 65:2; 73:2; 84:2). Pê-Bīt-Kuššu (^{I}*pe-*(*e-*)É-*ku-uš-šú*), son of

[18] Cf. **Vananta-* (masc., Tavernier 2007, 336–7, 4.2.1790).

Ṣaḫarturu (PBS 2/1 198:16, apparently with Bīt-Kuššu as theophoric element, in which case the name would denote 'By the command of Bīt-Kuššu'; cf. ^{I}*pe-e-*(É)*-ku-ú-šú* in TMH 2/3 188:6–7, l.e.), Basišuanaki (^{I}*ba-si-šú-a-na-ki*, BE 9 31:2, l.e. 27), B/Puk/qtâ (^{I}*b/puk/q-ta-a*) or Muk/qtâ (^{I}*muk/q-ta-a*, BE 9 66:8), and Ratla'iturû (^{I}*rat*$^{?}$*-la-*$^{?}$*-i-tu-ru-ú*, PBS 2/1 226:3, 4, 10, 11: [. . .]-$^{?}$) are recorded in the Murašû archive (late fifth century BCE).

Several peculiar names are recorded in the small onomastic dossier from the Babylonian harbour town of Dūr-Yakīn (early Neo-Babylonian) which had intense commercial links to Elam and eastern Arabia, if not beyond that; they may be explicable in West Semitic terms like the majority of the local onomasticon (cf. Zadok 2013, 267–8). Fortunately, the list of unexplained anthroponyms is not too long.

Gentilics As Personal Names

Gentilics used as anthroponyms in first-millennium Babylonia are Quttāya 'Gutian' (^{I}*qu-ut-ta-a-a*; not 'Cuthean', as understood by Pearce and Wunsch 2014, 77b–78a), Ukkāya '(Man) from Ukku' (^{I}*uk-ka-a-a*, *Dar.* 434:17; Ukku was located south of the Armenian plateau), Šarrukkāya 'Man from Dūr-Šarrukki' (^{I}LUGAL*-uk-ka-a-a*, Nielsen 2015, 366; this is a *gentilicium a posteriori*),[19] Kešāya 'Man from Keš' (^{I}*ke-šá-a-a*, PBS 2/1 43:5), Gub/māya 'Man from Gubbu(?)' (^{I}*gu-ba/ma-a-a*, Nielsen 2015, 134), Lik/qimmāya (^{I}*li-qí-im-ma-a-a*, Nielsen 2015, 191; perhaps based on West Semitic N-Q-M with dissimilation of liquids/nasals), ^{f}Kudāya$^{?}$itu (^{f}*ku-*DA*-a-a-i-tu*, Nielsen 2015, 178), and perhaps B/Madabarrāya (^{I}*ma-da-bar-ra-a-a*, Pearce and Wunsch 2014, 42a). The type is extant in Neo-Assyrian Karmesāya (^{I}kar*-me-sa-a-*[*a*], PNA 2/I 607, from Kirmese?), Nimarkāya (^{I}*ni-mar-ka-a-a*, PNA 2/II, 963), and Šamandāya (^{I}*šá-man/niš-da-a-a*, PNA 3/II, 1188).

References

Baker, H. D. (ed.) 2000. *The Prosopography of the Neo-Assyrian Empire*, 2/I: Ḫ–K. Helsinki: The Neo-Assyrian Text Corpus Project.

Baker, H. D. (ed.) 2001. *The Prosopography of the Neo-Assyrian Empire*, 2/II: L–N. Helsinki: The Neo-Assyrian Text Corpus Project.

Baker, H. D. (ed.) 2002. *The Prosopography of the Neo-Assyrian Empire*, 3/I: P–Ṣ. Helsinki: The Neo-Assyrian Text Corpus Project.

[19] Cf. the Middle Babylonian female name ^{f}Dūr-Šarru-kīn$^{?}$ītu ($^{f.⌜uru⌝}$BÀD.LUGAL.GI.NA*-a-a-i-ti*, MNA I, i 14; see Paulus 2014, 534).

Baker, H. D. 2004. *The Archive of the Nappāḫu Family*, Archiv für Orientforschung Beiheft 30. Vienna: Institut für Orientalistik der Universität Wien.

Baker, H. D. (ed.) 2011. *The Prosopography of the Neo-Assyrian Empire*, 3/II: Š–Z. Helsinki: The Neo-Assyrian Text Corpus Project.

Balkan, K. 1954. *Kassitenstudien I. Die Sprache der Kassiten*, American Oriental Series 37. New Haven: American Oriental Society.

Brinkman, J. A. 1998. 'Nazi-Maruttaš', *Reallexikon der Assyriologie und Vorderasiatische Archäologie* 9, 190–1.

Brinkman, J. A. 2006. 'The use of occupation names as patronyms in the Kassite period: a forerunner of Neo-Babylonian ancestral names?' in A. K. Guinan, M. deJ. Ellis, A. J. Ferrara, et al. (eds.), *If a Man Builds a Joyful House: Assyriological Studies in Honor of Erle Verdun Leichty*, Cuneiform Monographs 31. Leiden: Brill, pp. 23–43.

Dillard, R. B. 1975. Neo-Babylonian Texts from the John Frederick Lewis Collection of the Free Library of Philadelphia. PhD dissertation: Dropsie University, Philadelphia.

Hinz, W. and H. Koch 1987. *Elamisches Wörterbuch*, Archäologische Mitteilungen aus Iran, Ergänzungsband 17. Berlin: Dietrich Reimer.

Hölscher, M. 1996. *Die Personennamen der kassitenzeitlichen Texte aus Nippur*, Imgula 1. Münster: Rhema.

Jursa, M. 1995. *Die Landwirtschaft in Sippar in neubabylonischer Zeit*, Archiv für Orientforschung Beiheft 25. Vienna: Institut für Orientalistik der Universität Wien.

Laroche, E. 1966. *Les Noms des Hittites*, Études linguistiques 4. Paris: C. Klincksieck.

Nielsen, J. P. 2015. *Personal Names in Early Neo-Babylonian Legal and Administrative Tablets, 747-626 BCE*, NISABA 29. Winona Lake: Eisenbrauns.

Paulus, S. 2014. *Die babylonischen Kudurru-Inschriften von der kassitischen bis zur frühneubabylonischen Zeit untersucht unter besonderer Berücksichtigung gesellschafts- und rechtshistorischer Fragestellungen*, Alter Orient und Altes Testament 51. Münster: Ugarit-Verlag.

Pearce, L. E. and C. Wunsch 2014. *Documents of Judean Exiles and West Semites in Babylonia in the Collection of David Sofer*, Cornell University Studies in Assyriology and Sumerology 28. Bethesda: CDL Press.

Powell, M. A. 1972. 'Der neubabylonische Familienname ašgandu und die Urkundengruppe Nbn 314, TCL XIII 122, Nbn 668', *Archiv Orientální* 40, 124–9.

Radner, K. (ed.) 1998. *The Prosopography of the Neo-Assyrian Empire*, 1/I: A. Helsinki: The Neo-Assyrian Text Corpus Project.

Radner, K. (ed.) 1999. *The Prosopography of the Neo-Assyrian Empire*, 1/II: B–G. Helsinki: The Neo-Assyrian Text Corpus Project.

Richter, T. 2016. *Vorarbeiten zu einem hurritischen Namenbuch. Erster Teil: Personennamen altbabylonischer Überlieferung vom Mittleren Euphrat und aus dem nördlichen Mesopotamien*. Wiesbaden: Harrassowitz.

Salvini, M. 1993–7. 'Menua', *Reallexikon der Assyriologie und Vorderasiatische Archäologie* 8, 63–4.

Shaked, S., J. N. Ford, and S. Bhayro (with contributions from M. Morgenstern and N. Vilozny) 2013. *Aramaic Bowl Spells: Jewish Babylonian Aramaic Bowls*, 1. Leiden/Boston: Brill.

Streck, M. P. 2000. *Das amurritische Onomastikon der altbabylonischen Zeit. 1: Die Amurriter, die onomastische Forschung, Orthographie und Phonologie, Nominalphonologie*, Alter Orient und Altes Testament 271/1. Münster: Ugarit-Verlag.

Tallqvist, K. L. 1905. *Neubabylonisches Namenbuch zu den Geschäftsurkunden aus der Zeit des Šamaššumukîn bis Xerxes*, Acta Societatis Scientiarum Fennicae 32/2. Helsinki: Societas Litteraria Fennica.

Tavernier, J. 2007. *Iranica in the Achaemenid Period (ca. 550–330 BC). Lexicon of Old Iranian Proper Names and Loanwords, Attested in Non-Iranian Texts*, Orientalis Lovaniensia Analecta 158. Leuven: Peeters.

Waerzeggers, C. 2014. *Marduk-rēmanni: Local Networks and Imperial Politics in Achaemenid Babylonia*, Orientalis Lovaniensia Analecta 233. Leuven: Peeters.

Weidner, E. F. 1939. 'Jojachin, König von Juda, in babylonischen Keilschrifttexten' in *Mélanges Syriens offerts à M. René Dussaud, secrétaire perpétuel de l'Académie des inscriptions et belles-lettres, par ses amis et ses élèves II*, Bibliothèque archéologique et historique 30. Paris: Geuthner, 923–35, pls I–V.

Wunsch, C. 2000. *Das Egibi-Archiv: Die Felder und Garten*, 2 Vols, Cuneiform Monographs 20a and 20b. Groningen: Styx.

Wunsch, C. 2014. 'Babylonische Familiennamen' in M. Krebernik and H. Neumann (eds.), *Babylonien und seine Nachbarn in neu- und spätbabylonischer Zeit. Wissenschaftliches Kolloquium anlässlich des 75. Geburtstages von Prof. Dr. Joachim Oelsner, 2.-3. März 2007 in Jena*, Alter Orient und Altes Testament 369. Münster: Ugarit-Verlag, pp. 289–314.

Zadok, R. 1978. *On West Semites in Babylonia during the Chaldean and Achaemenian Periods: An Onomastic Study*. Tel Aviv: Wanaarta.

Zadok, R. 1979. 'On some foreign population groups in first-millennium Babylonia', *Tel Aviv* 6, 164–81.

Zadok, R. 1981. 'Arabians in Mesopotamia during the Late-Assyrian, Chaldean, Achaemenian and Hellenistic periods', *Zeitschrift der Deutschen Morgenländischen Gesellschaft* 131, 42–84.

Zadok, R. 1984. *The Elamite Onomasticon*, Supplemento n. 40 agli Annali dell'Istituto Orientale di Napoli 44. Naples: Istituto Universitario Orientale.

Zadok, R. 1999–2000. 'Review of M. Salvini 1996. *The Habiru prism of King Tunip-Teshup of Tikunani*', *Archiv für Orientforschung* 46–7, 351–8.

Zadok, R. 2013. 'The onomastics of the Chaldean, Aramean and Arabian tribes in Babylonia during the first millennium' in A. Berlejung and M. P. Streck (eds.), *Arameans, Chaldeans, and Arabs in Babylonian and Palestine in the First Millennium BC*, Leipziger Altorientalische Studien 3. Wiesbaden: Harrassowitz, pp. 261–336.

Zadok, R. 2018. 'People from countries west and north of Babylonia in Babylon during the reign of Nebuchadnezzar II', *Hebrew Bible and Ancient Israel* 7, 112–29.

Male names and persons

*[. . .]zāta-, 244, 250
ˀAḫīqam, 161
ˀAḫīqar, 151, 161, 278
ˀAṣīl-Yāma, 144, 149
ˀAškōlā, 151
ˀbˁll, 170
ˀbḥll, 170
ˀElqānāh, 160
ˀḥˀb, 172
ˀḥˀm, 172
ˀOhŏlîˀāb, 160
ˀrš, 176
ˀUhl(ī)-Yāma, 145, 160
ˀŪr-Milk(i), 145, 154
ˀwšˁ, 140
ˀwšˁyh, 140
ˁAbd(i)-Yāḫû, 153, 157
ˁAbd-kulāl, 189
ˁAbd-śams, 189
ˁAmru, 188
ˁAq(a)b-Yāma, 146, 150
ˁAqb(ī)-Yāma, 159
ˁAqqūb, 151
ˁAqūb, 151
ˁAt(a)l-Yāma, 150
ˁAzar-Yāma, 144, 145
ˁAz(a)z-Yāma, 150
ˁbdḥmn, 172
ˁbdkllm, 189
ˁbdmlk, 172
ˁEdrā, 87
ˁUzzāya, 145
ˁUzzīyāh(û), 159
ˁzry, 175

Aba, 218
Ababa, 218
Abāya, 200
Abdā, 132
Abdia, 176
Abdi-Esi, 202, 207
Abdi-Iššar, 132
Abdu-Ḫmūnu, 172, 179
Abdu-Milki, 172
Abdūnu, 174
Ab-ḫalalu, 170
Abi-abi, 21
Abī-ḫazumu, 191
Abī-ilaḫī, 128, 131
Abī-ilāya, 128
Abī-lūmur, 31
Abī-râm, 87, 174
*Abisaukā-, 243
Abī-ul-īde, 31
Abī-ul-(t)īde, 99
Abi-ummi-aqar, 43
Abnī, 132
Abraham, 141
*Abṛta-, 244
Abši-Ešu, 116
Abu-Enlil-dāri-libūr, 43
Abu-lētī, 131
Abunāya, 73
Abunu, 21
Abu-nūr, 87
Abu-ul-īde, 43
Ada, 218
Adad-Būr, 129
Adad-dayyānu, 44
Adad-natan, 128
Adad-šikinī, 131
Adbi-il, 191
Adda-ten, 260
Addu-rapā, 128
Addu-yatin, 86, 131
Adūmê, 176
Agathoklēs, 227
Agāya, 289
*Agnifarnah-, 242, 245, 250
Aḫ-ˀabi, 172
Aḫ-abia, 21
Aḫḫē-iddin-Marduk, 100

Aḫḫē-lūmur, 44
Aḫ(ḫ)ūtu, 53
Aḫḫū-ṭābu, 207
Aḫi-abū, 132
Aḫī-šadi-ili, 44
Aḫšeti, 32
Aḫu-ālu-uṣur, 42
Aḫu-dūru, 44
Aḫu-iddin, 97
Aḫu-iddin-Marduk, 100
Aḫu-kî-Sîn, 44
Aḫu-lakun, 87, 131
Aḫu-līšir, 97
Aḫu-lūmur, 97
Aḫūšunu, 19, 33, 59
Aia-mātu-taqqin, 113
Aia-Mitūnu, 172
Alexander, 6, 32, 194, 224, 230, 232, 252
Alexandros, 227, 232
Alexippos, 227
Ālu-lūmur, 44
*Amâ-, 244
*Amadāta-, 242
Amanūnu, 175
*Amatavāta-, 250
Amba-ziniza, 269
Amedirra, 269
Amīl-Marduk, 27, 250
Amīl-Nanāya, 45
Ammēni-ilī, 44
Amnapi, 201, 207
*Āmṛda-, 243
Amukānu, 75
Amunu-tabunaḫti, 207
Amurru-ēṭir, 46
Amurru-šamaʕ, 145, 146
Amurru-šarru-uṣur, 82, 89
Amušeḫ (*see also* Hawšiʕ, Hosea, Hôšēʕa), 146
Amutu, 201
Ana, 218
Ana-Bēl-atkal, 43
Ana-Bēl-ēreš, 49, 50
(Ana-)DN-ēreš(šu), 97
Ana-muḫḫi-DN-āmur, 98
Anana(/i/u), 218
Andronikos, 227
Anḫapu, 207
Antigenēs, 227
Antiochos, 227, 232
Antipatros, 227
Anu-iddin, 39
Anu-šarru-uṣur, 88
Anu-uballiṭ, 225, 233
Anu-zēru-iddin, 231
Apkallu, 67
Aplāya, 54, 55
Aplu-iddin, 42
Aplu-uṣur, 97
Apollodōros, 226
Apollōnios, 226
Apōllonidēs, 226
Appuwašu, 214, 216
Aqab-il, 130
Aqqunnušu, 289
Aqru, 67
Arad-Bēl, 19, 88
Arad-Egalmaḫ, 26
Arad-Erua, 66
Arad-Gula, 158
Arad-ili-rabî, 45
Arad-Marduk, 54
Arad-Nergal, 45, 275
Arad-Zarpanītu, 66
*Ārāšta-, 243
Arbailāiu, 116
*Arbamihra-, 242, 245
*Arbamiθra-, 242, 250
*Arbarēva-, 250
Archelaos, 227
Archias, 227
Ardia, 54
Ardi-Aššu, 115
Ardi-Eššu, 115
Ariḫ, 147, 160, 161
Aristeus, 227
Aristoklēs, 227
Aristokratēs, 227
Aristōn, 227
Arisus, 176
Arīšu, 176
*Armaka-, 250
Arma-nāni, 219
Arma-Tarḫunta, 219
*Ārmati-, 250
Arma-ziti, 219
Arrab(t)u, 47
Arrakūtu, 47
Artabara, 153
Artaḫšar, 153
Artareme (*see also* *Ṛtarēva-), 251
Artarios, 250, 251
Artemidōros, 226, 227, 233
*Aryapā-, 252
Aryāramna-, 246
*Aryaušta-, 246
*Aspâ-, 244
Aspacanah-, 243, 246
*Aspaka-, 244
*Aspastāna-, 246, 252
*Aspazanta-, 248

*Astašēbarva-, 243
Astyages (*see also* Ištumegu), 239, 241
*Āsuraθa-, 243
Aṣûšu-namir, 28
Ašarēdu, 47, 53
Ašid-rummu, 172
Aššur-ālik-pāni, 110
Aššur-bēlu-uṣur, 110
Aššur-dannu, 110
Aššur-etel-šamê-erṣeti-muballissu, 38
Aššur-ēṭir, 110, 114
Aššur-ilāʾī, 110
Aššur-mātu-taqqin, 113
Aštartu-šēzib, 173, 176, 178
Atam-artais, 201
Ātanaḫ, 97
Ātanaḫ-DN, 97
Athēnodōros, 226, 227
Athēnophilos, 226, 227
*Atikāma-, 243
Atkal-ana-Marduk, 29
Atmanu (*see also* Atta-menu), 270
*Ātṛbānu-, 245
*Ātṛciθra-, 245
*Ātṛfarnah-, 245, 246
*Āθrina-, 244
Atta-luš, 260
Atta-menu (*see also* Atmanu), 270
Attar-ramât, 129
*Aujah-, 241
Aya-abū, 132
Aya-aḫu, 44
Aya-rimî, 75
Ayy-mitūnu, 172
Azabtī-il, 170
Aza-tiwada, 220

Bʿlytn, 168, 169
Bʿlrm, 172
Baal-rūm, 172
Bābilāya, 47
Bābu-alsiki-abluṭ, 43
B/Madabarrāya, 290
*Badrapārsa-, 246
Bâd-Yāma, 150
*Bagâ-, 244, 245
Bagābigna-, 245
Bagabuxša-, 242, 245
*Bagadāta-, Bagadāta, 203, 242, 243, 245, 248
*Bagadēna-, 250
*Bagā(h)uvīra-, 243
*Bagakāma-, 246
*Bagakāna-, 247
*Bagaina-, 244
*Bagāma-, 242
*Bagamihra-, 242, 245
*Bagapāta-, 242, 248
*Bagapitā, 248
*Bagasravā, 248
*Bagavanta-, 248
*Bagavinda-, 245
*Bagayāza-, 250
Bagazuštu, 195, 197
Baḫiriru (*see also* Maḫiriru), 288
Balāssu, 46, 95
Balāṭāya, 95
Balāṭu, 19, 41, 50, 51, 96, 101
Balīḫāya, 47
Balīḫû, 47
Baltam(mu), 189
*Bāmu-, 241
Banānu, 270
Banā-Yāma, 151, 158
Banī, 95, 127
Bānia, 54, 95, 127, 151, 158
Bānītu-iddin, 59
Banūnu, 47
Bānûnu, 47, 95
Barbaru, 47
Barak-Yāma, 144
Barik-Bēl, 132
Barikī, 132
Barik-il, 128
Barīk-Yāma, 144, 153, 154
Basišuanaki, 290
Batūlu, 47
Bayt-Il-šarru-uṣur, 82, 87
Bazizi, 287
*Bāzubaga-, 242, 245
Bazuzu, 38, 251, 287
Bēl-aḫu-ittannu, 52
Bēl-ammēni, 44
Bēl-bullissu, 251
Bēl-dannu, 43
Bēl-ēdu-uṣur, 29
Bēl-ēreš, 49, 50
Bēl-eṭēri, 46
Bēl-eṭēri-Nabû, 46
Bēl-ēṭir, 152, 175
Bēl-ibni, 75, 252, 259, 265, 269, 270
Bēl-iddin, 39
Bēl-ina-kāri-lūmur, 44
Bēl-ina-nakutti-alsika, 43
Bēl-iqbi, 84
Bēl-išdīa-ukīn, 30
Bēl-ittannu, 52, 251
Bēl-lēʾi, 286
Bēl-paṭēsu, 202
Bēl-rēmanni, 33
Bēl-šarru-uṣur, 27, 85, 158

Bēl-šimânni, 27
Bēlšunu, 50, 118, 251
Belteshazzar, 17
Bēltu-šarru-uṣur, 157
Bēl-uballiṭ, 176
Bēl-usātu, 44, 46
Bēl-yatūnu, 169
Benjamin, 141
Binān, 132
Bīt-Ašarra-šarru-uṣur, 82
Bīt-il-adar, 128
Bīt-il-dilinī, 122
Bīt-il-ḫanna, 128
Bīt-il-ḫisnī, 128
Bīt-Irʾanni-šarru-uṣur, 82
*Bṛziya-, 239, 244
B/Puk/qtâ, 290
Būr-Adad, 45, 129
Burāšu, 47, 63
Buwa, 289

Cambyses, 27, 162, 172, 182, 194, 197, 217, 239
Cincaxri-, 242
Cincaxriš, 240, 242, 249
*Ciθrabṛzana-, 243
*Ciθrantaxma-, 249
Cyaxares, 239

Dābibī, 46
Dādia, 53, 55, 177
Dādṛši-, 241
Dādṛšiš, 239
Dagal-Yāma, 153
Dagān-šarru-uṣur, 82
Daha-, 246
Daḫīr-il, 191
Dalatānī, 130
Dalīli-Eššu, 115
Damqāya, 67
Damqia, 95
Damqu, 42, 67
Dān-Eššu, 115
Dān-Ešu, 116
Dannāya, 154
*Dāraya-, 242
*Dātafarnā, 248
*Davantāna-, 248
Dayyān-Marduk, 77
Dayyānu, 48
*Dēfrāda-, 251
Demetrios, 6, 226, 227, 232
Dēmokratēs, 227
Diodōros, 227
Diogenēs, 227
Dioklēs, 227
Dionysia, 226, 233
Diophanēs, 226, 228
Diophantos, 226, 233
DN-aḫḫē-lūmur, 97
(DN-)aḫḫē-šullim, 104
(DN-)aḫu-bulliṭ, 104
DN-aḫu-iddin, 97
DN-aḫu-ittannu, 97
DN-ālik-pāni, 105
DN-amāt-šarri-uṣur, 82
DN-balāṭ-šarri-iqbi, 82, 88
DN-balāṭ-šarri-uṣur, 82
DN-balliṭ, 117
DN-banā, 127
DN-erība, 102
DN-ēṭir, 102
DN-ēṭir-napištī, 102
DN-ibni, 101
DN-iddin, 37, 97, 102
DN-iqbi, 101
DN-iqīša, 96, 101, 103
DN-iškun, 101
DN-ittannu, 97
DN-itti-šarri, 82
DN-kāṣir, 102
DN-kibsī-šarri-uṣur, 82
DN-kīn-šarrūssu, 83
DN-kīnu-uṣur, 98, 105
DN-kittu-irâm, 99
(DN-)kudurru-uṣur, 104
DN-lēʾû, 102
DN-linṭar, 131
DN-līšir, 97, 102
DN-lūmur, 102
DN-mār-šarri-uṣur, 83, 88
DN-mātu-taqqin, 113
(DN-)mātu-tuqqin, 104
DN-mukīn-apli, 105
DN-naʾid, 97
DN-nādin, 97
DN-nādin-aḫi, 97
DN-nāṣir, 97, 101, 102
DN-nāṣir-aḫi, 97
DN-natan, 127
DN-qajalu-išemme, 99
(DN-)qātēšu-ṣabat, 104
DN-rāʾim-šarri, 82
DN-šarru-bulliṭ, 82
DN-šarru-ibni, 82
DN-šarrūssu-ukīn, 83, 88
DN-šarru-ukīn, 82
DN-šarru-uṣur, 81, 82, 169
DN-šarru-utēr, 82
DN-šukun-rēmu, 100
DN-šul(l)um-šarri, 82

DN-šumu-līšir, 97
DN-šumu-ukīn, 98
DN-šumu-uṣur, 97, 103
DN-šūzubu-ile??i, 97
DN-tāriṣ, 102
DN-tattannu, 97
DN-tattannu-uṣur, 97
DN-tultabši-līšir, 97
DN-uballiṭ, 102
DN-udammiq, 102
DN-ukīn, 102
DN-upāq, 97
DN-uṣalli, 98
DN-uṣur, 101
DN-uṣuranni, 97
DN-uṣuršu, 97
DN-ušabši, 101
DN-ušallim, 102, 104
DN-ušēzib, 102
DN-utīr, 101
DN-zuqup-kīnu, 100
Dullupu, 47
Dummuqu, 47, 67
Dūrāya, 174

Ea-iddin, 39
Ea-mušallim, 93, 94
Eanna-iddin, 26
Eanna-līpī-uṣur, 26
Eanna-nādin-šumi, 26
Eanna-šarru-uṣur, 82, 88
Eašarra-šarru-uṣur, 82
Ea-šarru-bulliṭ, 88
Ea-ušallim, 93, 94
Ea-zēru-iqīša, 75
Ebabbar-šadûnu, 26
Ekur-šumu-ušarši, 73
Enlil-balāssu-iqbi, 46
Enlil-kidin, 44
Enlil-māku-pitin, 29
Enlil-supê-muḫur, 30
En-nigaldi-Nanna, 274
Erēbšu, 96
Erība-Aššur, 174
Erība-DN, 103, 117
Erība-Enlil, 43
Erībāya, 54, 94, 95
Esagil-amassu, 26
Esagil-kīn-apli, 278
Esagil-šadûnu, 26
Esagil-šarru-uṣur, 82
Ēšâ, 116
Eša-rṭeše, 116
Ēṭirāya, 96
Ēṭiru, 46
Eulmaš-šākin-šumi, 73
Ezida-šumu-ibni, 52
Ezra, 141

*Farnahuvara-, 245
*Farnaka-, 272
*Farnaini-, 244
Frāda-, 242
*Fradāta-, 242, 249
*Fratama-, 249
Fravarti-, 249

Gabbi-(ilāni)-bēlu-uṣur, 29
Gabbi-ilī-šarru-uṣur, 82, 87
Gadal-Yāma, 179
Gadû, 30
Gaggū, 289
Gaubar(u)va-, 243, 246, 248
Gaumāta-, 244, 46
*Gauniya-, 252
*Gausūri-, 244
Giddâ, 178
Gigīya, 288
Gilūa, 285
Gimil-DN, 103
Gimil-Gula, 46
Gimil-Nergal, 46
Gimillu, 21, 46, 101
Gīr-Yāma, 139
Gubāru, 33
Gub/māya, 290
Gubbanu(?)-Eššu, 115
Gudādû, 188
Gula-zēru-ibni, 59
Gultam, 289
*Gundaini-, 244
Gūsāya, 170
Gušam, 188
Gūzu-ina-Bēl-aṣbat, 30
Gūzūnu, 176

*Hadābāga-, 243, 277
*Hambāzu-, 269
*Hantu(h)ma-, 243
*Haθēbaga-, 242
*Haθya-, 244
*Haθyabaga-, 245
*Haθya-Bēl, 244
*Haθyāna-, 244
Hawšiˁ (*see also* Amušeḫ, Hosea, Hôšēˁa), 140, 142, 144, 145, 146, 149, 151, 160, 161
Hawšiˁ-Yāma, 145
Haxāmani-, 243
*Haxiyabānu-, 250
Heliodōros, 226, 227

Hephaistiōn, 226
Herakleidēs, 226, 233
Herotheos, 226, 227
*Hinduka-, 246
Hipponikos, 227
Hosea (*see also* Amušeḫ, Hawšiˁ, Hôšēˁa), 146
Hôšēˁa (*see also* Amušeḫ, Hawšiˁ, Hosea), 146
Hōšiˁ-Yāma, 145
Huban-haltaš, 260, 266
Huban-menanu (*see also* Menanu), 263
Huban-nikaš, 266, 269
(Huban)-untaš, 269
*(H)ufrata-, 243
*Humāta-, 243, 247
*Humēca-, 244
*(H)urauda-, 252
*(H)urāna-, 243
*(H)uvardāta-, 249
*(H)uvārava-, 244
Hwšˁl, 141
Ḥaggay, 141, 151, 161
Ḥăkalyāh, 159
Ḥanan(nī), 151, 152
Ḥannān(ī/ia), 151, 152
Ḥanūn-Yāma, 149
Ḥēlem, 146
Ḥēn, 160
Ḥillumūt, 151
Ḫaddāya, 67
Ḫaḫḫuru, 47
Ḫairān, 190
Ḫalabesu, 267
Ḫallušu, 267
Ḫallušu-Inšušinak, 267, 270
Ḫallutuš-Inšušinak, 263
Ḫalpa-mu, 220
Ḫalpa-muwa, 219
Ḫalpa-runtiya, 219
Ḫalpa-wasu, 220
Ḫalpa-ziti, 219
Ḫamadinnu, 202
Ḫammurapi, 278, 279, 286
Ḫan(n)an(u), 68
Ḫannatānī, 151
Ḫantili, 218
Ḫanṭušu, 179
Ḫanūnu, 32
Ḫaraḫak, 289
Ḫaraṣīnu, 176
Ḫarimā, 132
Ḫāriṣānu, 31
Ḫar-maṣu, 196, 197, 207, 209
Ḫarsisi, 200
Ḫaru-Ṣapūnu, 167, 173
Ḫašb-ilīm, 170
Ḫattušili, 219
Ḫazā-il, 128
Ḫazannu, 48
Ḫubaba, 287
Ḫuḫuḫi, 288
Ḫupišnuman, 219
Ḫur-ši-Ēšu, 116
Ḫūru, 200
Ḫušazakmu, 289

Ibnāya, 121
Ibni-DN, 103
Ibni-Ištar, 43
Idā-DN, 131
Idā-Nabû, 131
Iddia, 54
Iddināya, 20, 54, 87, 173, 177, 251
Iddin-DN, 97, 103
Iddin-Marduk, 42, 58
Iddin-Nabû, 21, 24, 54, 87, 173, 177, 251
Iddin-Šīḫu, 285
Iddinunu, 95
Igigi, 38, 287
*Ildāta-, 244
Iltabiya, 250
Il-ta-ma-mu, 87
Iltar-gadā, 129, 132
Iltehr-hanan, 87
Iltehr-idrī, 129
Iltehr-naqī, 131
Il-yadīn, 153, 251
Imba-dara?, 260
Ina-Esagil-mukīn-apli, 26
Ina-Esagil-šarru-uṣur, 82
Ina-Esagil-šumu-ibni, 26
Ina-Esagil-zēri, 26
Inaḫarû, 205
Ina-nemēli-kitti-ibašši, 31
Ina-qātē-bēli-lumḫur, 29
Ina-qātē-Nabû-bulṭu, 30
Ina-qibīt-DN-azziz, 98
Ina-ṣilli-Bēl, 83
Ina-ṣilli-Bīt-Akītu, 30
Ina-ṣilli-Eanna, 26
Ina-ṣilli-Esagil, 46
Ina-ṣilli-Nanāya, 177
Ina-ṣilli-šarri, 46, 83
Ina-tēšî-eṭir, 49, 50
Indabibi, 269
Indēšu, 289
Innin-šarru-uṣur, 85
Innû, 289
Iqbi-DN, 103
Iqīša-DN, 103, 104
Iqīša-Marduk, 54

Iqīšāya, 54, 95, 167
Irâš-ana-Akītu, 99
Irâš-ana-Esagil, 99
Isaiah, 139
*Īsgu-, 246, 250
Isidōros, 226, 227
Isitheos, 226, 227
Išbi-Erra-dannam-nādā, 81
Išrib-Yāma, 149
Iššar-dābibī-nēr, 46
Iššar-tarībi, 129
Ištar-ḫundu, 260, 264
Ištar-lēʾi, 43
Ištumegu (*see also* Astyages), 241
Ittannu-DN, 97
Itti-Bēl-abni, 251
Itti-Bēl-šarru-limmir, 82
Itti-Bēl-šarru-lūmur, 85
(Itti-)DN-balāṭu/ssu, 45, 97
Itti-DN-šarru-lūmur, 82
Itti-Eanna-būdia, 26
Itti-Marduk-balāṭu, 51, 55, 83
Itti-Nabû-balāṭu, 50, 51, 178
Itti-Nabû-īnīa, 83
Itti-Nusku-īnīa, 50
Itti-Šamaš-balāṭu, 50
Itti-šarri-balāṭu, 83
Itti-šarri-būnu, 83
Itti-šarri-īnīa, 83, 168, 169
Izirî, 175

Jacob, 141
*Jāmāspa-, 243
Jehoiachin (*see also* Yāḫû-kīn, Yəhôyākîn), 145, 147, 160
*Jīvaka-

Kadašman-Enlil, 285
*Kāka-, 241
Kalbāya, 19
Kalbi-Bābu, 45
Kallilû, 189
Kalūmu, 47
*Kāmaka-, 246
Kamuš-il, 179
Kamuš-šarru-uṣur, 178
Karmesāya, 290
Kāṣir, 96
Kaššâ, 167
Kaššû-šumu-iddin, 286
Kephalōn, 226, 227
Kešāya, 290
Kidin-Anu, 228
Kidin-Sîn, 46
Kikê, 214
Kikki, 218
Kilaladia, 289
Kiligug, 286
Kīnāya, 67, 95, 174
Kinūnāya, 47
Kīn-Yāma, 144
Kiribti-Marduk, 51
Kiribtu, 51
Kiruru, 287
Kiṣir-DN, 118
Kiṣir-Eššu, 115
*Kṛgaya-, 244
*Kṛgu-, 241
*Kṛmāniya-, 246, 252
*Kṛtaka-, 251
Kubburu, 33
Kukkunni, 218
Kulbību, 47
Kulūlu, 287
Kurigalzu, 23, 28, 72, 286
Kusisî, 288
Kuṣura, 153
Kutur (*see also* Kutur-Nahhunte), 264
Kutur-Nahhunte (*see also* Kutur), 263, 264

Lâbâši, 50, 231, 251
Lâbâši(-DN), 99
Lâbâši-Marduk, 27, 50
Lâbâši-Sîn, 50
Lala, 218
Lalê-Esagil-lušbi, 84
Lalê-šarri-lušbi, 83, 84
Layyanmua, 289
Lētka-idi-Zarpanītu, 100
Libluṭ, 51
Līdānu, 47
Lik/qimmāya, 290
Līšir, 94, 97
Lukšu, 219
Lūmur-pāni-Marduk-itti-balāṭu, 38
Lūṣi-ana-nūr-DN, 97
Lūṣi-ana-nūr-Marduk, 44, 53, 99
Luttûa, 289

Maˁśēh-Yāma, 144
M/Badabarrāya, 290
Madānu-bēlu-uṣur, 29
Maḫiriru (*see also* Baḫiriru), 288
Mal(a)k-Yāma, 150
Mamma-kî-Ezida, 44
Mamma-kî-šarri, 44
Manānu, 270
Mannu-(a)kî-Arbail, 116
Mannu-akî-bīt-Aššur, 114
Mannu-(a)kî-DN/GN/TN, 140

Mannu-akî-Nabû, 83
Mannu-akî-šarri, 83
Mannu-izkur, 44
Mannu-kî-ḫāl, 132
Mannu-kî-ilaḫī, 128
Mannu-kî-Nanāya, 44
*Manuštāna-, 251
Marduk-(aplu-)iddin, 68
Marduk-ibni, 175, 251
Marduk-nāṣir-apli, 55
Marduk-šumu-iddin, 52
Marduk-zākir-šumi, 72
Marḫarpu, 195
Mār-šarri-ilūʾa, 84
*Marza-, 250
*Masišta-, 241
Maše-Emūn, 87
Mattania, 151
Mattannāya, 177
Mattanu, 177
Mattan-Yāma, 142, 153
*Mazdaica-, 244
*Mazduka-, 249
Menahem, 141
Menandros, 227
Menanu (*see also* Huban-menanu), 263
Menashe, 141
Menodōros, 227
Menophilos, 227
Menostanes, 250
Menua, 287
Mesimesi, 228
Metrodōros, 228
Mī-kā-Yāma, 150, 152
Milki-izirî, 171
Milki-rām, 87, 172
Milkūmu-šarru-uṣur, 5, 82, 179
Minaššê, 177
Minua, 287
Mīnu-ēpuš, 95
Mīnu-ēpuš-ilī, 20, 44, 98
Miṣirāya, 73
*Miθra-abūa-, 244
*Miθradāta-, 242, 245, 248, 252
*Miθrapāna-, 242, 245
*Miθravasa-, 12, 242
*Miθraya-, 244
*Miθrāta-, 244, 248, 252
*Miθrâ-, 244
Mlkyʿzr, 171
Mlqrtʿzr, 171
Mnšy, 177
Mohammad, 187
*Mṛdu-, 241
Msms, 288
Mudammiq-DN, 102
Mukīn-DN, 97, 102
Muk/qtâ, 290
Mulili, 218
Multēširu, 97
Munaḫḫiš-Marduk, 55
Munaššê, 173, 177
Mūrānu, 47
Murašû, 24, 47
Murmura, 218
Mušallam, 154
Mušallim-DN, 102
Mušebši, 94
Mušebši-DN, 103
Mušēzib-DN, 103
Mut-Dagan, 286
Muwa, 218
Muwattalli, 218
Myrtolos, 228

Naʾdi-Šīḫu, 285
Naʾid-bēlanu, 75
*Nababṛzana-Nabān, 252
Nabê-ṣīru, 167, 173
Nabonidus, 27, 28, 85, 180, 186, 274
Nabû-alsika-abluṭ, 30
Nabû-alsi-ul-abāš, 33
Nabû-alsi-ul-āmur, 30
Nabû-aplu-iddin, 73
Nabû-aplu-uṣur, 19, 27
Nabû-ayyālu, 30
Nabû-bān-aḫi, 54
Nabû-bān-zēri, 21
Nabû-bēlšunu, 50
Nabû-bēl-usāti, 46
Nabû-būnu-šūtur, 83
Nabû-dilinī, 131
Nabû-dūr-ēdi, 29, 84
Nabû-ezrī, 22
Nabû-gabbi-ileʾʾi, 30
Nabû-iddin, 33, 39, 52
Nabû-ikṣur, 250
Nabû-iltala, 87
Nabû-ina-Esagil-lūmur, 44
Nabû-ina-kāri-lūmur, 99
Nabû-ina-tēšî-eṭir, 49
Nabû-ittannu, 55
Nabû-itti-ēdi-alik, 99
Nabû-itti-šarri, 85
Nabû-killanni, 30
Nabû-kudurru-uṣur, 21
Nabû-lū-salim, 30
Nabû-maqtu-idekke, 99
Nabû-mātu-taqqin, 113
Nabû-mītu-uballiṭ, 33, 83

Nabû-mutīr-gimilli, 46
Nabû-naˀid, 27
Nabû-nādin-aḫḫē, 72
Nabû-nādin-aḫi, 52
Nabû-nādin-šumi, 43, 52, 73
Nabû-nāṣir, 174
Nabû-natan, 122
Nabû-nūrka-lūmur, 44
Nabû-rapaˀ, 87
Nabû-rēmuˀa, 30
Nabû-šarrūssu-ukīn, 87
Nabû-šarru-uṣur, 85, 87, 88
Nabû-šukun-rēmu, 100
Nabû-šumu-iddin, 20, 43, 52, 105
Nabû-šumu-ukīn, 52
Nabû-šumu-uṣur, 19, 51
Nabû-tabni-šuklil, 69
Nabû-tabni-uṣur, 54
Nabû-talīmu-uṣur, 46
Nabû-ukīn, 84
Nabû-uṣur-napištī, 100
Nabû-uṣuršu, 51
Nabû-zabad, 130
Nabû-zēr-kitti-līšir, 43
Nabû-zēru-ibni, 75
Nabû-zēru-līšir, 23
Nabû-zuqup-kīnu, 100
Nadāya, 95
Nādin-aḫi, 52, 53, 55, 95, 97
Nadin-DN, 97
Nādinu, 52, 53, 55, 95, 97
Nadnāya, 97
*Nāfēna-, 244
Naḫḫūm, 151
Naḥimāya, 151
Naḥim-Yāma, 151
Naḥūm, 151
Namarī, 132
Nana, 218
Nanāya-dūrī, 131
Nanāya-uṣalli, 43
Nanni, 289
Nannia, 289
Nannûtu, 289
Naraggu, 287
Narām-Sîn, 28
*Naryābigna-, 251
Naṣir-DN, 97
Nāṣiru, 97
Natūn, 251
Nāṭi-Yāma, 149
Nazi-Marduk, 286
Nazi-Maruttaš, 286
Nazīya, 285
Nəḥemyāh, 149
Nenê, 287
Nenēa, 287
Nergal-aḫu-ittannu, 251
Nergal-ašarēdu, 53, 55
Nergal-ina-tēšî-eṭir, 43, 49, 50, 99
Nergal-rēṣûa, 30
Nergal-šarru-uṣur, 87
Nergal-tēšî-ēṭir, 49
Nergal-ušēzib, 53, 55
Nerikkaili, 219
Nia, 289
Nidintāya, 95
Nidinti-Anu, 45
Nidinti-Bēl, 51, 251
Nidinti-DN, 97
Nidinti-Marduk, 51
Nidinti-Šamaš, 251
Nidintu, 51, 55, 59, 95, 97, 172
Nikanōr, 227, 252
Nikarchos, 227, 233
Nikēratos, 227
Nikolaos, 227, 233
Nimarkāya, 290
Nīrāya, 151
Nīr(ī)-Yāma, 151, 153, 161
Nisḫur-DN, 103
Niya, 218
Nubāya, 151, 153, 161
Nuḫšānu, 67
Nummuru, 47
Nūnāya, 288
Nūr-Bēl-lūmur, 54
Nūr-DN, 103
Nūrea, 54, 96
Nūr?-gumê, 167
Nūrzānu, 86
Nusku-iddin, 23
Nusku-īnīa, 50
Nusku-rapē, 131

Pā, 228
Paḫatarê, 200
Pakaštu, 286
Pal(a)ṭay, 152
Palulu, 218
Pamūnu, 251
Pāni-Aššur-lāmur, 117
Pāni-Bēl-lāmur, 117
Pāni-Sîn-lūmur, 44
Pappāya, 289
Papsukkal-ša-iqbû-ul-īni, 38
Parˁōš, 145, 152
Paratir?, 289
Pariya-muwa, 219
*Parnu-, 241

*Paršava-, 244
Partammu, 32
*Parθava-, 246
Parysatis, 153
Pasia, 87
Pati-Esi, 200, 203
Patimḫa, 208
*Patināša-, 243
Patroklēs, 227
Paṭuastu, 207
Paṭumunu, 201
*Paurušāti-, 246
Pê-Bīt-Kuššu, 289
Philinos, 227
Philippos, 227, 232
Philos, 227, 231
Piḫa, 218
Piḫammi, 218
Piḫa-muwa, 219
Pirʾu, 52
Pisamiski, 208
Poseidōnios, 12, 226, 228
Psamtek, 5, 202, 203
Puḫḫuru, 53
Puk/qtâ, 290
Pupuli, 218
Puršû, 53, 55
Puwa, 218

Qanā-Yāma, 160
Qazizi, 287
Qēlāyāh, 149
Qī-lā-Yāma, 149, 159
Qīšti-DN, 104
Qīšti-Marduk, 45
Quttāya, 290
Qwhlʾl, 149

Raḫimī, 132
Raḫim-il, 128
Rakal, 250
Rammān-(mu)kīn-apli, 173
Rammān-šarru-uṣur, 173
Râmûa, 95
Rapaʾ-Yāma, 144, 145, 152, 161
Rappari, 289
Ratlaʾiturû, 290
*Raudaka-, 244
*Rauxšnapāta-, 242
*Razmahuarga-, 243
*Razmārva-, 249
*Raznamiθra-, 245
Reḫīm-Adad, 200
Rēmanni-Marduk, 72
Rēmu-šukun, 30
Rēmūt-Bābu, 46
Rēmūtu, 151
Rībātu, 46
Rīb(i)-DN, 117
Riḫat-Anu, 233
Ṛšāma-, 243, 272, 276
*Ṛšan-, 242, 246
*Ṛšita-, 244, 246, 250
*Ṛtâ-, 244, 245
*Ṛta-b-a-, 244
*Ṛtabara-, 250
*Ṛtabāna-, 245
*Ṛtabānu-, 242, 247
*Ṛtā(h)umanā, 240, 243
*Ṛtapātacā-, 244
*Ṛtarēva- (*see also* Artareme), 242, 251
Ṛtavardiya-, 240
*Ṛtavarziya-, 240
*Ṛtaviša-, 242
Ṛtaxšaça-, 245
*Ṛtaxšara-, 251
*Ṛta-xš-ara-, 244
*Ṛta-xš-ī-, 244
*Ṛtaya-, 252
*Ṛtima-, 244
*Ṛtuka-, 244

*Sakita-, 244
Samakāya, 151
Samak-Yāma, 151, 152, 161
Samannapir, 204
Sanda-mu, 220
Sarmâ, 219
*Satamēša-, 249
Satūr, 151
Seleucos, 227, 232
Sēpi, 207
Silim-Bābu, 59
Sîn-banā, 130
Sîn-kī-Nabû, 44
Sinnašu, 289
Sinqa-Eššu, 115
Sinqi-DN, 118
Sîn-qitri, 172, 178
Sîn-rīmanni-aḫu, 100
Sîn-šarru-uṣur, 87
Sîn-tabni-uṣur, 43
Siptaʾ, 208
Siptaḫu, 208
*Skudrava-, 246
Sōkin, 176
Sōsandros, 227
*Spitāma-, 249
*Sravanta-, 248
Stratōn, 227, 228

*Stūnā-, 249
Sūkinni, 176
Sukkuku, 67
Sulāya, 31
Sūqāya, 31, 173
*Suxra-, 240, 241
Ṣaḫarturu, 290
Ṣalam-šarri-iqbi, 83, 84
Ṣid(i)q-Yāma, 150
Ṣidqi-Yāma, 150
Ṣidqī-Yāma, 150
Ṣiḫā, 176
Ṣī-Ḫūru, 201
Ṣplyh, 159
Ṣūʾa, 289
Ṣūlūa, 177
Ṣūrāya, 166, 178, 180
Šabbātay, 141, 152
Šabbû, 189
Ša-Bēl-bāni, 29
Ša-Bēl-šū, 45
Šadi-redû, 262
Šaḫû, 30
Šalam-aḫi, 174
Šalam-Yāma/Šal(a)m-Yāma, 142, 144
Šalīm-Yāma, 144
Šalūma-x, 174
Šamaʿōn, 152
Šamaʿ-Yāma, 144, 145, 151
Šamandāya, 290
Šamaš-aplu-iddin, 54
Šamaš-balāṭu, 50
Šamaš-erība, 27, 46, 54
Šamaš-iddin, 54, 158
Šamaš-ina-tēšî-eṭir, 49
Šamaš-iqīša, 33
Šamaš-pirʾu-uṣur, 52
Šamaš-šarru-uṣur, 85, 87
Šamaš-šumu-ukīn, 28
Šamaš-uballiṭ, 51
Šammû, 209
Šamšu, 189
Ša-Nabû-šū, 45
Ša-Nabû-taqum, 131
Šandamû, 220
Šangû-Ninurta, 45
Šapān, 152
Ša-pî-Bēl, 46
Ša-pî-kalbi, 19, 31, 46, 59
Šāpiku, 94, 95
Šār-Issar, 116
Šar-kali-šarrī, 23
Šarru-dūru, 83, 84, 87
Šarru-ilūʾa, 83
Šarru-kīn, 28
Šarrukkāya, 290
Šarru-lū-dari, 43, 82, 87
Šarru-mītu-uballiṭ, 83, 88
Šarru-ukīn, 83, 84, 88
*Šātaina-, 248
*Šātaka-, 246
*Šātibara-, 246
*Šātibaxša-, 249
*Šātibr̥zana-, 250
Šauška-muwa, 219
Šbnyh, 159
Šelemyāh, 149
Šellebu, 47
Šēpētāya, 28
Šēpē(t)-Bēl-aṣbat, 28
Šēpē(t)-Ninlil-aṣbat, 28
*Šībava-, 244
Šikkû, 31, 62, 64
Šillēm, 149
Šil(l)im, 152
Šillīm, 152
Šillimu, 173, 176, 178
Šillim-Yāma, 144
Širikti-Marduk, 51
Širikti-Šamaš, 46
Širiktu, 51
Širku, 55
Šiu, 289
Šlm, 174
Šlmyh, 142
Šūbnā-Yāma, 159
Šullumāya, 95
Šullumu, 101
Šulum-ana-Bābili, 50
Šulum-Bābili, 50, 59
Šumāya, 20, 118
Šumma-Eššu, 115
Šumu-iddin, 52
Šumu-ukīn, 25, 52
*Šumu-uṣur, 103
Šutar-šarḫu, 260, 262
Šutruk-Nahhunte, 264
Šutur-Nahhunte, 260, 264
Šūzubu, 101, 167

Tā, 218
Tabalāya, 31
Tabnēa, 54
Taḫ-māya, 199, 208
Takelot, 202
Talīmu, 46
Tammaritu, 269
Tammeš-ilka, 131
Tammeš-linṭar, 131
Tamūnu, 201

Taqbi-līšir, 97, 103
Taqīš-Gula, 23
Tardennu, 47
Tarḫunta-piya, 220
Tarḫunta-warri, 219
Tarībi-Iššar, 174
Tatedidos, 233
Tattannu, 97, 250
Tattannu-bullissu, 97
Tattannu-uṣur, 97, 103
Teispes, 239
Tēšî-ēṭir, 49, 50
Theoboulos, 227
Theodōros, 227
Theodosios, 227
Theogenēs, 227
Theomelēs, 227
*Tīhūpardaisa-, 247
Tiḫut-arṭēsi, 199
Timotheos, 227
Timokratēs, 226, 227
*Tīrâ-, 244
*Tīrakāma-, 246
Tīrik-šarrūssu, 83
*Tīryāvauš, 242
Tū, 218
Tukubenu, 289
Tukulti-Marduk, 23
Tuqnu-Eššu, 115
Tuqūn-DN, 118
Tuqūnu-ēreš, 118
Tuqūnu-Eššu, 115
Tuqūnu-lāmur, 118
Tūtia, 288
Ṭābia, 54, 67
Ṭāb-ṣilli-Marduk, 54
Ṭāb-šār-Ezida, 26
Ṭāb-Uruk, 26
Ṭāb-utul-Enlil, 274
Ṭōb-Yāma, 149
Ṭūb-Yāma, 149

Uballissu-DN, 102
Uballissu-Marduk, 72
Ubār-Eššu, 115
Ubāru, 31
Ubbudu, 67
Udarnā, 151
Uggâ, 173, 174
Ukkâya, 200, 290
Ultu-pāni-Bēl-lū-šulum, 30, 38
Ulūlāya, 47
Umḫuluma?, 269
Ummanšibar, 269
Undadu, 269
Unzaraḫ-[. . .], 118
Unzarḫu, 118
Unzarḫu-Aššur, 118
Unzarḫu-Issar, 118
Upadarma-, 243, 249
Upāq, 97
Upāqa-ana-Arbail, 116
Upāq-(ana)-DN, 97
Upputu, 67
Uqūpu, 47
Urawanni, 219
Urdu-Eššu, 115, 117
Urtagu (*see also* Urtak), 263
Urtak (*see also* Urtagu), 263–264, 268, 269
Ur-Utu, 274
Usamunu, 208
Uṣuršāya, 97
Uṣuršu-DN, 97
*Uštapāna-, 243
Utāna-, 243

Vahyazdāta-, 240, 243
*Vanāta-, 244
*Varāza-, 241
Vaumisa-, 243
*Vēzdāta-, 240
*Vindafarnah-, 243, 252
*Vištāna-, 244
Vištāspa-, 246
Vivāna-, 241

Waliwali, 218

*Xaraina-, 244
Xerxes (*see also* Xšayaršan-, Xšayaršā), 24, 33, 71, 242
*Xratu-, 241
Xšaθrita-, 244
Xšayaršan-, 243
Xšayaršā, 246
*Xšēti-, 244

Yaˁăqōb, 159
Yadaˁ-Yāma, 153, 251
<Yā>ḫû-ˀamar, 145
Yāḫû-ˁaz, 159, 161
Yāḫû-ˁaz(a)r, 150
Yāḫû-ˁizr(ī), 145
Yāḫû-aḫu-ēreš, 153
Yāḫ<û>-ḫīn, 145, 151
Yāḫû-idr, 154
Yāḫû-kīn, 145
Yāḫû-lānû, 153
Yāḫû-laqīm, 142, 154
Yāḫû-lūnu, 170

Yāḫû-natan, 142, 145, 151
Yāḫû-nūr(ī), 154
Yāḫû-rām, 149
Yāḫû-šarru-uṣur, 82, 153, 157, 158
Yāḫû-šūˁ, 145, 161
Yāḫû-šūr(ī), 145
Yāḫû-zabad, 142
Yālû, 189
Yāma-ˁaqab, 159
Yamūš, 151
Yaqīm-Yāma, 149
Yāqīm-Yāma, 149
Yašeˁ-Yāma, 139
Yāšûb, 159
Yašūb-ṣidq(ī), 152
Yašūb-ṭill(ī), 152
Yatūnu, 168, 174
Yəhôyākîn, 144
Yḫw(ʾ)ln, 170
Yhwntn, 142
Yigdal-Yāma, 149
Yšwb, 159
Ytn, 174
Zababa-šarru-uṣur, 87
Zabad-Yāma, 151
Zabāya, 289
Zabdī, 122
Zabdia, 151
*Zabrakāna-, 248
Zabudā, 132
Zakar-Yāma, 157
*Zangāna-, 244
*Zānuka-, 244
Zaraḫ-Tammeš, 129
*Zātaica-, 244
Zazāya, 288
Zenophilos, 227
Zēr-Bābili, 26
Zēria, 49, 285
Zēr-kitti-līšir, 99
Zēru-līšir-Nusku, 100
Zidanna/i, 220
Zikaru, 47
Zizīya, 288
Zuḫru, 189
Zūzānu, 288
Zuzū, 288

Female names and persons

NB: initial superscript ^{f} indicates a female name recorded in cuneiform spelling; female names known from other writing cultures (e.g. the Greek name Antiochis) are rendered without the superscript ^{f}. In those cases, (f.) is added after the name.

ᶠḪamatāya, 68
ᶠḪanašu, 68
ᶠḪannā, 133
ᶠḪibuṣu, 67
ᶠḪilb/punnu, 175
ᶠḪilbunītu, 30
ᶠḪinnī, 133
ᶠḪiptāya, 68
ᶠḪuṭuatā, 153

ᶠImmertu, 62
ᶠIna-bāb-magāri-alsišu, 60
ᶠIna-dannāti-alsišu, 61
ᶠIna-Eigikalamma-lūmuršu, 26, 65
ᶠIna-Eimbianu-alsišu, 26
ᶠIna-Esagil-bēlet, 60, 64
ᶠIna-Esagil-ramât, 60, 63, 64
ᶠIna-Esagil-šimînni, 30
ᶠIna-Eturkalamma-alsišu, 26, 30, 65
ᶠInbāya, 30, 62
ᶠInbia, 62
ᶠInbi-DN, 62
ᶠIndu, 68
ᶠInṣabtu, 63, 64
ᶠInzaʾītâ, 286
ᶠInzayītāy, 286
ᶠIsḫunnatu, 30, 63
ᶠIsḫunnu, 63
ᶠIsinnāʾītu, 65
ᶠItti-Eturkalamma-būnūʾa, 30
ᶠItti-Nanāya-būnū'a, 60
ᶠItti-Nanāya-īnāya, 60
ᶠItti-Ninlil-īnāya, 66

ᶠKabtāya, 67
ᶠKallabuttu, 30, 63
ᶠKaššāya, 64, 157,
161, 286
ᶠKāribtu, 62
ᶠKēautu, 289
Kratō (f.), 233
ᶠKubbutu, 67
ᶠKudāyaʾitu, 290
ᶠKurunnam-tabni, 63, 66
ᶠKuttāya, 63

ᶠLā-magirtu, 31, 63,
68
Laodice (f.), 12, 233
ᶠLā-tubāšinni, 60
ᶠLēʾi-DN, 60
ᶠLēʾītu, 60
ᶠLillidu, 175
ᶠLū-balṭat, 60
ᶠLurindu, 63

ᶠMādumītu, 246
ᶠMammītu-ṭābat, 59
ᶠManantāya, 289
ᶠMannu-akî-ištaria, 30, 61
ᶠMaqartu, 67
ᶠMārat-Sîn-banât, 59
ᶠMarduk-ēṭirat, 59, 66
ᶠMarduk-uballiṭ, 66
ᶠMasiktum, 67
ᶠMīṣātu, 63
ᶠMulâ, 214
ᶠMurašītu, 30, 62
ᶠMūrānatu, 62

ᶠNanāya-ana-bītišu, 60
ᶠNanāya-bēlu-uṣrī, 29, 60, 64
ᶠNanāya-biʿī, 153
ᶠNanāya-damqat, 59
ᶠNanāya-dīninni, 60
ᶠNanāya-ittia, 31
ᶠNanāya-kānat, 152, 154
ᶠNanāya-kēširat, 59
ᶠNanāya-kilīlu-uṣrī, 29, 60
ᶠNanāya-rīšat, 59
ᶠNanāya-silim, 31, 64
ᶠNanāya-šarrat, 59
ᶠNanāya-šimînni, 60
ᶠNasikat, 133
ᶠNinlil-ilat, 59
ᶠNīr-ʾimmî, 171
ᶠNūptāya, 62, 64

Phanaia (f.), 233
ᶠPuʿullā, 152, 153

ᶠQudāšu, 63, 64
ᶠQunnabatu, 63

ᶠRēʾindu, 62, 95
ᶠRibarmeš, 289
ᶠRīšat, 67
ᶠRīminni-Ištar, 60
ᶠRīšāya, 67

ᶠSinūnu, 30, 287
ᶠSipparāʾītu, 65
Stratonice (f.), 233
ᶠSuluppāya, 30
ᶠSūqaʾītu, 31, 63
ᶠṢāṣiru, 63
ᶠŠaḫḫurratu, 67
ᶠŠamê-ramât, 233
ᶠŠeleppūtu, 30, 63
ᶠŠēpetaya, 60
ᶠŠēpet(/Šēpessu)-DN-aṣbat, 60

ᶠŠikkû, 31, 62, 64
ᶠŠikkūtu, 23, 62
ᶠŠilangītu, 31
ᶠŠūšāya, 288

ᶠTaslimu, 68
ᶠTašmētu-atkal, 60
ᶠTašmētu-tabni, 61
Thalassia (f.), 233
ᶠṬābatu, 62, 64, 67
ᶠṬābatu-Iššar, 62
ᶠṬubbutu, 67
ᶠṬuppuštu, 67

ᶠUbārtu, 63
ᶠUmmī-ṭābat, 33
ᶠUqūpatu, 62
ᶠUrbil-ḫammu, 117

ᶠYāḫ̮û-dimr(ī), 153, 154
ᶠYāḫ̮û-ḥīn, 152
ᶠYapaʕ-Yāḫ̮û, 152

Family names

Aba-Enlil-da-ri (*see also* Aba-Ninnu-da-ri, Mannu-kīma-Enlil-ḫātin), 277–279
Aba-Ninnu-da-ri (*see also* Aba-Enlil-da-ri, Mannu-kīma-Enlil-ḫātin), 278, 279
Absummu, 277
Abunāya, 73
Abu-ul-īde, 43
Amīl-Gula, 275
Amīl-Papsukkal, 284
Amīl-Sîn, 276
Aqar-Nabû, 73, 77
Arad-Ea, 72–73
Arad-Nergal, 45, 275
Ararru, 157
Arkât-ilāni-damqā, 43
Arrabtu, 37, 47, 74
Asarluḫi-mansum, 275, 278, 279
Asû, 48
Ašarēdu, 47
Ašgandu (*see also* Šugandu), 284, 285
Aššurāya, 117
Atkuppu, 74

Bā'iru, 175
Baba-utu, 276
Balāssu, 46, 95
Basia, 25

Dannēa, 67
Dābibī, 46

Ea-ilūtu-bāni, 24, 77
Ēdu-ēṭir, 33, 114
Egibatila (*see also* Egibi, Sîn-taqīša-libluṭ), 276–277
Egibi (*see also* Egibatila, Sîn-taqīša-libluṭ), 22, 24, 31, 67, 148, 166, 176, 277
Ekur-zakir, 77, 231
Esagil-mansum, 275
Eṭēru, 46, 54

Gaḫal, 275, 284
Gaḫal-Marduk, 284, 285
Gallābu, 24, 48, 53
Gibindu, 285
Gimillu, 21, 46, 101

Ḫullunu, 285
Ḫunzû, 77, 85
Ḫuṣābu, 47

Iddin-Papsukkal, 54, 77
Ile??i-Marduk, 54
Ilī-bāni, 53
Ilūtu-bāni, 53
Ina-ṣilli-sammî, 26
Ingallēa, 53
Ir'anni, 82
Iššakku, 275
Itinnu, 175

Kandar-Šamaš, 285
Kassidakku, 275
Kutimmu, 74

Lāsimu, 74
Lē'êa, 67
Lu-dumununna, 276
Lullubāya, 286

Mannu-kīma-Enlil-ḫātin (*see also* Aba-Enlil-da-ri, Aba-Ninnu-da-ri), 277
Maqartu, 37, 74
Mar/štuk(āta), 284
Mukallim, 78

Nabûnnāya, 23, 75
Nabû-šumu-iddin, 20, 43, 52, 105
Nana-šuḫi, 285
Nanna-utu, Nannûtu, 276
Nappāḫu, 21, 24, 148

Nâš-paṭri, 78
Nazi-Enlil, 285
Nazūa, 285
Nikkāya, 286
Nusku-iddin, 23, 275

Pilamdi, 285

Rē'i-alpi, 74
Rē'i-sisê, 74
Rīšûa, 95

Sagdidi, 288
Salāmu, 77
Sîn-ibni, 276
Sîn-leqe-unninnī, 24, 73, 77, 278
Sîn-taqīša-libluṭ, 22, 276
Ṣāḫit-ginê, 77
Ša-ɪ-luḫ, 54
Ša-alāli (*see also* Šalala), 288
Šabbâ/Šambâ, 284
Šagerīya, 284
Šalala (*see also* Ša-alāli), 288
Šamaš-abāri, 23
Šamaš-erība, 27, 46, 54
Ša-nāšišu, 24, 77
Šangû-(Bēlet-)Ninua, 114
Šangû-Dilbat, 77
Šangû-DN, 74, 115
Šangû-Ninurta, 45
Šangû-Sippar, 73, 77
Šangû-Šamaš, 49, 77
Šatarindi, 285
Šugandu (*see also* Ašgandu), 284
Šumu-libši, 78, 95

Tunâ, 284
Ṭābiḫ-kāri, 54
Ṭābiḫ-Marduk, 54
Ṭābiḫu, 48, 54, 74, 78

Ur-Nanna, 275, 278–279
Ur-Nintinuga, 275, 278

Zababa-utu, 276
Zannētu, 285
Zērāya, 54
Zērūtu, 276

Place names

ˁAlemet, 146
Abu Habbah (*see also* Sippar), 147
Adummatu (*see also* Dūmat), 185
Agade, 23, 25, 83
Al-ˁUlā (*see also* Dadān), 185, 187
Aleppo, 219, 220
al-Ḥā'iṭ, 186
al-Ḥuwayyiṭ, 187
al-Madīnah, 187
Ālu-ša-Arbāyi, 187
Ālu-ša-Našar (*see also* Našar), 174
Ālu-ša-Yāḫūdāyi (*see also* Yāhūdu), 178
Ammon, 5, 166, 179
Anatolia, 1, 213, 214, 216, 217, 220, 283
Arabia, 1, 185–188, 191, 290
Arbaʔil, 110, 116
Arwad, 177
Ashkelon, 126, 139, 169
Assur, 111, 115, 117
Assyria, 3, 4, 7, 38, 52, 109–115, 139, 284
Aššurītu, 117

Babylon, 4–6, 8, 24–27, 33, 41, 50, 59, 64, 65, 72, 77, 82, 84, 111, 112, 115, 122, 143, 147, 148, 154, 160, 166–169, 172, 176, 179, 195, 196, 217, 225, 250, 252, 270, 275, 276, 278, 279, 285–287
Banānu (*see also* Manānu), 270
Bāb-Nār-Kabari, 126
Bīt-Abī-râm, 123, 124, 135, 147
Bīt-Hullumu, 270
Bīt-Kikê, 214, 217
Bīt-Ṣūrāyi, 168, 178
Bīt-Tabalāyi, 217
Borsippa, 24–26, 65, 72–74, 77, 104, 148, 154, 175, 196, 217, 225, 275, 285, 286

Carchemish, 32
Chaldea, 3, 72, 75, 157
Cilicia, 31, 217, 221

Dadān (*see also* Al-ʿUlā), 185, 186, 188
Dilbat, 26, 72, 77
Dor, 174
Dūmat (al-Jandal) (*see also* Adummatu), 185
Duqulān, 173, 176, 177, 178, 181
Dūr-Abiešuḫ, 276
Dūr-Šarrukki, 290
Dūr-Yakīn, 290

Elam, 126, 270, 288, 290
Elephantine, 140, 159
Elymais, 252
Egypt, 1, 4, 31, 47, 116, 180, 194, 200, 201, 204, 214, 216, 217, 250, 283

Fadak, 186, 187
Fars, 259

Gandar, 31, 65
Gaza, 126, 169
Greece, 1, 283
Gubbu, 290

Hamath (Ḫamat), 32
Ḥigāz, 188
Ḫabur, 139
Ḫazatu (*see also* Gaza), 169
Ḫindanu, 86
Ḫupišna, 219

Idumea, 149
Imbuku, 32
India, 246
Indus, 283
Iran, 1, 258, 283
Isin, 3, 25, 65
Israel, 139, 140
Išqillūnu (*see also* Ashkelon), 169
Izalla, 177
Izeh, 259

Jazirah, 177, 284
Jerusalem, 139, 140
Judah, 4, 32, 130, 139–141, 154, 157, 160
Judean hills, 140

Kabaru Canal, 126
Keš, 290
Khaybar, 187
Khuzestan, 259
Kirmese, 290
Kish, 25, 26, 41, 77, 148, 232, 286
Kutha, 25

Larsa, 25, 65
Lebanon, 168
Libbāli, 111
Libya, 201, 202

Madaba, 188
Maḫazīn, 174
Manānu (*see also* Banānu), 270
Marad, 26, 65, 168
Moab, 166

Našar (*see also* Ālu-ša-Našar), 123, 124, 129, 130, 135, 147
Neirab, 129, 130
Nineveh, 110, 114–115, 277, 278
Nippur, 23–26, 41, 65, 77, 112, 123–126, 129, 132, 133, 140, 142, 143, 147, 148, 153, 161, 168, 170, 175, 176, 178, 187, 188, 195–197, 217, 270, 274, 276–279

Opis, 148

Palestine, 140
Palmyra, 189
Pamphylia, 214
Persia, 5
Philistia, 169
Phoenicia, 180
Pirindu, 214, 216
Pisidia, 213, 214, 221

Qadesh, 126

Saba?, 188, 190
Samarian hills, 140
Sealand, 83, 259, 270
Sippar (*see also* Abu Habbah), 4, 5, 24–26, 41, 65, 73, 77, 78, 85, 111, 129, 133, 140, 147–149, 160, 161, 168, 170–172, 174, 176, 196, 274, 276, 285
Sūḫu, 188
Sumuntunaš, 270
Susa, 126, 158, 166, 179, 261, 266
Susiana, 259, 270
Syria, 4, 126, 128, 129, 171, 185, 190, 214
Šapīya, 75

Tabal, 217
Taymā?, 185, 186, 189, 190
Tel Keisan, 176
Tell al-Maskhūṭah, 188
Transjordan, 5, 140–141, 170, 171, 175
Tyre, 139, 168, 178, 181

Udannu, 25
Ugarit, 176
Ukku, 200, 290
Ur, 4, 24, 25, 77, 148, 274, 276
Ura, 219
Uruk, 4, 6, 20, 21, 24–28, 65, 72, 75–77, 84, 85, 89, 110, 111, 113, 114, 119, 148, 170, 172, 176, 217, 225, 227, 228, 230–233, 278

Yāhūdu, 123, 124, 126, 129, 130, 135, 142–144, 146–148, 151–154, 157–162, 178, 181
Yemen, 185

Zagros mountains, 3, 259, 283, 286
Zaphon, 173

Names of gods

ˁAl, 130
ˁAnat, 130
ˁAštart, 178
ˁAttā, 130
ˁAttar, 129
Adad, 40, 65, 128, 154
Addu, 128
Adgi, 129
Agni, 242
A(h)ura, 245
Ama, 242
Amun, 199, 201, 207, 208
Amurru, 40, 89, 129, 130
Anšar, 114
Anu, 25, 26, 40, 65, 76, 84
Anubis, 199
Anunnītu, 66
Apis, 199, 207
Apladda, 129
Apollo, 226
Arma, 219
Ārmati, 245
Arta, 242–245
Artemis, 226
Aššur, 38, 110, 111, 113, 114, 119
Athena, 226
Ātr̥, 245
Atum, 199, 201
Aya, 25, 40, 65, 66, 118

Bābu, 25, 40, 65, 66
Baga, 242, 245
Bānītu, 40, 66, 94, 95
Bastet, 199, 207
Bēl, 25, 29, 40, 45, 46, 65, 66, 82, 84, 133, 154, 169, 244
Bēlet-Bābili, 65
Bēlet-Ninua, 114–115
Bēltia, 25, 29
Bēltu, 40, 66
Bes, 199
Bīt-il, 128, 130
Bīt-Kuššu, 290
Bunene, 25, 40
Būr(u), 40

Ea, 40, 65, 118
Enlil, 25, 40, 65, 66, 102, 133, 277
Erua, 66
Esi (*see also* Isis), 175
Ēši/Ēšu, 116
Eššu, 115–116, 118

Gad, 130
Gula, 25, 40, 66, 275, 279
GVs/š (quality of vowel unknown), 130

Hapy, 199
Hauma, 245
Herakles, 226
Horus, 173, 199–201, 203, 205, 207, 209
Huban, 260, 263, 264, 266, 267
(H)uvar, 245
Ḥamōn, 172

IGI.DU, 25, 40
Iltar, 129
Iltehr, 129
Inšušinak, 263, 264
Isis (*see also* Esi), 116, 175, 199, 200, 202, 203, 226
Issar, 110, 113, 116, 118
Iššar, 113, 118
Ištar, 20, 25–28, 40, 66, 113, 116, 118, 129, 227, 264
Ištar-of-Babylon, 25
Ištar-of-Nineveh, 114–115
Iya, 219

Kemosh, 167, 169, 179
Khnum, 199
Khonsu, 199
Kuna, 130
Kurunnam, 66

Kuruntiya, 219
Kusu, 25

Lugal-Marada, 65, 168

Madānu, 25, 40
Māhi, 245
Mammītu, 65, 66
Mār, 130
Mār-bīti, 25, 40
Marduk, 19, 22, 25, 26, 29, 40, 42, 64–66, 114, 133, 143
Mazdā, 245
Mehyt, 199, 208
Milki, 171, 172
Milkom, 5, 167, 169, 179
Milqart, 171
Min, 199
Mithra, 242, 245
Mitōn, 172
Mullēšu, 65

Nabê, 130
Nabû, 25, 26, 39, 40, 45, 65, 66, 73, 82, 130, 133, 143, 154, 175
Nahhunte, 263, 264
Nanāya, 25, 40, 60, 65, 66
Nanna, 274, 289
Našuh, 130
Nefertem, 199
Neith, 199
Nergal, 25, 40, 65, 133
Ninazu, 25
Ningal, 25, 66
Ningišzidda, 25
Ninlil, 25, 40, 65, 66
Ninnu, 277
Ninurta, 25, 40, 65, 133
Niraḫ, 25
Nusku, 25, 40, 130, 131, 154, 275
Nyr, 171

Onnophris, 199, 204
Osiris, 199

Poseidon, 226
Ptah, 199, 208

Qōs, 130

Ra, 199
Rammān, 130, 173
Rauxšna, 242
Runtiya, 219

Sē, 130
Sîn, 25, 40, 65, 66, 130, 133, 276, 277
Sobek, 199
Šadi (*see also* Šati), 262
Šamaš, 25, 28, 40, 65, 73, 118, 129, 154
Šamê, 130
Šanda, 219
Šati (*see also* Šadi), 262, 263, 264
Šē?, 130

Tammeš, 129, 131, 133
Tarḫunta, 219, 220
Tašmētu, 25, 60, 61, 66
Tepti, 263, 264, 266
Thoth, 199
Tīra, 245
Tīrī, 245
Tīrya, 245

Umunazu, 25
Uraš, 66
Urdimmu, 25

Yāw, 146
Yāma, 127, 146
Yāḫû, 144
Yhw, 141, 143, 166, 178
YHWH, 141–143, 151, 154–155, 159

Zababa, 25, 26
Zaphon, 173
Zarpanītu, 29, 65, 66
Zeus, 226

Temple names

Bīt-Akītu, 30, 41
Bīt-Papsukkal, 41

Eanna, 26, 28, 41, 78, 88, 89, 110, 113, 148, 170, 172
Ebabbar, 26, 65, 111, 154, 168, 171, 172, 174, 176, 196, 197
Egalmaḫ, 26
Egišḫurankia, 115
Eigikalamma, 26, 65, 168
Eimbianu, 26
Ekurgal, 89
Esagil, 8, 26, 41, 44, 46, 60, 63, 64, 252
Eturkalamma, 26, 65
Eulmaš, 83
Ezida, 26, 41, 44, 73, 78, 89, 175

General index

abbreviated name. *See* shortened name
abbreviation, 232
acculturation, 161, 180, 195, 228
acrophony, 22
adoption, 21, 175, 270
ancestor, 23, 48, 53, 72, 73, 74, 115, 179, 278, 279
  female ancestor, 37
Antiochos Cylinder, 225
ardu, 45, 117, 251
Astronomical Diaries, 8, 225, 232

Babylonian Chronicle (ABC 1), 259, 265, 266
Bible, 140, 141, 159, 166, 186, 188
birth, 19, 31, 38, 45, 47, 61, 63, 101, 102, 103, 152
birth order, 39, 41

chronicle, 216, 225, 269
city as name element, 26, 41, 117, 219
courtier, 85, 87, 160, 161, 168
Cyrus Cylinder, 111

deportation, 111, 126, 139, 168, 180
deportee, 4, 5, 32, 126, 129, 139, 148, 157, 160, 161, 169, 180, 283
determinative
  BE (BAD), 260, 265
  DINGIR, 118, 128, 143, 200
  LÚ, 37, 74, 288
  MUNUS, 21, 37, 58, 74
  Personenkeil, 12, 22, 37, 74, 167, 265, 288
disambiguation, 110, 167

Eanna archive, 28, 111, 148
Ebabbar archive, 111, 196
Egibi archive, 148
Epic of Creation (Enūma eliš), 22, 114
Epic of Gilgamesh, 72, 278
ethnonym, 187, 215

family name, 20, 21, 22, 24, 33, 37, 41, 85, 86, 110, 117, 124, 157, 179, 202, 228, 275, 276, 277, 278, 279, 284, 285, 286, 288
  ancestral family name, 74
  double family name, 53
  female name used as family name, 74
  hybrid family name, 285
  occupational family name, 37, 45, 47, 48, 74, 75
father's name (*see also* patronym), 20, 22, 33, 75, 76, 110, 228
filiation, 21, 48, 75, 157, 179, 202
  two-tier, 157, 179
flora and fauna, 30, 47, 62
foundling, 19, 31, 46

gender, 38, 58, 62, 64, 65, 66, 129, 199
genealogy, 72, 110
  four-tier, 48, 76
  three-tier, 20, 76, 179
  two-tier, 75
gentilic, 174, 176, 178, 286, 290
grandfather, 21, 202, 229
grandfather's name, 48, 228
grandmother, 175, 202
great-grandfather's name, 228

Harran stele, 186
homonym, 27, 276
hypocorism, 20, 176, 178, 220, 244, 261, 269
hypocoristic suffix, 51, 151, 244
  -ʔ, 189
  -ā, 53, 132, 151
  -ān, 53, 132, 190
  -ān > -ōn, 151
  -ay, 177
  -ay(ya), 151
  -āya, 53
  -ea or -ēa, 53
  -ī, 53, 175
  -ī/ē, 151
  -ia, 53, 63, 151, 158
  -t, 289
  -ūa, 285
  -ūt, 151
hypocoristicon. *See* hypocorism

Kasr archive, 196
kinship term, 29, 41, 62, 132, 143, 166, 219

Lallname, 218

mammonymy, 21
merchant, 32, 147, 160, 197
migration, 125
mother, 20, 60, 61, 175, 229
mother's name, 20, 202
Murašû archive, 21, 123, 124, 133, 147, 148, 160, 195, 241

N1 archive, 8, 147, 154, 159, 167
name
  animal name, 47, 62, 64, 152, 241
  Banana name, 19, 20, 38
  basilophorous name, 202, 203
  Beamtenname, 81, 153, 157
  biblical name, 159
  ceremonial name, 274
  clausal name. *See* sentence name
  compound name, 45, 51, 132, 134, 142, 154, 169, 218, 219, 220, 226, 227, 260
  dithematic name, 225
  double name, 19, 53, 63, 87, 158, 203, 231, 233, 252
  female name, 12, 22, 37, 133, 152, 167, 199, 225, 227, 233
  foreign name, 32, 33, 142, 144, 146
  genitive compound name, 149, 172
  historical name, 28
  hybrid name, 41, 127, 153, 154, 169, 173, 178, 202, 239, 244, 262, 285, 286
  interrogative name, 44
  interrogative sentence name, 150, 172
  male name, 12, 22, 58, 59, 61, 65, 265
  monothematic name, 225
  nickname, 47, 49, 53, 158, 203
  nominal sentence name, 131, 134, 149, 171
  non-compound name, 46, 154, 169, 174, 218, 225, 226
  patronymic name, 244
  plant name, 47, 62, 63, 152
  prefixed name, 243
  royal name, 22, 27, 227, 231, 232, 233, 240, 259, 263, 286
  sentence name, 42, 43, 44, 49, 50, 51, 59, 64, 131, 134, 201, 220
  shortened name, 20, 48, 49, 50, 51, 62, 63, 150, 203, 220
  simplex name. *See* non-compound name
  single-stem full name, 241
  slave name, 28, 29, 30, 33, 60, 64, 153
  theophoric name, 19, 25, 39, 59, 61, 103, 189, 191, 199, 219, 226, 233
  two-stem full name, 242
  verbal sentence name, 130, 149, 169
name change, 158, 195
Nappāḫu archive, 148
newborn child, 19, 38, 41, 42, 43, 62, 93, 101, 105
newborn girl, 61
Nikarchos Cylinder, 225, 234
normalisation, 12, 126, 146, 203, 229, 246

oblate, 20, 33, 65, 71, 88, 175, 196
Old Testament. *See* Bible
oronym, 173
orphan, 31, 46

papponymy, 21, 202, 229
patronym (*see also* father's name), 48, 75, 85, 86, 87, 124, 141, 157, 228
Personenkeil. *See* determinative
phoneme, 206, 207, 229, 258
phonology, 118, 206, 259, 265
physical features, 33, 47, 63, 66, 67, 152
prayer, 29
priest, 74, 85, 88, 89, 115, 274, 275, 278
  ērib bīti, 73
  kalû, 72
  šangû, 24, 73
  šatammu, 24, 27, 73, 89, 252
priestess, 274
prisoner, 32, 126, 167, 197, 217

qīpu, 82, 83, 85, 88, 110, 168, 174
queen, 153, 233

royal inscription
  Achaemenid, 238, 239, 240, 241
  Neo-Assyrian, 109, 113
  Neo-Babylonian, 274
  Seleucid, 225

ša rēš šarri, 161, 168
ša rēš šarri bēl piqitti, 85
ša rēši, 86, 160
Sabbath, 141, 152
scholar, 23, 24, 77, 274, 275, 278
sēpiru, 86, 161
sibling, 34, 41, 44, 62, 161
slave, 28, 29, 31, 33, 48, 64, 67, 68, 71, 88, 117, 152, 157, 161, 196, 197, 250, 251
slave woman, 64, 68
spelling, 246
  (in)consistent spelling, 143
  alphabetic, 129, 142, 224, 229, 247
  archaising, 23, 204, 279

spelling (cont.)
  bisyllabic, 150
  cuneiform orthography of YHWH, 142
  defective, 152, 177
  logographic, 22, 28, 39, 93, 94, 96, 98, 99, 100, 101, 102, 103, 104, 117, 143, 264, 274
  phonetic markers, 93, 94, 95, 101, 102, 103
  segholite, 150
  syllabic, 93, 94, 98, 101, 103, 113, 229
status
  elite, 21, 24, 284
  elite woman, 64
  foreign, 32, 168
  free, 23, 28, 33, 48, 63, 64, 161, 196, 197
  high, 250, 278
  lower, 21, 175
  semi-free, 153, 161
  servile, 24, 71
  social, 23, 32, 39, 64, 71
  socio-economic, 160, 196
  urban elite, 25, 110, 124, 148, 157, 168, 179, 283, 286
Susa Acropole Archive, 261

Tattannu archive, 21, 196
temple as name element, 26, 41, 64, 82
theophoric element, 39, 45, 49, 65, 66, 76, 81, 105, 112, 114, 115, 118, 127, 128, 129, 130, 133, 140, 141, 142, 151, 154, 158, 160, 166, 169, 170, 171, 173, 178, 191, 219, 226, 245, 263, 264, 265, 266, 285, 290
toponym, 173, 180, 186, 188, 219
  hybrid, 126
  toponym as name element, 41, 116, 218, 219, 246

uncle, 21

wawation, 186, 188, 189, 190

Yāhūdu archive, 123, 124, 126, 147, 148, 152

Printed by Printforce, United Kingdom